ONE WEEK LOAN

Human Rights, Constitutional Law and the Development of The English Legal System: Selected Essays

This is a selection of Lord Irvine, the former Lord Chancellor's major lectures and articles since 1995. It surveys the constitutional revolution that has taken place in Britain since the Labour Government came to power in 1997, taking in devolution and House of Lords reform, but with a particular focus on human rights. The evolution of a new human rights culture is traced, from the policy underlying the Human Rights Act 1998, through the scheme of the legislation and the preparations for implementation, to an analysis of the impact of the Act during its first two years. The work is of particular interest because Lord Irvine chaired the four main Cabinet Committees on constitutional change and introduced the Human Rights Bill to Parliament.

Lord Irvine also considers the development and practice of public and administrative law, and the constitutional role of the British judiciary and the Lord Chancellor within our unique separation of powers. Alongside forays into criminal, commercial, and medical law, the collection also embraces an international perspective, with essays on the influence in Britain of European law; comparative analyses of key aspects of English, American and French jurisprudence; and a discussion of the continuing relevance of Magna Carta in Britain and Australia.

This collection is a timely contribution to the debate on human rights, constitutional law and the English legal system at the turn of the new millennium, and will be of interest to judges, academics, practitioners and students.

Human Rights, Constitutional Law and the Development of the English Legal System

Selected Essays

Lord Irvine of Lairg, PC, QC

·HART·
PUBLISHING
OXFORD AND PORTLAND OREGON
2003

Published in North America (US and Canada) by
Hart Publishing
c/o International Specialized Book Services
5804 NE Hassalo Street,
Portland, Oregon
97213-3644
USA

Hart Publishing is a specialist legal publisher based in Oxford, England.
To order further copies of this book or to request a list of other
publications please write to:

Hart Publishing, Salters Boatyard, Folly Bridge,
Abingdon Rd, Oxford, OX1 4LB
Telephone: +44 (0) 1865 245533 Fax: +44 (0) 1865 794882
email: mail@hartpub.co.uk
WEBSITE: http//:www.hartpub.co.uk

British Library Cataloguing in Publication Data
Data Available

ISBN 1-84113-411-2 (hardback)

Typeset by Olympus Infotech Pvt. Ltd., India, Sabon 11/14 pt
Printed and bound in Great Britain by
Biddles Ltd, www.biddles.co.uk

Contents

*Part 4:   Miscellaneous Essays on the
Development of the English Legal System*

Foreword

Lord Irvine appears likely to be the last person to have exercised all the executive, legislative and judicial functions of the office of Lord High Chancellor of Great Britain. During his six years of office he presided over great changes in the constitution of the United Kingdom, of which Scottish and Welsh devolution and the domestication of the Human Rights Convention are perhaps the leading instances. He also made important innovations in the administration of justice, the outstanding example being a new system for the public funding of litigation.

Some of these achievements are documented and discussed in this volume of collected essays and speeches. But Lord Irvine has not attempted to draw any general conclusions. His writings are left to speak for themselves. But they do in my opinion convey a message about the function of the office of Lord Chancellor in the modern British constitution. Lord Irvine's invitation to contribute a foreword gives me the opportunity to offer a personal view about what that message is.

There have been Lord Chancellors for a very long time and there has been nominal continuity in many of the functions of the office. Beneath the surface, however, much has changed. That is the way of the British constitution, which has evolved organically over the centuries without ever being wholly redesigned upon abstract principles. A disdain for mere labels and a preference for practice over theory has given the British people the unique privilege of institutional continuity, enabling them to adapt to the needs of the present without breaking their links with the past.

The organic and evolutionary nature of British institutions means that it is unwise to assume that a full description of the functions of any organ of government will be found in the law books. Constitutional changes which appear to give effect to approved political theories may have unintended consequences when it is found that they have an adverse effect upon the practical role which an institution plays in regulating the health of the body politic. This may be found to be true of the office of Lord Chancellor.

The executive, legislative and judicial functions of the Lord Chancellor are said to infringe the principle of the separation of powers. The objection is not so much to the combination of executive and legislative functions—that, after all, is and always has been pervasive in the British constitution—but to the Lord Chancellor's personal exercise of judicial functions and his responsibility for the appointment of judges. But this is to apply the principle of the separation of powers with a fundamentalist rigour which would have astonished its eighteenth century inventors: for example, Montesquieu, who was (as James Madison afterwards pointed out) entirely familiar with the British constitution of his day and nevertheless regarded Great Britain as a supreme example of the principle's practical application.

In recent years the Lord Chancellor's other duties, particularly in the case of Lord Irvine when he was close to the centre of government, have left him little time to participate in the sittings of the Appellate Committee of the House of Lords. He has delivered some notable judgments and no one could suggest that the quality of his learning or the independence of his judgment was in the slightest degree influenced by his other official duties. It is nevertheless true to say that it is not necessary for the proper functioning of the Appellate Committee that the Lord Chancellor should occasionally preside over its business. But that is not the point. What did matter was that it was a necessary qualification for the office of Lord Chancellor that the holder should be a lawyer of sufficient seniority and distinction to be able to sit without causing or feeling embarrassment as a judicial member of the House of Lords

The fact that these qualities have always been regarded as necessary for a Lord Chancellor has enabled him better to discharge the other duties of his office. It has given him the strength and discipline to act independently, though a member of the government, in the way the British constitution expects the Lord Chancellor and the law officers to act. It has certainly enabled both Lord Irvine and his predecessor to make appointments to the Bench with a fearless independence which has made the United Kingdom judiciary the envy of Europe. And in more general terms, it has enabled the Lord Chancellor, as a member of the government, to defend the rule of law and the independence of the judiciary.

These have been the practical strengths which the British constitution has gained from the existence of the office of Lord Chancellor in modern times. But they depended heavily upon the personal qualifications of the holder of the office. What this collection of essays demonstrates is the intellectual qualities which enable Lord Irvine, up to the very end, to discharge with distinction the constitutional duties of his historic office.

Lord Hoffmann
House of Lords
November 2003

Acknowledgments

Chapter 1 was first published under the title 'Response to Sir John Laws' in *Public Law* (1996: 636) and is published with the kind permission of Sweet & Maxwell.

Chapter 2 is reproduced with the permission of The Stationery Office.

Chapter 3 is based on the Tom Sargant Memorial Lectures delivered on 16 December 1997. The article was first published in *Public Law* (1998: 221) and is published with the kind permission of Sweet & Maxwell.

Chapter 4 is based on the National Heritage Lecture (1998).

Chapter 5 is based upon the 1999 Paul Sieghart Memorial Lecture, and was first published in the *European Human Rights Law Review* (1999 (4)) and is published here with the kind permission of the editor and Sweet & Maxwell.

Chapter 6 is based on a speech to the Canadian Institute of Advanced Legal Studies at Queen's College, Cambridge on 16 July 1999.

Chapter 7 is based on a Fabian Lecture delivered in 2000.

Chapter 8 is based upon the inaugural Irvine Human Right Centre Lecture, delivered on 1 November 2002, at Durham Human Rights Centre, Durham University, first published in *Public Law* (2003: 308). It is published here with the kind permission of Sweet & Maxwell.

Chapter 9 is based on the Administrative Law Bar Association lecture delivered on 16 October 1995. It was first published in *Public Law* (1996: 59) and is published with the kind permission of Sweet & Maxwell.

Chapter 10 was delivered as a lecture in Hong Kong, 18 September 1998, and was first published in the *Hong Kong Law Journal*. It is published here with the kind permission of the editors.

Chapter 11 was first published in *The Clifford Chance Millennium Lectures* (Hart Publishing, Oxford, 2000) and is published with kind permission of the editor, Professor BS Markesinis.

Chapter 12 is based upon a lecture given at the Third Worldwide Common Law Judiciary Conference held in Edinburgh in July 1999.

Chapter 13 was originally published in *The English Legal System in the 21st* Century, (The Honourable Society of the Inner Temple).

Chapter 14 is based upon the 31st Annual James Madison Lecture on Constitutional Law delivered at New York University Law School on 17 October 2000, first published in the *New York University Law Review* (April 2001, Vol 76, no 1). It is published here with the kind permission of the editors.

Chapter 15 is based on the inaugural Magna Carta Lecture delivered in Canberra, Australia on 14 October 2002 and first published in the *Law Quarterly Review* (2003: 227); it is published here with the kind permission of the editor and Sweet & Maxwell.

Chapter 16 is based upon a lecture delivered before the French Cour de Cassation on 26 March 2003.

Chapter 17 was delivered as a lecture at the Worldwide Advocacy Conference, 19 June 1998.

Chapter 18 is based on the KPMG lecture given by Lord Irvine on 24 June 1998.

Chapter 19 was first published in the *Medical Law Review* (1999: Vol. 7, 255) and is published here with the permission of the editor and Oxford University Press.

Chapter 20 was originally published in the *Sydney Law Review* (23 March 2001) and is published here with kind permission of the editors.

Chapter 21 is based on a lecture delivered to the British Academy on 22 November 2000. It was first published in *The Modern Law Review* (2001: Vol 64, No 3) and is published here with the kind permission of the editors.

Part 1

Human Rights and Constitutional Reform

1

The Philosophical Case for a Bill of Rights: A Response to Sir John Laws 1996 *

NOT SINCE I studied Moral Philosophy—more years ago than I care to remember—in my first University, north of the Border[1]—do I recall so strong a re-affirmation of individual autonomy in the Kantian sense: the basic concept that the ultimate source of moral principle is the rational will of moral agents, with each owing to every other duties of fundamental respect for persons as ends in themselves. Unsurprisingly, as a classicist, Sir John's starting point is Aristotelian: that rights are logically secondary to the morality which underpins them.

Sir John has argued that the well constructed state is a comfortable home for individuals, as Kantian autonomous agents; and this because the individual cannot be an independent actor on the moral state, unless protected within a sphere of secure freedom, from interference with his basic negative rights, for example, freedom of speech. That accepted on an ethical plane, the problem ever remains how to draw the line in practice, both where negative rights conflict with each other (for example, where unrestricted freedom of speech would sanction incitement to racial hatred) and where a positive right conflicts with a negative right (for example, where the positive right of a society to protect itself through armed forces, collides with a claimed negative right not to be taxed excessively).

Sir John has set out, with great force, his exposition of the philosophical underpinnings of a principled constitution. His starting point, as I have said, is the concept of man as an autonomous moral being,

* The 1996 Mishcon lecture was published in *Public Law*. Lord Irvine was present at the Mishcon lecture and delivered this response thereafter.
[1] The University of Glasgow.

and the Kantian notion of the individual as an end in himself, never a means. The starting point for a constitution, he asserts, must be a recognition of the sovereign autonomy of the individual. The alternative, he implies, is fascism.

Next, I welcome how Sir John has placed the autonomous individual in the context of a community, with his argument that the communal notion of mutual respect goes hand in hand with the proposition that every individual is an end in himself. For myself, I would say that a society which considers its values to be defined by its rights, rather than its rights defined by its values, is a society that is likely to fail to recognise the value of community and, in particular, the role of individual duty within that community. It may be that Sir John has suggested a Mishcon Lecture of tomorrow—a fuller communitarian critique of the classic liberal notion of the autonomous moral agent, on the basis that the individual can only be fully comprehended within the context of communities.

Obviously, within any society tensions arise between the protection of individual autonomy through the assertion of negative rights—rights of the individual not to be interfered with—on the one hand; and the achievement of positive communal goals—though the assertion of positive rights-on the other. A good example of a negative right is the right to dispose of one's property as one wills. An example of a positive right is the right to a clean environment. An untrammeled negative right—to dispose of one's property as one chooses—may conflict with a positive right to a clean environment: so the positive right could override the negative right; and pollution of the atmosphere might have to be outlawed.

Sir John identifies as the central problem, which he has set out to solve in his lecture: 'When is the state justified in curtailing the individual's negative rights in the pursuit of positive rights?' He has formulated his answer in this way:

(1) There is a presumption against any interference with negative rights. (2) Any such interference stands in need of objective justification. (3) An interference will be justified if (a) there would otherwise be a real though direct threat to the general enjoyment of negative rights by the people, or (b) the gain for positive rights, measured against the interference with negative rights in the particular case, is so great that the latter should give way to the former.

This second justification requires the application of a doctrine of proportionality in assessing a proposed interference with a negative right.

Sir John has been kind enough to refer to my own recent foray into the debate about the proper balance between parliamentary supremacy and judicial intervention.[2] He has observed that the doctrine of parliamentary sovereignty is a curious one if it conflicts with the fundamental philosophical imperative of minimal interference with negative rights. The doctrine of parliamentary sovereignty, in its absolute form, would seem to subjugate individual rights to the will (or tyranny) of the majority. I would myself add that it was through taking control of the legislature that Hitler first came to power in Germany.

Sir John asserts, and I think we would all here agree, that the need for the protection of fundamental rights is now universally accepted by those who oppose the subjugation of the individual to an oppressive state. The question, which I believe remains open, however, is how best to achieve the protection of the individual.

One means of protecting individual rights is through the incorporation of a democratically-validated Bill of Rights, enacted by a sovereign Parliament. That in my judgment is the way forward. This will have the virtue of setting out explicitly the rights which we, as a society, recognise are in need of protection, as well as (if the European Convention is used as a model) the circumstances in which positive rights, such as national security, may override the negative rights spelled out in the Bill of Rights.

Certainly an alternative, independent of a Bill of Rights, could be to make the judges the arbiters of our rights, in accordance with the basic principles formulated by Sir John. The central difficulty that I see, however, is that, whilst the fundamental importance of individual rights is almost universally recognised, the nature and content of those rights is not. Sir John himself recognises that even the boundary between negative and positive rights often becomes blurred. Some may see the right to a good education as a positive right; others may claim that it is an essential component of, say, the right to freedom of speech, since without education, we are disabled from communicating our opinions to others effectively.

The view, which I must say is my preference, is that the protection of rights can only be secured effectively if these rights are crystallised in a democratically validated Bill of Rights. However great a consensus there may be about the primacy of individual negative rights in general, there is no consensus as to which particular rights are fundamental;

[2] [1996] *PL* 59.

what their content is; when they may be overriden; and what hierarchy, if any, should exist among them. Unless the sole source of the protection of individual rights is a democratically validated Bill of Rights, then we may be compelled to inhabit a Tower of Babel of conflicting rights theories.

Sir John has given us an admirable account of the philosophical basis of the adherence by modern Western society to the notion of rights—so often taken as given in everyday debate, but without sufficient reflection, which he has provided, on its origins. That, I think, leaves unsettled the question how (and through what constitutional institutions) we identify, articulate and protect those rights in practice. There are two things of which I am sure: that the debate will continue; and that we have heard a major contribution to it.

2

The Human Rights Bill, House of Lords 2nd Reading

THE LORD CHANCELLOR (Lord Irvine of Lairg): My Lords, I have it in command from Her Majesty the Queen to acquaint the House that Her Majesty, having been informed of the purport of the Human Rights Bill, has consented to place Her prerogative and interest, so far as they are affected by the Bill, at the disposal of Parliament for the purposes of the Bill.

I beg to move that this Bill be now read a second time. I am sure that the whole House looks forward to the maiden speech of the noble Baroness, Lady Amos, in this debate. I am delighted that she, a former chief executive of the Equal Opportunities Commission, has chosen this occasion for what I am sure will be a distinguished début.

I chair many Cabinet committees, but none that has given me greater satisfaction than the committee whose labours have brought this Bill forward in the first legislative Session. It occupies a central position in our integrated programme for constitutional change. It will allow British judges for the first time to make their own distinctive contribution to the development of human rights in Europe. It is today a happy reflection that British jurisprudence will shortly flow into an inspired modern building, the European Court of Human Rights in Strasbourg. The architect chosen after an international competition is that great British architect, Richard Rogers, my noble friend Lord Rogers of Riverside, who recently took his place on the Government Benches.

I look forward especially to the contribution today of the noble Lord, Lord Lester of Herne Hill. His major role in the development of the anti-discrimination legislation of the 1970s under the future Lord Jenkins of Hillhead is well known. I should also acknowledge from this position, as did the White Paper, that he has perhaps for 30 years been a tireless campaigner for legislation on human rights. His has not been a silent but an eloquent vigil, and his day has now almost arrived.

It is also a great pleasure to see the noble and learned Lord, Lord Scarman, in his place today and to note that he is to speak in the debate. He has an even longer record of distinguished advocacy on human rights legislation than that of the noble Lord, Lord Lester of Herne Hill.

This is a Government who see Britain's future as a strong and leading participant in the Council of Europe and the European Union. This Bill is further evidence of that. It was not edifying to begin Friday, 24th October by hearing the shadow Home Secretary, Sir Brian Mawhinney, on the 'Today' programme railing at judges from Albania and Bulgaria sitting with other judges in the European Court to determine human rights. I acquit the noble Lord, Lord Kingsland, of any xenophobia. He is incapable of it. I know that when he speaks in support of this Bill he speaks strongly for himself. I doubt, however, whether he speaks for his party. Tory policy before the election was clear: outright rejection of the case for incorporation. From the mouth of the then Prime Minister we had this miracle of sapience:

We have no need of a Bill of Rights because we have freedom.

My Lords, what enervating insularity—and what nonsense!

The traditional freedom of the individual under an unwritten constitution to do himself that which is not prohibited by law gives no protection from misuse of power by the state, nor any protection from acts or omissions of public bodies which harm individuals in a way that is incompatible with their human rights under the convention. Our legal system has been unable to protect people in the 50 cases in which the European Court has found a violation of the convention by the United Kingdom. That is more than any other country except Italy. The trend has been upwards. Over half the violations have been found since 1990. I have no doubt that with his distinguished European background the noble Lord, Lord Kingsland, will reject as absurd the proposition that because we have liberty, we have no need of human rights. This is a Home Office Bill. I invite the noble Lord, Lord Kingsland, to define in his speech what is the policy, what is the position in principle of the Shadow Home Secretary and of the Conservative Party on this Bill.

This Bill will bring human rights home. People will be able to argue for their rights and claim their remedies under the convention in any court or tribunal in the United Kingdom. Our courts will develop human rights throughout society. A culture of awareness of human rights will develop. Before Second Reading of any Bill the responsible Minister will make a statement that the Bill is or is not compatible with convention rights. So there will have to be close scrutiny of the human rights implications of all legislation before it goes forward. Our standing will rise internationally. The protection of human rights at home gives credibility to our foreign policy to advance the cause of human rights around the world.

Our critics say the Bill will cede powers to Europe, will politicise the judiciary and will diminish parliamentary sovereignty. We are not ceding new powers to Europe. The United Kingdom already accepts that Strasbourg rulings bind. Next, the Bill is carefully drafted and designed to respect our traditional understanding of the separation of powers. It does so intellectually convincingly and, if I may express my high regard for the parliamentary draftsman, elegantly.

The design of the Bill is to give the courts as much space as possible to protect human rights, short of a power to set aside or ignore Acts of Parliament. In the very rare cases where the higher courts will find it impossible to read and give effect to any statute in a way which is compatible with convention rights, they will be able to make a declaration of incompatibility. Then it is for Parliament to decide whether there should be remedial legislation. Parliament may, not must, and generally will, legislate. If a Minister's prior assessment of compatibility (under Clause 19) is subsequently found by declaration of incompatibility by the courts to have been mistaken, it is hard to see how a Minister could withhold remedial action. There is a fast-track route for Ministers to take remedial action by order. But the remedial action will not retrospectively make unlawful an act which was a lawful act—lawful since sanctioned by statute. This is the logic of the design of the Bill. It maximises the protection of human rights without trespassing on parliamentary sovereignty.

Before I turn to the detail of the Bill, I am determined to address concerns that have recently been expressed by the press. First, the Government are not introducing a privacy statute. They have resisted demands that they should. They believe that strong and effective self-regulation is the best way forward in the interests of both the press and the public. It is well known, and deserves to be better known, that the noble Lord, Lord Wakeham, the Chairman of the Press Complaints Commission, with which I was myself associated until May as a member of the appointments commission which appoints its members, has begun the necessary work of strengthening self-regulation.

Although much remains to be done, there have already been significant improvements which are as welcome to government as to the wider public. We look forward to the noble Lord's good work continuing and prospering. It is strong and effective self-regulation if it—and I emphasise the 'if'—provides adequate remedies which will keep these cases away from the courts.

I want, however, to address directly the concerns of the press about how the courts will deal with Article 10 (freedom of expression, a central part of which is freedom of the press) and Article 8 (privacy) once the convention is incorporated. I am a strong upholder of the freedom of the press; and I am a member of a Government who, as a whole, give the highest value to upholding the freedom of the press. The European Court has in terms declared that Article 10,

> constitutes one of the essential foundations of a democratic society.

The Court is hostile to any attempt to restrict press freedom when the complainant is a public figure. Our highest courts have said the same. In 1990 the noble and learned Lord, Lord Bridge, said:

> In a free democratic society it is almost too obvious to need stating that those who hold office in Government and who are responsible for public administration must always be open to criticism. Any attempt to stifle or fetter such criticism amounts to political censorship.

In 1990 the noble and learned Lord, Lord Goff, declared that in the field of freedom of speech there was no difference in principle between English law and Article 10. In 1993 the noble and learned Lord, Lord Keith, stated uncompromisingly:

> It is of the highest—I emphasise—the highest—public importance that … any Governmental body should be open to uninhibited public criticism.

The European Court in 1991 in *Sunday Times v The UK (No 2)*—the Spycatcher case—declared:

> the dangers inherent in prior restraints are such that they call for the most careful scrutiny on the part of the Court. This is especially so as far as the press is concerned for news is a perishable commodity and to delay its publication even for a short period—and I emphasise 'even for a short period'—may well deprive it of all its value and interests.

I agree with that and so, I believe, does every British judge.

I say as strongly as I can to the press: 'I understand your concerns, but let me assure you that press freedom will be in safe hands with our British judges and with the judges of the European Court'. I add this, 'You know that, regardless of incorporation, the judges are very likely to develop a common law right of privacy themselves. What I say is that any law of privacy will be a better law after incorporation, because the judges will have to balance Article 10 and Article 8, giving Article 10 its due high value'.

More practically, I do not envisage the press going down to late Friday or Saturday privacy injunctions, disruptive of publishing timetables, if the press has solid grounds for maintaining that there is a public interest in publishing. The doors of my officials and of my right honourable friend the Home Secretary have been open throughout the summer to anyone interested to discuss the practical implications of incorporation. There were many who walked through our doors. They remain open. I say emphatically to editors and media lawyers, interested to discuss with us appropriate arrangements for handling these cases, where self-regulation has failed to nip them in the bud, 'You are welcome to come and make your views known to us'.

I now turn to the detail of the Bill. Clause 1 lists the convention rights that are to be given further effect in the United Kingdom by the Bill. They range from the right to a fair trial to the right to life itself; and they are all fundamental human rights. The text is set out in Schedule 1 to the Bill. Also, Clause 1 makes it possible for the rights contained in other protocols to be added to the Bill if the United Kingdom becomes a party to them in future.

Clause 2 requires courts in the United Kingdom to take account of the decisions of the convention institutions in Strasbourg in their consideration of convention points which come before them. It is entirely appropriate that our courts should draw on the wealth of existing jurisprudence on the convention.

Clauses 3 to 5 are concerned with the relationship between the convention rights and other legislation. Clause 3 provides that legislation, whenever enacted, must as far as possible be read and given effect in a way which is compatible with the convention rights. This will ensure that, if it is possible to interpret a statute in two ways—one compatible with the convention and one not—the courts will always choose the interpretation which is compatible. In practice, this will prove a strong form of incorporation.

As I have said, however, the Bill does not allow the courts to set aside or ignore Acts of Parliament. Clause 3 preserves the effect of primary legislation which is incompatible with the convention. It does the same for secondary legislation where it is inevitably incompatible because of the terms of the parent statute.

Clause 4 provides for the rare cases where the courts may have to make declarations of incompatibility. Such declarations are serious. That is why Clause 5 gives the Crown the right to have notice of any case where a court is considering making a declaration of incompatibility and the right to be joined as a party to the proceedings, so that it can make representations on the point.

A declaration of incompatibility will not itself change the law. The statute will continue to apply despite its incompatibility. But the declaration is very likely to prompt the Government and Parliament to respond.

In the normal course of events, it would be necessary to await a suitable opportunity to introduce primary legislation to make an appropriate amendment. That could involve unacceptable delay when Parliamentary timetables are crowded. We have taken the view that if legislation has been declared incompatible, a prompt parliamentary remedy should be available. Clauses 10 to 12 of the Bill provide how that is to be achieved. A Minister of the Crown will be able to make what is to be known as a remedial order. The order will be available in response to a declaration of incompatibility by the higher courts. It will also be available if legislation appears to a Minister to be incompatible because of a finding by the European Court of Human Rights.

We recognise that a power to amend primary legislation by means of a statutory instrument is not a power to be conferred or exercised lightly. Those clauses therefore place a number of procedural and other restrictions on its use. First, a remedial order must be approved by both Houses of Parliament. That will normally require it to be laid in draft and subject to the affirmative resolution procedure before it takes effect. In urgent cases, it will be possible to make the order without it being approved in that way, but even then it will cease to have effect after 40 days unless it is approved by Parliament. So we have built in as much parliamentary scrutiny as possible.

In addition, the power to make a remedial order may be used only to remove an incompatibility or a possible incompatibility between legislation and the convention. It may therefore be used only to protect human rights, not to infringe them. And the Bill also specifically provides that no person is to be guilty of a criminal offence solely as a result of any retrospective effect of a remedial order.

So far I have spoken about the relationship between the convention rights and legislation and about what happens if they cannot be reconciled. That is only the first way in which the Bill brings rights home. On its own that would be insufficient. I turn now to the second way, which is in Clauses 6 to 9. Clause 6 makes it unlawful for a public authority to act in a way which incompatible with the convention. Before I explain what that means in practice, I should say something about our approach to the application of this Bill to public authorities. We decided, first of all, that a provision of this kind should apply only to public authorities, however defined, and not to private individuals. That reflects the arrangements for taking cases to the convention institutions in Strasbourg. The convention had its origins in a desire to protect people from the misuse of power by the state, rather than from the actions of private individuals. Someone who takes a case to Strasbourg is proceeding against the United Kingdom Government, rather than against a private individual. We also decided that we should apply the Bill to a wide rather than a narrow range of public authorities, so as to provide as much protection as possible to those who claim that their rights have been infringed.

Clause 6 is designed to apply not only to obvious public authorities such as government departments and the police, but also to bodies which are public in certain respects but not others. Organisations of this kind will be liable under clause 6 of the Bill for any of their acts, unless the act is of a private nature. Finally, Clause 6 does not impose a liability on organisations which have no public functions at all.

If people believe that their convention rights have been infringed by a public authority, what can they do about it? Under Clause 7 they will be able to rely on convention points in any legal proceedings involving a public authority; for example as part of a defence to criminal or civil proceedings, or when acting as plaintiff in civil proceedings, or in seeking judicial review, or on appeal. They will also be able to bring proceedings against public authorities purely on convention grounds even if no other cause of action is open to them.

If a court or tribunal finds that a public authority has acted in a way which is incompatible with the convention, what can it do about it? Under Clause 8 it may provide whatever remedy is available to it and which seems just and appropriate. That might include awarding damages against the public authority. We have concluded that if a court is considering an award of damages for an act which is incompatible with the convention, then it should have regard to the principles applied by the European Court of Human Rights. Our aim is that people should receive damages equivalent to what they would have obtained had they taken their case to Strasbourg.

Clause 9 is concerned with what happens when a court or tribunal acts in a way which is incompatible with the convention. Here we have preserved the existing principle of judicial immunity and have provided that proceedings against a court or tribunal on convention grounds may be brought only by an appeal or application for judicial review. I have spoken at some length about the two main ways in which the Bill brings right home. I now deal more briefly with the other provisions of the Bill.

Clauses 14 to 17 are concerned with derogations from, and reservations to, articles of the convention. The United Kingdom has one derogation and one reservation in place, relating to Article 5(3) of the convention and Article 2 of the first protocol, respectively, and those articles have effect subject to them. The text of the derogation and reservation is set out in Schedule 2 to the Bill. They will have domestic effect in accordance with the provisions of the Bill. Any future derogation and reservations may also be given domestic effect under the Bill. For domestic purposes they will be subject to periodic renewal in the case of derogation, or review in the case of reservations.

Clause 18 stands apart from the other provisions of the Bill. It is concerned with the appointment of judges to the European Court of Human Rights. That Court is being reconstituted next year as a new permanent Court and one of its member judges will come from the United Kingdom. In drawing up nominations for that post, we want to be able to select from a wide field of suitably qualified candidates. One disincentive which might discourage some potential candidates from coming forward is that sitting full-time as a judge at Strasbourg would be incompatible with performing the duties of a judge in the United Kingdom. Under our present law, a judge would have to resign his office here in order to take up the appointment at Strasbourg, with no guarantee of reinstatement at the end of the term of office. Clause 18 is designed to remove that obstacle, so that if a judge is appointed to the European Court he will have the right to return to the bench in the United Kingdom after his term at Strasbourg.

Clause 19 imposes a new requirement on government Ministers when introducing legislation. In future, they will have to make a statement either that the provisions of the legislation are compatible with the convention or that they cannot make such a statement but nevertheless wish Parliament to proceed to consider the Bill. Ministers will obviously want to make a positive statement whenever possible. That requirement should therefore have a significant impact on the scrutiny of draft legislation within government. Where such a statement cannot be made, parliamentary scrutiny of the Bill would be intense.

Finally, Clauses 20 to 22 are concerned with various supplemental provisions with which I need not detain the House.

Lastly, the Bill does not provide for the establishment of a human rights commission. I appreciate that this will cause disappointment to some. It is suggested that a commission would have a useful role to play in promoting human rights and advising individuals how to proceed if they believe their rights have been infringed. Although we have given this proposal much thought, we have concluded that a human rights commission is not central to our main task today, which is to incorporate the convention as promised in our election manifesto. There are questions to be resolved about the relationship of a new commission with other bodies in the human rights field; for example, the Equal Opportunities Commission and the Commission for Racial Equality. Would a human rights commission take over their responsibilities, or act in partnership with them, or be an independent body independent of them? We would also want to be sure that the potential benefits of a human rights commission were sufficient to justify establishing and funding for a new non-governmental organisation. We do not rule out a human rights commission in future, but our judgment is that it would be premature to provide for one now.

We have, however, given very positive thought to the possibility of a parliamentary committee on human rights. This is not in the Bill itself because it would not require legislation to establish and because it would in any case be the responsibility of Parliament rather than the Government. But we are attracted to the idea of a parliamentary committee on human rights, whether a separate committee of each House or a joint committee of both houses. It would be a natural focus for the increased interest in human rights issues which Parliament will inevitably take when we have brought rights home. It could, for example, not only keep the protection of human rights under review, but could also be in the forefront of public education and consultation on human rights. It could receive written submissions and hold public hearings at a number of locations across the country. It could be in the van of the promotion of a human rights culture across the country.

I have tried to explain why the Government want to bring rights home and how we propose to do it. This Bill represents a major plank in our programme for constitutional change and invigoration. I have for many years been downcast by the want of protection for human rights in the United Kingdom. In a democracy it is right that the majority should govern. But that is precisely why it is also right that the human rights of individuals and minorities should be protected by law.

I am convinced that incorporation of the European convention into our domestic law will deliver a modern reconciliation of the inevitable tension between the democratic right of the majority to exercise political power and the democratic need of individuals and minorities to have their human rights secured. I commend this Bill to the House and look forward to the whole of our debate today.

Moved, That the Bill be now read a second time.—(*The Lord Chancellor.*)

3

The Development of Human Rights in Britain under an Incorporated Convention on Human Rights*

O N OCTOBER 23, I introduced the Human Rights Bill into Parliament. It will incorporate into the domestic law of the United Kingdom the rights and liberties guaranteed by the European Convention on Human Rights. It will mean that our citizens can secure their rights from our own United Kingdom courts. They will not have to take the long slow road to the Court in Strasbourg. It is one of the major constitutional changes which this Government is making.

I want to consider the significance the Human Rights Bill has for individuals, but also to go beyond the extensive area in which the Act will bite and to consider how the Human Rights Bill will influence and mould the process of law making and the content of the law in other and wider areas. It will be a constitutional change of major significance: protecting the individual citizen against erosion of liberties, either deliberate or gradual. It will also help develop a process of justice based on the promotion of positive rights.

Today we talk readily of Human Rights law. There is now a corpus of law, international and national, recognising fundamental freedoms, International Human Rights law. Fifty years ago it would not have been possible to talk of such a body of law. Until then very few issues would have been regarded in any way as the province of international law. Piracy and slavery were the major exceptions. For many years the existence of internationally recognised norms of human rights was simply inconsistent with central propositions of international law, the positivist doctrines of state sovereignty and domestic jurisdiction.

---

* This article is based on the Tom Sargant Memorial Lecture delivered on 16 December 1997. I am indebted to Peter Goldsmith QC for the great assistance he gave me in the preparation of this Lecture.

This view was particularly expounded by John Austin in his *Lectures on Jurisprudence*, delivered at the newly founded University College London between 1828 and 1832. He brought together many of the ideas scattered through Bentham's own voluminous works.[1] Law, according to Austin's definition, was a body of rules fixed and enforced by a sovereign political authority. There could be no such thing as international law, it followed, since there was no sovereign political authority over the individual sovereign States themselves to set or enforce any rules of conduct. It also followed that under the doctrine of state sovereignty, individuals received no protection under international law. Their protection had to come in courts of purely domestic jurisdiction. It was a breach of international law for one State to intervene in another State's sphere of exclusive domestic jurisdiction, unless authorised by permissive rules to the contrary.[2] The idea of state sovereignty was not new. The Dutch lawyer, Hugo Grotius, usually, but not universally,[3] recognised as the father of contemporary international law, had in his great work on the *Law of War and Peace*[4] accepted the sovereign State as the basic unit of international law over 200 years before. Yet the exaggerated importance Austin was to attach to the theory of sovereignty was easily exploitable by despots to justify resisting outside 'interference' in their oppressive domestic conduct towards their own peoples. It can be powerfully argued that the acceptance by lawyers of this view of state sovereignty did much to hold back the development of international norms of human rights.[5]

It took the horrors of the Second World War and the Holocaust to start a decisive transformation in international law. The United Nations Charter recognised specifically an international obligation to secure human rights. Its Preamble identifies one of the United Nations' own primary purposes as 'Promoting and encouraging respect for human rights and for fundamental freedoms for all without distinction as to race, sex, language or religion'.[6] The enlightened draftsmen of the Charter, determined to do all in their power to remove the threat of a

---

[1] See Sabine, *A History of Political Theory* 3rd ed (London Harrap, 1968), p 684.
[2] See for example Schwarzenberger, *A Manual of International Law* 5th ed, (London Stevens, 1967) at p 65
[3] *Schwarzenberger, ibid* p 19.
[4] *Dr Jure Bellis ac Pacis* (1625).
[5] For example by FS Nariman, Chairman of the Executive Committee of the International Commission of Jurists in an address to the International Bar Association given at the United Nations, New York in June 1977.
[6] Charter of the United Nations, Preamble 3; UNTS xvi; UKTS 67 (1946) Cmd 7015.

return to conflict and genocide, saw the need for these fundamental freedoms not only as common justice but also as part of the process of guaranteeing peace. And so Article 55 of the Charter placed on the United Nations an obligation to promote 'Universal respect for, and observance of, human rights and fundamental freedoms for all without distinction as to race, sex, language, or religion'; and to do so, in the words of the Charter, 'With a view to the creation of conditions of stability and well being which are necessary for peaceful and friendly nations based on respect for the principle of equal rights and self-determination of peoples'.[7] The members themselves pledged cooperation with the United Nations and to take joint and separate action to achieve those purposes.[8]

In the five years that followed the agreement of the Charter, international law moved in a decisive new direction. The Genocide Convention,[9] the Geneva Conventions for the Protection of Victims of War,[10] Relative to the Protection of Civilian Persons in Time of War[11] and in relation to Conditions of Wounded Servicemen[12] were all promulgated and agreed during this fertile legislative period. So also was the Universal Declaration of Human Rights itself.[13] It celebrates its half centenary in 1998.

Two other important events occurred in the same period. First, the judgment at the Nuremberg Trials, presided over by Lord Justice Lawrence, gave concrete evidence that victims of crimes against humanity committed even by their own Governments were entitled to the protection of international criminal law.[14] The significance of these trials cannot be underestimated. Yet the decision to stage them had not been lightly reached. Churchill, for one, had been against them. But the Allies had committed themselves in the Declarations of St James of 1942 and the Moscow Declarations of November 1943.[15] The United

---

[7] *Ibid*, Arts 55 and 56.

[8] Above n 6, Art 56.

[9] Convention on the Prevention and Punishment of the Crime of Genocide (1948) 78 UNTS 277; Cmnd 2904.

[10] Geneva III, (1949) 75 UNTS 31.

[11] Geneva IV, (1949) 75 UNTS 31, Cmnd 550.

[12] Convention for the Amelioration of the Condition of Wounded and Sick in Armed Forces in the Field (1949); Convention for the Amelioration of the Condition of Wounded and Sick and Shipwrecked Members of Armed Forces at Sea (1949) Geneva II.

[13] General Assembly Resolution 217A (III), UN Doc A/810 at 71 (1948).

[14] See generally Davies, *Europe, A History*, (London Pimlico, 1997).

[15] *Ibid*, and see HL Deb, v 124, pp 577, *et seq*; and 38 *American Journal of International Law* (1944), suppl p 3.

Kingdom has been a strong supporter of the successors to that first international war crimes tribunal, now sitting to deal with events in the former Yugoslavia and Rwanda. The present Government showed our own strong commitment to this process when earlier this year British soldiers were involved in the arrest of suspected war criminals.

It was during the same fertile period that the Council of Europe, established as part of the Allies' programme to rebuild Europe, produced the European Convention on Human Rights.

As the White Paper introducing the Human Rights Bill[16] records, the simple power of the language of its articles led Sir Edward Gardner QC, the Conservative MP, to say in 1987, when introducing an earlier attempt to incorporate the Convention:

> It is language which echoes down the corridors of history. It goes deep into our history and as far back as the Magna Carta.[17]

The history of the United Kingdom's quickness to ratify the Convention but slowness to adopt the jurisdiction of the Court of Human Rights for individual petition, and even greater slowness to incorporate its provision into domestic law, have been chronicled by Lord Lester of Herne Hill QC.[18] I pay tribute to his long campaign to see the Convention given greater effect in the United Kingdom.

So, spurred by the urgent need to reconstruct civilisation after the winter of World War II, in this short period legal innovation had turned the individual citizen into a subject of international law. In 1950, Hersch Lauterpacht, later judge of the International Court of Justice, was able to assert that 'The individual has now acquired a status and a stature which have transformed him from an object of international compassion into a subject of international right'.[19]

I have dealt with this background because it is right to remind ourselves of our history and of the roots of the Convention. It is right to remind ourselves that these rights are part of the bedrock laid down after 1945 for a safe and just society. It is also right to remind ourselves of the strong justification for recognising in domestic law international human rights obligations.

---

[16] Rights Brought Home: The Human Rights Bill, Cm 3872, 1997.
[17] HC Deb, 6 February 1987, col 1224.
[18] A Lester, 'Fundamental Rights. The United Kingdom Isolated' (1984) *PL* 46.
[19] Lauterpacht, *International Law and Human Rights* (London, Longman, 1950).

I. A RIGHTS BASED SYSTEM

Against this background, I turn to the Human Rights Bill and its effects.

A major change which the Act will bring flows from the shift to a rights based system. Under this system a citizen's right is asserted as a positive entitlement expressed in clear and principled terms. For example, under Article 5 of the Convention 'Everyone has the right to liberty and security of person'. Whilst there are reservations to that right, the reservations take effect as explicit exceptions and derogations which must be justified according to the terms of the Article. They represent exceptions which, in the public interest, are justified and reasonable. For example, the basic right in Article 5 is qualified by a list of the defined and circumscribed cases where a person may be deprived of his liberty. So, where a national authority wants to justify a detention, it will need to show how the facts fit into one of those defined categories and how it has met other requirements of the Convention; for example, the fair trial guarantees in Article 6.

This approach contrasts with the traditional common law approach to the protection of individual liberties. The common law treats liberty only as a 'negative' right. As explained by Lord Donaldson MR in one of the *Spycatcher* cases[20] this negative approach means that 'the starting point of our domestic law is that every citizen has a right to do what he likes, unless restrained by the common law or by Statute.' The liberty of the subject is therefore the 'negative' right of what is left over when all the prohibitions have limited the area of lawful conduct.

Dicey saw merit in this negative approach. He believed that the absence of writing lent the common law a flexibility to develop to meet changing conditions. But the approach has disadvantages which are greater. By proposing this law the Government has decisively demonstrated its view that the more serious threat to liberty is an absence of written guarantees of freedom. For the negative approach offers little protection against a creeping erosion of freedom by a legislature willing to countenance infringement of liberty or simply blind to the effect of an otherwise well intentioned piece of law. As Dworkin has argued, the challenge to liberty is not only from despots. A Government may have 'a more mundane and corrupting insensitivity to liberty'.[21] The Human Rights Bill is our bulwark against that danger. The traditional freedom

---

[20] *AG v Guardian Newspapers (No 2)* [1990] 1 AC 109.
[21] R Dworkin, *A Bill of Rights for Britain?* (London, Chatto, 1988) pp 9–10.

of the individual under an unwritten constitution to do himself that which is not prohibited by law gives no protection from misuse of power by the State, nor any protection from acts or omissions by public bodies which harm individuals in a way that is incompatible with their human rights under the Convention. Our legal system has been unable to protect people in the 50 cases in which the European Court has found a violation of the Convention by the United Kingdom. The view that because we have liberty we have no need of human rights must be rejected.

II.   THE IMPLICATIONS OF THE CHANGE

What then are the practical implications of this change to a rights based system within the field of civil liberties?

A.   Domestication of Freedom

First, the Act will give to the courts the tools to uphold freedoms at the very time their infringement is threatened. Until now, the only remedy where a freedom guaranteed by the Convention is infringed and domestic law is deficient has been expensive and slow proceedings in Strasbourg. They could not even be commenced until after all the domestic avenues of complaint and appeal had been exhausted. The courts will now have the power to give effect to the Convention rights in the course of proceedings when they arise in this country and to grant relief against an unlawful act of a public authority (a necessarily widely drawn concept). The courts will not be able to strike down primary legislation. But they will be able to make a declaration of incompatibility where a piece of primary legislation conflicts with a Convention right. This will trigger the ability to use in Parliament a special fast-track procedure to bring the law into line with the Convention.

This innovative technique will provide the right balance between the judiciary and Parliament. Parliament is the democratically elected representative of the people and must remain sovereign. The judiciary will be able to exercise to the full the power to scrutinise legislation rigorously against the fundamental freedoms guaranteed by the Convention but without becoming politicised. The ultimate decision to amend legislation to bring it into line with the Convention, however, will rest with Parliament. The ultimate responsibility for compliance with the Convention must be Parliament's alone.

B.   Prioritising Rights

That point illustrates the second important effect of our new approach. If there are to be differences or departures from the principles of the Convention they should be conscious and reasoned departures, and not the product of rashness, muddle or ignorance. This will be guaranteed both by the powers given to the courts but also by other provisions which will be enacted. In particular, Ministers and administrators will be obliged to do all their work keeping clearly and directly in mind its impact on human rights, as expressed in the Convention and in the jurisprudence which attaches to it. For, where any Bill is introduced in either House, the Minister of the Crown, in whose charge it is, will be required to make a written statement that, either, in his view, the provisions of the Bill are compatible with the Convention rights; or that he cannot make that statement but the Government nonetheless wishes the House to proceed with the Bill. In the latter case the Bill would inevitably be subject to close and critical scrutiny by Parliament. Human rights will not be a matter of fudge. The responsible Minister will have to ensure that the legislation does not infringe guaranteed freedoms, or be prepared to justify his decision openly and in the full glare of parliamentary and public opinion.

That will be particularly important whenever there come under consideration those articles of the Convention which lay down what I call principled rights, subject to possible limitation. I have in mind Articles 8–11, dealing with respect for private life, freedom of religion, freedom of expression, and freedom of assembly and association. These articles confer those freedoms subject to possible limitations, such as, for instance in the case of Article 10 (freedom of expression)

> are prescribed by law and are necessary in a democratic society in the interests of national security, territorial integrity or public safety, for the prevention of disorder or crime, for the protection of health or morals, for the protection of the reputation or rights of others, for preventing the disclosure of information received in confidence, or for maintaining the authority and impartiality of the judiciary.

In such cases, administrators and legislators will have to think clearly about whether what they propose really is necessary in a democratic society, and for what object it is necessary. Quite apart from the concentration on the Convention and its jurisprudence this will require, the process should produce better thought-out, clearer and more transparent administration.

The important requirements of transparency on Convention issues that will accompany the introduction of all future legislation will ensure that Parliament knows exactly what it is doing in a human rights context. I regard this improvement in both the efficiency and the openness of our legislative process as one of the main benefits produced by incorporation of the Convention.

C.   Substantive Rights

Thirdly, the Convention will enable the courts to reach results in cases which give full effect to the substantive rights guaranteed by the Convention. It would not be appropriate for me to deal with individual aspects of the law which may come up for decision in the courts in future, but some general observations are possible.

The courts have not ignored the Convention rights. As long ago as 1972 in *Cassell v Broome*[22] Lord Kilbrandon referred to the Convention as supporting the existence of 'A constitutional right to free speech' when warning against holding the profit motive to be sufficient to justify punitive damages for defamation.

But the courts have only had limited ability to give effect to those rights. Lord Bingham in his maiden speech in the House of Lords on taking the office of Lord Chief Justice, enumerated six ways in which the courts have been able to take the Convention rights into account.[23] Of these, the first and the most important has been as an aid to construction. 'Where', as Lord Bingham explained, 'a United Kingdom statute is capable of two interpretations, one consistent with the Convention and one inconsistent, then the courts will presume that Parliament did not intend to legislate in violation of international law.' A further instance is in developing the common law where it is uncertain, unclear or incomplete.[24]

But the courts are not enforcing the Convention when they act in this way. They are enforcing statutory or common law. It follows—and it is emphasised in all the authorities—that recourse cannot be had to the

[22] [1972] 1 All ER 801.
[23] HC Deb 3 July 1996, col 146.
[24] See eg, the Court of Appeal in *R v Secretary of State for the Home Department, ex parte Brind* [1991] 1 AC 696.

terms of the Convention unless the terms of the Statute, or the content of the common law[25] is uncertain or ambiguous. If Parliament has spoken with sufficient certainty, in terms that exclude or contradict the Convention, the latter, under our present arrangements, has no place.[26] The decision of the House of Lords in *ex parte Brind* is a case in point. That concerned a challenge by a group of broadcasters to the restrictions then imposed preventing the broadcast of the voices of members of proscribed organisations, notably Sinn Fein. The Secretary of State had acted under a power broadly drawn in the Broadcasting Act 1981 empowering him to prohibit the broadcast of 'any matter or classes of matter specified in the notice'. The Applicants tried, unsuccessfully, to persuade the Court to impose a limitation on those words to make them consistent with the right of freedom of expression in Article 10 of the Convention. The House of Lords could find no ambiguity allowing them to read in such words of limitation.

It is moreover likely—although individual cases will be for the courts to determine and I should not attempt to prejudge them—that the position will in at least some cases be different from what it would have been under the pre-incorporation practice. The reason for this lies in the techniques to be followed once the Act is in force. Unlike the old Diceyan approach where the Court would go straight to what restriction had been imposed, the focus will first be on the positive right and then on the justifiability of the exception. Moreover, the Act will require the courts to read and give effect to the legislation in a way compatible with the Convention rights 'so far as it is possible to do so ...'[27] This, as the White Paper makes clear, goes far beyond the present rule. It will not be necessary to find an ambiguity. On the contrary the courts will be required to interpret legislation so as to uphold the Convention rights unless the legislation itself is so clearly incompatible with the Convention that it is impossible to do so.[28] Moreover, it should be clear from the Parliamentary history, and in particular the Ministerial statement of compatibility which will be required by the Act, that Parliament did not intend to cut across a Convention right. Ministerial statements of compatibility will inevitably be a strong spur

---

[25] 'Courts in the United Kingdom should have regard to the provisions of the [Convention] ... where our domestic law is not firmly settled', *AG v BBC* [1981] AC 303, at 352, *per* Lord Fraser.

[26] *R v Home Secretary, ex parte Brind* [1991] 1 AC 696.

[27] Clause 3(1).

[28] Clause 3(1).

to the courts to find means of construing statutes compatibly with the Convention.

Whilst this particular approach is innovative, there are some precedents which will assist the courts. In cases involving European Community law, decisions of our courts already show that interpretative techniques may be used to make the domestic legislation comply with the Community law, even where this requires straining the meaning of words or reading in words which are not there. An illustrative case is *Litster*[29] concerning the construction of the Transfer of Undertakings Regulations.[30] The issue was whether protection in the Regulations, limited to those employed in the business 'immediately before' the time of the transfer, extended to employees unfairly dismissed very shortly before the transfer. The applicants had clearly not been employed in the business immediately before the transfer as those words would normally be interpreted. Nor were the words ambiguous. Yet the House of Lords interpreted the Regulations (so as to accord with the European Court's existing interpretation of the underlying Community obligation which the Regulations were intended to implement) by implying additional words 'or would have been so employed if they had not been unfairly dismissed [by reason of the transfer]'. This implication of appropriate language into an apparently unambiguous provision is the sort of tool which could have led to a different result in a case like *Brind*. It shows the strong interpretative techniques that can be expected in Convention cases.

Guidance may also be found in the jurisprudence of the New Zealand courts. Under the New Zealand Bill of Rights Act 1990 a meaning consistent with the rights and freedoms contained in the Bill of Rights is to be given in preference to any other meaning 'wherever an enactment can be given [such] a meaning'. The existing New Zealand decisions seem to show that the only cases where the legislation will *not* be interpreted consistently with the protected rights are those where a statutory provision contains a clear limitation of fundamental rights.[31] The difference from the approach until now applied by the English courts will be this: the Court will interpret as consistent with the Convention not only those provisions which are ambiguous in the sense

[29] *Litster v Forth Dry Dock and Forth Estuary Engineering* (1990) 1 AC 546.
[30] Transfer of Undertakings (Protection of Employment) Regulations 1981.
[31] See especially *R v Laugalis* (1993) 10 CRNZ; and also *Ministry of Transport v Noort* [1992] 3 NZLR 260; *R v Rangi* [1992] 1 NZLR 385; see also the valuable analysis by Jason Coppel [forthcoming 2003].

that the *language* used is capable of two different meanings, but also those provisions where there is *no* ambiguity in that sense, unless a *clear* limitation is expressed. In the latter category of case it will be 'possible' (to use the statutory language) to read the legislation in a conforming sense because there will be no clear indication that a limitation on the protected rights was intended so as to make it 'impossible' to read it as conforming.

D.   Principled Decision-Making

The fourth point may be shortly stated but is of immense importance. The courts' decisions will be based on a more overtly principled, and perhaps moral, basis. The Court will look at the positive right. It will only accept an interference with that right where a justification, allowed under the Convention, is made out. The scrutiny will not be limited to seeing if the *words* of an exception can be satisfied. The Court will need to be satisfied that the *spirit* of this exception is made out. It will need to be satisfied that the interference with the protected right *is* justified in the public interests in a free democratic society. Moreover, the courts will in this area have to apply the Convention principle of proportionality. This means the Court will be looking *substantively* at that question. It will not be limited to a secondary review of the decision making process but at the primary question of the merits of the decision itself.

In reaching its judgment, therefore, the Court will need to expand and explain its own view of whether the conduct is legitimate. It will produce in short a decision on the *morality* of the conduct and not simply its compliance with the bare letter of the law.

III.   THE INFLUENCE ON OTHER AREAS OF LAW

I believe, moreover, that the effects of the incorporation of the Convention will be felt way beyond the sphere of the application of the rights guaranteed by the Convention alone. As we move from the traditional Diceyan model of the common law to a rights based system, the effects will be felt throughout the common law and in the very process of judicial decision-making. This will be a healthy and dynamic development in our law.

There is good precedent for this sort of influence on the common law in the effect which European Community law has already produced. Under the European Communities Act, the precedence accorded to European law can lead to legislation being suspended[32] or disapplied[33] or declared to be unlawful.[34] As I pointed out in a Lecture I delivered to the Administrative Law Bar Association in October 1995[35] British Courts are as a result now required to perform a number of tasks which would have been unthinkable even 20 years ago.

Although the legislative technique adopted under the Human Rights Bill is different from that under the European Communities Act, the effect on the general process of deciding cases will, I believe, be as influential. Courts will, from time to time be required to determine if primary or secondary legislation is incompatible with the Convention rights.[36] They will decide if the acts of public authorities are unlawful through contravention, perhaps even unconscious contravention, of those rights.[37] They may have to award damages as a result.[38]

These are all new remedies for our courts to apply and, as they begin to develop the tools and techniques to apply them, an influence on other areas of law and judicial decision making is, I believe, inevitable.

This spillover effect has been seen already from the application here of European Community law. Cases may be seen where the very exposure of practitioners and judges to a new body of law presents new solutions even for purely domestic problems. A good example, was the reliance by Lord Goff of Chieveley on principles of German law in deciding in the House of Lords the question of the responsibility to the disappointed beneficiary of an English solicitor who failed to draw up a will before the demise of the would-be testators.[39] Another example is *Woolwich Equitable Building Society v Inland Revenue Commissioners*.[40] The House of Lords had to decide whether the Inland Revenue was liable to pay interest when it returned tax

---

[32] *R v Secretary of State for Transport, ex parte Factortame Ltd (No 2)* [1991] 1 AC 603.
[33] For example, *Marshall v Southampton and South West Area Health Authority (No 2)* [1994] 2 WLR 292.
[34] *R v Secretary of State for Employment, ex parte Equal Opportunities Commission* [1995] 1 AC 1.
[35] 'Judges and decision-makers—The theory and practice of Wednesbury review' [1996] PL 59.
[36] Clause 4.
[37] Clause 6.
[38] Clause 8(2).
[39] *White v Jones* [1995] 2 AC 207.
[40] [1993] AC 70.

originally paid by the tax payer under regulations held to be invalid. This was a purely domestic question and no issue of Community law arose. Classic common law principles suggested interest would only be payable where the tax had been paid under compulsion or mistake of fact and not (as here) through a payment made voluntarily under a mistake of law. Yet the majority of the House concluded that interest was payable by the Revenue by extending the categories of obligation to repay money to cases where money was paid pursuant to an unlawful demand by a public authority. A comparison with community law seems to have played a part in this decision to change the common law of England. Lord Goff noted in terms that the European Court of Justice had held[41] that a person who pays charges levied by a member State contrary to community rules is entitled to repayment of the charge. He went on to say:

> ... at a time when Community law is becoming increasingly important, it would be strange if the right of the citizen to recover overpaid charges were to be more restricted under domestic law than it is under European law.[42]

The spillover influence of Community law in the field of procedure and judicial decision making is as marked. In *Pepper v Hart*[43] the long established convention that the courts do not look at *Hansard* to discover the parliamentary intention behind legislation was reversed. It is strongly arguable that this was a consequence of the influence of Community law, where it is common to look for the purpose of a law in order to interpret that law and to look for that purpose in the legislative history. That Community influence can be seen when examining how *Pepper v Hart* came to be decided. Its direct precursor was the earlier decision in *Pickstone v Freemans*.[44] That was a Community law case. There the House of Lords referred to passages in Hansard to understand national regulations made by the United Kingdom Parliament to give effect to Community law. The justification for that unusual approach was the special position of Community law.[45] Yet the very basis of allowing that exceptional approach in *Pickstone* was discarded

---

[41] In Case 199/82 *Amministrazione delle Finanze dello Stato v SpA San Giorgio* [1983] ECR 3595.
[42] *Woolwich Equitable Building Society v IRC* [1993] AC 70 177.
[43] [1993] AC 593.
[44] *Pickstone v Freemans plc* [1989] AC 66.
[45] See eg, *per* Lord Keith of Kinkel at pp 111–12.

in *Pepper v Hart* as being 'logically indistinguishable from the similar exercise of statutory interpretation of purely national legislation'.[46]

So too it is becoming increasingly hard not explicitly to recognise in English administrative law the Community law doctrine of proportionality. That doctrine, drawn from German administrative law principles, is a tool for judging the lawfulness of administrative action. It amounts to this: Excessive means are not to be used to attain permissible objectives. Or, as it was more pithily put by Lord Diplock, 'a steam hammer should not be used to crack a nut'.[47] There has been much argument whether this principle now forms a part of the criteria for review of public decisions generally since Lord Diplock opened that door in 1985.[48] It seemed to have been slammed shut by the *Brind* decision in 1991. This is not the occasion to trace those developments. Yet, by whatever name, it seems undeniable that the traditional common law concepts converge with their continental cousins. This is but another example of the inevitable incremental effects of introducing another system of law to be applied alongside traditional common law principles.

One other example will illustrate the point. In *M v Home Office*[49] a contempt application was made against the Secretary of State for failure to procure the return of an applicant for political asylum. The Court had to consider the extent of its powers over the Executive. In purely domestic cases these were traditionally narrow. But in cases where Community law obligations were at issue it had been shown that the powers were wider. They extend to granting interlocutory injunctions against the Crown as shown in the *Factortame* case.[50] This distinction troubled the Court. Although both the Court of Appeal (and ultimately the House of Lords)[51] found a way round the concerns, Lord Donaldson M R was driven to condemn as 'anomalous and ... wrong in principle' distinctions in the powers of the court to hold the ring by interlocutory injunctions which depended on the identity of the defendant; and it was even more anomalous that the extent of those powers over central government should depend on whether the obligation in question arose under Community law or purely domestic law.

---

[46] *Pepper v Hart* [1993] AC 593 at 635, *per* Lord Browne-Wilkinson.
[47] *R v Goldstein* [1983] 1 WLR 151 at 155.
[48] *Council of Civil Services Unions v Minister for the Civil Service* [1985] AC 374.
[49] *M v Home Office* [1992] QB 270.
[50] Above n 32.
[51] *M v Home Office* [1992] 3 WLR 433.

This illustrates the difficulty of maintaining a rigid distinction between two differing sets of principles of law, co-existing side by side.[52] Nor would I want in all cases to maintain rigid distinctions. The greatness of the common law lies in its flexibility and ability to adapt to changing economic and social conditions. It is enriched by drawing on the principles and solutions found in other developed legal systems.

IV.   THE EMERGENCE OF A NEW APPROACH

I have referred to the effect the introduction of European Community law has had on the development of our own domestic law. I believe that incorporation into our own law of the Convention rights will have an equally healthy effect.

Any court or tribunal determining any question relating to a Convention right will be obliged to take into account the body of jurisprudence of the Court and Commission of Human Rights and of the Council of Ministers.[53] This is obviously right; it gives British courts both the benefit of 50 years careful analysis of the Convention rights and ensures British courts interpret the Convention consistently with Strasbourg. The British courts will therefore need to apply the same techniques of interpretation and decision-making as the Strasbourg bodies. I have already mentioned recourse to parliamentary materials such as *Hansard*—where we are now more closely in line with our continental colleagues. I will mention three more aspects. As I do so, it should be remembered that the courts which will be applying these techniques will be the ordinary courts of the land. We have not considered it right to create some special human rights court alongside the ordinary system; the Convention rights must pervade all law and all court systems. Our courts will therefore learn these techniques and inevitably will consider their utility in deciding other non-Convention cases.

First there is the approach to statutory construction. The tools of construction in use in mainland Europe are known to be different from those the English courts have traditionally used. I will refer to just one: the teleological approach, which is concerned with giving the instrument its presumed legislative intent. It is less concerned with the

[52] See further on this topic the valuable discussion in O'Neill, *Decisions of the European Court of Justice and their Constitutional Implications* (1994), ch 5.
[53] See Clause 2.

textual analysis usual to the common law tradition of interpretation.[54] It is a process of moulding the law to what the Court believes the law should be trying to achieve.[55] It is undoubtedly the case that our own domestic approach to interpretation of statutes has become more purposive. Lord Diplock had already identified this trend 20 years ago when he noted that:

> If one looks back to the actual decisions of the [House of Lords] on questions of statutory construction over the last 30 years one cannot fail to be struck by the evidence of a trend away from the purely literal towards the purposive construction of statutory provisions.[56]

This trend has not diminished since then, although there are cases where the courts have declined to adopt what was in one case described as an 'over purposive' approach.[57]

Yet as the courts, through familiarity with the Convention jurisprudence, become more exposed to methods of interpretation which pay more heed to the purpose, and less to whether the words were felicitously chosen to achieve that end, the balance is likely to swing more firmly yet in the direction of the purposive approach.

Secondly, there is the doctrine of proportionality, to which I have already referred. This doctrine is applied by the European Court of Human Rights.[58] Its application is to ensure that a measure imposes no greater restriction upon a Convention right than is absolutely necessary to achieve its objectives. Although not identical to the principle as applied in Luxembourg, it shares the feature that it raises questions foreign to the traditional *Wednesbury*[59] approach to judicial review. Under the *Wednesbury* doctrine an administrative decision will only be struck down if it is so bad that no reasonable decision-maker could have taken it.

Closely allied with the doctrine of proportionality is the concept of the margin of appreciation. The Court of Human Rights has developed this doctrine which permits national courts a discretion in the application of

---

[54] The Court of Human Rights also adopts a dynamic approach which enables it to take account of changing social conditions.

[55] See Lord Denning's description in *James Buchanan v Balxo* [1977] 2 WLR 107, 112.

[56] *Carter v Bradbeer* [1975] 1 WLR 1204 at 1206–7.

[57] By Dillon L J in *R v Poplar Coroner, ex parte Thomas* [1993] 2 All ER 381 at 387; and see the criticism by Bennion in *The All England Reports Annual Review*, 1996, of the House of Lords decision in *R v Preddy* [1996] 3 All ER 481.

[58] See *eg, Soering v UK* (1989) Series A, v 161.

[59] *Associated Provincial Picture Houses v Wednesbury Corporation* [1948] KB 223.

the requirements of the Convention to their own national conditions. This discretion is not absolute, since the Court of Human Rights reserves the power to review any act of a national authority or court; and the discretion is more likely to be recognised in the application of those articles of the Convention which expressly include generally stated conditions or exceptions, such as Articles 8–11, rather than in the area of obligations which in any civilised society should be absolute, such as the rights to life, freedom from torture and freedom from slavery and forced labour that are provided by Articles 2–4.

The margin of appreciation was first developed by the Court in a British case, *Handyside v UK*.[60] It concerned whether a conviction for possessing an obscene article could be justified under Article 10(2) of the Convention as a limitation upon freedom of expression that was necessary for the 'protection of morals'. The court said:

> By reason of their direct and continuous contact with the vital forces of their countries, state authorities are in principle in a better position than the international judge to give an opinion on the exact content of those requirements [of morals] as well as on the 'necessity' of a 'restriction' or 'penalty' intended to meet them ...[61]

Although there is some encouragement in British decisions for the view that the margin of appreciation under the Convention is simply the *Wednesbury* test under another guise[62] statements by the Court of Human Rights seem to draw a significant distinction. The Court of Human Rights has said in terms that its review is not limited to checking that the national authority 'exercised its discretion reasonably, carefully and in good faith'. It has to go further. It has to satisfy itself that the decision was based on an 'acceptable assessment of the relevant facts' and that the interference was no more than reasonably necessary to achieve the legitimate aim pursued.[63]

That approach shows that there is a profound difference between the Convention margin of appreciation and the common law test of rationality. The latter would be satisfied by an exercise of discretion done 'reasonably, carefully and in good faith' although the passage I have cited indicates that the Court of Human Rights' review of action is not

---

[60] (1976), Series A, v 24.
[61] *Ibid*, paras [48]–[49].
[62] See *eg, R v Home Secretary, ex parte Patel* [1995] Imm AR 223; *R v Home Secretary, ex parte Mbatube* [1996] Imm AR 184.
[63] *Vogt v Germany*, Series A, No 323 (1996), para 52; (1996) 21 EHRR 205, 235.

so restricted. In these cases a more rigorous scrutiny than traditional judicial review will be required. An illustration of the difference is to be found in the speech of Simon Brown L J in *ex parte Smith* (the armed forces homosexual policy case):

> If the Convention for the Protection of Human Rights and Fundamental Freedoms were part of our law and we were accordingly entitled to ask whether the policy answers a pressing social need and whether the restriction on human rights involved can be shown proportionate to its benefits, then clearly the primary judgment (subject only to a limited 'margin of appreciation') would be for us and not for others; the constitutional balance would shift. But that is not the position. In exercising merely a secondary judgement, this court is bound, even though acting in a human rights context, to act with some reticence.[64]

The question I pose is how long the courts will restrict their review to a narrow *Wednesbury* approach in non-Convention cases, if used to inquiring more deeply in Convention cases? There will remain distinctions of importance between the two categories of case which should be respected. But some blurring of lines may be inevitable. I expressed my views in my Administrative Law Bar Association Lecture in 1995[65] on how the courts ought properly to regard the dividing line between their function and that of Parliament. But the process is not one way. British influence on the application of the Convention rights is likely to increase. British officials were closely involved in the drafting of the Convention. When our British courts make their own pronouncements on the Convention, their views will be studied in other Convention countries and in Strasbourg itself with great respect. I am sure that British judges' influence for the good of the Convention will be considerable. They will bring to the application of the Convention their great skills of analysis and interpretation. But they will also bring to it our proud British traditions of liberty.

V.   THE SHIFT FROM FORM TO SUBSTANCE

So there is room to predict some decisive and far reaching changes in future judicial decision making. The major shift may be away from

---

[64] *R v Ministry of Defence, ex parte Smith* [1996] QB 517, at 541.
[65] See n 35, above.

a concern with form to a concern with substance. Let me summarise the reasons.

In the field of review by judges of administrative action, the courts' decisions to date have been largely based on something akin to the application of a set of rules. If the rules are broken, the conduct will be condemned. But if the rules are obeyed, (the right factors are taken into account, no irrelevant factors taken into account, no misdirection of law and no out and out irrationality) the decision will be upheld, usually irrespective of the overall objective merits of the policy. In some cases much may turn—or at least appear to turn—on the form in which a decision is expressed rather than its substance. Does the decision as expressed show that the right reasons have been taken into account? Does it disclose potentially irrational reasoning? Might the court's view be different if the reasoning were expressed differently so as to avoid the court's *Wednesbury* scrutiny?

Now, in areas where the Convention applies, the Court will be less concerned whether there has been a failure in this sense but will inquire more closely into the merits of the decision to see for example that necessity justified the limitation of a positive right, and that it was no more of a limitation than was needed.[66] There is a discernible shift which may be seen in essence as a shift from form to substance. If, as I have suggested, there is a spillover into other areas of law, then that shift from form to substance will become more marked.

This may be seen as a progression of an existing and now long standing trend. In modern times, the emphasis on identifying the true substance at issue has been seen in diverse areas: in tax where new techniques have developed to view the substance of a transaction overall rather than to be mesmerised by the form of an isolated step,[67] or in the areas of statutory control of leases, where the Courts are astute to prevent form being used to obscure the reality of the underlying transaction.[68] In what may seem at first blush a very different area, that of interpretation of contracts, recent decisions also emphasise the need to cast away the baggage of older years where literal and semantic analysis was allowed to override the real intent of the parties.[69] In a

[66] Albeit within the margin of appreciation left to the public authority.
[67] *Ramsay v IRC* [1982] AC 300. *Furniss v Dawson* [1984] AC 474.
[68] See for example *Street v Mountford* [1985] AC 809.
[69] See *Mannai v Eagle Star Life Assurance Co Ltd* [1997] 2 WLR 945 and *Investors Compensation Scheme v West Bromwich Building Society*, 24 June 1997.

very broad sense we can see here a similarity of approach: to get to the substance of the issue and not be distracted by the form.

These are trends already well developed but I believe they will gain impetus from incorporation of the Convention. In addition the courts will be making decisions founded more explicitly and frequently on considerations of morality and justifiability.

This Bill will therefore create a more explicitly moral approach to decisions and decision making; will promote both a culture where positive rights and liberties become the focus and concern of legislators, administrators and judges alike, and a culture in judicial decision making where there will be a greater concentration on substance rather than form.

If that is so, we will more readily be able to refute TS Eliot's sardonic version of the lawyers' motto cited by one of my predecessors: 'The spirit killeth, the letter giveth life'.[70]

---

[70] Lord Hailsham, *Hamlyn Revisited: The British Legal System Today* (1983) (Hamlyn Lectures) at p 49.

4

*Constitutional Change in the United Kingdom: British Solutions to Universal Problems**

I.   UNIVERSAL PROBLEMS

ALL LEGAL SYSTEMS have to confront the way individuals and governments interrelate. In countries which maintain democracy and uphold the rule of law, attachment to these fundamental values must find expression in the constitutional framework which regulates the relationship between the individual and the state. The United States of America stands as a pre-eminent example of a society which has striven to order its constitutional arrangements in this way. My theme this evening is the importance of securing this objective by means sensitive to national political and legal cultures.

In the United States this task was begun by those who came together, over two hundred years ago, in Philadelphia, to draft the text of the Constitution. However, the framers of the Constitution must share the credit for its success with the way it has been interpreted and applied by the US Supreme Court. Former Chief Justice Hughes famously remarked that '[t]he Constitution is whatever the judges say it is'. More recently it has been said that 'the obverse is true as well: if the judges are not prepared to speak for it, a constitution is nothing'. I can assure you that on our side of the Atlantic we are well aware that *Marbury v Madison* is not merely of historical significance. We know that the Supreme Court has in the last few months re-affirmed that the constitution is superior and paramount law, whose protections cannot be impaired by shifting legislative majorities. It is this commitment to the Constitution which explains, more than any other factor, the ample protections which now

* The 1998 National Heritage Lecture.

inhere in the relationship between the US institutions of government and American citizens.

The incidents of that relationship, dictated by the demands of democracy and the rule of law, are numerous. Foremost must be the protection of fundamental rights; the accountability of, and public participation in, the governmental process; and an ethos of open government which acknowledges that true democracy is incompatible with an unthinking culture of institutional secrecy.

That these objectives are pursued in the United States is apparent beyond doubt. The human rights guarantees in the federal and state Constitutions; the federal structure itself which locates government closer to the governed; and the freedom of information legislation which has been adopted both at national and state levels demonstrate, in the clearest terms, a concern to imbue relationships between citizen and state with characteristics based firmly on democracy and the rule of law.

The pursuit of these goals is not, of course, the exclusive preserve of the United States. In the sphere of human rights, many transnational agreements demonstrate international recognition of the high value given to respect for fundamental rights. The Universal Declaration of Human Rights is a distinctive example, in this, the year of its fiftieth anniversary. The International Charter on Civil and Political Rights, and the European Convention on Human Rights, are important, too, as is the legal system of the European Union. In its short history it has developed its own doctrine of fundamental rights. National legal orders also increasingly recognise the need to uphold human rights. This is witnessed by the adoption of the Canadian Charter of Rights and Freedoms in 1982 and the New Zealand Bill of Rights Act in 1990, as well as by the assertion by the Australian High Court of a jurisdiction to review primary legislation which interferes with basic rights.

As with human rights, so too with the other necessary ingredients of a proper relationship between the individual and the state. Through their federal arrangements, many legal systems enhance the accountability of and public participation in the business of government. The importance of this policy is also recognised in the legal order of the European Union, finding expression in the principle of subsidiarity. Similarly, there exists broad recognition that it is necessary to dismantle the culture of secrecy which has so often enveloped government. In 1982, Australia, Canada and New Zealand all moved to enact legislation to create public rights of access to official information.

II. BRITISH SOLUTIONS

It is a strong ambition to fashion solutions to these fundamental problems that underlies the constitutional changes we are now carrying into effect in the United Kingdom. Since its election to office, just over twelve months ago, the new British Government has embarked on a comprehensive programme of constitutional renewal as a major political priority. My central point this evening is that, although the impetus for these reforms is a set of problems universal in character, the solutions being adopted in the United Kingdom are, of necessity, tailored to the particular needs of the British constitution. Let me try to substantiate this argument by reference to the Government's proposals to enhance human rights protection in the UK. I begin, however, by offering two other examples which illustrate my thesis.

I have already spoken of the way in which federal arrangements—as those of the United States—promote governmental accountability and public participation in the governmental process by locating that process closer to the people. The same objective informs the United Kingdom Government's proposals to create devolved legislatures in Scotland and Wales—proposals approved by referendums in those countries last summer. Similarly our plans for a strategic authority for London, led by an elected mayor, were approved by Londoners as recently as last Thursday, 7 May, which demonstrates the continuing support for our constitutional reforms. In the longer term, if there is a local demand for it, we propose to devolve power to the English Regions. And a central element of the peace agreement, recently reached in Northern Ireland, will be a local Assembly, substantially a hybrid of the Scottish and Welsh patterns of devolution, which will also be put to a referendum later this month.

At present, all primary legislative power resides in the Westminster Parliament. Scotland and Wales are administered by executive departments which are accountable to that Parliament. Following referendums last year, the Government is promoting legislation to create a Scottish Parliament and a Welsh Assembly whose members will be directly elected by the people of Scotland and Wales. In turn, these arrangements will provide a more democratic framework for the government of those parts of the Union.

I know that the British are often accused of not understanding what 'federalism means', perhaps something as elusive as British theories of Parliamentary sovereignty. However I do not think our constitutional reform programme heralds a federal structure for the United Kingdom in the United States sense. Although a strictly federal approach has been adopted successfully in many countries, it would not be right for Britain. The needs of the various parts of the Union differ. It is the diversity of the countries which make up the United Kingdom that constitutes one of its greatest strengths. This is reflected in the system of devolution which is planned. Rather than imposing a pure federal structure on the UK as a whole, varying degrees and types of power will be devolved to different parts of the Union in light of their needs and desires. It is for this reason that the reform packages planned for Scotland and Wales are fundamentally different. The Scottish legal system is already substantially independent of that of England and Wales. This tradition will be built upon by the new Scottish Parliament, which will have the power to pursue a distinctive legislative agenda for Scotland over an extensive range, including the law, economic development, industrial assistance, universities, training, transport, the police and the prosecution system. However, in spite of this broad competence, fundamental human rights are 'ring fenced'. The new Scottish Parliament will not have competence to infringe fundamental rights. In contrast to the Scottish Parliament, however, the Welsh Assembly will have no power to enact primary legislation; rather, it will serve an executive function, exercising the executive powers previously exercised by the Secretary of State for Wales, so providing a more transparent and democratic framework for the government of Wales.

Only by adopting this pragmatic approach has it been possible to fashion a devolution scheme appropriate to the special circumstances of each part of the United Kingdom.

The same point can be made about freedom of information. Before publishing its proposals, the Government considered the regimes which operate in other countries—the United States, Canada, Australia and New Zealand. Although this comparative analysis was illuminating, it was appreciated that a unique approach would be needed in the UK, to take account of the particular circumstances of the British legal system. For instance, there presently exists in Britain a non-statutory freedom of information regime (much weaker than the new statutory framework that is being constructed). No other country, in developing statutory rights of access to official information, has had to do so against this kind of background. It has also been necessary to consider all the many existing statutory provisions giving rights of access to personal information, as well as those which restrict disclosure of official information on, for example, national security grounds.

So, the development of the new freedom of information system illustrates that, although the United Kingdom legal order is highly receptive to fresh ideas through processes of cross-fertilisation—we have recognised that ultimately we must respond to universal problems by cultivating domestic solutions suitable to national conditions, rather than simply transplanting approaches favoured elsewhere.

Nowhere is this plainer than in the area of human rights protection.

III.   PROTECTING FUNDAMENTAL RIGHTS

A.   Introduction: The Problem and the Solution

It is well known that the United Kingdom today is without a systematic human rights regime. So the protections of human rights in Britain today are the fruit of a number of different legislative and judicial initiatives.

In certain contexts, Parliament has stepped in to provide a statutory framework for the protection of human rights, sometimes borrowing ideas from elsewhere. For example, British legislation on gender and race equality was modelled on State anti-discrimination legislation, introduced in the aftermath of the Second World War, starting with the State of New York, followed closely by Massachusetts and then Pennsylvania. The law of the European Union also plays an important part in the field of human rights both in terms of trans-European legislation and the indigenous doctrine of fundamental rights developed by the Community Court.

Although they lack any comprehensive human rights jurisdiction, the contribution of the British courts has been central to the protection of individuals' rights in the United Kingdom. In limited areas, the judges have been able to develop common law rights to safeguard against legislative and executive encroachment, relying on basic postulates of a democracy under the rule of law, for example, the existence of courts and the necessity of access to justice. More generally, the courts have considerably enhanced their powers of judicial review in recent decades. They have begun to scrutinise a broader range of decision-making powers, holding that all governmental functions are in principle amenable to review, irrespective of the legal source of the power in question. Also, the courts have dispensed with a range of technical fetters which previously limited their jurisdiction, for example by relaxing the standing requirements and boldly resisting occasional legislative attempts to curtail judicial scrutiny of executive action. Although the British courts are constrained by the doctrine of Parliamentary sovereignty from reviewing primary legislation itself, their supervisory powers nevertheless contribute substantially to human rights protection in two key ways. First, by imposing requirements of fairness and rationality on public decision-makers, judicial review ensures that individuals are not subjected to arbitrary treatment by those entrusted with governmental power. Secondly, the courts subject executive action which impacts on fundamental rights to particularly thoroughgoing scrutiny.

Notwithstanding these advances, United Kingdom law is undoubtedly deficient. Let me outline some of the main problems. First, British law possesses no statute which systematically sets out citizens' rights. Secondly, there exists no obligation on governmental and other public authorities to respect substantive human rights. When our courts have taken account of the European Convention on Human Rights in certain limited contexts, they are ultimately powerless to apply the Convention in the face of a clear infringement of fundamental rights where statute sanctions what has been done. More generally, the UK lacks a legal culture of rights: for instance, no institutional procedure exists which seeks to ensure that new legislation conforms to human rights norms.

The former Prime Minister, John Major, in a major speech opposing a Bill of Rights for Britain, famously declared, 'We have no need of a Bill of Rights because we have freedom.' While it is true that British citizens have a *residual* freedom to do that which is not prohibited by law, Mr Major overlooked the capacity of Acts of Parliament to invade basic human rights. His claim also gave away an enervating insularity.

It is precisely for these reasons that the new British Government has introduced into Parliament a Human Rights Bill. It will, for the first time, provide the United Kingdom with a modern charter of fundamental rights, enforceable in national courts. The rights which the Bill enshrines are those defined by the European Convention on Human Rights. Mechanisms will be established which aim to ensure the compatibility of new legislation with these rights. The courts will be directed to interpret all legislation as being consistent with the Convention so far as is possible, and, where this is truly interpretively impossible, the higher courts will be given a unique competence to declare a provision of an Act of Parliament incompatible with the Convention. Moreover, public authorities will be placed under an entirely new obligation to act in a way that does not violate human rights.

Not only will the Human Rights Bill substantially enhance the protection and profile of fundamental rights in Britain. It will also resolve an historic anomaly which is of more than academic relevance. The UK played an important part in drafting the European Convention on Human Rights. It was among the first group of countries to sign the Convention. It was the very first State to ratify it, in March 1951. In spite of this, the aberrant position has been reached that the United Kingdom is virtually the only state party to the Convention which has failed to give proper effect to it in domestic law. This has arisen through a combination of the British duellist tradition, according to which international treaties become part of domestic law only through legislative incorporation; and the long standing unwillingness of successive governments within our separation of powers to legislate to confer 'excessive' powers on the judiciary at the expense of an elected Parliament. This has disadvantaged the British people by requiring them to vindicate their human rights not in their own courts but before the European Commission and Court in Strasbourg. In turn, this has imposed considerable expense and delay on litigants, and has tended to insulate Britain from the culture of fundamental rights which the Convention regime has developed. The enactment of the Human Rights Bill will change this position radically by giving effect in national law to the human rights guaranteed by the European Convention.

I began by underlining the significance of infusing the relationship between the individual and the state with values based on democracy and the rule of law, whilst taking account of the nuances of national legal systems. The Human Rights Bill secures these dual objectives by combining the well known and well proven principles of our constitutional democracy with modernity, harnessing both in its quest to fashion a regime of fundamental rights protection in harmony with our British political and legal culture. Thus, the Bill fully respects the principle of Parliamentary sovereignty and, as a result, will not require the courts radically to reinvent their role by adjudicating on the validity of legislation. However, as well as respecting these well proven principles of the British constitution, the Government's proposals are equally consistent with a series of more modern trends in British public law thinking, particularly the shift towards a more substantive conception of the rule of law; a greater awareness of the relevant of rights-based adjudication;

and the increasing receptiveness of United Kingdom law to the influences of other legal systems.

Let me set out these ideas in a little more detail, beginning with the way in which the Human Rights Bill reconciles its objectives with the fundamental principle of the sovereignty of Parliament.

B.   Maintaining Constitutional Tradition: Parliamentary Sovereignty in a Rights-Sensitive Environment

The omnicompetence of the British Parliament has long been regarded as the cornerstone of the UK's constitutional structure. However, many commentators have argued that Parliamentary supremacy is inconsistent with the effective protection of human rights. I recognise, because of the importance of judicial review of legislation in the US—the subject of Justice Breyer's Lecture only last week at Oxford in memory of Professor Herbert Hart—I appreciate that it may appear paradoxical from the American perspective even to countenance the enactment of a bill of rights without even attempting formally to entrench it.

However, a British approach based on strict entrenchment would overlook the realities of the our constitution. It would be anathema to the political and legal culture of the United Kingdom under which ultimate sovereignty rests with Parliament. That is why the Government has instead adopted a model which accommodates the sovereignty principle.

The need to find a solution sensitive to domestic circumstances has been recognised elsewhere, too, as can be seen from the divergent approaches to rights protection which operate in different legal systems. So, in its recent human rights legislation, New Zealand favoured an essentially interpretive approach, which has proved successful and appropriate to that legal culture. In contrast, the Canadian model confers greater powers on the judges by allowing them to strike down unconstitutional legislation, while preserving the ultimate power of the legislature to infringe the Charter of Rights and Freedoms where this is thought necessary. The American system is, of course, different again, assigning full supremacy to the Constitution by denying to the legislative branch any power to override, other than by amendment.

It is therefore clear that a broad spectrum of solutions may be adopted to uphold fundamental rights. Each country must embrace an approach appropriate to its own circumstances. The American model, providing for judicial review of legislation, and motivated substantially by considerations arising from the federal structure of the United States, would be unsuited to Britain with its long history of legislative supremacy and its non-federal arrangements.

This unequivocal commitment to the ultimate sovereignty of Parliament will not, however, reduce the efficacy of the new British human rights system in practice. The want of any jurisdiction to strike down incompatible primary legislation will not, in the vast majority of cases, impair the ability of the courts to ensure that the executive and other public authorities exercise their discretionary and rulemaking powers consistently with human rights. Also, although the sovereignty of Parliament is preserved, the Human Rights Bill will impact significantly on how it is exercised in practice. In particular, a declaration by a higher court that British law is incompatible with the European Convention is likely to create immense political pressure to amend the offending legislation to secure in national law the protection of the relevant right. The Bill encourages corrective action by providing a 'fast-track' procedure for that purpose. Also, the Bill will require ministers, when introducing new legislation, to state to Parliament whether it is compatible with the European Convention. Parliament will, no doubt, scrutinise closely any draft legislation which risks infringing human rights. So, while the ultimate sovereignty of Parliament is undisturbed by the Human Rights Bill, that sovereignty will in future have to be exercised within an environment highly sensitive to fundamental rights.

There are clear precedents for this approach, by which constitutional innovation is reconciled with the ultimate sovereignty of the British Parliament. The most striking illustration is the reception of European Union law into United Kingdom law. It is an axiom of European Union law that it must take priority over any inconsistent national provision. This requirement is normally met simply by interpreting national legislation as being consistent with Community law. In the *Factortame* litigation, however, the British courts were presented with an irreconcilable conflict between United Kingdom legislation and European Union law. The national legislation provided that fishing vessels could only be registered as British, so gaining the right to exploit the United Kingdom fishing quota, if 'a genuine and substantial connection with the United Kingdom' could be demonstrated. It was argued that this requirement conflicted with certain guarantees set out in the Treaty of Rome, such as the right not to be discriminated against on grounds of nationality and the right of individuals and businesses to establish themselves anywhere in the Community. After receiving guidance from the European

Court of Justice, it was held that an English court could disapply national legislation which conflicted with Community law. However, this does not impair the ultimate sovereignty of Parliament, because, in giving effect in this way to Community law, the courts are simply heeding Parliament's intention—as expressed in the legislation which facilitated British membership of the Community—that European law should take priority. This creative solution was inspired by the fact that the Treaty of Rome makes it a *requirement* of Community membership that European law should be accorded priority over municipal law. Moreover, it is well recognised that Parliament's ultimate sovereignty remains undisturbed, since it is unquestioned that it may enact legislation to withdraw the UK from the European Union.

This reconciliation of constitutional innovation with the orthodox theory of sovereignty is also apparent in the human rights sphere. For example, although the courts have expressed a particularly strong commitment to the common law right of access to the courts, they have emphasised that respect for parliamentary sovereignty dictates that this right is enforced only by interpretive means. The same kind of accommodation can be discerned in the vindication of procedural values by way of judicial review. The ultra vires doctrine, which is the foundation of the review jurisdiction, provides that those values must ultimately be related to, and therefore reconciled with, the sovereign will of Parliament.

Thus, the first strength of the Human Rights Bill is its ability to accommodate fully the axiom of parliamentary sovereignty. In doing so, it draws on the long-established practice in English public law of reconciling constitutional innovation with established principle.

C.   The Human Rights Bill and the New Public Law Culture in Britain

a.   Introduction

The Human Rights Bill is equally is equally in tune with a series of *contemporary* strands in public law thinking which favour a shift towards rights-based adjudication. Some believe there exists an unbridgeable divide between these more novel aspects of British public law and its traditions, so that a modern regime of rights protection can be achieved only at the expense of discarding established constitutional principle. The Human Rights Bill disproves that. Its capacity to harness both constitutional principle and the new ethos of public law is its defining characteristic. This is the single most important factor which will ensure its success in forging a politically acceptable system of rights protection in harmony with British political and legal structure.

b.   *Building on the Common Law's Commitment to Fundamental Rights*

I have already referred to the common law's commitment to fundamental rights. Its respect for liberty has a long history. Neither the absence of a written catalogue of rights nor the doctrine of parliamentary sovereignty has made British judges impotent to protect fundamental rights. The courts have shown particular confidence in recent years in the field of access to justice, applying a strong presumption that Parliament does not intend to interfere with the citizen's right of access to the courts. Thus, when the previous Government sought to increase significantly the court fees which must be paid by intending litigants, it was held that this measure was unlawful because of its considerable adverse impact on the right of access to justice. Notwithstanding its essentially interpretive character, this approach secures a high degree of protection for those rights to which it applies. Precisely the same point can be made in relation to the procedural rights which are safeguarded by way of judicial review.

It is therefore apparent that the contribution of the Human Rights Bill will be to strengthen and enlarge an already existing edifice of rights protection in English law, the foundations of which are to be found in the common law itself. In this way the Human Rights Bill is wholly in tune with the current nature of public law in the UK, given that both the Bill's objective of promoting rights and its interpretive methodology are already, and increasingly, embraced by the courts.

c.   *Changing Conceptions of the Rule of Law*

The growing confidence of the judiciary in articulating and enforcing a limited catalogue of common law rights can be related to a broader development in English public law. It has long been recognised that the rule of law is a fundamental of the unwritten British constitution. The Victorian jurist, Albert Venn Dicey, famously wrote that the rule of law is one of 'the two principles which pervade the whole of the English constitution'. The other, of course, is the doctrine of parliamentary sovereignty.

The rapid development in recent decades of the High Court's supervisory jurisdiction reflects a growing judicial awareness of the need to vindicate the rule of law by imposing standards of legality on public authorities. However, while British judges have steadily extended the *procedural* rights which individuals enjoy as they interact with the state, this has not been matched by the development of a jurisdiction to check executive action for compliance with *substantive* human rights norms.

There are some signs that this position is slowly changing. In a number of lectures and articles, senior members of the judiciary have displayed their appetite for a shift in British public law away from exclusively procedural concerns and towards an adjudicative approach which also upholds substantive rights. It is clear that this desire is born of a wish to give effect to a conception of the rule of law which has both procedural and substantive dimensions. Thus, the judges have called for the incorporation of the European Convention on Human Rights into British law, and, in the meantime, the recognition of a more developed indigenous jurisdiction to uphold human rights.

This extra-curial discourse has to some extent been given practical effect through the courts' willingness to subject to particularly intensive scrutiny executive action which is alleged to have interfered with fundamental rights.

However, it is important to appreciate the limits of this approach. An example concerned with the right of freedom of expression is illustrative. Some years ago, the then Government issued regulations imposing restrictions on the broadcasting of interviews with representatives of particular terrorist organisations. The impact of the regulations was relatively minor, effectively prohibiting only live interviews with these individuals. Still, it was alleged, in judicial review proceedings, that these regulations improperly interfered with freedom of expression. The House of Lords refused to deal directly with the substantive question whether this interference was justifiable or proportionate to the Government's objective. Apart from asking whether the adoption of the regulation was manifestly irrational or perverse—a test which is very hard to satisfy—the court focused exclusively on the propriety of the decision-making *procedure* which had led to the adoption of the regulation.

This example demonstrates that, at the heart of the human rights debate in the UK, lies a paradox. Undoubtedly there is a ground swell of enthusiasm for the protection of fundamental rights under a more substantive conception of the rule of law. Nevertheless, the courts consistently hold back from giving full effect to this trend, preferring instead to perpetuate an almost exclusively procedural approach to the rule of law. Thus, in spite of the widespread recognition in judicial and other circles of the importance of upholding fundamental rights, English courts still possess no comprehensive jurisdiction capable of securing this objective in substantive terms.

The reason for this paradox lies in the uncertainties of the unwritten British constitutional order. The United States Constitution guarantees to citizens that certain fundamental rights are paramount, beyond even the reach of the legislative branch. The existence of such an explicit catalogue of rights carries with it, as Chief Justice Marshall recognised almost two hundred years ago, important implications for the judicial function. In particular, it is recognised as conferring on the courts a constitutional warrant to vindicate these rights through judicial review. The exercise of this jurisdiction by the Supreme Court is often the subject of public debate and even controversy. Crucially, however, the Constitution provides a focal point for discussion and is the benchmark against which the legitimacy of the Court's development of American public law can be evaluated.

In contrast, the disparate and largely unwritten character of the British constitution makes it harder to delineate the respective functions of the different branches of government. It is this problem with which the judges are grappling in relation to human rights. Although they clearly wish to give effect to a substantive theory of the rule of law by affording direct protection to fundamental rights, the courts are ultimately deterred from doing so by a concern to avoid transgressing the bounds of their allotted constitutional province.

Judicial adoption of a substantive theory of the rule of law would involve a much greater exercise of power by the courts. The judges would become exposed to the charge of claiming for themselves a jurisdiction which is not properly theirs. The attendant increase in the intensity of review would at least raise the spectre of improper judicial interference with executive functions. And judicial determination of which rights are sufficiently fundamental to quality for legal protection would create the appearance of judicial law-making in the sphere allocated to an elected Parliament.

These considerations have led me, in the past, to argue that 'it is the constitutional imperative of judicial self-restaint which must inform judicial decision-making in [English] public law'. In the United Kingdom—unlike the United States—the three branches of government are not equal and co-ordinate: it is, ultimately, Parliament which is the senior partner. It is for this reason that, if, as I think it must, the judiciary is to set about the task of protecting substantive rights, the content of those rights and the nature of the courts' function in upholding them, must be 'crystallised in a democratically validated Bill of Rights', which is what our Human Rights Bill is.

The success of the US Constitution in delivering a developed system of human rights protection is, I am sure, because it supplies individuals and the courts with a catalogue of rights which has a consensual basis and provides the judiciary with the constitutional warrant it needs to uphold those rights. Those characteristics also underlie the new rights protection which will be instituted in the United Kingdom. It is the Human Rights Bill which will resolve the paradox to which I referred earlier and which has hitherto stunted the development of a proper human rights jurisdiction in Britain. The Bill will harness the growing trend towards human rights protection and a substantive conception of the rule of law, while giving democratic impetus to that development. Against this background, the courts will be able to begin the important task of forging a substantive rights-based jurisprudence without any fear of exceeding their proper constitutional province.

d.   Changing Conceptions of the Judicial Function

Thus far, I have explained how the Human Rights Bill, while respecting constitutional principle, also intersects with more contemporary features of British public law such as the development of common law rights and the movement towards a more substantive notion of the rule of law. I would like to mention two further aspects of public law thinking which the Human Rights Bill embraces. Let me begin by saying something about changing conceptions of the judicial function.

It would be misleading to suggest that a concern for civil liberties is the exclusive preserve of the *modern* judiciary in Britain. In *Dr Bonham's Case* in 1603, Chief Justice Coke argued that 'when an act of parliament is against common right and reason, or repugnant ..., the common law will control it, and adjudge such act to be void'. Although this case predates the constitutional settlement which affirmed the sovereignty of Parliament and therefore does not form part of the modern law, it nevertheless serves to illustrate that the protection of fundamental values has traditionally been viewed in England as an aspect of the judicial function.

It is fair to say, however, that the extent to which the judges have felt obliged to speak up for these values has varied considerably over time.

The history of English administrative law in the twentieth century is the litmus paper of this phenomenon. During the earlier part of the century the judges often attached little weight to protecting the rights of the individual. A classic example is the decision of the House of Lords in *Liversidge v Anderson* in 1941. The Secretary of State was empowered to make an order detaining any person whom he had reasonable cause to believe was, in some way, a threat to public safety or national security. The majority of the court held that, provided the Minister had acted in good faith, they could enquire no further into the propriety of his action. In particular, it was said that the court could not determine whether the detention order was, in fact, justified on objective grounds. It was only Lord Atkin, in his historic dissenting speech, who spoke up for the protection of liberty as an important component of the judicial function I quote:

> In this country, amid the clash of arms, the laws are not silent. They may be changed, but they speak the same language in war as in peace. It has always been one of the pillars of freedom, one of the principles of liberty for which on recent authority we are now fighting, that the judges are no respecters of persons and stand between the subject and any attempted encroachments on this liberty by the executive, alert to see that any coercive action is justified in law.

Fortunately, the attitude of the English courts has since changed almost beyond recognition from the decision of the majority in *Liverside v Anderson*. In 1979, the House of Lords acknowledged that the decision in *Liversidge v Anderson* was simply wrong. Beginning in the 1960s, the judges started to rediscover constitutionalism as part of their function. This renaissance, seen principally in the field of judicial review, has been described in colourful language by Mr Justice Sedley. Speaking extra-judicially, he has remarked that by the early 1980s, 'the courts were waiting with refined instruments of torture for ministers and departments...who took their public law obligations cavalierly'.

English law is not, of course, unique in witnessing alterations across time in the conception of the judicial function, as the jurisprudence of the US Supreme Court demonstrates. It is hardly necessary to mention the rejection of the old, 'equal but separate' doctrine, of *Plessy v Ferguson* by the Supreme Court in *Brown v Board of Education*. What may have changed between 1896 and 1954 was not the concept of equal protection, but perhaps rather a change in the conception of the judicial function and the court's perception and understanding of the requirements for the practical implementation of equal protection. In the United Kingdom, we are traditionally more wedded to the concept of *stare decisis*. But the United States Supreme Court is prepared to depart from prior decisions when adherence to them involves a collision with principle which is 'intrinsically sounder, and verified by experience'.

Britain and America are not alone in having experienced, particularly during the latter part of this century, the 'constitutionalisation' of the judicial function. It is the massive expansion of the administrative state which, more than any other factor, has prompted the judges to reassess their constitutional role. As the comparative lawyer Mauro Cappelletti has observed, the courts in many jurisdictions are 'becoming themselves the 'third giant' to control the mastodon legislator and the leviathan administrator'.

It is this emerging view of the judicial function with which the British human rights legislation not only intersects but also legitimates. The United States Constitution permits—and requires—the American courts to recognise that duties of a constitutional character inform the nature of their judicial function. United Kingdom law has hitherto possessed no analogue. It is the Human Rights Bill which will capture the current *zeitgeist* of British public law favouring the constitutionalisation of the judicial function. By conferring democratic legitimacy upon this development, the new legislation will allow the judges to fulfil a stronger constitutional role in a wholly constitutional way.

And it is not only the Human Rights Bill which will contribute to this process. The other constitutional reforms, which I outlined earlier, will have similar consequences. Thus, it is the courts, through their judicial review jurisdiction, which will have the last word on freedom of information. Moreover, the devolution of governmental power will confer on the British judiciary a wholly new function of a constitutional character, since it is the judicial system which will bear ultimate responsibility for ensuring that the Scottish Parliament does not transgress the bounds of its legislative competence.

Of course, the American courts have, since the inception of the federal Constitution, exercised this kind of function by resolving demarcation disputes between Congress and the state legislatures. By conferring on UK courts an analogous jurisdiction, the devolution regime will contribute to the further constitutionalisation of the judicial function in Britain.

e. The Trend towards Cross-Fertilisation of Legal Norms

The final trend in UK public law which I mention is this: the increasingly outward-looking attitude of the courts. In recent years, English law has grown more receptive to the influences of other legal orders, both domestic and transnational.

British membership of the European Union has been a major catalyst. The UK was required, as a condition of membership, to receive Community law into its national legal system. However, the impact of this 'incoming tide'—as Lord Denning, the former Master of the Rolls, once famously referred to European Law—has been felt not only in areas governed directly by Community law: it has also exerted a more general, indirect influence on national law. In a number of important decisions— dealing with issues as diverse as the liability of the Crown to be restrained by injunction and the interpretation of ambiguous national legislation—the indirect influence of European law on the development of domestic law has been clear.

This more outward-looking attitude of the English courts is to be seen in other areas, too. For instance, they are increasingly willing to look to other national legal orders to help them resolve hard cases. There are also some indications that the English courts are beginning to refer more readily to international law, both customary and conventional. This is particularly true of international human rights law. Thus, despite its unincorporated status, the European Convention on Human Rights has exerted an indirect influence on the jurisprudence of domestic courts in the UK, which have used it to guide their development of the common law and as an aid to the construction of ambiguous legislation.

It is within this context that the issue of human rights has now taken centre stage in public law discourse in the UK. As British public lawyers increasingly look at the experiences of other legal systems, they become more acutely aware of the shortcomings of their domestic law in the field of human rights.

Against this background, it is appropriate that the institution of a British system of fundamental rights protection is to involve recourse to the European Convention on Human Rights, an *international* human rights instrument. By adopting this solution, the Human Rights Bill once again intersects with an important aspect of modern thinking in British public law. Now, more than ever, it is apparent that the

British legal system exists within a broader European—and, ultimately, international—community of legal families. Just as English law has long exerted important and valuable influences on other legal orders, so it is increasingly recognised that other legal orders are a rich source of inspiration for English courts. Crucially, however, this permeation of English law is to occur through the subtle influences of cross-fertilisation, rather than by crudely transplanting into English law a regime which is unsuited to its political and legal culture.

IV.   CONCLUSION

Professor Ronald Dworkin recently wrote that:

> Great Britain was once a fortress for freedom. It claimed the great philosophers of liberty—Milton and Locke and Paine and Mill. Its legal tradition is irradiated with liberal ideas: that people accused of crime are presumed to be innocent, that no one owns another's conscience, that a man's home is his castle, that speech is the first liberty because it is central to all the rest.

The programme of constitutional reform now being undertaken in the United Kingdom will provide a modern institutional framework capable of giving contemporary effect to this proud libertarian tradition. I began, this evening, by observing that all legal systems must confront the relationship between the individual and the state. It is precisely that issue which is tackled by the current reforms of the British constitution. Individuals will acquire a legal right of access to official information. Government itself will become more accessible through the devolution of executive and, where appropriate, legislative power. British citizens will, at long last, be empowered to vindicate their fundamental rights before British courts. In these ways, the relationship between the individual and the state will acquire a new, constitutional dimension. It will be imbued, far more than ever before, with values—based on democracy and the rule of law—which the British constitution has traditionally championed.

It is axiomatic that this process of renewal will take full account of the contours—ancient and modern—which shape the landscape of British public law. Thus, the Human Rights Bill accommodates both the constitutional orthodoxy of parliamentary sovereignty and the series of contemporary, rights—oriented trends in public law thinking which

I have identified this evening. Far from being an uneasy compromise, this accommodation which the Bill achieves is its foremost strength. It is the means without which it would not have happened. By placing principle and modernity side by side in harness, the Human Rights Bill ensures a catholic approach which will lead to the strongest possible foundation for a uniquely British regime of human rights protection.

The importance of adopting an approach of this kind should not be underestimated. It is widely known that Canada's Bill of Rights, passed in 1960, largely failed to achieve any genuine constitutional status. Neither the Canadian Supreme Court nor the federal government displayed the enthusiasm which is necessary to ensure the success of a human rights regime. As Professor Harry Arthurs observed some years ago, 'Only when [a] Bill [of Rights] begins to command the loyalty of individuals—will its aspirations be translated into reality.' This reality was realised by Canada through the Charter of Rights and Freedoms which it adopted in 1982, by which time the political and legal culture was ready to receive a human rights regime. Similar factors help to explain the success which the New Zealand Bill of Rights has enjoyed since its inception in 1990. As the New Zealand commentator Paul Rishworth observes, the enactment of the Bill 'coincided with a spring tide of judicial enthusiasm for the enforcement of fundamental rights and control of governmental power'.

These experiences are of great relevance to Britain as it renews its own constitution. They underscore the importance of achieving a synthesis between political and legal culture and the measures by which the constitution is reformed. The foundations of this synthesis are established by the capacity of the Human Rights Bill to harness both the strengths of our democratic principles and the new ideologies of British public law.

I fully acknowledge, however, that the institution of a new human rights regime is a hugely complex undertaking. While the characteristics of the Human Rights Bill which I have discussed this evening provide an excellent starting point, much work remains to be done. The proof of this, as with every pudding, will be in the eating. Politicians, public servants, lawyers and citizens all have their distinct roles to play to ensure that a new culture of respect for fundamental rights comes to prevade all our public authorities, including the courts, and extend throughout the whole of our society.

It is, though, the judges who will probably bear the the heat of the day in this collective endeavour. The task which now lies before the

British judiciary is one which was begun by the Justices of the United States Supreme Court over two hundred years ago. The magnitude of the task appears from the many fraught and courageous decisions the Supreme Court has taken during its history. I am confident that the British courts will rise to the challenge they now face with wisdom and enthusiasm. In doing so, however, they will do well to look to the long experience of the American courts and the impressive body of jurisprudence which they have amassed in the field of human rights.

Still, in discharging their new constitutional duties, the ultimate task of the British courts will be to build on the foundations laid by Parliament in the Human Rights Bill, by upholding human rights in a manner appropriate to our national political and legal culture. This will be their contribution to the development of a uniquely British solution to this most universal of issues—the proper balance of power and right between the individual and the state in a democracy under the rule of law.

5

Activism and Restraint: Human Rights and the Interpretative Process*

I. INTRODUCTION

L ET ME BEGIN by paying tribute to the life and work of Paul
      Sieghart, which this Annual Lecture celebrates. Paul Sieghart was
      an exceptional man, a distinguished lawyer, and as Lord
Browne-Wilkinson has recalled a tireless campaigner for human rights.
He arrived in this country as a schoolboy speaking no English, but
French and German—a refugee from Nazi persecution. He was called
to the Bar in 1953 and soon earned recognition for his strong advocacy.
His lucid intellect combined with superb skills of communication in
quite different media—in the spoken word, as a writer and on televi-
sion—made him a compelling campaigner. He was driven by a passion
for the protection of human rights and civil liberties both in Britain and
abroad. His own background and personal experience, I am sure, drove
him on. An illustration is his arrest and deportation by the Czechs in
1968 when he went to Prague as an Amnesty observer at a dissident's
trial. As a young barrister he became heavily involved with Justice, serving for 10 years as the Chairman of its executive committee. He
presided over numerous working parties and produced well argued and
brilliantly written reports. Two of his campaigns became law. First, the
Rehabilitation of Offenders Act, which he joked was the first law to
allow people to tell a lie lawfully, and secondly the Data Protection Act.
He was passionate about constitutional reform. I am sure that the

---

* I am indebted to Mark Elliott, Research Student at Queens' College, Cambridge, for
his high quality assistance in the preparation of this lecture. Note: Mark Elliott is now
a lecturer in law and Fellow of St Catherine's College, Cambridge.

incorporation of the ECHR into domestic law would have delighted him as would strong Freedom of Information legislation. In short, he was a man of many, many talents. How appropriate it is that we should be here in the Great Hall of this College in his own University where he received the honour of a personal Chair.

My subject tonight is 'Activism and Restraint: Human Rights and the Interpretative Process'. When scholars begin to write the legal history of the twentieth century, they will need to allocate a considerable space to their chapters on public law. Judicial activism in the development of a mature system of public law is likely to come to count as the century's single greatest judicial achievement.

Lord Diplock expressed his view that he regarded the progress towards a developed system of administrative law as 'one of the greatest achievements of the English courts' in his judicial lifetime.[1] But it has been on the anvil of interpretation of statutory materials by judges that much of this progress has been made. In developing their powers of judicial review, and in beginning to articulate a doctrine of common law constitutional rights, the judges have been careful to explain that their creativity has been an interpretative one. The activism which has driven the dramatic expansion of public law has thus been tempered by the restraint which our constitution requires.

The tendency in the United Kingdom towards growing judicial supervision of the executive finds its broader, international counterpart in the increasing importance which is attached—at both national and transnational level—to the protection of human rights. As the United Nations High Commissioner for Human Rights remarked last December, on the occasion of the fiftieth anniversary of the Universal Declaration of Human Rights, we have seen in the last 50 years that 'a culture of human rights is growing throughout the world'. Although a wide range of factors determines the extent to which this culture can take effect in any particular legal system, the trend—in recent years—towards the legalisation of human rights has been central. The eminent jurist, Hersch Lauterpacht, was in the vanguard of those who recognised the importance of embracing fundamental rights not merely as aspirational rhetoric, but as enforceable legal principle.[2]

---

[1] *Inland Revenue Commissioners v National Federation for Small Businesses and Self-Employed Ltd* [1982] AC 617 at 641.
[2] See *eg, An International Bill of the Rights of Man* (New York, Columbia University Press, 1945).

It is the task of translating the text of the European Convention on Human Rights into principles of domestic law upon which British courts will soon embark: and, just as the interpretative process has been crucial, during the twentieth century, to the development of administrative law, so it will also take centre stage when our courts begin to exercise a more substantive public law jurisdiction as the new millennium dawns.[3] However, while the centrality of interpretation will remain constant, the nature of the interpretative challenge faced by the courts will evolve. They will be confronted, for the first time, with an instrument that enumerates—in the expansive terms which are the universal language of constitutional texts—the fundamental rights of people.

It is, therefore, timely to examine the nature of the interpretative process in the human rights arena. I shall turn, shortly, to the experiences of other jurisdictions, since there is much which a comparative perspective can offer. I will also address the prospects for human rights adjudication in the United Kingdom. Let me begin, however, by focusing on the particular challenges which fundamental rights interpretation poses and the factors which shape the judiciary's response.

II.   TEXTUAL PRESCRIPTION AND JUDICIAL RESPONSE: THE ALCHEMY OF HUMAN RIGHTS INTERPRETATION

A.   The Special Challenge of Human Rights Adjudication

Interpretation is, at root, an exercise in textual analysis. It is, therefore, the words of a bill of rights with which judges must primarily be concerned as they seek to adjudicate in cases which engage fundamental norms. Although many eminent judges held that the judicial function entailed nothing other than this literal approach to construction,[4] this

---

[3] It is the courts' interpretative duty, under the Human Rights Act 1998, s 3(1), to construe national law in a manner which is consistent with the Convention rights which lies at the heart of the legislative scheme. Indeed, it is this interpretative approach to fundamental rights which facilitates the coexistence of strong rights protection and respect for parliamentary sovereignty. See further Cm 3782, *Rights Brought Home: The Human Rights Bill* (London, 1997), pp 9–11, and my 1998 National Heritage Lecture to the Historical Society of the United States Supreme Court, 'Constitutional Change in the United Kingdom: British Solutions to Universal Problems' (now chapter 4 in this volume).

[4] Lord Simonds was a forceful exponent of the declaratory theory of the judge's role. See *eg*, his remarks in *Scruttons v Midland Silicones Ltd* [1962] AC 446 at 467–69. Lord Devlin expressed similar views in 'Judges and Lawmakers' (1976) 39 *MLR* 1.

declaratory theory long ago gave way to more open recognition that lawmaking—within certain limits—is an inevitable and legitimate element of the judge's role.[5] Acceptance of this truism reveals the real nature of the interpretative process. In particular, it indicates that, when construing a statutory provision, the judge may well have to choose between competing meanings by reference, for instance, to the underlying rationale of the legislative scheme. Lord Simonds famously rebuked the late Lord Denning for advocating such an approach, commenting that it would be 'a naked usurpation of the legislative function under the thin disguise of interpretation'.[6] In this, as in so many other matters, Lord Denning was rather ahead of his time; yet, as was sometimes although not inevitably the case, Lord Denning's heterodoxy came, in time, to be accepted as the new orthodoxy.[7]

These truths concerning the nature of the interpretative process apply with particular force to human rights instruments. As the Chief Justice of Hong Kong observed, in a case about which I shall have a good deal more to say later, 'A constitution' or, for that matter, a bill of rights 'states general principles and expresses purposes without condescending to particularity and definition of terms. Gaps and ambiguities are bound to arise ...'.[8] As he approaches the interpretation

---

[5] See *eg*, Lord Reid, 'The Judge as Law Maker' (1972) 12 *Journal of the Society of Public Teachers of Law* 22. For a relatively early articulation of the legislative function of the courts, see B Cardozo, *The Nature of the Judicial Process* (New Haven, Yale University Press, 1921), pp 98–141; for more recent perspectives, see A Lester, 'English Judges as Lawmakers' [1993] *PL* 269; Lord Bingham of Cornhill, 'The Judge as Lawmaker: An English Perspective' in P Rishworth (ed), *The Struggle for Simplicity in Law* (Wellington, Butterworths, 1997).

[6] *Magor and St Mellons Rural District Council v Newport Corporation* [1952] AC 189 at 191.

[7] A good example of this in the public law field is the approach which Lord Denning took to the scope of judicial review. In *Laker Airways Ltd v Department of Trade* [1977] QB 643 at 705, he said that, 'Seeing that the prerogative is a discretionary power to be exercised for the public good, it follows that its exercise can be examined by the courts just as any other discretionary power which is vested in the executive.' The House of Lords accepted this conclusion some years later in *Council of Civil Service Unions v Minister for the Civil Service* [1985] AC 374. In *The Discipline of Law* (London, Butterworths, 1979), p 61, Lord Denning wrote that, 'The great problem before the courts in the twentieth century has been: In an age of increasing power, how is the law to cope with the abuse or misuse of it?' It was this healthy attitude to the supervision of governmental power which underpinned Lord Denning's valuable contributions to the development of English public law; and it was his equally keen awareness of the scope for abuse of power in relationships between citizen and citizen which was the impetus for many of his decisions in the private law sphere.

[8] *Ng Ka Ling v Director of Immigration* [1999] 1 HKLRD 315 at 339–40, *per* Li C J, giving the unanimous judgment of the Court of Final Appeal.

of a constitutional text, the task of the judge is therefore a delicate one. Two particular imperatives weigh upon him, and pull in different directions.

First, it is important that the courts are not so timid in their interpretation of a rights instrument that it loses its utility as an effective guarantee of the citizen's fundamental entitlements. The dictum which one New Zealand commentator[9] has dubbed 'the celebrated Cardozo-via-Wilberforce aphorism' is often cited, but remains as pertinent as ever. According to this formulation, rights texts must be given 'a generous interpretation avoiding what has been called the 'austerity of tabulated legalism', suitable to give individuals the full measure of [their] fundamental rights and freedoms'.[10]

However, it is equally crucial that human rights are not stretched by courts so far that they become distorted caricatures. As Lord Woolf remarked in a Privy Council decision[11] on the Hong Kong Bill of Rights Ordinance, 'it is necessary to ensure that disputes as to the effect of the Bill are not allowed to get out of hand. The issues involving the ... Bill of Rights should be approached with realism and good sense, and kept in proportion. If this is not done the Bill will become a source of injustice rather than justice and it will be debased in the eyes of the public.'[12] This is wise counsel, and it will apply to our own Human Rights Act just as it does to Hong Kong's Bill of Rights.

B.   The Role of the Judiciary and the Courts' Interpretation of Human Rights Texts

The challenge for the courts is to work out where the correct balance lies between these competing imperatives of activism and restraint. A rich and complex alchemy of factors impacts upon this judicial balancing exercise. But a crucial factor is the prevailing conception in society of

---

[9] P Rishworth, 'Lord Cooke and the Bill of Rights' in P Rishworth (ed), *The Struggle for Simplicity in Law* (Wellington, Butterworths, 1997), p 321.
[10] *Minister of Home Affairs v Collins MacDonald Fisher* [1980] AC 319 at 328, *per* Lord Wilberforce.
[11] The Privy Council ceased hearing appeals from Hong Kong upon the transfer of sovereignty to the People's Republic of China on 1 July 1997. The Hong Kong Special Administrative Region's Court of Final Appeal is now the highest appellate tribunal in the jurisdiction.
[12] *Attorney-General of Hong Kong v Lee Kwong-kut* [1993] AC 951 at 975.

the role and function of the courts within the broader legal and constitutional order. The more keenly it is felt that the judges are guardians of fundamental rights who serve a central role in ensuring accountable government, the more likely they are to take an interventionist approach, broadly reading the rights themselves while narrowly construing any provisions which appear to inhibit their application. In contrast, a judiciary which less readily perceives that it is part of a constitutional machinery which secures individuals' rights against legislative encroachment and executive abuse is likely to take a very different approach to the interpretation of a human rights instrument.

I need hardly point out to so distinguished an audience that there can be no clearer illustration of this than the historic judgment of the United States Supreme Court in *Marbury v Madison*.[13] The vacuum created by the US Constitution's silence on the courts' powers over unconstitutional legislation had to be filled by judicial decision. The Supreme Court's conclusion, that the judicial branch could set aside such legislation, was inspired by a particular conception of the purpose and role of the courts and the nature of their relationship with the other institutions of government.

However, to acknowledge the particular importance and sensitivity of the judicial decision-making process in the field of human rights interpretation does not mean that the judges have carte blanche to do as they please.[14] This follows for a number of reasons. First, the text itself provides, to some extent, a limit on the judges' freedom. Although the expansive language of human rights instruments means that they cannot constitute precise directions which judges simply enforce, they do at least point towards the acceptable parameters within which constitutional adjudication may occur.[15] The text thus reminds that judge that, in the words of Cardozo J, 'even when he is free, [he] is not wholly free ... He is not a knight-errant, roaming at will in pursuit of his own

[13] (1803) 1 Cranch 137.

[14] For further discussion, from the perspective of English law, of the limits which the constitution imposes on judicial decision-making in the public law field, see s 4 below, and my lectures 'Judges and Decision-Makers: The Theory and Practice of *Wednesbury* Review' [1996] *PL* 59 and '*Principle and Pragmatism: The Development of English Public Law under the Separation of Powers*' (Hong Kong, September 1998; now chapter 10 in this volume).

[15] By stating such parameters, the text of human rights legislation also serves a democratic function by furnishing the judges with a catalogue of rights which has received the imprimatur of an elected legislature: see further my 'Response to Sir John Laws' [1996] *PL* 636.

ideal of beauty or of goodness'.[16] Secondly, the conclusions which previous courts have reached also constitute—through the doctrine of precedent—a significant limit on the scope of the judges' interpretative freedom. But in this regard as in so many others, human rights are something of a special case. Professor Jack Beatson, in his inaugural lecture at Cambridge, pointed out that 'in its application on any date the language of [an ordinary] Act [of Parliament], though necessarily embedded in its own time, is nevertheless to be construed in accordance with the need to treat it as current law'.[17] This same principle applies—but with much greater force—to human rights instruments. To quote Cardozo again: 'Statutes are designed to meet the fugitive exigencies of the hour ... A constitution'—or a bill of rights—' states or ought to state not rules for the passing hour, but principles for an expanding future.'[18] It is for this reason that the European Convention on Human Rights is regarded as 'a living instrument which ... must be interpreted in the light of present day conditions'.[19] Consequently, while past decisions on the meaning of human rights texts furnish judges with invaluable guidance, they certainly do not fix any immovable limit on the courts' interpretative freedom,[20] as the US Supreme Court's volte-face in *Brown v Board of Education* on the constitutionality of racial segregation illustrates.[21]

Finally, the jurisprudence of constitutional courts in other jurisdictions is a useful source of guidance to any judge seeking to give meaning to a human rights instrument. The South African Constitutional Court has embraced this comparative ethos with particular zeal.[22]

---

[16] Cardozo, n 5 above, at p 141.

[17] 'Has the Common Law a Future?' [1997] *CLJ* 291 at p 302.

[18] Cardozo, n 5 above, at p 83.

[19] *Tyrer v United Kingdom* (1978) Series A, v 26, para 31.

[20] British courts, when they begin to adjudicate on the ECHR, will, of course, benefit from the existence of a ready-made body of case law in the form of the jurisprudence of the European Commission and Court of Human Rights. Although s 2(1) of the Human Rights Act 1998 requires British courts to have regard to these decisions, they will not constitute 'precedent' in the technical sense.

[21] Compare *Plessy v Ferguson* (1896) 153 US 537 and *Brown v Board of Education of Topeka* (1953) 347 US 483.

[22] The Master of the Rolls has noted that English courts, too, are becoming increasingly outwardlooking, suggesting in his 1991 FA Mann Lecture that it would not be long before 'England ... ceased to be a legal island, bounded to the north by the Tweed, and joined, or more accurately rejoined, the mainstream of European legal tradition, at least as an associate member'. See Sir Thomas Bingham, '"There is a World Elsewhere": The Changing Perspectives of English Law' (1992) 41 *ICLQ* 513 at p 514.

Thus we reach the position that, while there are many factors which, quite properly, shape and guide the interpretation of human rights instruments, their linguistic texture and their evolutive nature necessarily leave the judges with a significant margin of interpretative autonomy. As I have already suggested, it is the prevailing conception of the constitutional role of the judiciary which shapes its behaviour within this area of decision-making freedom.

Before I develop this theme further, I enter an important caveat. The content of this perception of the courts' role should emphatically not be determined by the attitudes of individual judges. While there will always exist subtle differences of emphasis and opinion between members of the Bench, the overarching conception of the judiciary's role, which determines the premise on which it approaches constitutional texts, necessarily consists in a complex amalgam of strands within a wider consensus in society about the nature and purpose of the judicial function.

This phenomenon can be observed in the development of English public law over the course of the twentieth century. As I noted at the outset, the growth of judicial review is one of the pre-eminent legal innovations of recent decades. And, although the courts fashioned our modern system of administrative law, it would be misleading to suggest that these developments occurred at their unilateral instance. The expansion of judicial review must be understood within a broader constitutional setting. The explosion of regulatory power led to the courts coming to be regarded as a central part of a broader constitutional mechanism securing responsible government. In this manner, the growth of review, and the perception of the judicial function upon which it is founded, constituted a mature response to the changing needs of good governance.[23]

The role of the judiciary in this context is also shaped by the perception of judicial independence. I regard independence, along with judicial impartiality and open justice, as a closely related trinity. Judicial independence is a fundamental article of Britain's unwritten constitution. It is a critical aspect of the doctrine of separation of powers. In their own

---

[23] See further Sir Stephen Sedley, 'Governments, Constitutions, and Judges' in G Richardson and H Genn (eds), *Administrative Law and Government Action* (Oxford, Clarendon Press, 1994) and 'The Sound of Silence: Constitutional Law Without a Constitution' (1994) 110 *LQR* 270. For a broader perspective, see M Cappelletti, *The Judicial Process in Comparative Perspective* (Oxford, Clarendon Press, 1989), ch 1.

sphere the judges are independent, free of executive influence or control. There is no higher duty of the office I occupy than to ensure from within Government that judicial independence is both respected and maintained absolutely. And, as you know, under our arrangements, the fulfillment of that duty is strengthened and supported by my separate, but related, roles as Cabinet Minister and Head of the Judiciary. So, judges are independent of Government, with an absolute power over the decisions within their own courts, which can only be overturned by the equally absolute decisions of senior judges in higher courts. In return, the trust we place in our judiciary is that they will carry out their duties impartially. Judicial impartiality, which I would define as the absolute recognition and application by judges of an obligation of fidelity to law, is the *quid pro quo* from the judiciary for the guarantee from the state of their judicial independence in their distinct sphere within the separation of powers.

But just as judicial impartiality is the other side of the coin of judicial independence, so open justice, as witnessed by an attentive media, is a strong spur to judicial impartiality in practice. And each element in this trinity is especially highlighted in a period in which the importance of public law adjudication in the United Kingdom is heightened. I will return to the position in the U K later. First, however, let me draw upon the experiences of other jurisdictions to illustrate my thesis in comparative perspective.

III.   PERSPECTIVES ON ACTIVISM AND RESTRAINT IN THE INTERPRETATION OF HUMAN RIGHTS

A.   The Immigrant Children Cases: Interpretation in Hong Kong's New Constitutional Order

a.   Introduction

Hong Kong is my first port of call. Its courts are still coming to terms with a new set of constitutional arrangements. It is only eight years since the International Covenant on Civil and Political Rights (ICCPR) was incorporated into Hong Kong law,[24] and it is less than two years

---

[24] This was effected by the Hong Kong Bill of Rights Ordinance. For an interesting discussion of the Hong Kong courts' early Bill of Rights jurisprudence, see J M M Chan, 'Hong Kong's Bill of Rights: Its Reception of and Contribution to International and Comparative Jurisprudence' (1998) 47 *ICLQ* 306.

since the Basic Law, which now forms the written constitution of the Hong Kong Special Administrative Region, entered into force upon the transfer of sovereignty from the United Kingdom to the People's Republic of China.[25]

The most challenging questions of construction which have arisen under Hong Kong's new constitutional texts relate to the rights of permanent residence and abode which Article 24 of the Basic Law confers upon certain categories of persons. The issues raised by these Immigrant Children cases[26] can be divided into two broad categories. Before I turn to the substantive questions about the scope of the entitlements granted by the Basic Law, however, let me examine two broader issues which arose, concerning the interrelationship of Hong Kong's institutions of government.[27]

b.　*The Institutional Issues*

First, the scope of the Court of Final Appeal's competence to interpret Hong Kong's constitution had to be decided. The Basic Law requires the Court to refer to the National People's Congress the interpretation of matters which relate to the responsibilities of the central government or

---

[25] Following the transfer of sovereignty, the ICCPR remains part of Hong Kong's domestic law by operation of Article 39 of the Basic Law.

[26] There are two separate *Immigrant Children* decisions. The first case, *Ng Ka Ling v Director of Immigration (sub nom: Cheung Lai Wah (An Infant) v Director of Immigration)* [1997] 3 HKC 64 (Court of First Instance); [1998] 1 HKC 617 (Court of Appeal); [1999] 1 HKLRD 315 (Court of Final Appeal), dealt with a particularly broad range of issues, and it was in this case that the Court of Final Appeal took the opportunity to explain, in some detail, its approach to constitutional adjudication (on which see below). The other *Immigrant Children* decisions are cited as *Chan Kam Nga v Director of Immigration* [1998] 1 HKLRD 142 (Court of First Instance); [1998] 1 HKLRD 752 (Court of Appeal); [1999] 1 HKLRD 304 (Court of Final Appeal).

[27] A further institutional issue also arose, regarding the constitutionality of Hong Kong's Provisional Legislative Council. This question had been the subject of considerable dispute in earlier cases before the lower courts. In *Hong Kong Special Administrative Region v Ma Wai Kwan David* [1997] 2 HKC 315, the Court of Appeal held that the provisional legislature had been lawfully constituted in accordance with the requirements of the Basic Law. The issue was raised again in *Cheung Lai Wah (An Infant) v Director of Immigration (No 2)* [1998] 2 HKC 382, but the Court of Appeal held itself bound by its earlier decision. The question was authoritatively determined by the Court of Final Appeal in *Na Ka Ling v Director of Immigration* [1999] 1 HKLRD 315 at 355–57, which held that the Provisional Legislative Council was lawfully constituted.

which impact upon its relationship with Hong Kong.[28] The way in which this issue was approached by the Court was crucial, since a broad construction would have transferred a substantial degree of interpretative competence from the Hong Kong judiciary to the mainland authorities.[29] After due consideration, the Court held that the duty to refer questions of interpretation related only to a very narrow range of issues and that it was a matter for the Court to determine whether, in any particular case, such an issue was properly engaged.[30] While this construction did not place unbearable strain on the text of the Basic Law, it did not necessarily constitute the most natural construction of the relevant words.

Three principal factors underpinned the Court of Final Appeal's approach, each of which affected its underlying conception of the constitutional role and function of the judicial branch. First, the Court held that the construction of constitutional texts calls for a particular interpretative method. A 'literal, technical, rigid or narrow approach' had to be rejected; instead, it was said that Hong Kong's courts should 'give a generous interpretation to the ... constitutional guarantees' enshrined in the Basic Law, 'in order to give to Hong Kong residents the full measure of [their] fundamental rights and freedoms'.[31] Secondly, Li CJ—giving the judgment of the Court—held that constitutional adjudication called for a 'purposive approach' which recognised that one of the fundamental objectives of the Basic Law was 'to implement the unique principle of "one country, two systems"'.[32] This policy, said the Court, was advanced by the Basic Law's conferral of 'a high degree of

---

[28] Basic Law, Art 158(3). This had not been in issue when the case was before the lower courts, since Art 158(3) applies only to courts which make 'final judgments which are not appealable'.

[29] Such a construction was urged by counsel for the Director of Immigration who suggested that, even when the predominant question related to a provision of the Basic Law not falling within one of the special categories delineated by Art 158(3), reference should still be made to the National People's Congress if another provision of the Basic Law, which did relate to one of the matters mentioned in Art 158(3), was arguably relevant to the interpretation of the predominant provision. See *Ng Ka Ling v Director of Immigration* [1999] 1 HKLRD 315 at 343–44.

[30] *Ibid*, at 344–45. Thus the reference duty arises only when the Court concludes that the 'predominant' provision of the Basic Law requiring interpretation relates to one of the matters set out in Art 158(3). The fact that other provisions of the Basic Law which do relate to Art 158(3) issues are arguably relevant to the construction of the predominant provision is insufficient to trigger the duty to refer.

[31] Above n 29, at 340, *per* Li C J.

[32] Above n 29, at 339, *per* Li C J.

autonomy' upon Hong Kong and its courts.[33] Thirdly, and most explicitly, the Court of Final Appeal emphasised that it is the 'constitutional role' of Hong Kong's courts to act 'as a check on the executive and legislative branches of government to ensure that they act in accordance with the Basic Law'.[34]

It is not my purpose to analyse the correctness or otherwise of the decision at which the Court actually arrived. The determination of the constitutional dynamics of a particular legal order is properly for its own institutions to determine. My point is simply this: that, in light of the manner in which the Court perceived its function, it is wholly unsurprising that it favoured a construction of the Basic Law which emphasised the role of the judiciary as the primary interpreter of the constitution. Naturally, in considering this, attention was paid to the text of the constitution; but it is undeniable that the premises on which the Court approached the terms of the Basic Law exerted a strong influence on the conclusion which it reached.

The same ethos pervaded the Court's treatment of the second institutional issue, which concerned the competence of the judiciary to review the validity of legislation on the ground of its incompatibility with the Basic Law or the ICCPR. Although the Court's comments on this point were *obiter*, they are nevertheless important given both the authoritative source from which they issued and the light which they shed on the Court's broader approach to constitutional adjudication.

While the Court said that it 'undoubtedly' had jurisdiction to set aside enactments of Hong Kong's own Legislative Council,[35] the more controversial question was whether a similar jurisdiction could be exercised over legislation passed by China's National People's Congress. In an earlier case before a lower court, Chan CJHC had suggested that the relationship between the courts of the Hong Kong Special Administrative Region and the National People's Congress was analogous to that which had previously existed between the colonial courts and the Westminster Parliament.[36] On this view, there was no

---

[33] Above n 29 at 337, *per* Li C J.
[34] Above n 29 at 337.
[35] *Ng Ka Ling v Director of Immigration* [1999] 1 HKLRD 315 at 337.
[36] *Hong Kong Special Administrative Region v Ma Wai Kwan David* [1997] 2 HKC 315 at 334–35. This suggestion was based upon Art 19(2) of the Basic Law which directs that, 'The courts of the Hong Kong Special Administrative Region shall have jurisdiction over all cases in the Region, except that the restrictions on their jurisdiction imposed by the legal system and the principles previously in force in Hong Kong shall

jurisdiction in the courts to review the legislative acts of the sovereign. The Court of Final Appeal disagreed fundamentally, stating that the Court's jurisdiction to review legislation for consistency with the Basic Law extends to legislation passed by the National People's Congress, though this jurisdiction was subject to the provisions of the Basic Law itself, including the provision that the power of interpretation of the Basic Law, vesting in the Standing Committee of the National People's Congress, was paramount.

These different approaches to the sovereignty question disclose a broader shift in ethos which, to date, has been evident during the short history of Hong Kong's new constitutional order. The earlier decisions of the lower courts disclosed what may be termed a 'sovereigntist' approach to constitutional adjudication, which places less emphasis on the role of the court as a guardian of fundamental rights and as part of a constitutional machinery which supervises the other branches of government. This approach can be detected not only in the early decisions on the Basic Law, but also in some of the colonial courts' judgments, prior to the transfer of sovereignty, on the Bill of Rights Ordinance. In contrast, the *Immigrant Children* decision marks a shift away from a 'sovereigntist' view of the adjudicative function, towards a constitutionalist conception which underscores the courts' role as a constitutional check on the legislature and the executive. The Court's decision that it has jurisdiction to invalidate legislation passed by the National People's Congress thus stands as an important symbol of this change of ethos; in particular, it will serve as a useful marker for the lower courts as they continue to adjust to the demands of Hong Kong's new constitutional order.

However, before leaving the institutional implications of the *Immigrant Children* decision, I wish to offer one further thought. While the Court of Final Appeal's assertion of jurisdiction over mainland legislation is of symbolic importance for the future direction of constitutional

---

be maintained.' Chan CJHC opined that, following the transfer of sovereignty, the National People's Congress replaced the Westminster Parliament as Hong Kong's sovereign legislature, so that the courts' incapacity to question enactments of the latter transferred, by operation of Art 19(2), to the former. It should be pointed out that Chan CJHC later expressed doubts as to the correctness of these comments. In *Cheung Lai Wah (An Infant) v Director of Immigration (No 2)* [1998] 2 HKC 382 at 395, he said that, 'It may be that in appropriate cases ... the HKSAR courts do have jurisdiction to examine the laws and acts of the NPC which affect the HKSAR for the purpose of, say, determining whether such laws or acts are contrary to or inconsistent with the Basic Law ... '

jurisprudence in Hong Kong, the rejection of the notion of a sovereign legislature whose enactments cannot be questioned is not an ineluctable element of a shift from a 'sovereigntist' to a constitutionalist approach. It is quite possible for courts to adopt a more constitutionalist ethos in the public law sphere without questioning the ultimate supremacy of the legislature. The jurisprudence of the courts in New Zealand and the United Kingdom, to which I shall turn shortly, are cases in point.

c.   The Substantive Issues

First, let me make some brief remarks about the substantive issues raised by the *Immigrant Children* decision. The Basic Law provides that Chinese nationals, at least one of whose parents is a permanent resident of Hong Kong, should themselves be regarded as permanent residents: importantly, acquisition of this status triggers a right of abode.[37] Shortly after the transfer of sovereignty, the Provisional Legislative Council, mindful of the possibility of a huge influx of people possessing—or claiming to possess—the status of permanent residency, enacted legislation to regulate and impose order upon the immigration process.[38] The effect of this legislation was twofold. First, it defined, in greater detail than the Basic Law, the conditions which had to be satisfied in order to establish permanent residency by descent; the applicants contended that this definition was unduly narrow and, hence, unconstitutional. Secondly, the legislation directed that those seeking to exercise a right of abode should, before going to Hong Kong, prove their status as permanent residents and obtain permission to travel from the mainland authorities; breach of these regulations entailed the commission of a criminal offence, and this provision took effect retroactively.

The lower courts upheld all of these legislative initiatives, apart from one aspect of the definition of permanent residency.[39] In stark contrast, the Court of Final Appeal held that all but one of them was invalid for

---

[37] Basic Law, Art 24(2) and (3).

[38] See Immigration (Amendment) (No 2) Ordinance (No 122 of 1997); Immigration (Amendment) (No 3) Ordinance (No 124 of 1997).

[39] See *Ng Ka Ling v Director of Immigration (sub nom: Cheung Lai Wah (An Infant) v Director of immigration)* [1997] 3 HKC 64 (Court of First Instance) and [1998] 1 HKC 617 (Court of Appeal); *Chan Kam Nga v Director of Immigration* [1998] 1 HKLRD 142 (Court of First Instance) and [1998] 1 HKLRD 752 (Court of Appeal). The part of the legislative scheme referred to in the text which the lower courts, in *Ng Ka Ling,*

breach of either the Basic Law or the ICCPR.[40] The text of those constitutional instruments did not alter as the litigation progressed up the appellate hierarchy. Rather, the Court of Final Appeal reached conclusions which differed from those of the lower courts because it adopted a particularly constitutionalist conception of its function which impacted fundamentally on its interpretative approach. So, the dissimilar treatment of these substantive aspects of the *Immigrant Children* cases further illustrates the relationship between a courts' perception of its constitutional role and the ultimate decisions which it reaches on the scope of fundamental rights.[40a] Let me outline a further example of this phenomenon.

B. South Africa and the United Kingdom: Access to the Courts' Supervisory Jurisdiction

The conception of the judicial function which prevails in a society is revealed with particular clarity by the courts' treatment of legislative attempts to attenuate their jurisdiction. The more acutely it is felt that courts are guardians of individual liberties, the more likely they are to construe ouster provisions in a way which preserves the judiciary's capacity to adjudicate in disputes between the citizen and the state.

impugned as unconstitutional related to a provision which recognised an illegitimate child as the descendent only of its mother (unless the child was legitimated by subsequent marriage of both parents, in which case the child would then be recognised as the descendent of its mother and its father). It should also be noted that, in *Chan Kam Nga*, the Court of First Instance held unconstitutional a legislative provision which refused to recognise a child as having been 'born of' a permanent resident if the parent became a permanent resident only after the birth. However, the Court of Appeal upheld the constitutionality of this provision.

[40] The only aspect of the legislative scheme upheld by the Court of Final Appeal, in *Ng Ka Ling* n 39, was a requirement that persons claiming to be permanent residents had to substantiate their claims to the satisfaction of Hong Kong authorities based on the mainland before travelling from the mainland to Hong Kong. The further requirement, that permission to travel had to be obtained from mainland authorities, was impugned as unconstitutional.

[40a] Since this lecture was delivered, the Standing Committee of the National People's Congress has exercised its power under the Basic Law, Art 158(1), by re-interpreting certain of the provisions of the Basic Law which were at stake in the *Immigrant Children* cases. For the present purposes, it is sufficient to observe that these developments do not detract from the fact that the courts' decisions in these cases clearly illustrate my argument that the judicial response to a constitutional text turns on, *inter alia*, the judiciary's perception of its constitutional function.

English courts attach great importance to the citizen's right of access to justice; and judges have now come to speak of this as a constitutional right.[41] The locus classicus of this genre is still the seminal *Anisminic*[42] decision in which the House of Lords went to considerable lengths to preserve the availability of judicial review in the face of a statutory provision which, on a literal construction, appeared to preclude it. My theme is usefully illuminated by comparing *Anisminic* with the 1988 judgment of the South African Appellate Division in the *UDF* case.[43] The two decisions concerned very similar ouster clauses, yet the respective courts reached sharply contrasting conclusions.

It is well known that the Foreign Compensation Act 1950 provided that the determinations of the Commission established under that Act could 'not be called in question in any court of law'.[44] The Law Lords, in *Anisminic*, held that this only immunised valid determinations of the Commission: that is, determinations within jurisdiction. 'What would be the purpose,' asked Lord Wilberforce, 'of defining by statute the limit of a tribunal's powers if, by means of a clause inserted in the instrument of definition, those limits could safely be passed'[45] By interpreting the ouster provision in this way, it was possible for the House of Lords to set aside a decision made under a jurisdictional error of law.

This decision has provoked considerable debate and disagreement ever since it was handed down. Many commentators have suggested that the House of Lords ignored Parliament's intention and treated the right of access to court as a constitutional fundamental which not even Parliament could abrogate.[46] It is not my intention, this evening, to address this aspect of *Anisminic* in any detail.[47] It is sufficient for me to say that I do not share this view; but to add that, although the courts are right to presume that Parliament does not intend to attenuate access to justice, there must exist some formulation which is strong enough to

---

[41] See eg, *R v Secretary of State for the Home Department, ex parte Leech (No 2)* [1994] QB 198; *R v Lord Chancellor, ex parte Witham* [1998] QB 575.
[42] *Anisminic Ltd v Foreign Compensation Commission* [1969] 2 AC 147.
[43] *Staatspresident v United Democratic Front* (1988) (4) SA 830.
[44] S 4(4).
[45] [1969] 2 AC 147 at 208.
[46] HWR Wade, 'Constitutional and Administrative Aspects of the *Anisminic* Case' (1969) 85 *LQR* 198; HWR Wade and CF Forsyth, *Administrative Law* (Oxford, Clarendon Press, 1994), (7th ed) pp 734–39.
[47] My views on the subject of sovereignty can be found in 'Judges and Decision-Makers: The Theory and Practice of *Wednesbury Review*' [1996] *PL* 59.

overcome that presumption.[48] This proposition follows straightforwardly from Parliament's sovereign status. For present purposes, my interest in *Anisminic* lies simply in the fact that the House of Lords went to such lengths in order to hold that jurisdiction was preserved in the face of a preclusive clause.

The *UDF* case[49] reveals a very different approach. Section 3 of the South African Public Safety Act 1953 conferred broad emergency powers on the State President. Relying on these powers, regulations were made which imposed severe restrictions on the freedom of the press. The United Democratic Front challenged these provisions on the ground that they were unacceptably vague. However, section 5B of the Act provided that 'no court shall be competent to enquire into or give judgment on the validity of any proclamation' made under section 3. Had the Appellate Division desired to effect judicial review in spite of this preclusive provision, the necessary conceptual tools lay ready to hand. The *ultra vires* doctrine had long been regarded as the juridical basis of review in South Africa.[50] It was therefore open to the court to hold that the vague regulations had been made beyond jurisdiction with the consequence that—by analogy with *Anisminic*—the ouster clause did not protect vague regulations from review. However, the Appellate Division rejected this analysis, choosing not to accept the concept of jurisdiction as the organising principle of administrative law. By holding that vagueness was not a jurisdictional matter, the court precluded itself from applying *Anisminic* logic.

Thus, the preclusive provision in the Public Safety Act succeeded before the Appellate Division where the equivalent provision of the Foreign Compensation Act had spectacularly failed before the House of Lords. As with the divergent conclusions of the various courts in the

---

[48] As the Divisional Court recognised in *R v Lord Chancellor, ex parte Witham* [1998] QB 575.

[49] The judgments in this case are in Afrikaans. For discussion in English, see N Haysom and C Plasket, 'The War Against Law: Judicial Activism and the Appellate Division' (1988) 4 *South African Journal on Human Rights* 303; E Mureinik, 'Administrative Law' [1988] *Annual Survey of South African Law* 34; J Grogan, 'The Appellate Division and the Emergency: Another Step Backward' (1989) 106 *SALJ* 14; ML Matthews, 'Vandalizing the *Ultra Vires* Doctrine' (1989) 5 *South African Journal on Human Rights* 481; C F Forsyth, 'Of Fig Leaves and Fairy Tales: The *Ultra Vires* Doctrine, the Sovereignty of Parliament and Judicial Review' [1996] *CLJ* 122.

[50] See L Baxter, *Administrative Law* (Cape Town, Juta and Co, 1984), p 303: 'The *ultra vires* doctrine was adopted at the Cape almost as soon as the Supreme Court was established.'

Hong Kong *Immigrant Children* decisions, the reason for this difference cannot be attributed to textual considerations, since the two ouster provisions were almost identical. It is the different premises upon which the two courts approached their interpretative task—and, in particular, their divergent perceptions of their constitutional functions—which explains the radically different conclusions at which they arrived. This much is apparent from the respective historical contexts in which the decisions were reached.

Professor Wade has written that, during the middle part of the twentieth century, 'a deep gloom settled on [English] administrative law.... The courts showed signs of losing confidence in their constitutional function...and they showed little stomach for continuing their centuries-old work of imposing law upon government.'[51] There can be no better illustration of this than the House of Lords' decision in *Liversidge v Anderson*.[52] The majority's conclusion—strongly opposed by Lord Atkin[53]—that a subjective language clause could preclude any proper judicial scrutiny of the decisionmaking process stands in stark contrast to the modern judiciary's attitude in this field. As subsequent decisions have demonstrated,[54] it would have been relatively easy to interpret the subjective provision in a manner which preserved a meaningful role for judicial review. Ascribing such an interpretation to the clause in *Liversidge* would certainly have involved considerably less difficulty than the House of Lords' creative construction of the much stronger ouster clause in *Anisminic*.[55]

The substantial differences in approach which these cases disclose can be explained only by reference to the sea change which had taken place, in the intervening 25 years, in the prevailing conception of the courts' public law role. To quote Sir William Wade again, 'In the 1960s the judicial mood completely changed. It began to be understood how

[51] HWR Wade and CF Forsyth, *Administrative Law* 7th ed (Oxford, Clarendon Press, 1994), pp 17–19.
[52] [1942] AC 206.
[53] For discussion of—and a fascinating insight into—the disagreement between Lord Atkin and the majority, see RFV Heuston, '*Liversidge v Anderson* in Retrospect' (1970) 86 *LQR* 33.
[54] Eg, *Secretary of State for Education and Science v Tameside Metropolitan Borough Council* [1977] AC 1014. See further HWR Wade and CF Forsyth, *Administrative Law* (7th ed) (Oxford, Clarendon Press, 1994), pp 442–59.
[55] The fact that *Liversidge v Anderson* was a wartime decision naturally had some impact on the House of Lords' approach; but this cannot constitute a full explanation. This decision formed part of a much broader retreat from effective judicial supervision of government which extended well beyond the period 1939–45.

much ground had been lost and what damage had been done to the only defences against abuse of power which still remained.'[56] The courts realized—more clearly than ever before, in light of the rate at which the state was expanding—that their public law jurisdiction was a crucial cornerstone in the constitutional machinery for securing responsible government. The decision in *Anisminic* formed an integral element of the courts' reinvention of their constitutional function; and the House of Lords' unwillingness interpretatively to denude itself of the power to adjudicate on disputes between the citizen and the state clearly illustrates the conception of the judicial function which underpinned the renaissance of English administrative law.

The *UDF* case formed part of a very different—and particularly dark—chapter in the history of South African public law. The state of emergency was ongoing, and the courts were beginning to adopt an unduly deferential attitude to the executive and legislative branches. By the time of the *UDF* case a culture was developing within some parts of the judiciary which tended to overlook the courts' duty to impose standards of legality on government. There was at least the risk of South Africa's courts becoming 'more executive minded than the executive'.[57] A South African critic used stronger language still, arguing that the court had displayed 'an excess of enthusiasm for the preservation of the powers of the State President, a reckless neglect of the consequences for the legal system and, indeed, a suicidal disregard for the functions of the judiciary'.[58] The attributability of the *UDF* judgment to a change in the conception of the courts' role is made all the more apparent by the fact that, as I have already explained, the appeal court chose to reject an orthodox jurisdictional analysis, which would have reduced the impact of the ouster clause,[59] in favour of a wholly novel approach which had the opposite effect.

The *Immigrant Children* case demonstrates that the way in which a court perceives its constitutional function can impact fundamentally on how it interprets the text of a human rights instrument. Taken together, the *Anisminic* and *UDF* decisions illustrate that this conception of the

[56] HWR Wade and CF Forsyth, *Administrative Law* 7th ed (Oxford, Clarendon Press, 1994), p 19.
[57] Lord Atkin levelled this criticism at the majority in *Liversidge v Anderson* [1942] AC 206 at 244.
[58] ML Matthews, 'Vandalizing the *Ultra Vires* Doctrine' (1989) 5 *South African Journal on Human Rights* 481.
[59] For an example of such orthodox reasoning, see the earlier decision in *Minister of Law and Order v Hurley* 1986 (3) SA 586.

judicial function exerts similar influence on the construction of ordinary legislation which touches individuals' rights. Each of these points will assume a heightened relevance in this country as our courts begin both to attribute meaning to the European Convention and to construe municipal statutes against that background. Before I deal with these domestic prospects in more detail, let me refer, briefly, to the experiences of two other jurisdictions.

C.   Canada and New Zealand: Constitutional Innovation and Judicial Reaction

It is widely acknowledged that the Canadian Bill of Rights 1960 largely failed in its attempt to engender in Canada a culture of fundamental rights; even the draftsman admitted that it 'received a very poor reception from the legal profession'.[60] This was in spite of the fact that a strong approach to the protection of human rights was envisaged, according to which the Bill of Rights would prevail over incompatible legislation.[61] In fact, this situation was held to have arisen in only one case[62] in spite of the fact that, according to Canadian academic opinion, the courts could have reached this conclusion on many more occasions.[63]

---

[60] EA Driedger, 'The Meaning and Effect of the Canadian Bill of Rights: A Draftsman's Viewpoint' (1977) 9 *Ottawa Law Review* 303. See also J Black-Branch, 'Entrenching Human Rights Legislation under Constitutional Law: The Canadian Charter of Rights and Freedoms' [1998] *EHRLR* 312 at pp 315–19.

As is well known, Canada's experience with its Charter of Rights and Freedoms 1982 has been markedly different. Although—as would be expected—there exists a diversity of opinion in Canada concerning the extent to which the Charter has succeeded in protecting individuals' rights, there can be no doubt that it has been received with immeasurably greater enthusiasm than the earlier Bill of Rights. Although space does not permit detailed consideration of this matter, the divergent attitudes of the judiciary to the Bill of Rights and the more recent Charter certainly provide at least a partial explanation for the failure of the former and the success of the latter. The literature on the Charter is enormous; however, a useful overview of its impact to date can be found in R Penner, 'The Canadian Experience with the Charter of Rights: Are there Lessons for the United Kingdom?' [1996] *PL* 104.

[61] Canadian Bill of Rights, s 2. See further Driedger, n 60 above, at pp 307–10. The Bill was not fully entrenched, since it was possible for legislation, by express provision, to take effect notwithstanding conflict with the Bill of Rights; a similar approach is to be found in s 33(1) of the Canadian Charter of Rights and Freedoms 1982.

[62] *R v Drybones* [1970] SCR 282.

[63] See especially H Arthurs in 'Minutes of Evidence taken before the Select Committee on a Bill of Rights' (House of Lords, 1977).

As Professor Zander remarks, Canada's experience in the 1960s shows that the 'mere enactment' of a Bill of Rights 'changes nothing'.[64]

New Zealand's Bill of Rights Act 1990 provides an interesting counterpoint.[65] This modest[66] measure operates only by interpretation and confers no powers on the courts to invalidate or declare the incompatibility of legislation which infringes human rights.[67] Many commentators predicted, on this basis, that the legislation would have little effect.[68] History, however, has proved them wrong.

The key to the success of the New Zealand fundamental rights legislation was the manner it which it was approached by the courts.[69] Under the Presidency of Sir Robin Cooke, whose views on the importance of protecting human rights are well-known,[70] New Zealand's

---

[64] M Zander, *A Bill of Rights?* 4th ed (London, Sweet and Maxwell, 1997), p 127.

[65] For an overview, see M Taggart, 'Tugging on Superman's Cape: Lessons from Experience with the New Zealand Bill of Rights Act 1990' in J Beatson, C F Forsyth and I C Hare (eds), *Constitutional Reform in the United Kingdom: Practice and Principles* (Oxford, Hart Publishing, 1998).

[66] It had originally been intended that New Zealand should have a fully entrenched rights instrument, but this proposal did not win sufficient public support. The 1990 Act rose from the ashes of the failed attempt at entrenchment. See further P Rishworth, 'The Birth and Rebirth of the Bill of Rights' in G Huscroft and P Rishworth (eds), *Rights and Freedoms* (Wellington, Brooker's, 1995), Ch 1.

[67] See New Zealand Bill of Rights Act 1990, ss4 and 6. The New Zealand measure is, in terms of its text, weaker than the United Kingdom's Human Rights Act 1998 in two respects. First, the interpretative duty under s 6 of the New Zealand Act appears to be slightly less robust than the formulation found in s 3 of the United Kingdom legislation. Secondly, the British Act's declaration of incompatibility and fast-track amendment machinery (see ss 4 and 10, respectively) have no analogues in the New Zealand legislation.

[68] However, cf P Rishworth, 'The Potential of the New Zealand Bill of Rights' [1990] *NZLJ* 68.

[69] For detailed discussion, see A Adams, 'Competing Conceptions of the Constitution: The New Zealand Bill of Rights Act 1990 and the Cooke Court of Appeal' [1996] *New Zealand Law Review* 368. Adams identifies three distinct 'discourses' within the Court of Appeal's Bill of Rights jurisprudence during the period 1990–95. She locates Lord Cooke of Thorndon firmly within the first such discourse which emphasises the constitutional status of the Bill of Rights. Although Adams argues that the judges within the other two discourses approached the Bill of Rights with less enthusiasm, it was the generous, constitutional approach to the legislation which determined the outcome of many of the leading cases.

[70] Lord Cooke of Thorndon has, both judicially and extra-curially, consistently asserted that certain norms are so fundamental that they lie beyond the competence of even a sovereign Parliament. See *L v M* [1979] 2 NZLR 519 at 529; *Brader v Ministry of Transport* [1981] 1 NZLR 73 at 78; *New Zealand Drivers' Association v New Zealand Road Carriers* [1982] NZLR 374 at 390; *Fraser v State Services Commission* [1984] 1 NZLR 116 at 121; *Taylor v New Zealand Poultry Board* [1984] 1 NZLR 394 at 398; 'Fundamentals' [1988] NZLJ 158. For discussion see P Rishworth, 'Lord Cooke and the Bill of Rights' and M Kirby, 'Lord Cooke and Fundamental Rights' in P Rishworth (ed), *The Struggle for Simplicity in the Law* (Wellington, Butterworths, 1997).

courts took it upon themselves to act—in the words of Hardie Boys J—as 'the ultimate guardians of personal liberty'.[71] It was this view of the judicial function which ensured that the Act's potential as a guarantee of civil liberties was realised. The best illustration of this is to be found in *Baigent's* case.[72] In spite of the facts that the Bill of Rights lacked a remedies clause and that there were certain oblique indications that this omission was deliberate,[73] the Court nevertheless created, in this case, a new public law remedy for breach of the Bill of Rights. It is quite clear that it was the Court's view of its constitutional duty which led it to take this activist step: it refused to countenance a Bill of Rights that constituted 'no more than legislative window dressing',[74] holding instead that judges must have power to take remedial action when they discover human rights abuses.

As one commentator has observed, the New Zealand courts' response to the Bill of Rights demonstrates that 'entrenchment no longer seems as important ... as it once did';[75] rather, what mattered was that the enactment of the Bill of Rights 'coincided with a springtide of judicial enthusiasm for the enforcement of fundamental rights and control of government power'.[76]

IV.   ACTIVISM, RESTRAINT AND THE PROSPECTS FOR HUMAN RIGHTS ADJUDICATION IN THE UNITED KINGDOM

A.   The Human Rights Legislation: A Constitutional Balancing Act

Let me conclude this address by turning to the prospects for human rights adjudication in the United Kingdom. The Human Rights Act is founded upon a division of functions between the different branches of government, which reflects the British conception of the separation of powers principle on which our constitution is based. Under the Act our

---

[71] *R v Te Kira* [1993] 3 NZLR 257 at 275.
[72] *Simpson v Attorney-General (Baigent's Case)* [1994] 3 NZLR 667.
[73] Specifically, the White Paper had included a remedies clause, but the legislation did not. This may be thought to indicate an intention to exclude remedies from the Bill of Rights.
[74] [1994] 3 NZLR 667 at 691, *per* Casey J.
[75] P Rishworth, 'Affirming the Fundamental Values of the Nation: How the Bill of Rights and the Human Rights Act affect New Zealand Law' in P Rishworth and G Huscroft (eds), *Rights and Freedoms* (Wellington, Brooker's, 1995), p 71.
[76] *Ibid*, at p 76.

courts have to interpret statutes 'so far as possible' to be compatible with Convention rights; if this is impossible they have been given a unique power to declare legislation to be incompatible, but then it is for the executive to initiate, and Parliament to enact, remedial legislation, with a fast track process available for that purpose.[77] This balance which inheres in the text of the Act can be secured in practical terms only by a measured judicial response to the challenge of seeking, so far as is possible, to Interpret national law consistently with the Convention.

If the courts were to adopt a very narrow view of this duty of consistent construction, their ability interpretatively to guarantee Convention rights would be severely curtailed. Instead of reading municipal law in a way which gave effect to individuals' rights, the courts would tend to discover irreconcilable conflicts between United Kingdom law and the Convention which would then require legislative correction. In contrast, a judiciary which took an extremely radical view of its interpretative duty would be likely to stretch legislative language, beyond breaking point, if necessary, in order to effect judicial vindication of Convention rights. Such an approach would yield virtually no declarations of incompatibility: the judges would, in effect, be taking it upon themselves to rewrite legislation in order to render it consistent with the Convention, and so excluding Parliament and the executive from the human rights enterprise.

Both of these approaches would be wrong. The constitutional theory on which the Human Rights Act rests is one of balance. It requires courts to recognise that they have a fundamental contribution to make in this area, while appreciating that the other elements of the constitution also have important roles to play in securing the effective protection of the Convention rights in domestic law. Thus the Act, while significantly changing the nature of the interpretative process, does not confer on the courts a licence to construe legislation in a way which is so radical and strained that it arrogates to the judges a power completely to rewrite existing law: that is a task for Parliament and the executive. The interpretative duty which the courts will soon begin to discharge in the human rights arena is therefore a strong one; but it is nevertheless subject to limits which the Act imposes, and which find

---

[77] See principally, ss 3, 4 and 10.

still deeper resonance in the doctrine of the separation of powers on which the constitution is founded.[78]

It is my view that the manner in which English courts have developed public law to date discloses a well-balanced conception of the judicial function which will provide a sound foundation for the judiciary as it begins to work out the precise content of its interpretative duty under the Human Rights Act. Let me illustrate by highlighting three specific contexts in which the courts have successfully balanced the competing imperatives of activism and restraint in their recent public law jurisprudence.

B.   The Existing Judicial Review Jurisdiction

I began, this evening, by commenting on the remarkable growth of judicial review over recent decades. Although this is a striking example of judicial activism, the judges have nevertheless striven to find constitutional balance as they have pushed public law forward, tempering their interventionism with appropriate restraint.

For instance, the courts have, in general, been careful to preserve the distinction between appeal and review, appreciating that it would be an affront to Parliament's sovereignty, according to which the legislature can choose on whom to confer discretion, for the judges to arrogate to themselves primary decision-making power by enquiring into the merits of executive action. These issues recently crystallised in the context of legitimate expectation.[79] In the *Hamble Fisheries* case,[80] Sedley J had

---

[78] A different, but related, challenge will arise once the Scottish Parliament begins to legislate. According to the Scotland Act 1998, s 28(6), the courts must seek to avoid reaching the conclusion that Scottish legislation is invalid (on the ground of its being *ultra vires*) by construing it narrowly. Although this interpretative duty is different in nature from that which the Human Rights Act creates, the importance of balance will remain constant: the courts will have a fundamental contribution to make in seeking to ensure that the Scottish Parliament's legislation is effective (in the sense of being *intra vires*) while preserving the integrity of the distribution of legislative competence between Westminster and Edinburgh which the Scotland Act embodies. Thus, by utilising interpretative methodology to secure the protection of fundamental rights and the efficacy of Scottish legislation, both the Human Rights Act and the Scotland Act recognise that the interpretative process will be of central importance to the success of the constitutional reform programme.

[79] On the subject of legitimate expectation, see generally C F Forsyth, 'The Provenance and Protection of Legitimate Expectations' (1988) *CLJ* 238.

[80] *R v Ministry of Agriculture, Fisheries and Food, ex parte Hamble (Offshore) Fisheries Ltd* [1995] 2 All ER 714.

expressed the view that whether an agency could depart from a substantive expectation was 'ultimately a matter for the court'.[81] It is clear to me that—at the present stage of the development of English administrative law—this did constitute an unduly interventionist approach. Orthodoxy has now been restored by the Court of Appeal which held, in *Hargreaves*,[82] that it is not for a court to determine that an agency may not depart from the substance of its policy. Only if frustration of the expectation would be *Wednesbury* unreasonable may a court intervene on substantive grounds.[83] This reflects a proper balance between judges and decision-makers, and demonstrates the capacity of the courts to temper activism with restraint.[84] Although the Human Rights Act will shift that balance, it is crucially important that this will occur pursuant to legislative intervention, rather than at the unilateral instance of the judicial branch. I shall return to this subject shortly.

The importance of maintaining balance also pervades the law of judicial review at the level of constitutional theory. Although some academics,[85] and certain judges in their extracurial capacity,[86] have questioned the contemporary relevance of the *ultra vires* doctrine, British courts[87] consistently adhere to it as the juridical basis of

---

[81] *Ibid*, at 735.

[82] *R v Secretary of State for the Home Department, ex parte Hargreaves* (1997) 1 WLR 906.

[83] See *ibid* at 921, *per* Hirst LJ, 'On matters of substance ... *Wednesbury* provides the correct test.' Similarly, at 924, Pill LJ explained that a court would prevent departure from the substance of a policy 'only if ... the decision to apply the new policy in the particular case was unreasonable in the *Wednesbury* sense'.

[84] See further my comments in 'Judges and Decision-Makers: The Theory and Practice of *Wednesbury* Review'(1996) *PL* 59 at pp 71–2. For a different view, see PP Craig, 'Substantive Legitimate Expectations in Domestic and Community Law' [1996] CLJ 289.

[85] See *eg*, D Oliver, 'Is the *Ultra Vires* Rule the Basis of Judicial Review?' [1987] *PL* 543; PP Craig, '*Ultra Vires* and the Foundations of Judicial Review' [1998] *CLJ* 63; D Dyzenhaus, 'Reuniting the Brain: The Democratic Basis of Judicial Review' (1998) 9 *Public Law Review* 98.

[86] See *eg*, Lord Woolf of Barnes, '*Droit Public*—English Style' (1995) *PL* 57; Sir John Laws, 'Law and Democracy' (1995) *PL* 72 and 'Illegality: The Problem of Jurisdiction' in M Supperstone and J Goudie (eds), *Judicial Review* 2nd ed (London, Butterworths, 1997); Sir Stephen Sedley, 'The Common Law and the Constitution' in Lord Nolan and Sir Stephen Sedley (eds), *The Making and Remaking of the British Constitution* (London, Blackstone Press, 1997), pp 16–18.

[87] Unlike some of their Commonwealth counterparts. For instance, the High Court of Australia now regards certain principles of judicial review as autonomous common law rules rather than as interpretative constructs. See, principally, *Kioa v Minister for Immigration and Ethnic Affairs* (1985) 159 CLR 550 and, for discussion, P Bayne, 'The Common Law Basis of Judicial Review' (1993) 67 *ALJ* 781. South African courts also

review.[88] In this way, the judiciary has been able to confer considerable protection on citizens, as they interact with the state, in a manner that respects the ultimate sovereignty of the legislature.[89] Moreover, by postulating a relationship between legislative intention and judicial review, the *ultra vires* principle demonstrates that the prevention of maladministration is a cooperative endeavour which involves both Parliament and the courts.

C.   The Doctrine of Common Law Constitutional Rights

In recent cases, such as *Leech*[90] and *Witham*,[91] the courts have conferred particularly strong protection on the individual's right of access to justice, by characterising it as a 'constitutional right'. Two aspects of this discourse exemplify the judiciary's careful balancing of the activist expansion of public law against the restraint which constitutional propriety demands.

At a structural level, the courts have been careful to reconcile their decisions with orthodox constitutional theory,[92] acknowledging that, in a state based on an acceptance of Parliamentary supremacy, constitutional rights can subsist only as interpretative constructs, which take effect by way of presumption and which yield in the face of clear contrary enactment.[93] This is of a piece with both the courts' adherence to the *ultra vires* doctrine and the scheme of the Human Rights Act.

---

went down this path in the 1980s (see the UDF decision, discussed above), although judicial review in South African law now rests on new constitutional foundations, on which see AJH Henderson, 'The Curative Powers of the Constitution: Constitutionality and the New *Ultra Vires* Doctrine in the Justification and Explanation of the Judicial Review of Administrative Action' (1998) 115 *SALJ* 346.

[88] For recent and authoritative confirmation of the centrality of *ultra vires*, see *Boddington v British Transport Police* [1998] 2 WLR 639.

[89] On the constitutional importance of the *ultra vires* doctrine, see CF Forsyth, 'Of Fig Leaves and Fairy Tales: The *Ultra Vires* Doctrine, the Sovereignty of Parliament and Judicial Review' [1996] *CLJ* 122; MC Elliott, 'The *Ultra Vires* Doctrine in a Constitutional Setting: Still the Central Principle of Administrative Law' [1999] *CLJ* 129; MC Elliott, 'The Demise of Parliamentary Sovereignty? The Implications for Justifying Judicial Review' (1999) 115 *LQR* 119.

[90] *R v Secretary of State for the Home Department, ex parte Leech* (No 2) [1994] QB 198.

[91] *R v Lord Chancellor, ex parte Witham* [1998] QB 575.

[92] See MC Elliott, 'Reconciling Constitutional Rights and Constitutional Orthodoxy' [1997] *CLJ* 474.

[93] This reasoning is especially clear in Laws J's judgment in *Witham*, above n 91.

On the plane of substance, the judiciary has shown similar sensitivity. Take, for instance, the *Lightfoot* case[94] The applicant, who wished to present a petition for bankruptcy, was unable to afford the court fees which she was first required to pay. Claiming that this was an infringement of her constitutional right of access to justice, she sought judicial review of the delegated legislation which determined the level of the fees.[95] After careful consideration, Laws J concluded that the applicant was seeking recourse to an essentially administrative regime rather than a core judicial function and, for this reason, held that the right of access to justice was not properly engaged. Thus, while this constitutional right is of great significance, it is important to recognise its limits. As Laws J observed, 'A sound principle may be undermined, even destroyed, if it is pressed into service in areas to which it does not necessarily belong.'[96] Although this case was concerned with the scope of an unwritten common law right, the courts will have to conduct precisely the same type of balancing exercise as they begin to interpret the norms which the Convention enumerates.

D.   Human Rights and the European Convention in English Courts

Let me offer one final example of the judiciary's willingness to balance activism and restraint in the public law field. English courts have not been impervious to the growing international trend towards the legalisation of human rights. The judicial review jurisdiction and the doctrine of common law rights both contribute to the protection of fundamental rights in the United Kingdom. Moreover, the courts have ascribed some relevance to the European Convention,[97] using it to resolve ambiguities in legislation[98] and to develop the common law where it is incomplete or uncertain.[99] However, the judiciary has consistently refused to embrace

---

[94] *R v Lord Chancellor, ex parte Lightfoot* [1998] 4 All ER 764. For comment, see MC Elliott, '*Lightfoot*: Tracing the Perimeter of Constitutional Rights' [1998] *Judicial Review* 217.

[95] Specifically, she claimed that the relevant provisions of the Insolvency Fees Order 1986 (SI 1986 No 2030) were *ultra vires* their putative legal basis (*viz* Insolvency Act 1986, s 415(3)).

[96] [1998] 4 All ER 764 at 773.

[97] For a useful summary of the present relevance of the ECHR in English law, see Lord Bingham of Cornhill, H L Debs, cols 146–1467, July 3, 1996.

[98] See *R v Secretary of State for the Home Department, ex parte Brind* [1991] 1 AC 696.

[99] See *Attorney-General v British Broadcasting Corporation* [1981] AC 303 at 352, *per* Lord Fraser.

the Convention as a direct limit on the decision-making powers of the executive.[100] Notwithstanding that they have been described as 'straining at the leash' to do so,[101] the courts have recognised that to take such a step unilaterally would substantially affront the separation of powers, at a stroke reducing agency autonomy and usurping Parliament's constitutional responsibility for the domestication of international treaties.[102] Once again, activism in public law yields to the restraint of constitutional propriety.[103]

V.   CONCLUSION

Over the course of the twentieth century, the changing nature of governance within the United Kingdom has substantially altered the prevailing conception of the judicial function. As Lord Mustill said of the courts' public law jurisdiction:

> To avoid a vacuum in which the citizen would be left without protection against a misuse of executive powers the courts have had no option but to occupy the dead ground [left by Parliament] in a manner, and in areas of public life, which could not have been foreseen 30 years ago.[104]

On this view, we have witnessed a shift from what I have termed a 'sovereigntist' to a constitutional perception of the role of the judiciary,

---

[100] See especially *Brind*, n 98 above; *R v Ministry of Defence, ex parte Smith* [1996] QB 517. For an interesting empirical study, see F Klug and K Starmer, 'Incorporation through the Back Door?' [1997] *PL* 223, especially pp 228–32.

[101] M J Beloff and H Mountfield, 'Unconventional Behaviour: Judicial Uses of the European Convention in England and Wales' [1996] EHRLR 467 at 495.

[102] See further my 'Constitutional Change in the United Kingdom: British Solutions to Universal Problems' (now chapter 4 in this volume) and n 3, above.

[103] The Court of Appeal's decision in *R v Secretary of State for the Home Department, ex parte Ahmed and Patel* [1998] INLR 570, does not detract from my thesis. In this case, it was held—by applying reasoning similar to that of the High Court of Australia in *Minister of State for Immigration and Ethnic Affairs v Teoh* (1995) 183 CLR 273— that British accession to a treaty, such as the ECHR, can found a legitimate expectation that the executive, in exercising its prerogative powers, will respect the provisions of the treaty. However, given that, as I have already mentioned, substantive expectations can be protected only through the doctrine of *Wednesbury* unreasonableness, the *Ahmed and Patel* judgment does not place administrators under a directly enforceable duty to act consistently with the Convention rights. It will be the Human Rights Act which does that.

[104] *R v Secretary of State for the Home Department, ex parte Fire Brigades Union* [1995] 2 AC 513 at 567.

6

*Britain's Programme of Constitutional Change**

CHAIRMEN, JUDGES, DISTINGUISHED Guests, thank
you very much for your introduction. I am delighted to be
here at Queen's College, Cambridge—a College in which—
more years ago than I care to remember—I used to supervise, to teach
the law students—to participate in this meeting of the Canadian
Institute of Advanced Legal Studies. I know that the last Labour Lord
Chancellor, Lord Elwyn Jones, was present at the inaugural meeting
convened in 1978, by the then Canadian High Commissioner, Paul
Martin. So, it is a great pleasure, to be present in 1999, in Lord Elwyn
Jones' footsteps.

My subject today is 'Britain's Programme for Constitutional Change'.

This Government has committed itself to an unprecedented programme of major constitutional change. Our objective is to put in place
an integrated programme of measures to decentralise power in the
United Kingdom; and to enhance the rights of individuals within a more
open society.

No other British Government this century has embarked upon so significant, or wide-ranging, a programme of constitutional reform. So, I
am especially pleased, as the member of the British Cabinet entrusted
with driving forward development of constitutional policy, to speak to
you this afternoon about that programme.

I want to describe the problems we inherited, which made constitutional reform so imperative; the coherent structure of our programme
of reforms; and the profound and beneficial effects which I am confident they will produce.

---

*Speech to the Canadian Institute of Advanced Legal Studies, Queen's College,
Cambridge on 16 July 1999

The world's democracies face many challenges in common. Public disillusionment with politics is one of the most critical. From country to country, our circumstances may differ, but we share a common challenge—the perception by people that government serves the governors, not the people. It is the duty of those in government to demonstrate that democratic politics are not just better than the alternatives—but that they merit respect in their own right.

The United Kingdom has suffered from a long drift towards ever greater centralisation of political power. This has caused many to feel that they have little or no opportunity to influence the important decisions that affect their daily lives. The accountability of government to the people has been damaged by a culture of secrecy. And human rights cases in Britain have had to be taken to the European Court of Human Rights in Strasbourg, instead of being pursued in our domestic courts, because the United Kingdom, the earliest signatory to the European Convention on Human Rights, failed, for almost half a century, to incorporate it into its domestic law.

Before the Election in May 1997, we identified a range of problems:

— A government that was over-centralised, inefficient and bureaucratic:
— Local government in need of reform:
— Something approaching a national crisis of confidence in our political system:
— Excessive secrecy that both encouraged and reflected the arrogance of power and a lack of accountability:
— A want of principled protection for human rights:

Parliament itself at risk of falling into disrepute, with the House of Commons in need of modernisation, and a House of Parliament, the House of Lords, with an inbuilt Conservative majority from the hereditary peerage, which was unsustainable at the end of the twentieth century:

A country that was in danger of being sidelined in Europe, for a perceived lack of decisive leadership and commitment.

The people of the United Kingdom have suffered from a range of unsatisfactory constitutional practices. I give two examples. One relatively recent—the abolition of the Greater London Council a decade or so ago, which robbed London of any city-wide strategic government. The other—reform of the hereditary component of the House of Lords—dates back far longer. It is unfinished business from the last century.

Our solutions are based on the incremental development of a mature, democracy, where government is brought closer to the people. And where individuals can readily gain access to their basic rights with ease. Our approach is one of pragmatism based on principle

The reforms are sensible incremental responses, based on liberal constitutional principles, reconciling mature demands for reform with the status quo in the most appropriate way. Thus, our approach is consistent with a long line of constitutional reform, which gave Britain what was until recent decades widely regarded as Europe's most progressive and stable constitutional settlement. What runs counter to the grain of our history, however, is the notion that the constitution cannot be changed to meet changing demands. What we are about is improving our traditions whilst we transmit them.

Many countries have experienced a growing desire for greater local autonomy. Sometimes this has led to civil war and anarchy, not greater democracy. But this is *not* the inevitable consequence of pressure for greater local self-determination. Strong, established democracies, such as Britain's, must respond to this pressure, by modernising and reforming its political processes.

A nation of such diverse parts as the United Kingdom requires structures sensitive to place and people, not a uniform pattern of powers devolved from the centre for the sake of uniformity. Intellectually satisfying neatness and tidiness is not the cement which makes new constitutional arrangements stick. What are required are arrangements to which people can give their continuing consent, because they satisfy their democratic wishes for themselves.

Faced with so much to reform, we needed to determine a workable agenda. Our first Session of Parliament concentrated on devolution and human rights, while taking important preparatory steps on Freedom of Information, on reform of the House of Lords, and on consultation over electoral reform of the House of Commons, the elected Chamber of our Parliament.

We needed to consider a range of issues.

— **Institutional change,** to the House of Commons, the House of Lords, and the system of government itself, by dispersing power away from the United Kingdom Parliament; and also by giving the Bank of England operational responsibility for setting interest rates;

— **Changes in the law,** to establish a clear framework of rights, and to ensure greater openness and transparency in the activities of government;

— **Adjustments to our electoral systems** to ensure that voting— the central democratic act—occurs on a basis reflecting a consensus of what is fair; and

— **Changes in our political and administrative culture**—in particular, to move from a bureaucratic, centralised and closed system to a culture of rights, openness and accountability.

We also needed to ensure that the main elements of our reform programme added up to a coherent and effective overall prescription for change. What are these elements?

I.   DEVOLUTION

We have brought devolution to Scotland, and to Wales. As part of the historic Belfast Agreement, we set out a scheme for devolution to Northern Ireland. The Government of Wales Act 1998, the Scotland Act 1998 and the Northern Ireland Act 1998, are all on the statute book. Elections were held in Scotland and Wales in May; and administrations have been formed in both countries; and only two weeks ago I was privileged to be present at the historic opening of the new Scottish Parliament.

We are not promoting a federal style uniform devolution of powers. Our differential approach to the arrangements for each country reflects the different histories and contemporary circumstances of England, Scotland, Wales and Northern Ireland.

The Scottish Parliament has the power to pursue a distinct legislative agenda for Scotland over an extensive range, including the legal system, economic development, industrial assistance, education, training, transport, the police and the penal system. In contrast, the National Assembly for Wales has no power to enact primary legislation. Instead it now exercises the executive powers previously exercised by the Secretary of State for Wales, so providing a more transparent and democratic framework for the government of Wales. These two systems reflect what was sought by the majority of citizens of Scotland and Wales respectively and represents what they voted for in referendums.

The Northern Ireland Act system is different again. The Act of 1998 provides for the Northern Ireland Assembly to have extensive devolved powers, including social security, but initially excluding police and criminal justice. Northern Ireland is unique: because it is a divided community, it is imperative to secure wide consent for constitutional change; and there is the special relationship with the Republic of Ireland. Both governments accept there can be no change in the status of Northern Ireland without the consent of the majority of its people.

The Belfast Agreement seek to introduce new institutions, to reflect the totality of relationships within these islands. They include:

— A Northern Ireland Assembly, which will enable locally elected representatives to exercise real responsibility and bring power closer to the people, with special provisions to ensure that key decisions are only taken with cross-community support;

— A new North-South Ministerial Council, which will help to deepen relationships and improve practical cooperation within the island of Ireland, delivering real benefits to all its people. There will also be a number of cross-border **implementation bodies** to implement policies agreed in the Council.

— A British-Irish Council, which will being together the two Governments and the devolved institutions in Northern Ireland, Scotland and Wales, as well as the Channel Islands and the Isle of Man, to discuss and cooperate on matters of mutual interest. Also there will be a British-Irish Intergovernmental Conference.

Those of you who have been following recent events in Northern Ireland in the media will be aware that earlier this week the Government published a Bill designed to give effect to proposals put on 2 July in Belfast by our Prime Minister Tony Blair and Ireland's Bertie Ahern. The Bill implements the 'fail safe' mechanism in the proposals, by which key institutions of the Good Friday Agreement would be suspended if there was any default on commitments in relation to decommissioning or devolution. The Bill completed all its stages in the House of Commons on Tuesday of this week, and received its Second Reading in the House of Lords on Wednesday. The intention had been that it would complete its remaining stages in the House of Lords yesterday. The Government responded to concerns expressed in the Commons by preparing to introduce amendments to the Bill. Regrettably, notwithstanding these proposed amendments, the Ulster Unionist Party decided not to nominate Ministers for the new Northern Ireland Executive.

It is a matter of deep regret that the efforts of all those concerned in recent days have not led to devolution in Northern Ireland this weekend as envisaged in the proposals of the two Government of 2 July. Despite the setbacks, the Government remains firmly committed to the search for a lasting solution adapted to accommodate the totality of relationships within these islands.

II.   LONDON

No other capital city in the world with the stature of London has to manage without a city-wide authority to secure its strategic interests. Yet that has been the position of London since 1986. The Greater London Authority Bill, which is currently in Committee Stage in the House of Lords will give London the voice it needs and deserves by creating a city-wide strategic authority, consisting of a powerful directly-elected mayor and a separately elected Assembly by May 2000.

III.   THE ENGLISH REGIONAL DIMENSION

The interests of the English regions have been neglected in recent years, and we aim to remedy that. Our first step was to establish Regional Development Agencies, to improve competitiveness and to provide for effective coordination of economic development. We remain committed to more accountable regional government in England. But we can do a great deal already, within the present democratic structures, to build up the voice of the regions. Local authorities are joining with business and other partners, to form voluntary regional chambers, and so create a more integrated regional approach. When there emerges clear popular consent for directly elected regional government in England, we are ready to create that too. But, we accept that finding the *right* solutions may take time. We are not in the business of imposing change but offering change in response to popular demand.

IV.   REFORM OF LOCAL GOVERNMENT

Councils are local, directly elected bodies uniquely placed to make things happen on the ground. But in a White Paper called 'In Touch with the

People' we made clear that a fundamental shift of culture throughout local government is essential. Our aim is a radical refocusing of councils, both to give local people a bigger say about the affairs of local communities, and to give them a better deal on local services. We have embarked on a programme of reforms to liberate local government from a centrally-imposed, uniform, national structure. It will be for local people to choose the local arrangements that they feel best suit the needs of their local areas.

Our proposals for a Scottish Parliament; a Welsh Assembly; a Mayor and Authority for London; and the new political settlement in Northern Ireland were, in each case, put to the people of the Regions affected in separate referendums. In each case, the Government's proposals were endorsed. And any further proposals for regional government in England will be subject to approval in a referendum.

We are also committed to have a referendum before we would join our European partners in Economic and Monetary Union. We would only join a single currency if the Government, Parliament and the British people agree we should. The wider use of referendums in the United Kingdom marks our insistence that people have a determinative say in major constitutional change.

V.   MODERNISATION OF THE HOUSE OF COMMONS

It is vital to the health of our democracy that we reverse some of the ineffective and old-fashioned working practices of our Parliament. We have therefore begun the modernisation of procedures in the House of Commons, through a special parliamentary committee. This has already produced a fuller and clearer explanatory note for Bills, replacing the notes on clauses. A special Standing Committee was set up to consider the Asylum and Immigration Bill. Pre-legislative scrutiny of the Financial Services and Markets Bill took place at the beginning of the year in a joint committee of both Houses of Parliament. And greater pre-legislative consultation and scrutiny will improve the quality of legislation. That is currently taking place on the Freedom of Information Bill in separate Select Committees in each House of Parliament.

VI.   REFORM OF THE HOUSE OF LORDS

We have a bi-cameral system, as do you. We introduced a Bill this session to remove the right of hereditary peers to sit and vote, in a

House of Parliament, the House of Lords, as a self-contained reform. The Bill completed its passage through the House of Commons before Easter and has now completed its Report Stage in the House of Lords.

You may find it extraordinary that, on the threshold of the millennium, the hereditary principle still applies in one part of the British legislature. We agree. We believe that the time of hereditary parliaments has long gone. We do not have hereditary poets, hereditary rocket scientists, or hereditary football managers. Why then hundreds of hereditary legislators?

The government believes that longer-term reform of the House of Lords should take into account the widest possible range of views on the issues involved, which are of great constitutional importance and complexity. Successful proposals will have an impact on every part of our political structure. That is why we thought it appropriate to appoint a Royal Commission to analyse the options.

The terms of reference of the Royal Commission are:

Having regard to the need to maintain the position of the House of Commons as the preeminent chamber of Parliament and taking particular account of the present nature of the constitutional settlement, including the newly devolved institutions, the impact of the Human Rights Act and developing relations with the European Union:
To consider and make recommendations on the role and functions of a second chamber; and To make recommendations on the method or combination of methods of composition required to constitute a second chamber fit for that role and those functions.
To report by 31 December 1999.

We have made it clear that the Royal Commission's proposals must preserve three key elements of our constitutional settlement:

A general election to the House of Commons, the elected House of Parliament, must determine who forms the government, and the ability of the government to retain the confidence of the House of Commons is alone crucial to its right to remain in office;

The House of Commons must continue to have sole powers over the provision of financial support for the government;

The government must ultimately have the right to secure any of its legislation introduced in the House of Commons with the consent of the House of Commons alone, except for a Bill to extend the life of a Parliament.

The role of the second chamber should continue to complement rather than duplicate the role of the House of Commons. The House of Lords provides a valuable function of scrutiny—we call it the revising Chamber—without which the burden on the House of Commons would be greater and the quality of legislation diminished. Over the past ten years, for example, the House of Lords has made nearly 2,000 amendments a year to government legislation. These are very often brought forward as government amendments, frequently in response to critical analysis made in both Houses. Legislative scrutiny will continue to be a major function of a reformed second chamber. Whether a fully reformed House of Lords will remain wholly nominated, but became a House of all the talents of the nation fairly appointed through a new Appointment Commission, or become wholly elected, or remain nominated but part elected, in particular to represent the devolved institutions and regions of the nation, is within the remit of the Royal commission. When it reports, —Parliament will decide.

VII.   FREEDOM OF INFORMATION

Openness is fundamental to good government. Confidence in government has been undermined in the United Kingdom by a culture of secrecy. Our Manifesto therefore included a commitment to introduce a Freedom of Information Act, to open up public organisations and make the whole of government more accountable to people.

Our predecessors had established a non-statutory code of practice on access to government information. Its coverage was limited to central government. Its exemptions were broad, tending to err in favour of protecting information from disclosure. The code was simply not strong enough to guarantee genuine openness. And it conferred no legally enforceable rights.

Our first legislative programme did not include a Freedom of Information Bill. There were those who thought that we had lost our appetite for openness, at the first taste of office. In fact, we simply wanted sufficient time to devise from within government, a regime across government, which would be as liberal as possible consistent with the protection of the national interest. Complex problems do not benefit from hasty solutions. One advantage in delaying the introduction of Freedom of Information legislation is that we have been able to consider, and to learn from the experience of other countries. A draft

Bill has been published and is currently undergoing pre-legislative scrutiny by separate Committees in both Houses of Parliament.

When enacted, during the life of this Parliament, the Freedom of Information Act will provide a legal right to see documents, not just information in a form decided by Government bodies. The Act will apply right across the public sector, including some private sector organisations in the areas where they carry out statutory functions.

It will provide for more information held by government bodies to be published as a matter of course. Most importantly, public bodies wanting to withhold information will have to demonstrate that its disclosure would cause real prejudice to one of a number of specified public interests—for example, national security or commercial confidentiality. In other words, the system will be weighted as heavily as possible in favour of openness.

This Act will mark a watershed in the relationship between the government and people of the United Kingdom. The British people will, at last, have the right to know what is being said and done in their name; and they will be better equipped to be active participants in political discourse on the future of their country.

Finally, to deliver effective Government, this sweeping programme of constitutional reform must be matched by a radical modernisation of the machinery of Government. Our objective is to secure strategic policies, working across government boundaries rather than within individual departmental limits. We want to see, what we have started to call in the UK, 'joined up' government. Our vision is of a Government focusing on the outcomes it wants to achieve, devolving responsibility to those who can achieve these outcomes, and so intervening in inverse proportion to success. A Cabinet Committee was established to carry this project through and a 'Modernising Government' White Paper published. All government Departments are now charged with carrying through the Modernising Government agenda.

So, I would dispute any proposition that our programme lacks coherence. We made decisions, based on empirical evidence, about precisely which aspects of our constitution needed earliest attention, and on what basis. We are conscious of the way different elements of any constitutional settlement can impact on each other. Of course, many parts of the package are not interdependent. They address particular problems, which are the product of lengthy and complex pre-histories of their own. Each strand of our constitutional reform programme is soundly justified on its own merits, and as part of the whole package. They are united by common themes and objectives—modernisation; decentralisation; openness; accountability; the protection of basic human rights; the sharing of authority within a framework of law. All of this will fundamentally change the fabric of our political and administrative culture, and for the better.

VIII.   THE HUMAN RIGHTS ACT

The Human Rights Act, which I piloted through Parliament, occupies a special place in our programme of reform. The guiding principle was our need to secure human rights protection, whilst respecting constitutional propriety generally, and our doctrine of Parliamentary sovereignty in particular. In making the Convention rights enforceable in our domestic courts, our key challenge was to determine its status in relation to domestic legislation. How could we reconcile the superior status of Convention rights—to be enforced by British judges in our courts—with Parliamentary sovereignty?

I know this is a challenge which you in Canada faced in the early 1980s; and that the Charter of Rights and Freedoms of 1982 included your solution: Section 33(i), the 'notwithstanding clause' procedure. This effectively provides for judicial authority to be exercised as I understand it, subject to Parliamentary override. Anyone whose rights or freedom, guaranteed by the Charter, have been breached may apply to the courts to 'obtain such a remedy as the court considers appropriate and just in the circumstances.' To our minds that might seem to give the courts a right to legislate. As a supreme law it prevails, however, over all existing and future legislation which may conflict with it. The Charter, therefore, placed some limitations on the concept of Parliamentary sovereignty, as the validity of laws passed through Parliament can now be tested before the courts to assess compliance with the Charter; and you courts, again as I understand it, now have the power to declare legislation ultra vires. However, Section 33 of the Charter also allows the federal Parliament or any provincial legislature to declare, for five year renewable periods, that legislation should be given effect by the courts regardless of the fact that it infringes certain (prescribed) rights.

So you have devised your own way of preserving Parliamentary sovereignty. Our approach was different, because the doctrine of Parliamentary sovereignty is so uncompromisingly embedded in our political and legal culture. I doubt that consent to the Human Rights Act could have been achieved if it gave the judiciary the right to strike down Acts of Parliament in whole or part.

Our Human Rights Act introduces a new rule of interpretation. As far as it is possible to do so, primary and subordinate legislation must be interpreted by the courts and effected in a way which is compatible with Convention rights; and that applies to both primary and subordinate legislation.

If primary legislation is held to be incompatible, the courts will still have to enforce it, but the higher courts will be able to make a declaration that it is incompatible with Convention rights. This is a wholly unique remedy. It will create acute pressure to amend the incompatible law, to bring it back into line through a fast-track remedial procedure, subject to Parliamentary approval, or otherwise through new primary legislation.

Also, from the start of the current Parliamentary Session, every Minister in charge of a Bill has had to make and publish a written statement before the Second Reading in each House—Second Reading is the first substantive Parliamentary debate on a proposed law—about its compatibility with the Convention rights. Just before Christmas I did just that, for a major piece of legislation for which I am responsible, the Access to Justice Bill.

For every Bill the responsible Minister will have to ensure that the legislation does not infringe guaranteed rights or freedoms; or be prepared to justify its incompatibility with the Convention—openly, in the full glare of Parliamentary and public opinion. We have brought this important provision into force ahead of the rest of the Act. It will make a significant contribution towards the creation of a culture of respect for human rights at the heart of our democracy.

Both a declaration of incompatibility by the courts, and the statement of compatibility by Ministers, are pragmatic measures. The first reconciles judicial power with Parliamentary sovereignty. The second causes Ministers to stand up and be counted for human rights.

The Act provides a modern reconciliation of the inevitable tension between the democratic right of the majority to exercise political power through the legislative process; and the democratic need of individuals and minorities to have their human rights respected.

We have also made changes to our electoral systems. As a result there are a number of different electoral systems in play. No one electoral system is perfect. Each has advantages and disadvantages. Our objective is—as it should be—to find the electoral system appropriate for the elected institution concerned.

For example, in Northern Ireland it is not surprising that the parties to the Belfast Agreement concluded that Proportional Representation, using the single transferable vote in multimember constituencies, was the best system for their Assembly. It will help to secure a fair and proportional result within a constituency, because secondary and subsequent preferences are counted, and a relatively high proportion of votes affect the result. It is also a system with which the people of Northern Ireland are familiar, since it has been in use for some time for District Council and European Parliamentary Elections. It is also in use in the Republic of Ireland.

The system does, however, have drawbacks. It may not necessarily achieve a fully proportional result. And, since it requires multi-member constituencies, it does not achieve the close identification with constituencies which single member systems do. But it is pragmatic—it builds on prior history and experience. On balance, it was thought right for Northern Ireland.

When we came to decide the electoral system for the Scottish Parliament, the National Assembly for Wales and the London Assembly, the importance of single member constituencies weighed strongly with us. In the absence of community tensions like those in Northern Ireland, the most important consideration was that these bodies will perform functions which will have a very direct impact on the lives of the people of Scotland, Wales and London respectively. It was therefore thought important that voters should have a single representative to whom they could turn with their problems. That is why the majority of members of each have been, or will be, directly elected in individual constituencies using the first past the post system.

However we took the view that it was also important that these three bodies should truly represent the people of Scotland, Wales and Greater London. We were anxious to ensure that all points of view and all sections of the community would be reflected in the elected institutions concerned. Consequently, voters in each area are able to exercise two votes, the second being used to elect the additional, 'top-up' members. For example, in the recent elections to the Scottish Parliament, 73 members were elected from single person constituencies, with 56 additional members being elected from regional lists based on the European Parliamentary Constituencies. The regional seats were allocated so that the overall result, taking account of the outcome of the constituency elections, more accurately reflected the share of votes cast for each party. The system is designed to ensure that overall each party wins a share of the total seats broadly proportionate to its share of the total of votes in the region. It thus retains the advantages of a significant proportion of members from single member constituencies, with a much more proportional result than would be achieved by first past the post alone.

By contrast, for the directly elected Mayor of London, we decided on a supplementary vote system: that is, in effect, a system of improved first past the post. We did this because the Mayor will be in a unique position. Never before has so large an electorate in our country voted for a single individual. The Mayor will be charged with protecting the interests of 7 million people in one of the most diverse cities in Europe. The Mayor must represent a broad cross section of Londoners. The supplementary vote system allows voters to record both their first choice, and their second choice, with second preference votes used to ensure that the more popular of the top two candidates wins. The Mayor's authority will be enhanced by the fact that he or she will enjoy a broader base of support than might be achieved by first past the post alone. All this demonstrates our hostility to uniformity or symmetry for its own sake.

So I hope that what I have said illustrates my firm view, that our constitutional reform programme—though it covers much diverse ground—is nonetheless coherent, structured and strategic. The diversity of the separate parts of the United Kingdom, and the singularity of its histories—though crucially interwoven—are inevitable barriers to any uniform, imposed solutions.

Devolution is not a form of either federalism or independence for Scotland, Wales, or Northern Ireland. The United Kingdom Parliament will remain sovereign. The Union will be renewed, not weakened by devolution. It will be able to evolve in a way which decentralises power, recognises a strong sense of identity where that exists, and extends political accountability.

Devolution needs political courage. But it will forge a new Britain. A strong, multi-national, multi-cultural, multi-ethnic, country—where our strength will come not from uniformity but from our diversity. Not from a constraining process of programmed assimilation, but from democratic renewal, through mutual tolerance and respect.

To succeed, we must of course retain that unity and continuing cooperation among our several parts. There will be arrangements to ensure that the UK Government and the devolved administrations co-operate on issues of mutual interest. We are establishing of a Joint Ministerial Committee, in which the UK Government and the devolved administrations will be represented. As part of its terms of reference this Committee will consider non-devolved matters which impinged on devolved responsibilities, and devolved matters which impinge on non-devolved responsibilities. And there will also be Concordats, agreements, between Whitehall Departments and their counterparts in the devolved institutions which will be models for their future cooperation.

IX.   CONCLUSION

The United Kingdom Government believes that it is not enough simply to put measures reforming the constitution, the justice system, or any other area of public policy on to the statute book. We must work through a coherent programme of reform, based on sound principles. Only in this way can the benefits be real and lasting. That is why we have taken great care to consult widely, to encourage public debate, and to involve as many different groups and individuals in the process of policy making as possible.

We have set out to be an inclusive Government—a Government truly of the people, for the people, and by the people. We have set out to be a Government which returns power to the people from whom power ultimately derives. We have set out to build an inclusive society. A strong, decent, outward-looking society. A society which gives people opportunities, and the confidence to use them. And we have set out to improve the future of Britain by modernising our institutions and renewing confidence in our constitution.

Our reforms will reinforce our ability to play a full, creative, constructive role in world affairs. We in Britain look forward to continuing and building on the strong relationships we already enjoy with our European partners with the Commonwealth, and all our friends and allies across the world.

After many sterile and stagnant decades, we are at last driving forward an unprecedented programme of constitutional change. We are realigning the most fundamental relationships between the State and the citizen, in ways that will secure the consent of the people affected, because they deliver what the people want.

Each principled step takes us further, but safely and successfully, along a winning route to constitutional renewal, in unity and in peace.

7

A New Constitution—A New Citizenship*

F OR TOO MANY people, the business of conventional politics is a distant thing, nothing to do with them. For too many people, the idea of becoming a local councillor or an MP or MEP is inconceivable. It is something *other* people do. And even if their scepticism is overcome, even if they are persuaded that they could have a role working actively in politics, then their work, family or financial commitments can discourage them from throwing their hats into the ring.

The Government's programme of constitutional reform is designed to increase public engagement in democracy. Though radical, it remains true to the essential characteristics of our historical tradition. It is designed to regenerate our national identity. By restoring people's sense of belonging to a country with a coherent vision of its past and its future, we will achieve a better engagement between people and government, and revive people's interest in public affairs.

In planning these reforms, we had a strong concept of what 'British' means. That gives them their coherence. It is also what will make them work for people. Our constitutional renewal is a patriotic renewal.

'British' means the unity and intermingling of the four nations that make up our society. It means a long historical legacy that should always find constitutional expression. It means a strong civic society; and vibrant communities with an influential local voice. It means being internationalist in spirit, learning from our neighbours and providing an example to them in turn. Most of all, it should mean fairness and equality for all our citizens before the law, tolerance for the many cultures of our multi-racial society—not a flattening process of simila-tion—and a strong underpinning by the rule of law, implemented by an independent and impartial judiciary.

* Fabian Lecture.

The best of Britain has always resisted the excesses of selfish individualism. One of the great British qualities has always been our strong sense of personal and civic responsibility and reciprocity. It is time to rejuvenate that.

Our reform programme will show that constitutional structures, to engage the community, cannot be fossilised because of a false idea of our heritage. People's regard for our national inheritance should not be hijacked to preserve constitutional structures which have had their day.

There are two broad schools of thought about our national identity. One school says that the whole idea of 'Britishness' is an artificial concept; that consciousness of Britain and the United Kingdom as a single entity was only forged by the opportunities of Empire and the threat from wars abroad. It is significant that although Britain is often called 'England' abroad, the Empire was always called the *British*, not the *English*, Empire. Now that we are free of Empire and no longer plagued by continuous war, the claim is that the idea of 'Britain' is breaking down, and people are defining themselves according to their regions, or the component nations of the United Kingdom. The other school of thought is that Britain does have a special identity: strong local communities, democratic values, creativity, an enterprising spirit, diversity, tolerance, and the ability to draw the best from a wide range of cultures.

This Government believes that we do have a national identity. People who argue that Labour's reform programme is moving this country away from its heritage completely miss the point: that what we are doing is drawing on the best of what is British to rejuvenate our democracy, build a society that includes and celebrates differences and revives people's sense that public bodies are relevant to their beliefs, their lives and their ambitions for themselves and their families.

Despite what some claim—and very vocally—being British does *not* mean:

— having 750 hereditary legislators sitting in the House of Lords;
— being anti-European and inward-looking;
— having Westminster hold an 'England first' strait-jacket over the diversity of the regions and nations in the Union;
— having no principled protection for human rights; and
— having our great national institutions, which represent our community spirit, like the NHS, privatised.

Let me start with devolution. The charge is: 'Labour demolishes Britain'. It is true that we have devolved more power from the centre than any other British government in modern history—an odd form of 'control freakery' that. But, to cling to an unchanging constitution, as some would have had us do, would have been to deny expression to the regions and nations of the United Kingdom, and restrain the opportunity for different cultures and centres of initiative each to enrich the other.

We must instead adapt our institutions to reflect our values, since otherwise people will be increasingly alienated from structures that they see as anachronistic and distant. There is nothing essentially British about having the Union completely dominated by Westminster. In fact, it goes against something that is far more essentially British: democracy. For Scotland, for example, to have had a Conservative Government at Westminster when there were hardly enough Conservative MPs in Scotland to fill the Scottish Ministerial posts, and no devolved administration to give the people another voice, could not be truly democratic or good for the cohesion of the Union. The people's reaction was clear. When we came to power, the Conservatives—the party of no change—were left without a single seat in Scotland or in Wales.

We have tailored our programme of devolution to the different regions—to make sure that people's aspirations are reflected in their institutions—and to strengthen, not weaken, the Union itself. Our approach reflects the diverse histories of England, Scotland, Wales and Northern Ireland. That does make our devolution arrangements asymmetrical. But we are constitutional pragmatists: in the light of historical experience we do not look for perfect symmetry.

Scotland has historically had its own separate identity. It was an independent European nation until 1707, although there had been the Union of the Crowns in 1603. After 1707, Scotland enshrined many of the attributes of nationhood—its own common law, court system, Judges, Church and educational system. The Scottish Parliament and Executive today reflect this historical legacy in their very high level of autonomy, over the legal system, economic development, industrial assistance, education, training, transport, the police and the penal system. That reflects popular demand in Scotland, as proved by the people's votes in a referendum.

Wales's association with England is of longer standing. It was between 1536 and 1543 that the two countries were merged fully into a single entity, after developments over many years. The National

Assembly for Wales reflects the distinctive characteristics of the two countries, but also the closeness of their association. It cannot enact primary legislation. But it exercises the executive powers previously held by the Secretary of State for Wales, and so provides a more transparent framework for the government of Wales. This too reflects what the people wanted, proved by their votes in a referendum.

In Northern Ireland, the special relationship with the Irish Republic and the divided nature of the community dictated a different settlement. Power-sharing is a distinctive feature of the Northern Ireland arrangements. Special voting arrangements make sure that legislation and other decisions of the Assembly cannot be passed without the support of both sides of the Northern Ireland community, whom we are keen to see as heavily involved as possible in the process. As you all know, it is an uphill struggle.

We have also begun to remedy the neglect of the English regions. New Regional Development Agencies (RDAs) will improve competitiveness and coordinate economic development and regeneration more effectively. Regional chambers of local councillors and other partners will give each region a focused voice.

Then, of course, there is London. No other capital city in the world with the stature of London has had to manage without a city-wide authority to secure its strategic interests. Yet that has been London's position since 1986, despite what the people who live in London wanted. The Greater London Authority Act has at last given London the voice it deserves.

And, in time, if we are satisfied that popular demand is there, we will introduce legislation to enable people, region by region, to decide whether they want directly elected regional government elsewhere. Again, we are not clinging to our own preconceptions, but listening where there is clear popular demand and responding to what people want. If people are allowed to be the masters of their institutions—not the reverse—then active citizenship will be able to thrive. We are moving from a centralised Britain, where power flows top-down, to a more devolved and plural state.

And devolution will allow the United Kingdom to draw strength from its diversity. Under the new settlement, the UK will be far more than the sum of its parts. Devolution does not signal antagonistic confrontation, but beneficial diversity; and diversity is not to be feared, but embraced, as a source of strength and innovation. The proposed Drug Enforcement Agency for Scotland may show the rest of Britain how to tackle the scourge of drug addiction and trafficking. 'The Welsh Assembly's new services for the elderly may point the way forward in that area of care. The RDAs in the English Regions are making pioneering advances in regional development and attracting inward investment, from which other parts of the UK could learn. Diversity is about the distinct parts of a whole learning each from the other.

Devolution will free the nations and regions of the United Kingdom to find innovative local solutions for local problems, and learn from each other.

Some seem to think that every time the Assembly in Wales or the Executive in Scotland acts in a different way, or has a different idea to Westminster, that is a defeat for the Government. In fact, it is the *opposite*. To see the devolved institutions, elected by people in their own regions and nations, taking forward policies that will best improve life in their own areas, cooperating with the Westminster Parliament but not wholly dictated to by it, influenced by the other devolved institutions, but not slavishly copying them—that is the Government's aim. It shows that devolution works. It shows people that their devolved administrations are working for them, and encourages them to become involved.

Some have argued that devolution creates new identities within Britain; and that it will lead to the break-up of the Union. But the reverse is true. Our British identity is rooted in the intermingling of our constituent nations. Devolution will strengthen the Union because it gives expression to existing identities. To try to stifle those identities would be to fuel the arguments of those who want to tear the Union apart. Instead, under our devolution settlement, a new Britain is emerging with a revised conception of citizenship, that recognises the mix of cultures and traditions that form our Union. It is intrinsic to the nature of our Union of four nations over hundreds of years, that we have multiple political allegiances. We can be Scottish and British; or Pakistani and British; or Cornish and British and European. Devolution could be described as a journey towards a revived sense of ourselves, applying to modern life and our political institutions historic British values and qualities—creativity, built on tolerance; openness and adaptability; strong communities, and an outward looking approach to the world.

Our British identity is also based on a strong understanding of diversity, and the desire to protect and give expression to the vulnerable elements of our society, so ensuring a society that is fair. This country has consistently led the European field on anti-discrimination and equality legislation. We have progressive race relations legislation, reviewed comprehensively in the MacPherson report; and progressive sex discrimination legislation.

Our British identity also includes protecting the vulnerable; and that includes against State action that tramples on basic human rights. Until the Human Rights Act, we have had no principled protection for human rights. John Major famously said, reflecting the views of the last government, 'We have no need of a Bill of Rights because we have freedom'. What enervating insularity! In the traditional British scheme of things, 'freedom' was no more than what was left over after all the law's prohibitions had been obeyed. And the critical point is: statute is perfectly capable of, and occasionally does, trample on basic human rights.

What our modern British society needs is a formal shared understanding of what is fundamentally right and fundamentally wrong if it is to work together in unity and confidence. The Human Rights Act provides that understanding, in an ethical language we can all recognise. Our traditional affinity with freedom and the protection of the vulnerable should put us in the vanguard of new developments in human rights protection.

Britain's influential role in the development of the Convention fifty years ago is a source of pride for this Government. The Convention has achieved positive development after development in rights protection. But for fifty years after our signing of the Convention, we failed to incorporate the Convention into our domestic law. But in just over a week's time, British citizens will become able to enforce their rights under the Convention in their national courts, where they will be more effectively and intensively enforced, and not have to take the costly, time-consuming road to Strasbourg, which very few in practice took. A new culture of respect for human rights will infuse our public institutions in a more direct, immediate and intensive way than access to Strasbourg could.

The new powers of the higher courts to issue declarations of incompatibility, and the duty incumbent on Ministers under section 19 of the Act to draw Parliament's attention to the human rights implications of legislation as it is brought forward, stating whether it is ECHR compliant or not, will focus legislators' minds more sharply than ever before on fundamental rights issues. When a Minister assures Parliament that new legislation being brought forward is ECHR compliant, and then the higher courts declare it not to be—I predict a very rare event—the pressure to make it compliant, by the special procedures the Human Rights Act provides, is obvious.

By incorporating the ECHR we are *not* taking on a burdensome European regime and moving away from anything naturally British. On the contrary, what we are doing is advancing the traditional British respect for human rights by giving our people for the first time proper, principled, protection, by implementing what British lawyers and human rights experts were influential in promoting and agreeing over fifty years ago.

By incorporating the Convention we are also giving our British courts the opportunity to develop a body of human rights case law that will inform what is done in Strasbourg and across the European Community. So, we will contribute to the development of European jurisprudence, and not just obey its dictates. We have traditionally been a nation of internationalists, whose law still informs the constitutions of many countries. Our legal sector is one of our most successful national exports. Our judges and lawyers have real expertise in human rights law to offer Europe. Those who believe that we should preserve what they think to be our 'traditional' lack of principled protection for human rights would not only deprive our people of individual protection, but also Britain the opportunity to make its mark on a critically important area of European law. This Government takes pride in Britain's place in Europe, and believes that we should assume a leadership role in developing human rights jurisprudence.

Another British institution which the Government has been accused of attacking, contrary to our heritage, is the House of Lords. It is true that the hereditary peers had a great historical legacy; but they were an anachronism at the end of the 20th Century, not to mention the end of the 19th. Our reform to remove them, subject to a temporary right for one tenth to remain, is not a blow to any symbol of our nation. The hereditary peers certainly did not define 'Britishness' even though their tenacity in clinging to power is quite amazing. Queen Elizabeth the First's initial Privy Council of nine men included a Cecil, a Herbert, a Russell, a Stanley and a Talbot—families still active politically four hundred years later.

No, what is British is our multi-cultural society. In that diverse society—which we celebrate—it cannot be right to give some a privileged place in our Parliament simply because their ancestors came from the old British nobility. We should be freeing up our public institutions, allowing them to be strengthened by the diversity and innovation within our society. Everyone should have the opportunity to achieve a place in the Upper House—no matter who their ancestors were, or where they came from, or who they slept with. The principles of inclusiveness, and of fair play and equality of opportunity, are far more *British* than the exclusivity represented by the hereditary peers. A far greater British institution than the hereditary peers is *democracy* itself.

Those who argue that reform of the House of Lords is destroying our historical legacy have—let me say it—a narrow, elitist view of what our legacy is. It was no more than a reflection of the needs of the British people at one time. It was not an eternal expression of the British character. To change it does not mean that something quintessentially British has been destroyed. Not at all.

On the contrary, it is quintessentially British, and one of our distinguishing characteristics as a people, that we have always been willing to adapt our institutions to changing circumstances. In the 19th century, in response to tumultuous economic and social change, we reformed the suffrage not once but three times. One of the earlier attempts to remove the hereditary peers from the House of Lords dates back to 1888, 112 years ago, when Lord Rosebery, before he became Prime Minister, tabled a Motion that would have deprived them of the automatic right to vote. He did this because he thought the right was an anachronism in modern 19th century society, only six years after married women had won the right to own property; and thirty years before women got the right to vote.

It is not staying true to a British institution to trap it in a time warp that was thought anachronistic in the 19th century; just as it is not helpful to Britain to deny the House of Lords the opportunity to be part of the fullest development of all the talents of our nation.

Finally, the most important characteristic of the British at their best is strong communities, which exercise their rights and fulfil their responsibilities. There is a strong case for saying that, in the age of Enlightenment, Britain invented the idea of a civic society, rooted in what the Scottish philosopher, Adam Fergusson, called our 'civil responsibilities'. But the Union cannot hold together effectively when this civic society is divided, and too many of its citizens have strong legitimate grievances against each other, or against the centre. I do believe our new constitutional resettlement will work and will stand the test of time.

8

The Impact of the Human Rights Act: Parliament, the Courts and the Executive

WHEN I INTRODUCED the Bill in the House of Lords, where it began, on 3 November 1997, I expressed my conviction that it would 'deliver a modern reconciliation of the inevitable tension between the democratic right of the majority to exercise political power and the democratic need of individuals and minorities to have their human rights secured'.[1] I believe that statement to have been well justified over the two years since the Act came into force.

The Act has proved to be of profound significance. A measure of its impact has been the range of idiom with which commentators have tried to describe it. It has been, variously, a dog that has not yet barked, a litmus test, rights that dare not speak their name, a magnetic field, a powerful solvent, and even an iatrogenic disease.[2] But it is no surprise that the Act has stretched the traditional language of legal commentary. It is unique. Like all legislation, it changes the law and asks to be interpreted by the courts. But unlike most legislation, it is also concerned with our constitutional order.

The purpose of this article, therefore, is to look at the impact the Act has had on our constitution as well as on our law. It should be celebrated by all those who believe in our tradition of freedom under the law. As Lord Woolf has recently said, and rightly: '[t]he recognition of the need to adhere to the rule of law by protecting human rights is essential to the proper functioning of democracy'.[3] In order to respond to the

---

[1] HL Deb, col 1234, 3, November 1997.
[2] Laws L J, reportedly during the course of argument, in *R v Spear, Hastie and Boyd* [2001] QB 804 (Courts-Martial Appeals Court).
[3] Lord Woolf C J, 'Human Rights—Have the Public Benefited', The British Academy Thank-Offering to Britain Lecture, 15 October 2002 (available at *www.britac.ac.uk* and in the *Proceedings of the British Academy*, 2002).

Act's doubters and detractors, I will also look at what it has *not* done, and what it was *not* intended to do, either to our constitution or our law.

The Act has a clear starting point—a pragmatic view of our constitutional arrangements. That view is of an accommodation between the state and the individual; and of a new and dynamic cooperative endeavour that is developing between the executive, the judiciary and Parliament; one in which each works within its respective constitutional sphere to give ever developing practical effect to the values embodied in the Act. I will examine each of these branches of government, its role under the Act, and its relationship with its partners. I will look too at how the invigoration of our law and institutions, brought about by the Act, can have an effect on the international legal order and our place in it. But first, let me set the scene.

I.   HISTORY AND BACKGROUND

In the aftermath of the Second World War, Britain played a crucial role in the conception and drafting of the European Convention on Human Rights. We were one of the first countries to sign the Convention. Yet for 50 years, we failed to incorporate it into our domestic law, due to a historic hostility based on two misconceptions. First, an outdated—and exaggerated—view of the efficacy of political accountability as a means of securing the protection of fundamental rights. Secondly, a fear of undermining parliamentary sovereignty and transferring power to unelected judges. John Major famously said, '[w]e have no need of a Bill of Rights because we have freedom'. That encapsulated the complacency and insularity that beset successive Conservative governments. Prior to the Act, 'freedom' was no more than what was left over after all the law's prohibitions had been obeyed. And that freedom gave no specific protection against the acts or omissions of public bodies that harmed fundamental rights. Neither Parliament nor our legal system had been strong enough in the face of the legislative and executive activity associated with modern governance, both of which proved well capable of trampling on basic human rights. No doubt the majority of the statute book was Convention compliant, but in some key areas it was certainly not. That is why, prior to the Act, the European Court of Human Rights in Strasbourg found against the United Kingdom more times than against any other country except Italy. And that is why one of the first acts of the new government in 1997 was to bring forward a Bill incorporating the Convention into domestic law, so that British citizens, like citizens in almost every other European country, could rely on their Convention rights in their own courts, before their own judges; and so that they would no longer have to take the long road to Strasbourg—a road that often took more than five years to travel.

II.   THE ROLE OF PARLIAMENT

Parliament has two principal interests in the Human Rights Act. The first is to defend its legislation and its right to legislate, if it wishes, in spite of the Act; that is, to maintain parliamentary sovereignty. The second is Parliament's role in scrutinising legislation. The former shapes Parliament's relationship with the courts, the latter with the executive.

The Act expressly protects parliamentary sovereignty. Section 4(6), for example, makes it clear that if a statute is declared incompatible, it nevertheless continues to be enforceable. Unlike the United States, we do not have a Constitutional Court with the power to strike down Acts of Parliament. So it is for Parliament to decide whether it should pass remedial legislation; and it is under no *legal* obligation to do so. Further, s 6(3) excludes Parliament from the definition of 'public authority', so that if Parliament acts incompatibly with the Convention, that is not made unlawful by s 6(1). Parliament can therefore legislate incompatibly if it chooses. Let me enter this caveat, however. My discussion is confined to domestic law. Parliament's ability to legislate in contravention of the Convention has carried a prohibition in *international* law since 1951. And I will not address the implications for parliamentary sovereignty of European Community law.[4]

But how do we reconcile parliamentary sovereignty in domestic law, with the notion of fundamental, or superior, rights? In Canada, the enactment of the Charter of Rights and Freedoms took that country, in the words of a Supreme Court Judge,[5] from a system of parliamentary

---

[4] See European Communities Act 1972. Further, I am referring to the Westminster Parliament only. The Scottish Parliament, Northern Ireland Assembly and Welsh Assembly are different. Legislation passed by those bodies that is incompatible with the Convention is not only unlawful by virtue of the Human Rights Act 1998, it is also beyond the powers conferred on the devolved legislatures by the Scotland Act 1998, Northern Ireland Act 1998, and the Government of Wales Act 1998.

[5] Iacobucci J cited by Laws L J, n 6 below.

supremacy to one of constitutional supremacy. Laws L J has made this comparison:

> In its present state of evolution, the British system may be said to stand at an intermediate stage between parliamentary supremacy and constitutional supremacy, to use the language of the Canadian case. Parliament remains the sovereign legislature; there is no superior text to which it must defer (I leave aside the refinements flowing from our membership of the European Union); there is no statute which by law it cannot make. But at the same time, the common law has come to recognise and endorse the notion of constitutional, or fundamental, rights. These are broadly the rights given expression in the European Convention on Human Rights, but their recognition in the common law is autonomous ...[6]

It may be that Sir John's description of 'an intermediate stage' is a prediction that we are only halfway on a constitutional journey and that, in the fullness of time, we will leave parliamentary supremacy behind altogether. If so, I do not join in that prediction. The present arrangements were crafted as a settlement. They do not call for, or imply, further legislation, and I do not predict any. They represent our reconciliation of effective rights protection with parliamentary sovereignty. The balancing of these is central to the Act. It retains Parliament's *legal* right to enact legislation which is incompatible with the Convention. But it dramatically reduces its *political* capacity to do so. It does this by introducing, through the declaration of incompatibility, a limited form of constitutional review, which serves as a political and perhaps moral disincentive to legislate incompatibly.[7] As Professor David Feldman has said: 'Parliament may legislate in such a way, but has a heavy responsibility to ensure that it does not do so lightly, or for inadequate reasons, or inadvertently'.[8]

That is why s 19 of the Act is important. It requires the minister introducing a Bill to Parliament, to make a statement, either that, in his view, the Bill *is* compatible with the Convention; or that, although he is unable to give that assurance, the government nevertheless wishes the House to proceed with the Bill. This guarantees an informed consent on

[6] *International Transport Roth GmbH v Secretary of State for the Home Department* [2002] EWCA Civ 158; [2002] 3 WLR 344 at [71].
[7] Human Rights Act 1998, s 4.
[8] D Feldman, 'Parliamentary Scrutiny of Legislation and Human Rights' [2002] *PL* 323. Professor Feldman argues that a declaration of incompatibility implies a degree of legal impropriety in what Parliament has done even if it does not amount to illegality.

the part of Parliament. It will not legislate incompatibly with the Convention, without being absolutely clear that it is doing so.

Section 19 also triggers Parliament's second principal interest under the Act: its scrutiny function. The Act enhances this role by giving Parliament a basic set of standards against which to scrutinise all legislation that comes before it. This is good for the democratic process, and it strengthens Parliament's claim to the courts that its assessments should be left alone.

III. ROLE OF THE COURTS—WHAT HAS *NOT* HAPPENED

So let me turn now to the courts, whose role under the Act has, from the very beginning, attracted the most comment and controversy. That is understandable, for it was always bound to be in the courts that the essential parameters of the Act would be worked out. What is less understandable is that so much of the comment has been negative: predictions of chaos; a politicised judiciary; and the inauguration of the rule of lawyers. None of that has happened. The prophets of doom have been proved wrong. Let me tell you why.

A. Chaos in the Courts

In the two years since the Act came into force, the judicial system has matched up well to the demands placed on it by the Act. That is the result of a carefully drafted Act and two years of intense preparation by the government and the courts.

Research published in October 2002 showed that, one year after implementation, the Act had still *not* had the effect that many had anticipated, in terms either of the number or complexity of challenges on human rights grounds.[9] The overall impression that has emerged is that human rights arguments are mostly used to add to, bolster, or put a fresh slant on, preexisting lines of challenge. The great majority of cases in which a human rights point has been raised would have gone forward in any event, most typically in judicial review.

[9] John Raine and Clive Walker, 'The Impact on the Courts and the Administration of Justice of the Human Rights Act 1998', Lord Chancellor's Department Research Series No 9/02, p 53.

B.   Politicising the Judiciary

Critics of the Human Rights Act also argued that it would politicise our higher judiciary. It has not. Of course it has raised politically controversial cases. The cases on the Home Secretary's power to fix the tariff element of a mandatory life sentence for murder provide a topical example.[10] But the law is no stranger to that over the centuries. Think of the landmark cases in civil liberties. Think of the development of the law in relation to trade unions and the development by Parliament of immunities for industrial action which were then interpreted by the judges in controversial ways. Think of *Liversidge and Anderson*,[11] the Regulation 18B case. Think of the development of judicial review and of natural justice. Think of *Brind*,[12] which excluded certain politicians from media appearances but allowed actors to stand in. Think of the cases about homosexuality in the armed forces.[13] Think about whether the life support machine should be turned off.[14] Think of every controversial decision in the criminal law. Our judges have always had to decide cases in areas of political controversy. The Human Rights Act has ushered in only a difference of degree, not of kind.

But based on the erroneous belief that the Act *would* politicise the judiciary, and detract from judicial impartiality, some called for an injection of parliamentary scrutiny into the judicial appointments process. That, however, would open the way for judges to be appointed on political grounds. And I am convinced that the country does not want that, and that it would be wrong. The country wants impartial judges chosen through a merits-based system and would be opposed to political hearings prior to appointment, which would subject judges' judicial track records or attitudes to appraisal by politicians in terms of changing fashions for political correctness. I have no doubt at all that our higher courts should not be sculpted to conform to some notion of social, gender or political balance. The Human Rights Act does nothing to change that judgment.

Nor were our courts unfamiliar with Convention principles. They had, for many years prior to the Act, applied the Convention in limited but important situations: for example, where a statute was capable of

[10] See *eg, R v Secretary of State for the Home Department Ex parte Anderson* [2002] UKHL 46; [2002] 3 WLR 46.
[11] *Liversidge v Sir John Anderson* [1942] AC 206.
[12] *R v Secretary of State for the Home Department Ex parte Brind* [1991] 1 AC 696.
[13] *R v Ministry of Defence Ex parte Smith* [1996] QB 517.
[14] See *eg, Airedale NHS Trust v Bland* [1993] AC 789.

two interpretations, one consistent with the Convention and one inconsistent, the courts would presume that Parliament intended to legislate in conformity with the Convention, and would interpret the statute accordingly.[15]

C.   The 'Rule of Lawyers'

So concerns about our judges were unfounded. But what of the lawyers? There were fears that over-enthusiastic lawyers would make excessive use of the Act, as they tested its scope and implications, and that this would undermine longstanding law and policy. But such fears were well wide of the mark. They underestimated both the ability of our judges to deal sensibly with unmeritorious arguments; and the degree to which most—but certainly not all—of our laws were already compliant with the Convention. As I have said, our judges were not unfamiliar with Convention principles. And this country already had a much greater respect for human rights than many others in Europe: we had been a signatory to the Convention for over 50 years. Most of our laws and procedures generally reflected that, and the judiciary have recognised that. As Lord Hoffmann neatly put it, the Act was intended to strengthen the rule of law without inaugurating the rule of lawyers.[16] A few months after implementation, the *Financial Times* wrote:

> The Human Rights Act, which became law in October, was condemned by many who claimed it would create a legal nightmare—jamming the courts with worthless cases and rendering centuries-old British traditions illegal. But such predictions have proved to be wide of the mark. Judges have shown a commendable willingness to throw out bad cases while expediting more serious claims.[17]

What has happened in the courts—or more accurately what has *not* happened—justified the government's own confidence in the majority of existing practices and procedures. We were wary of counsel advising government departments to make seismic changes. They were often over-reacting, donning the mantle of judges and enjoying the experience

[15] See Lord Bingham's Maiden Speech to the House of Lords, HL Deb, col 1466, 3 July 1996.
[16] *R (on the application of Alconbury Development Ltd) v Secretary of State for the Environment, Transport and the Regions* [2001] UKHL 23; [2001] 2 WLR 1389 at [1427].
[17] *Financial Times*, 27 December 2000.

of quasi-legislating through their opinions. So, yes, we paused from the date the Act was passed in November 1998 to implementation on 2, October 2000, to ensure that public bodies, including the courts, were well prepared. But we did not undertake a rewrite of the statute book because that was not necessary. We believed the overwhelming majority of our legislation, procedures and practices would prove to be Convention-compliant. So we engaged in sensible auditing, training and moderate reform, with the aim of achieving sufficient, rather than excessive, compliance.

IV.   THE ROLE OF THE COURTS—WHAT *HAS* HAPPENED

And what *has* happened in the courts has borne out the wisdom of that approach.[18] Just as those who predicted catastrophe in the courts have been proved wrong, so have those who said the Human Rights Act would add nothing. In examining what impact the Act has had on the courts, and on our system of law, the overriding theme that emerges is *balance*: balance between scrutiny and deference; between the individual and the community; and between interpretation and declarations of incompatibility.

A.   The Development of a Domestic Margin of Appreciation

First, we have seen the development of a domestic version of the 'margin of appreciation', long recognised in Strasbourg. The concept reflects the willingness of the European Court, when assessing whether a restriction on a Convention right is justified under the Convention, to extend leeway to domestic authorities, on the basis that they are, generally speaking, in a better position to make that assessment. As the court recognised in *Handyside v UK*:

> By reason of their direct and continuous contact with the vital forces of
> their countries, State authorities are in principle in a better position than

---

[18] For a recent example, see *R v Secretary of State for the Home Department Ex parte Saadi* [2002] UKHL 41; [2002] 1 WLR 3131. The case concerned the use of Oakington Reception Centre. The House of Lords held that short-term detention of asylum-seekers for the purpose of rapidly processing their claims was permitted by Art 5(1)(f). Further, in practice, the detention was neither arbitrary nor disproportionate. It was therefore lawful.

the international judge to give an opinion on the … 'necessity' of a 'restriction' or 'penalty' … it is for the national authorities to make the initial assessment of the reality of the pressing social need implied by the notion of 'necessity' in this context.[19]

The domestic version addresses when, why, and the degree to which, the domestic courts defer to the decisions of Parliament and the executive, rather than seek to weigh up the merits of those decisions themselves. 'Judicial deference', as it is also known, does not mean that the courts are subordinate partners in the tripartite relationship, but that they recognise that, in certain areas, the government or Parliament are better placed to make judgments because of the knowledge and experience available to them.

Nor does deference represent an abdication of the responsibility, given by Parliament to the courts, to scrutinise executive conduct and guard against unjustified interference with Convention rights. Certainly the government would not want that. The Human Rights Act constitutes a promise to citizens that public bodies will, subject to parliamentary sovereignty, act compatibly with their rights.[20] And the guarantee backing that promise is that citizens can take the government to court if they believe government has failed.[21]

The courts have not been slow to utilise the enhanced form of scrutiny provided for by the Human Rights Act, and called for by the European Court in Strasbourg. In *Smith and Grady v UK*—decided by the European Court after the passing of the Human Rights Act, but before it came into force—the court examined the treatment of a group of servicemen and women.[22] It found that the Ministry of Defence's policy of excluding homosexuals from the armed forces had violated their Art 8 rights to respect for private and family life. But the court also held that there had been a violation of Art 13, since challenging the MoD policy in the domestic courts could not provide an effective remedy, given the limitations of judicial review. The domestic courts could only interfere with the exercise of administrative discretion on substantive grounds where a decision was unreasonable in the sense that it was beyond the range of responses open to a reasonable decision-maker. They were precluded, therefore, from considering whether the interference with

---

[19] *Handyside v UK* (1979–80) 1 EHRR 737 at 753.
[20] Human Rights Act 1998, s 6(1).
[21] *Ibid*, s 7(1).
[22] (2000) 29 EHRR 493.

the applicants' rights answered a pressing social need or was proportionate to the national security and public order aims pursued. Now the Act did not incorporate Art 13, because the Act itself provided the effective remedy that was previously lacking. But what *Smith and Grady* illustrated was that the courts would need to use the Act to extend the traditional parameters of judicial review to enable greater scrutiny of the proportionality of decisions being challenged.

Consequently, in the case of *Daly*, a prisoner claimed that searches of legally privileged correspondence in his cell, carried out in his absence, violated his rights under Art 8.[23] The House of Lords, allowing his appeal, recognised the need for these searches to take place and—on occasion—to take place in the prisoner's absence. But it held that the policy of routinely excluding *all* prisoners during these searches could not be justified. The infringement of the prisoner's rights represented by the policy was greater than the legitimate public objectives behind it. In short, it went further than necessary. The judgment in that case is an instructive example of how the courts view their enhanced role under the Act. Lord Steyn, for example, identified three general differences between the traditional grounds of review and an approach based on proportionality:

> First, the doctrine of proportionality may require the reviewing court to assess the balance which the decision maker has struck, not merely whether it is in the range of rational or reasonable decisions. Secondly, the proportionality test may go further than the traditional grounds of review in as much as it may require attention to be directed to the relative weight accorded to interests and considerations. Thirdly, even the heightened scrutiny test developed in *ex parte Smith* is not necessarily appropriate to the protection of human rights.[24]

In the 'prison babies' case the appellants challenged the Prison Service's policy of not allowing babies to remain with their mothers in prison beyond the age of 18 months.[25] Again, the case concerned Art 8. The Court of Appeal followed the *Daly* approach and considered whether the application of this policy in the cases before it was really proportionate to the legitimate aims it sought to pursue. It held that the Prison Service was entitled to operate this policy but that it was not

[23] *R (on the application of Daly) v Secretary of State of the Home Department* [2001] UKHL 26; [2001] 2 AC 532.
[24] *Ibid*, at 547.
[25] *R (on the application of P) v Secretary of State of the Home Department* [2001] EWCA Civ 1151; [2001] 1 WLR 2002.

permitted to do so in a rigid fashion: the policy must admit of greater flexibility. Since the aim of the policy was to promote the welfare of the child, that aim was not fulfilled if the effect of the policy on a particular child was catastrophic. The policy therefore required that individual consideration be given to each case. In considering whether the interference with Convention rights was proportionate to its legitimate aims in each case, the Prison Service would have to strike a fair balance between those aims—the aims being: the necessary limitations on the mother's rights and freedoms brought about by her imprisonment; the extent to which any relaxation in the policy would cause problems within the prison or Prison Service generally; and the welfare of the individual child. The Court of Appeal dismissed one prisoner's appeal, but allowed the other's. And it is notable that the Master of the Rolls, Lord Philips, said: '[b]efore the introduction of a rights-based culture into English public law these applications for judicial review would have been quite unarguable'.[26]

It is all about balance. The balance between intense judicial scrutiny and reasonable deference to elected decision-makers is a delicate one to strike. But the judiciary have struck it well; and I welcome that. Whilst scrutiny is undoubtedly an important aid to better governance, there are areas in which decisions are best taken by the decision-makers entrusted by Parliament to make them. This may be for reasons of democratic accountability, expertise or complexity. But we recognise that we cannot simply recite the need for 'deference' or 'self-restraint'. Rather, we must, where appropriate, argue the case for it carefully and persuasively. This often involves 'policy advocacy'—the equivalent of 'Brandeis briefs' in the US Supreme Court—by which government counsel gives the court a thorough analysis of the policy behind legislation.

Our judges have been receptive to this approach. Lord Bingham demonstrated that in the Scottish case of *Brown v Stott*.[27] The case was about drink driving, and the rule in s 172 of the Road Traffic Act 1988 requiring a suspect to declare who had been driving a car at the material time. The defendant argued that the rule infringed her right to a fair trial, and in particular her privilege against self-incrimination. In the Privy Council, Lord Bingham accepted evidence of the social menace presented by drink driving, and was persuaded that the Road Traffic

[26] *Ibid*, at 2020.
[27] [2001] 2 WLR 817. Note, the ECHR point in this case was considered under the Scotland Act 1998, rather than the Human Rights Act 1998.

Act was a fair way of countering and punishing that behaviour. The case ceased to be a legalistic debate about self-incrimination. Instead, it showed an astute awareness by our judges of the needs of the community and the responsibilities of government.

That awareness was very evident in the *Alconbury* planning cases in the House of Lords.[28] The applicants argued that the Secretary of State's role in policy-making meant that when a planning decision was 'called in' for determination by the Minister himself, rather than by an inspector appointed by him, he was not an 'independent and impartial' tribunal under Art 6. They argued that the relevant sections of the Town and Country Planning Act 1990 were therefore incompatible with Art 6. The Administrative Court agreed. But the House of Lords allowed the government's appeal unanimously. It held that the availability of judicial review meant that the process *as a whole* complied with Art 6. And, crucially, it held also that, in a democratic society, it was entirely appropriate that the determination of planning policy and its application in particular cases should be entrusted to the Secretary of State, who was answerable to Parliament on policy aspects of his decision and to the High Court on the lawfulness and fairness of his decision-making process.

That brings me to the decision reached by the Court of Appeal in the '*SIAC*' case.[29] Eleven foreign nationals who had been detained under the Anti-Terrorism, Crime and Security Act 2001 brought the case. They were suspected of links to terrorist activity or organisations, but could not be deported because of the danger they might face if returned to their country of nationality. The applicants argued that the legislation was unlawful and incompatible with Art 14 of the Convention, in that it discriminated against them on the ground of their nationality. The Special Immigration Appeals Commission agreed, but the Court of Appeal did not. It held that foreign nationals *could* be distinguished from British nationals: first, they had no right to remain in this country, only a right (for the time being) not to be removed for their own safety; secondly, it was well-established in international law that states could distinguish between nationals and non-nationals in times of emergency; and thirdly, Parliament had been entitled to limit the measures to foreign nationals only, because the Convention permits meaures that derogate only 'to the extent strictly required by

---

[28] See n 16 above.
[29] *A, X, Y v Secretary of State for the Home Department* [2002] EWCA Civ 1502; [2003] HRLR 3.

the exigencies of the situation'.[30] The Court of Appeal said it had been mindful of its duty under the Human Rights Act to scrutinise legislation and governmental action in the light of Convention rights; but it showed itself mindful too of the need to balance this against recognition that Parliament and the executive were the appropriate fora for decisions that go to the heart of national security. Lord Woolf said:

> Whether the Secretary of State was entitled to come to the conclusion that action was only necessary in relation to non-national suspected terrorists, who could not be deported, is an issue on which it is impossible for this court in this case to differ from the Secretary of State. Decisions as to what is required in the interest of national security are self-evidently within the category of decisions in relation to which the court is required to show considerable deference to the Secretary of State because he is better qualified to make an assessment as to what action is called for.[31]

So the court followed the House of Lords in *Secretary of State for the Home Department v Rehman*.[32] This case concerned a Pakistani national who was refused indefinite leave to remain, when he would otherwise have qualified, because he was believed to be a danger to national security. The House of Lords allowed the government's appeal from SIAC and found that, in assessing whether there was a risk to national security, even a fact-finding tribunal such as SIAC must respect the primary decision-maker's judgment and assessment of risk. In Lord Hoffmann's view, the events of 11 September 2001 (which fell after the hearing in this case) underlined the need for the judiciary to respect the decisions of ministers on whether support for terrorist activities in a foreign country constituted a threat to national security. Not only did the executive have access to special information and expertise in these matters, but such decisions required a legitimacy which could only be conferred by entrusting them to those responsible to the community through the democratic process.[33]

B. Balancing Individual Rights with the Wider Public Interest

Both *SIAC* and *Rehman* are notable as classic examples of the courts striking the right balance, not only between scrutiny and deference, but

---

[30] Art 15 ECHR.
[31] See n 29 at 1159.
[32] [2001] 3 WLR 877.
[33] *Ibid*, at 897.

between the rights of the individual and the wider public interest. The latter is entirely consistent with the jurisprudence of the European Court, which has often said that it is inherent in the Convention that a fair balance must be struck between the general interest of the community and the protection of the individual's fundamental rights.[34] This is also an important express requirement of Arts 8, 9, 10 and 11 of the Convention, each of which is subject to limitation or restriction clauses which enable the general public interest to be taken into account. The leading cases show, contrary to views expressed in sections of the press, that the courts have not sacrificed the wider public interest in favour of the rights of individuals. Rather, they have applied a principled approach and have sought to strike a fair balance between the two. So, in the case of *Roth* a German road transport carrier challenged the civil penalty scheme under the Immigration and Asylum Act 1999.[35] The scheme imposed a fixed penalty on carriers who brought in illegal immigrants unless they could show, not only that they had no knowledge of having carried the entrants, but that they had an effective system for preventing this, which was operated properly on the occasion in question. A majority of the Court of Appeal held that the scheme was incompatible with Art 6 because the fixed nature of the penalties offended the right to have a penalty determined by an independent tribunal. In addition, the scale and inflexibility of the penalty constituted an interference with an individual's property rights under Art 1, Protocol 1, that was disproportionate to the public interest objectives it sought to achieve.

But in *Farrakhan* the balance struck by the court was in favour of the wider public interest.[36] The case involved an American national who was refused entry to the United Kingdom, by the Home Secretary, on the grounds that his presence in the country might provide a catalyst for public disorder, given his publicly pronounced views, which could be seen to be racially divisive. The Court of Appeal found against Farrakhan because, although Art 10 was engaged, the Home Secretary had struck a proportionate balance between the public interest aim of preventing disorder and Mr Farrakhan's freedom of expression.

---

[34] See *eg, Klass v Germany* (1978) 2 EHRR 214; *Brogan v UK* (1988) 11 EHRR 117; *Goodwin v UK* (2002) 35 EHRR 447. See also *R v Manchester Crown Court Ex parte M* [2002] UKHL 39; [2002] 2 WLR 1313, in which Lord Hope said, at 1330, that it is a theme running right through the Convention that the exercise of freedoms carries with it duties and responsibilities.

[35] See n 6 above.

[36] [2002] 3 WLR 481.

C.   The Tension between Ss 3 and 4 of the Act

These cases and trends illuminate the modern relationship that is developing, as a result of the Act, between the three branches of government. And that is never in sharper focus than when the courts grapple with the tension between ss 3 and 4 of the Act. In drafting these sections as we did, we were again asking the courts to chart a careful course between two extremes. Once again, they are doing that well; they are striking a sound balance.

Section 3 requires the court to interpret legislation compatibly with the Convention wherever that is possible. It is a new and powerful tool of interpretation and that is exactly what it was intended to be. Where the ordinary, or accepted, meaning of a statute would give rise to an incompatibility, the courts must use s 3 to look for other possible meanings that are compatible. But if that is impossible they must consider turning to s 4 and issuing a declaration of incompatibility. The two, of course, have very different results. Section 3 takes effect between the parties in the particular case. By interpreting the legislation, damages may be awarded, convictions quashed, and injunctions imposed. Section 4, on the other hand, passes the matter over to Parliament. It is an illustration of how the new cooperative relationship between the three branches of government works in practice: the court's declaration triggers Parliament's power to pass fast-track remedial orders or amending legislation brought before it by the executive, in response to the court. This is what happened following the Court of Appeal's decision in the *MHRT* case.[37] The court declared s 73 of the Mental Health Act 1983 incompatible with Art 5, because it placed the burden of proof on the patient to establish that the criteria for his continuing detention were *not* met. The incompatibility was corrected by the first remedial order made under the Act: the burden is now on the hospital to prove that the criteria for continuing detention *are* met. So declarations of incompatibility enable Parliament to put the law right in the way it thinks best; or, if it wishes, to leave it as it is. The latter is of course entirely consistent with the Act. But let me say this. Where a declaration of incompatibility is made, in respect of legislation passed since the Act, and which was accompanied by a s 19 statement of compatibility by the minister, the minister must inevitably come under

[37] *R (on the application of H) v Mental Health Review Tribunal, North and East London Region* [2002] QB 1.

some moral pressure to reconsider the position. After all, the declaration will mean that the view he presented to Parliament has been proved wrong in a fully reasoned judgment of a higher court.

Section 3 enables the courts to iron out incompatibilities throughout the statute book. It means that the courts are equipped with a set of basic legal norms, provided by Parliament, to aid statutory interpretation. But s 3 has its limits. Section 4 makes plain that not all provisions in primary legislation can be rendered Convention-compliant by s 3. So s 4 must come into play where the interpretation that would be necessary to hold a statutory provision compatible with Convention rights, is either intellectually indefensible, or would amount to a usurpation of Parliament's legislative function. In this way, s 4 is a necessary recognition of parliamentary supremacy in the right case. There is clearly a creative tension between the two.

An early use of s 3 came in *R v A (No 2)*.[38] In this case, the House of Lords looked at the prohibition, under s 41 of the Youth Justice and Criminal Evidence Act 1999, on cross-examining an alleged rape victim about her sexual history. It used s 3 to interpret s 41 as providing for such evidence to be admitted, where it was so relevant to the issue of consent, that failure to admit it might result in a breach of the defendant's right to a fair trial under Art 6. This was an expansive use of s 3, and one which surprised many observers. It appears to have been the most extreme use of the interpretative power, and the House of Lords has subsequently made clear the limits of s 3.

In *Re S* the House of Lords firmly established the principle that s 3 cannot be used in a way which amounts to legislation rather than interpretation, or which undermines a fundamental aspect of the statute in question.[39] The case concerned care orders under the Children Act 1989. The Court of Appeal had propounded a new procedure, by which the essential milestones of a care plan would be elevated to 'starred status'. If such a milestone was not achieved within a reasonable time after the date set at trial, the court could intervene. In effect, this amounted to a new supervisory jurisdiction for the court, which the Court of Appeal created using s 3. So the question before the House of Lords was whether it was legitimate to introduce into the working of the Children Act a range of rights and liabilities not sanctioned by Parliament. The House of Lords' answer was no. The starring system departed

---

[38] [2001] UKHL 25; [2002] 1 AC 45.
[39] *Re S (Minors) (Care Order: Implementation of Care Plan)* [2002] UKHL 10; [2002] 2 AC 291.

substantially from a fundamental principle of the Children Act: that courts are not empowered to intervene in the way local authorities discharge their parental responsibilities under final care orders. As such, it crossed the boundary between interpretation and legislation, and so was not a legitimate use of s 3. The House of Lords reversed the Court of Appeal's decision.

But *Re S* does not preclude s 3 from producing unexpected, yet acceptable results; results that clarify and improve the law, and achieve compliance with the Convention. With s 3, Parliament has invited the courts to use the Convention creatively in order to find the right answer. Our judges have embraced this innovation skilfully. In a recent case the same-sex partner of a mental health patient sought to be recognised as the patient's 'nearest relative' under s 26(1) of the Mental Health Act 1983, thus assuming important carer responsibilities.[40] Her arguments, based on Arts 8 and 14, succeeded. By way of consent order, the court recognised that the critical phrase in s 26(6), 'person living with the patient as the patient's husband or wife, as the case may be', could include a same-sex partner if that interpretation avoided an incompatibility.

D.   Reinvigorating the Common Law

My analysis so far has focused on statute-based cases, for it is there that the dynamics of the modern relationship between Parliament, the executive and the courts are most clearly observed. But let us consider, for a moment, the common law, for here too we have seen the Human Rights Act have a profound effect. The Convention rights are far from alien to our legal system; but the status and force now given them by the Act has brought a clarity and coherence to our concept of fundamental rights. Clarity because the rights can now be seen free of the pre-Act limitations on the use of the Convention: the condition, for example, that a statute must be capable of two interpretations—one consistent with the Convention and one not—before the Convention could be applied.[41] And coherence because for each part of the United Kingdom, and for each citizen, and each branch of law, the rights are the same and the language is the same.

---

[40] *R (on the application of Summerfield-Gee) v Liverpool City Council*, CO/1220/2002, 22 October 2002. Maurice Kay J (consent order).
[41] See n 15 above.

Even where not decisive, the rights in the Act have proved valuable. In a case about commercial confidentiality and freedom of expression, Sedley L J commented:

> In the present case, as one would hope in most cases, the human rights highway leads to exactly the same outcome as the older road of equity and common law. But it may be said that it is in some respects better signposted, and it is therefore helpful that it has played a central role in that argument.[42]

Many of the cases have revealed that, as with the statute book, much of our common law is already consistent with the Convention.[43] Others have seen the common law evolving to reflect the Convention. The best examples are the cases involving the privacy of public figures, and the balance that must be struck between their right to respect for private life under Art 8, and the press's right to freedom of expression under Art 10.[44] The case law is still developing but, already, we have been reminded of the inherent capacity of the common law to develop, and we have seen the Human Rights Act providing both the impetus and the direction.

In a further category of case, we have seen the common law adjusted or reformulated, but only implicitly or partially in response to the Convention. These cases use the language of rights and responsibilities; and they are often pleaded in terms of the Act. But the developments they bring can seem autonomous and are not expressly framed in Convention terms. These cases are important because, although their significance is less obvious, they illustrate how the concepts and principles of the Act have begun to permeate our legal culture.

---

[42] *London Regional Transport v Mayor of London* [2001] EWCA Civ 1491 at [62]; [2003] EMLR 4.

[43] *Eg*, the early days of the Human Rights Act saw the defence of qualified privilege in defamation emerging unchanged after being tested against the right to freedom of expression in Art 10 of the Convention: *Loutchansky v Times Newspapers Ltd* [2002] QB 321. The Court of Appeal held that the current scope of the defence, as articulated in *Reynolds v Times Newspapers Ltd* [1998] 3 WLR 862, was compatible with Art 10. The rules of public interest immunity, allowing a judge in a criminal trial to order the non-disclosure of unused material, were found to be compatible with the right to a fair trial in Art 6: *R v Joe Smith* [2001] 1 WLR 1031. And where a mother applied for an order allowing her to remove a child from the jurisdiction, the Court of Appeal confirmed that the principles of our family law were not affected by any separate consideration of the father's rights under Art 8: *P v P (Removal of Child to New Zealand)* [2001] EWCA Civ 166; [2001] Fam 473.

[44] The leading cases include *Douglas v Hello! Ltd* [2001] QB 967; *A v B (a firm)* [2002] EWCA Civ 337; [2002] 3 WLR 542; and *Naomi Campbell v Vanessa Frisbee* [2002] EWCA Civ; 1374; [2003] EMLR 3.

In *Marcic v Thames Water*, for example, the court at first instance found the common law of nuisance to be inadequate in that it failed to provide a property owner with a remedy against a statutory sewerage undertaker. The court filled that gap with a remedy derived from the Human Rights Act: the owner's right to peaceful enjoyment of his property. The Court of Appeal agreed with this conclusion under the Convention, but found that the common law was sufficient to provide the same remedy.[45]

E.   Exporting the Common Law

The Human Rights Act has also, finally, enabled the reverse to take place. For too long, the qualities of our common law were kept away from the very Convention which British jurists helped to draft. Incorporation has changed that. Now, we do not expect cases to be taken from the United Kingdom to Strasbourg unless the Convention issues have been tested in our own courts first. So our judges can now influence and contribute to the development of Strasbourg jurisprudence.

The relationship between Strasbourg and our own growing human rights jurisprudence is in its infancy. But already there are signs that the legal reasoning applied here carries weight in Strasbourg—as we hoped it would when drafting the Bill. For example, in the *Alconbury* case that I have already mentioned, the House of Lords analysed the Art 6 case law and its underlying principles carefully.[46] The cases on the application of Art 6 to administrative decision-making had already confirmed that review of a decision by a judicial body 'with full jurisdiction' could remedy a lack of independence in the original decision-maker.[47] But, with no disrespect to Strasbourg, the House of Lords explored the concept of 'full jurisdiction', the justification for departing from the Art 6 paradigm, and the circumstances in which that departure would be tolerated, more thoroughly than the Strasbourg Court had done in earlier cases. The House of Lords, in other words, took the jurisprudence forward. And the subsequent decision in Strasbourg, in which the applications by one of the parties to the case was ruled inadmissible, was an endorsement.[48]

---

[45] [2002] EWCA Civ 64; [2002] QB 929. Note, the defendants have been granted leave to appeal to the House of Lords.
[46] See n 16 above.
[47] *Albert and Le Compte v Belgium* (1983) 5 EHRR 533, and *Bryan v UK* (1996) 21 EHRR 342.
[48] *Holding & Barnes plc v UK*, 12 March 2002.

There is also the tragic case of Diane Pretty.[49] Mrs Pretty, who suffered from motor neurone disease, sought an assurance that her husband would not face prosecution under s 2 of the Suicide Act 1961, if he assisted her suicide. She claimed that if s 2 did prohibit his assistance—or prevented the Director of Public Prosecutions from undertaking not to prosecute—it was incompatible with the Convention. The House of Lords was therefore asked to consider the application of Art 2 (and also Arts 3, 8, 9 and 14) to a situation that had not previously been the subject of litigation. They concluded that s 2 of the Suicide Act was not incompatible with the Convention, that the DPP could not give an assurance not to prosecute, and that Art 2 did not guarantee the right to end life. Shortly afterwards, following an expedited hearing, the Strasbourg Court came to the same conclusion,[50] and, in doing so, relied extensively on Lord Bingham's reasoning in the House of Lords.

So Strasbourg now gains the full benefit of British Convention analysis, and our jurisprudence is now at the heart of the international human rights legal order.

V.   THE ROLE OF THE EXECUTIVE

Let me turn finally to the executive's role under the Human Rights Act. Its role involves engaging positively with Parliament and the courts, to give real weight to the cooperative endeavour I have described.

This means the executive must continue to build Convention standards into decision-making at all levels, so that decisions are proportionate, rational and respectful of fundamental rights. And it means the executive must be robust in the face of human rights challenges, so that it can vigorously demonstrate and defend the merits of its decisions. After all, contested cases are sometimes necessary to help develop the rights based culture we want.

But what about when the courts disagree with the executive? In a democracy under the rule of law, it is not mature to cheer the judges when a win is secured and boo them when a loss is suffered. Under the previous administration, the public would have been forgiven for thinking that on occasions the executive and the judiciary had ceased to be on speaking terms. In the latter two years of the last

---

[49] R *(on the application of Pretty) v DPP* [2001] UKHL 61; [2002] 1 AC 800.
[50] *Diane Pretty v UK* (2002) 35 EHRR 1.

government, there was unprecedented antagonism between judiciary and government over judicial review of ministerial decisions. Some Conservative politicians even went so far as to call judicial review itself into question.

We have come a long way since then and the Human Rights Act has helped us do so. It was drafted sensitively to the balance of forces within our substantially unwritten constitution. And that means the government can accept adverse court decisions, not as defeats, but as steps on the road to better governance. The working out of the Act is not an obstacle to good administration, but an essential element in the path to achieving it. So where domestic decisions go against the government, it will appeal where sensible. And where not, it will ask Parliament to change the law, or it will proceed and implement the decision.

Losing is not necessarily bad for government, or for the citizen. There have been Strasbourg cases over the years that have prompted reforms which we now take for granted. The same dynamic can be expected in domestic human rights litigation, with the added benefit that decisions by our own courts are bound to be more sensitive to the British context. The childcare cases I mentioned earlier drew attention to a possible gap in the protection we give vulnerable children.[51] That has now being filled by the Adoption and Children Act 2002. It is therefore a first class example of major social benefit flowing from intense judicial scrutiny of legislation.

So the government does not see successful challenges in court as affronts to our constitutional arrangements. Nor are the thorough and careful reports on government Bills prepared by the Joint Parliamentary Committee on Human Rights. Both show the Act being worked out, in a spirit of cooperation, between the bodies with responsibility for that task.

VI.   CONCLUSION

One commentator asked recently why the Human Rights Act is still disliked.[52] It is a good question. Is it that Parliament has explicitly recognised the role played by the judiciary in our constitution? Surely not. In giving greater responsibility to our judges, we are merely confirming that ours is a society governed by the rule of law. Is it that the

[51] See n 39 above.
[52] Francesca Klug, *Guardian*, 3 October 2002.

Act has given rise to an uncontrollable flood of absurd or mischievous litigation? It cannot be—because it has not. Or is it simply that individual decisions have been unpopular? Perhaps, because in almost all litigation there must be a winner and a loser. We ask our judges to decide many difficult cases. Some are between private citizens. Some are criminal appeals. Others are against ministers; and of these, some are lost and some are won. That is neither avoidable nor unconstitutional. It is simply proof that 'be you ever so high, the law is above you'.

I think that it is time to start celebrating the Human Rights Act. It has set out the terms on which power is to be exercised, and reinvigorated the rule of law in the United Kingdom. It is true to our constitutional heritage from Magna Carta through to the Petition of Right 1672, the Habeas Corpus Act 1679 and the Bill of Rights. The Act represents one small manageable step for our courts; but it is a major leap for our constitution and our culture. It has transformed our system of law into one of positive rights, responsibilities and freedoms, where before we had only the freedom to do what was not prohibited. It has corrected a 50-year long anomaly, by which British people *had* rights but could only access them in Europe, not at home. In doing so, it has moved public decision-making in this country up a gear, by harnessing it to a set of fundamental standards. And it has breathed new life into the relationship between Parliament, government and the judiciary, so that all three are working together to ensure that a culture of respect for human rights becomes embedded across the whole of our society.

Part 2

Judges and the Development of English Public Law

9

Judges and Decision-Makers: The Theory and Practice of Wednesbury *Review**

MY SUBJECT IN this article is the foundation on which the practice of administrative law is based. How much discretion do public bodies really have in the exercise of their decision-making powers? How ready will the courts be to intervene to overturn decisions which are challenged before them? The answers to these questions encapsulate the constraints within which all of us—advocates, academics and judges—carry on the day to day business of administrative law.

Let me begin with a recognition that the consequences of the 'democratic deficit', the want of Parliamentary control over the executive in recent years, have been, to an important degree, mitigated by the rigours of judicial review. I pay tribute to the high quality of judicial review in this country. It has so often rightly held the executive to account and improved the quality of administrative decision-making.

Now is a timely moment to evaluate the legal relationship between the decision-makers and the courts. Many longstanding assumptions about the ability and the desire of government to provide for its citizens have had to yield in the face of a frequently unedifying conflict over scarce resources, a conflict for which the High Court has increasingly provided the battleground.[1] As the pressure on public funds grows ever greater, and staff levels are reduced, so the resources available not only for public spending but also for decision-making itself are squeezed.

* This article is based on the 1995 Administrative Law Bar Association lecture delivered on 16 October 1995, in Lincoln's Inn Old Hall. The author would like to thank Jason Coppel for his assistance in the preparation of this lecture.
[1] See for example, *R v Home Secretary, ex parte P and G, The Times,* 19 May 1994; *R v Home Secretary, ex parte Fire Brigades Union* [1995] AC 513; *R v Gloucestershire County Council, ex parte Mahfood, The Times,* 21 June 1995.

Public authorities in the 1990s take an ever growing number of potentially reviewable decisions, often under considerable pressure, and in an environment where the time and resources to reach and reflect on them is reducing. Inevitably the quality of public decision-making is put at risk.

Unquestionably, judicial review has caught the imagination of those affected by controversial public decisions (and perhaps more importantly their legal advisors) and the number of applications for judicial review continues to grow apace. These challenges come not only from individuals but increasingly also from pressure groups, who seek to use judicial review as a means of influencing the policy of government when conventional tactics of political persuasion have failed.[2]

I.   THE PRINCIPLES OF *WEDNESBURY* REVIEW

I start with a restatement of the principles which are generally accepted to be axiomatic of the system of judicial review in this country. They have come to sum up the constitutional role of the courts in public law cases. These principles in large part inter-relate. They are that judicial review is not an appellate procedure; the court must not substitute its opinion for that of the decision-maker; the court must rule only upon the legality of a decision and not upon its correctness; the court will concern itself with the manner in which a decision is reached rather than with the substantive merits of the decision itself.

These principles undoubtedly have superficial appeal, condensing complex constitutional choices into user-friendly slogans. In reality, however, they offer only limited assistance in determining the true limits of judicial review. To say that the courts will merely concern themselves with the legality of decisions and not with their merits tells us nothing about the circumstances in which a decision will be held to be illegal. These circumstances are to be defined by the courts and it says much about the misleading nature of the aphorisms of public law that they are as widely accepted now as they were 50 years ago, yet the range of circumstances in which decisions may be struck down has been

---

[2] See for example, *R v Inspectorate of Pollution, ex parte Greenpeace Ltd (No 2)* [1994] 4 All ER 329; *R v Secretary of State for Foreign Affairs, ex parte World Development Movement Ltd* [1995] 1 WLR 386; C Harlow and R Rawlings, *Pressure Through Law* (London, Routledge, 1992)

extended beyond recognition. I would suggest that the ritual incantation of these legalistic home truths has done much to obscure notable developments in the scope and intensity of judicial review.

A considered analysis of the intensity of judicial review must include two additional elements: first, an understanding, and an account, of why it is that judicial review should never be an appellate process, that the court should adjudicate only upon the legality of a decision and not upon its merits; and second, a formulation of substantive principles of judicial review which truly reflect the constitutional underpinnings which are so readily attributed to them.

A. The Constitutional Basis of Judicial Review

These principles rest upon the constitutional imperative of judicial self-restraint. There are at least three bases for this imperative.

First, *a constitutional imperative*: public authorities receive their powers from Parliament which intends, for good reason, that a power be exercised by the authority to which it is entrusted. This is because each and every authority has, within its field of influence, a level of knowledge and experience which justifies the decision of Parliament to entrust that authority with decision-making power.[3] Secondly, *lack of judicial expertise*: it follows that the courts are, in relative terms, ill-equipped to take decisions in place of the designated authority. This is all the more true where the decision in question is one of 'policy'; and the further into the realm of 'policy' an issue lies, the more reluctant a court should be to interfere with the authority's decision.[4] Thirdly, *the democratic imperative*: it has long been recognised that elected public authorities, and particularly local authorities, derive their authority in part from their electoral mandate. The electoral system also operates as an important safeguard against the unreasonable exercise of public powers, since elected authorities have to submit themselves, and their decision-making records, to the verdict of the electorate at regular intervals.[5]

---

[3] *Associated Provincial Picture Houses v Wednesbury Corporation* [1948] 1 KB 223, 230 (*per* Lord Greene M R).
[4] *CREEDNZ Inc v Governor General* [1981] NZLR 172, *per* Richardson J at pp 197–8; *R v Ministry of Defence, ex parte Smith, The Times,* 6 November 1995, *per* Bingham M R
[5] *Slattery v Naylor* (1888) 13 AC 446; *Kruse v Johnson* [1898] 2 QB 91.

What this reduces to is a doctrine of judicial self-restraint in deference to the sovereignty of Parliament. The traditional doctrine of separation of powers requires that the three basic functions of government—legislative, executive and judicial—are the distinct preserve of separate branches. The courts may not decide either on the validity or the desirability of legislation. It was not ever so. In *Bonham's Case* in 1610 Coke C J maintained that:

> when an act of parliament is against common right and reason, or repugnant, or impossible to be performed, the common law will control it, and adjudge such act to be void.[6]

So also five years later, in *Day v Savadge*, Hobart C J said:

> even an act of parliament made against natural equity … is void in itself; for *jura naturae sunt immutabilia*, and they are *leges legum*.[7]

Such notions form no part of the modern law, though I will discuss later the attempt by some to revive them as part of the law of judicial review. They became obsolete when the supremacy of Parliament was finally established by the revolution of 1688.[8] As Willes J put it in 1871, the judges could not 'act as regents over what is done by Parliament with the consent of the Queen, Lords and Commons'.[9] In 1986, Lord Templeman spoke of 'Parliament exercising the supremacy of power conferred on Parliament by the unwritten constitution of the United Kingdom, subject to quinquennial democratic control and to the daily force of public opinion.'[10] There is a superfluity of judicial statement to this effect.[11]

The legislative supremacy of Parliament is not merely a legal concept, a principle of the common law, recognised and applied by the decisions of the courts. It 'is also the result of political history and is ultimately based on fact, that is, general recognition by the people and the courts'.[12] It is Professor Hart's 'ultimate rule of recognition'.[13]

---

[6] (1610) Co Rep 113b.
[7] *Day v Savadge* (1614) Hob 85, 97.
[8] *Pickin v British Railways Board* [1974] AC 765, *per* Lord Reid at p 782.
[9] *Lee v Bude & Torrington Railway* (1871) LR 6 CP 576, 582.
[10] *R v Secretary of State for the Environment, ex parte Nottinghamshire CC* [1986] 1 AC 240, 265.
[11] See O Hood Phillips, *Constitutional and Administrative Law* 7th ed, (London, Stevens, 1987), p 521.
[12] *Ibid*, at p 50.
[13] H L A Hart, *The Concept of Law* 2nd ed, (Oxford, Clarendon Press, 1995), p 108.

B.   The Substantive Principles of Judicial Review

The final element of a normative description of judicial review is the formulation of substantive principles of judicial review which faithfully reflect the constitutional imperative of judicial self-restraint.

This exposition of public law principles is neither novel nor surprising. It is drawn directly from the speech of Lord Greene in the *Wednesbury* case, the *locus classicus* of British administrative law.[14] Lord Greene started with a maxim: that the court does not act as an appellate authority, but as a judicial authority concerned only with the issue of whether the public authority has contravened the law by acting in excess of the powers which Parliament has confided in it. Its justification is that the public body is entrusted by Parliament with the decision on a matter with which the knowledge and experience of that authority can best be trusted to deal.

He then outlined substantive principles of judicial review which truly reflect the constitutional basis which he ascribed to them. First, that a decision-maker has a broad discretion as to the factors which are to be taken into account before a decision is made, a discretion which is only restricted if the governing statute clearly requires that a particular factor *must* be considered, or *must not* be considered. Second, the celebrated principle of *Wednesbury* unreasonableness, that once the decision-maker has properly determined the range of relevant considerations, the weight to be given to each consideration is a matter within its discretion and a decision will only be struck down as unreasonable where it is so unreasonable that no reasonable decision-maker could have made it.

Lord Scarman observed in the *Nottinghamshire* case that 'no question of constitutional propriety arose in *Wednesbury*'.[15] His further observation, that 'the Master of the Rolls was not concerned with the constitutional limits for the exercise of judicial power in our parliamentary democracy' cannot, however, be sustained. Lord Greene MR was unquestionably addressing the boundaries of judicial review beyond which it would be constitutionally inappropriate to trespass. The court was not a court of appeal which could substitute its decision for that of the decision-maker, who acted under powers conferred by Parliament. This would amount to 'a wrongful usurpation of power by the judiciary'.[16]

---

[14] Above n 3.
[15] *Ex parte Nottinghamshire CC*, above n 10, at p 249.
[16] *R v Secretary of State for the Home Department, ex parte Brind* [1991] 1 AC 697, *per* Lord Ackner at p 757.

Since 1948, '*Wednesbury* review' has come to be used as shorthand for that constitutional school of thought which advocates judicial self-restraint in public law matters. Moreover, it is shorthand which the vast majority of lawyers would still acknowledge to be the guiding principle of our system of judicial review.

The very restrictiveness, however, of the *Wednesbury* principles has put them under attack. First, there have been attempts to modify them, in cases where fundamental rights are said to have been restricted and where national economic policy has come under challenge. Secondly, various grounds for judicial review, developed by the courts in the years since *Wednesbury*, including improper purpose, breach of natural justice and failure to respect legitimate expectations, have been treated as hard-edged principles. There, the opinion of the court is determinative and the opinion of the decision-making body must conform to it if its decision is to survive challenge. *Wednesbury* review, in contrast, expresses a strong preference for soft-edged decisions, in which the opinion of the decision-making body may differ from that of the court yet still fall within a band of legitimate responses.[17] Thirdly, the legal systems of the European Union and of the European Convention on Human Rights, whose approach to judicial review is markedly different from our own, have had an increasing influence, both direct and indirect.

II.   THE CHALLENGE TO THE *WEDNESBURY* PRINCIPLES

The standard of *Wednesbury* unreasonableness, which has been renamed (as irrationality) and reformulated, but until recently not challenged, sets an onerous standard for review of the merits of public decisions: There is, however, recent authority which could support the contention that a class of case may exist where it would be appropriate for there to be 'a conceptual shift away' from *Wednesbury* in the direction of a lower threshold of unreasonableness. On the other hand there is also recent authority which could support movement in the opposite direction: that another class of case may exist where it would be appropriate for there to be a higher threshold of unreasonableness ('super-*Wednesbury*' as Simon Brown L J in the Divisional Court

---

[17] For the use of this terminology, see *R v Monopolies and Mergers Commission, ex parte South Yorkshire Transport Ltd* [1993] 1 WLR 23, *per* Lord Mustill at p 32; M Fordham, *Judicial Review Handbook* (Oxford, Hart, 1994), pp 107–15.

dubbed the concept in *R v Ministry of Defence ex parte Smith*).[18] I will consider each suggested class of case in turn.

A. Lower Threshold: Fundamental Rights Cases

Irked by the restrictiveness of Lord Greene M R in *Wednesbury* and Lord Diplock in *CCSU v Minister for the Civil Service*,[19] so that 'it might be thought that there was little room for conceptual development beyond the existing formulations', Laws J, in an important article, based on his 1992 ALBA Lecture,[20] has advocated that 'the greater the intrusion proposed by a body possessing public powers over the citizen into an area where his fundamental rights are at stake, the greater must be the justification which the public authority must demonstrate'. He maintained that, if accepted, this would be 'no more a usurpation of constitutional propriety than is the conventional *Wednesbury* approach itself'.[21]

Laws J lays claim, therefore, to 'a conceptual shift away from *Wednesbury* unreasonableness', but a shift as justifiable as *Wednesbury* itself. There is authority which may provide some support for these propositions.[22] Lord Bridge in *Brind* went as far as to suggest a judicially ordered hierarchy of values so that the court was 'perfectly entitled to start from the premise that any restriction of the right to freedom of expression requires to be justified and that nothing less than an important competing public interest will be sufficient to justify it'.[23] Such justification was a decision for the Secretary of State alone ('the primary judgment') but it was for the court to determine whether that decision could reasonably have been made ('the secondary judgment').

Lord Ackner, however, decided *Brind* on traditional *Wednesbury* grounds, whilst observing:

> In a field which concerns a fundamental human right—namely that of free speech—close scrutiny must be given to the reasons provided as justification for interfering with that right.[24]

[18] [1995] 4 All ER 427, 441 and 445.
[19] [1985] AC 374.
[20] 'Is the High Court the Guardian of Fundamental Constitutional Rights?' [1993] *PL* 59.
[21] *Ibid*, at p 69.
[22] *R v Secretary of State for the Home Department, ex parte Bugdaycay* [1987] AC 514, *per* Lord Bridge at p 531; *ex parte Brind*, above n 16.
[23] Above n 16, at pp 748–49.
[24] Above n 16, at p 757.

It is hard to see *Brind* as marking a 'conceptual shift' away from *Wednesbury*. There is now the authority of Neill L J in the *NALGO* case that the *Wednesbury* threshold of unreasonableness is not lowered in fundamental rights cases.[25] This must be correct. The effect of *Brind* is that, where the issue is whether an acknowledged fundamental right should be restricted, then the decision for the Secretary of State must be two-stage: first, to acknowledge the fundamental right; second, to decide whether there is an important competing public interest which justifies its restriction. Consistent with *Wednesbury*, however, the court can only require of the Secretary of State a decision-making process in this form where the fundamental right is unquestioned, representing an undoubted value of our democratic society. For example, an alleged right to hunt stags, a highly controversial activity which fell to be examined in the recent case of *R v Somerset County Council, ex parte Fewings*, would not qualify.[26]

Lord Bridge's presumption in *Brind* should therefore be read as no more than a recognition that it would be perverse for a Secretary of State to fail to recognise that such fundamental rights, as the right to life or freedom of expression, can be overridden only by 'an important competing public interest'. This approach should apply only to cases where by reason of the accepted values of our democratic society, it would be perverse to maintain otherwise—values that no democratic politician, consistently with his status as such, could be heard to deny.[27] The primary judgment where the balance of public interest lies should be for the Secretary of State.

There have been a number of recent judicial statements to the effect that the courts will be particularly alert when scrutinising the behaviour of the executive where fundamental rights are at stake, For example, Simon Brown L J stated in *ex parte Smith* that:

> When the most fundamental human rights are threatened, the Court will not, for example, be inclined to overlook some perhaps minor flaw in the

---

[25] *R v Secretary of State for the Environment, ex parte NALGO* [1993] Admin LR 785.
[26] [1995] 1 All ER 513 (DC); [1995] 1 WLR 1037 (CA). See Nardell [1995] *PL* 27.
[27] A similar approach already affects the law of legitimate expectation. Where an individual has proceeded on the basis that the Secretary of State has undertaken that he will enjoy a benefit if he satisfies certain conditions, it has been held that the Secretary of State 'should not ... be entitled to resile from that undertaking without affording interested persons a hearing and *then only if the overriding public interest demands it*' (emphasis supplied): *R v Home Secretary, ex parte Khan* [1984] 1 WLR 1337, *per* Parker L J at p 1334.

decision-making process or adopt a particularly benevolent view of the Minister's evidence, or exercise its discretion to withhold relief.[28]

However, such suggestions have been accompanied by a more general assertion that the courts will intervene more readily, and on the basis of a lower standard of *Wednesbury* unreasonableness in fundamental rights cases. Simon Brown L J himself stated in *R v Coventry Airport, ex parte Phoenix Aviation*,[29] that the courts would adopt a more interventionist role to protect and uphold the rule of law, just as it would in fundamental rights cases. On this approach, the court would be invited to exercise a much tighter control over the merits of a decision where it perceives a threat to fundamental rights.

This is to stray far beyond the limits laid down in *Brind*, and to lead the judges into dangerous territory. In practice, few cases which touch upon the protection of fundamental rights reflect the beguiling simplicity of the legal slogan. The political and legal choices which import consideration of fundamental rights protection are among the most difficult and the most subjective, and offer immense scope for political and philosophical disagreement. It cannot be right that such questions should be regarded as more rather than less suitable to judicial determination. The approach adopted in *Brind*, which states conclusively that the *Wednesbury* threshold of unreasonableness is not lowered in fundamental rights cases, must prevail.[30]

B. Higher Threshold: Decisions Concerning National Economic Policy

Two recent decisions of the House of Lords represent a high-water mark in judicial self-restraint, where decisions concerning national economic policy are concerned.[31] The House did not go so far as to hold that such decisions are non-justiciable but powerfully indicated that, in practice, they will be, unless in the most exceptional circumstances. The *Nottinghamshire* case concerned a report by the Secretary of State, approved by resolution of the House of Commons, specifying the limits of public expenditure by local authorities and

---

[28] Above n 18.
[29] [1995] 3 All ER 37, 62.
[30] See *ex parte NALGO*, above n 25, *per* Neill L J at p 798. This view is confirmed by Bingham M R in *ex parte Smith*, above no 4.
[31] *Ex parte Nottinghamshire CC*, above n 10; *R v Secretary of State for the Environment, ex parte Hammersmith* LBC [1991] 1 AC 521.

therefore the distribution of the tax burden between taxpayers and ratepayers. In the earlier part of the leading judgment, Lord Scarman appeared to hold that the decision under challenge was reviewable if there was a *prima facie* case of bad faith, improper motive or perversity, that is if 'the consequences of [the Secretary of State's] guidance were so absurd that he must have taken leave of his senses'[32] He appeared, however, then to exclude perversity in the operative part of his judgment. He held that since the proposed action complied with the statute and had been approved by the Commons:

> it is not for the judges to say that the action has such unreasonable consequences that the guidance upon which the action is based and of which the House of Commons had notice was perverse and must be set aside ... Judicial review is a great weapon in the hands of the judges: but the judges must observe the constitutional limits set by our parliamentary system upon their exercise of this beneficent power.[33]

In the next case, the *Hammersmith* case,[34] which also concerned a national economic policy choice, Lord Bridge appears to have reinstated perversity as a potential ground of challenge, but in some new and higher form. He held that *Nottinghamshire* meant that:

> [the decision] is not open to challenge on grounds of irrationality *short of the extremes of bad faith, improper motive or manifest absurdity* ... The courts would be exceeding their proper function if they presumed to condemn the policy as unreasonable. (Emphasis added)

Understandably, Simon Brown L J in *ex parte Smith* interpreted these decisions as defining a concept of 'super-*Wednesbury*' irrationality.[35]

The danger with Lord Bridge's judgment is that it suggests that there is a level of 'irrationality' short of manifest absurdity which may found judicial review *in the ordinary case*. This encourages applications on a false basis. Lord Diplock in the *GCHQ* case defined a *Wednesbury* unreasonable decision as one 'which is so outrageous in its defiance of logic or of accepted moral standards that no sensible person who had applied his mind to the question to be decided could have arrived at it'.[36] That leaves no scope for 'super-*Wednesbury*' irrationality.

---

[32] Above n 10 at p 247.
[33] Above n 10 at pp 250–51.
[34] Above n 31.
[35] Above n 18.
[36] Above n 19, at p 410.

If *Hammersmith* recognises such a concept then it is in principle unsound and went further than was necessary to express the judicial self-restraint appropriate to this class of case.[37]

In summary, the standard of *Wednesbury* reasonableness is, to some extent, under direct attack. A more subtle form of challenge is, however, the techniques by which the *Wednesbury* threshold is sidelined and ignored. Challenges based on *Wednesbury* unreasonableness rarely succeed. Successful challenges are typically put in terms of relevancy, illegality or procedural impropriety.

C. *Wednesbury* Relevance and Improper Purposes

Wednesbury insists that the merits of a decision are for the decision-maker. The *Wednesbury* principle of relevance is premised upon the view that the decision-maker is in the best position, by reference to the statute, its purposes and the powers it confers, to determine the range of factors which bear upon his decision. The statute may expressly, or by necessary implication, provide that some factors *must*, and some *must not*, be considered, but there is a margin of appreciation within which the decision-maker may decide for himself which considerations should play a part in his reasoning process.[38] Thus, there are three categories of consideration: those that must, those that must not and those that may, in the decision-maker's discretion, be taken into account. An important part of *Wednesbury* is the recognition of this free area of optional considerations.

In *Tesco Stores Ltd v Secretary of State for the Environment*, Lord Keith held that:

> It is for the courts, if the matter is brought before them, to decide what is a relevant consideration. If the decision-maker wrongly takes the view that some consideration is not relevant and therefore has no regard to it, his decision cannot stand and he must be required to think again. But it is entirely for the decision-maker to attribute to the relevant consideration such weight as he thinks fit, and the courts will not interfere unless he has acted unreasonably in the *Wednesbury* sense.[39]

---

[37] Bingham M R in *ex parte Smith*, above n 4, rightly held that the *Wednesbury* test was sufficiently flexible to cover all situations.
[38] See also Simon Brown L J dissenting in *ex parte Fewings* (CA), above n 26, at p 1049.
[39] *Tesco Stores v Secretary of State for the Environment* [1995] 1 WLR 759.

Lord Keith should not be taken to be denying the third category of optional considerations. He is holding only that it is for the courts to decide whether a consideration is mandatorily included or excluded by the statute.

With respect to Laws J, he went wrong at first instance in *ex parte Fewings*, the case in which Somerset County Council prohibited stag-hunting on land which it held 'for the benefit … of their area' because he failed to recognise this third category, of optional considerations, which *may* be taken into account consistently with the terms and the purposes of the statute. Having held staghunting to be lawful, he concluded that the court would hold moral considerations to be irrelevant unless there was express statutory authorisation for these to be taken into account. That is the wrong test. The true question was whether Somerset as the decision-maker was *prohibited* by the statute from taking these considerations into account when deciding the activities it would permit on land it held for the benefit of its area. Absent a statutory prohibition, these considerations were plainly permitted.

When Sir Thomas Bingham M R in the Court of Appeal held that he did not accept Laws J's view that moral considerations were 'necessarily irrelevant' to the decision whether stag-hunting promoted the benefit of its area, he was regarding such considerations as within the optional third category.[40] Simon Brown L J held that they were at least that but in addition he thought they were 'necessarily relevant'.[41]

The decision in *Padfield* has an important impact upon *Wednesbury* relevance.[42] Just as the court may construe a statute as requiring the inclusion or exclusion of a particular consideration, so also it is for the court to determine the policy and objects, or purpose(s), of the Act by construing it as a whole. The consequence is that the activities of public bodies are constrained not only by the express words of the statute but also by such purposes as the court may see fit to imply from the statute as a whole when a decision is challenged.

The determination of a statutory purpose is a hard-edged decision, a matter of law for the court. It arises prior to any assessment of the relevance of the factors which may have been taken into account by the authority,[43] and to a large extent will condition the outcome of that assessment. The characterisation by a court of what would undoubtedly

---

[40] Above n 26, at p 1046.
[41] Above n 26 at p 1049.
[42] *Padfield v Minister of Agriculture* [1968] AC 997.
[43] See for example, *ex parte World Development Movement Ltd,* above n 2.

qualify as a relevant consideration as the purpose of the statute plainly restricts the decision-maker's discretion to adopt other considerations as relevant.

In this context, the *Pergau Dam* case merits close attention.[44] The issue in that case was whether the grant of aid to fund the construction of the Pergau dam in Malaysia was 'for the purpose of promoting the development' of Malaysia within the meaning of section 1(1) of the Overseas Development and Cooperation Act 1980. The Divisional Court glossed the statute by inserting the word 'sound' before 'development purpose' in the statutory provision. That decided, it was 'a matter for the courts and not for the Secretary of State to determine whether, on the evidence before the court, the particular conduct was, or was not, within the statutory purpose'. Since the grant of aid was, in the court's view, economically unsound, that was the end of the matter and all the other 'political and economic considerations', such as the promotion of regional stability, good government, human rights and British commercial interests, which the Secretary of State had taken into account in deciding not to rescind the offer of aid, mattered not.

It is not obvious why the court's function was not spent in construing the statute as sanctioning the promotion of *sound* development, so that it would be for the Secretary of State on all the facts to decide, subject to *Wednesbury*, whether the proposed development was sound. True, on the strong facts of the case, the Secretary of State might well have acted perversely had he decided that this development was sound, but, in principle, this primary factual judgment should have been for the decision-maker, not the court. The general rule is that if, on its true construction, a statutory criterion is a flexible and evaluative one, whose rational application to the same facts may produce conflicting conclusions, it is the view of the rational decision-maker, and not the view of the court, which governs.[45] The soundness of a development in the context of an overseas aid statute requires evaluation and that should be for the Secretary of State not the court.

Even on its own terms—that the decision whether the proposed development was in fact sound was for the court—the *Pergau Dam* decision dramatically illustrates the impact of treating a factor, such as the soundness of a proposed development project, not as a mandatory

---

[44] Above n 2.
[45] *Edwards v Bairstow* [1956] AC 14; see also *ex parte South West Yorkshire Transport Ltd*, above n 17, *per* Lord Mustill at pp 32–3. On the *Pergau Dam* case see also L Collins [1995] King's College L J 20, at p 22.

relevant consideration for the Secretary of State to weigh alongside other relevant considerations, but as the purpose of the statutory provision. The courts should take care to abstain, under the mantle of construction, from elevating what is, in truth, a mere relevant consideration into *a* or *the* purpose of a statutory provision, thus curbing a valuable and legitimate facet of administrative autonomy.

III.   THE RISE OF OTHER PRINCIPLES OF HARD-EDGED REVIEW

A.   Natural Justice

Natural justice, or the duty to act fairly, has, since *Ridge v Baldwin* in 1964,[46] been extended to provide a procedural ground of review in most areas of public law.

> Where an Act of Parliament confers upon an administrative body functions which involve its making decisions which affect to their detriment the rights of other persons or curtail their liberty to do as they please, there is a presumption that Parliament intended that the administrative body should act fairly towards those persons who will be affected by their decisions.[47]

Few would disagree that the enforcement of procedural safeguards on behalf of those affected by public decision-making is one of the great advances of modern administrative law. Natural justice, however, like justice itself, is far from being a natural concept,[48] or one with an invariable content. The basic tenets of natural justice, that a man may not be judge in his own cause and that a man's defence must be fairly heard, are universally accepted but their detailed requirements in any specific context are always for debate. We are regularly told by the courts that the rules of natural justice are not engraved on tablets of stone, that the standards of fairness which they imply are not immutable, and that their demands will differ according to the particular circumstances.[49]

---

[46] *Ridge v Baldwin* [1964] AC 40.
[47] *R v Commission for Racial Equality, ex parte Hillingdon LBC* [1982] AC 779, 787; see also *R v Home Secretary, ex parte Doody* [1993] AC 154, 168.
[48] *Per* Megarry VC in *McInnes v Onslow-Fane* [1978] 1 WLR 1520, 1530.
[49] See for example, *Lloyd v McMahon* [1987] AC 625, *per* Lord Bridge at p 702; *R v Maze Prison Visitors, ex parte Hone* [1988] 1 AC 379, *per* Lord Goff at pp 391–2; *ex parte Doody* [1993] 3 WLR 154, *per* Lord Mustill at p 168.

Nonetheless, the Court of Appeal has insisted that, where natural justice applies, what it requires in context is a matter of law for the court, which is the 'author and sole judge' of procedural standards.[50] That is, natural justice as a ground of review is hard-edged. There is no room for a legitimate difference of opinion between the decision-maker and the court.

This proposition is highly disputable. It is clear that it is for the court to decide whether the duty to act fairly arises. It is also clear that the content of the duty will be variable and will depend on the nature of the decision and the surrounding circumstances. There is much authority, however, that the court should only intervene if the procedures applied by the decision-maker are so unfair that they could not have been reasonably adopted.[51] This alone is the approach which respects the *Wednesbury* doctrine. Not only that: the contrary view which currently prevails is highly inefficient. The hearing comes first, the court afterwards. Thus a lengthy hearing, conducted reasonably by the expert body concerned, may be set aside because the court's view of the requirements of fairness, within a band of reasonably fair procedures, differs from that of the decision-maker.

B.   Legitimate Expectations

The doctrine of legitimate expectations is another of the most significant judicial inventions in the field of public law.[52] Just as it is a hard-edged decision for the court to determine whether the duty to act fairly arises under a statute, so also whether a legitimate expectation exists is a hard-edged decision for the court because its existence is the foundation for the duty to act fairly. The decision, however, whether that legitimate expectation may be trumped because of an overriding public interest must be for the decision-maker, subject to *Wednesbury*.

Expectations created in an individual by the past conduct of a public authority may give rise to the right to be consulted before a decision is taken,[53] and also to *locus standi* for the purposes of challenging a public decision.[54] An issue, however, has arisen on the authorities

---

[50] *R v Panel on Take-overs and Mergers, ex parte Guinness plc* [1990] 1 QB 146, *per* Lloyd L J at p 183.
[51] *Halsburys Laws* 4th ed, (1989), v 1(1), para 84, p 160, n 14.
[52] See *Schmidt v Home Secretary* [1969] 2 ch 149 for the inception of the doctrine.
[53] *R v Liverpool Corporation, ex parte Liverpool Taxi Fleet Operators Association* [1972] 2 QB 299; *Attorney General of Hong Kong v Ng Yuen Shiu* [1983] 2 AC 629.
[54] *O'Reilly v Mackman* [1983] 2 AC 237; *Re Findlay* [1985] AC 318.

between Sedley J and Laws J (though others have been allowed to join in) whether there is a doctrine of both *substantive* and *procedural* legitimate expectation, or only of the latter. The issue is not unrelated to the fact that from the Bar they argued the case of *ex parte Ruddock* on opposite sides before Taylor J (as he then was) in 1986.[55] The legitimate expectation advanced in *Ruddock* was a substantive expectation, that the Secretary of State would only tap telephones in accordance with published criteria. Laws J had argued that the 'doctrine of legitimate expectation relates only to cases where the applicant's expectation is of being consulted or given the opportunity to make representations before a certain decision adverse to him is made'. That submission was rejected by Taylor J.[56] Simon Brown L J also accepted, in *R v Devon County Council, ex parte Baker*[57] that there can be a 'substantive' legitimate expectation, that is, an expectation capable of giving rise to an entitlement to a substantive benefit that the claimant asserts cannot be denied to him, and not merely a right to be consulted.

Laws J, however, returned to this issue in *R v Secretary of State for Transport, ex parte Richmond LBC*. He denied the utility of any concept of *substantive* legitimate expectation and held that:

> the law of legitimate expectation ... only goes so far as to say that there may arise conditions in which, if policy is to be changed, a specific person or class of persons affected must first be notified and given the right to be heard.[58]

Laws J was pressed by Counsel with *R v Home Secretary, ex parte Khan*.[59] In that case the Court of Appeal had held that if the Secretary of State 'undertakes to allow a person [into the country] if certain conditions are satisfied, [he] should not ... be entitled to resile from that undertaking without affording interested persons a hearing, *and then only if the overriding public interest demands it*'. Counsel argued that these *two* conditions had therefore to be satisfied before the Secretary of State could change tack. Not so, held Laws J: the *second* condition would make the court the judge of the merits of the proposed policy

---

[55] [1987] 1 WLR 1482.
[56] This was acknowledged by Dyson J in *R v The Governors of Haberdashers' Aske's Hatcham College Trust, ex parte Tyrell* (unreported, transcript, pp 20 and 24).
[57] [1995] 1 All ER 73, 88.
[58] [1994] 1 All ER 577, 595–6.
[59] Above n 27.

change and therefore the argument had to be rejected because 'the court is not the judge of the merits of the decision-maker's policy'.

With respect, this was no ground for rejecting Counsel's argument that the law recognised *substantive* legitimate expectations. The courts have held that fundamental rights (*Brind*) and substantive legitimate expectations (*Khan*) may only be trumped where the decision-maker is *Wednesbury* reasonable in deciding that an overriding public interest so demands. Yet as *Brind* shows, this does not mean that the court's view is substituted for that of the decision-maker: the primary judgment is for the decision-maker, the secondary for the court.

Sedley J had his opportunity to return to the fray in *R v Ministry of Agriculture, ex parte Hamble Fisheries.*[60] He expressly recalled his and Laws J's rival submissions as Counsel in *Ruddock* and, rightly in my view, held that the law did recognise a *substantive* legitimate expectation.[61] Sedley J then held that:

> ... it is the court's task to recognise the constitutional importance of ministerial freedom to formulate and to reformulate policy; but it is equally the court's duty to protect the interests of those individuals whose expectation of different treatment has a legitimacy which in fairness *out-tops* the policy choice which threatens to frustrate it.[62]

I would respectfully suggest that this is part right, part wrong.

It is part right in the sense that just as the availability of the protection of natural justice is a hard-edged decision for the court, so also it is for the court to decide whether a legitimate expectation exists and, if it does, what it requires.[63]

But, Sedley J is wrong, I submit, insofar as he holds that the issue whether the Secretary of State may override a legitimate expectation, properly recognised by him as such, is also a hard-edged decision for the court. This is surely contrary to the essence of the decisions in both *Wednesbury* and *Brind*, which hold that this kind of issue is for the designated decision-maker. To fail to recognise that, at this stage, the primary judgment is for the Secretary of State, and only the secondary judgment for the court, and to strike down the overall decision on the basis of the Secretary of State's refusal to treat a legitimate expectation acknowledge by him as trumping the policy change in the particular case,

[60] [1995] 2 All ER 714. See Himsworth, p 46 above.
[61] *Ibid*, at pp 723–4.
[62] Above n 60 at p 731.
[63] See for example, *per* Lord Diplock in the *GCHQ* case, Above n 19, at p 408.

is no more than judicial irredentism: it is to advance from a hard-edged decision on the existence and extent of a legitimate expectation (which is proper) to a hard-edged review of the merits of the Secretary of State's overall decision as to whether that legitimate expectation may be overridden (which is improper). The court may only properly intervene where it can hold that the Secretary of State in exercising his primary judgment was unreasonable in a *Wednesbury* sense in deciding that there was a public interest which should override a recognised legitimate expectation. Only thus can due weight be given to the constitutional imperative of respect for the merits of public decisions.

C.   Jurisdictional Error of Law

Error of law, the classic ground of review for illegality, is perhaps the most obvious example of hard-edged review, of the court substituting its view for that of the decision-maker. Allegations of error of law are generally concerned with the interpretation of statutory provisions and, whilst very many statutory provisions are susceptible of a range of reasonable interpretations, the tribunal must have selected that particular interpretation which is favoured by the court if it is not to be guilty of an error of law. The collapse of the distinction between jurisdictional and non-jurisdictional errors of law, so that any decision affected by any error of law made by an administrative tribunal or inferior court, is open to *certiorari* has broadened further the scope of hard-edged review.[64]

Where, for example, a tribunal has the power to confer benefits upon successors in title, as in *Anisminic*,[65] or upon people who carry out improvements amounting to structural alterations, as in *Pearlman*,[66] both of which terms do not by any means have a single clear meaning, the court may substitute its own view as to what constitutes a successor in title or a structural improvement, for that of the decision-maker. It is crucial to recognise, however, that decision-making powers are conferred by Parliament upon particular tribunals because it is envisaged that they will acquire experience and expertise in specialist matters. An interventionist approach to judicial review for error of law may, in part,

---

[64] *Page v Hull University Visitor* [1993] AC 682, *per* Lord Browne-Wilkinson at p 701.
[65] *Anisminic v Foreign Compensation Commission* [1969] 2 AC 147.
[66] *Pearlman v Keepers and Governors of Harrow School* [1979] QB 56.

undermine the *raison d'être* of the system of specialist administrative tribunals, which are intended by Parliament in most cases to replace, and not merely to supplement, the decision-making powers of the court.

In the *South West Yorkshire Transport* case the House of Lords insisted that statutory interpretation is exclusively for the court so that there can be only one right answer to a question of construction—what the court decides.[67] The House recognised, however, that certain statutory terms,[68] have an inherent vagueness so that even when the court has determined the correct interpretation to be placed upon them, their application in any factual situation still gives rise to a spectrum of permissible outcomes. This falls short of the American doctrine of 'rational choice' under which very many if not all statutory terms have a range of interpretations which may rationally be accorded to them so that it is sufficient for the tribunal to act on an interpretation within the range, although not the interpretation that the court itself would give.[69]

In English law, however, where the court-determined construction gives rise to a flexible and evaluative criterion, then it is for the decision-maker to apply it to the facts and the courts will not question that application provided it is *Wednesbury* reasonable. The dividing line between the two approaches in practice is distinct, although narrow. What is clear, however, is that our courts, as courts of construction only, should abstain from assuming any primary judgment over the application of the correct construction to the facts of the case.

IV.   THE INFLUENCE OF EUROPEAN LAW

Finally, I turn to the 'incoming tide' of European law which has inevitably had a significant impact on the theory and practice of judicial review.

A.   Proportionality

First, the range of potential grounds for judicial review has expanded, most controversially, in the shape of proportionality, the principle that

---

[67] Above n 17.

[68] In that case, 'substantial part of the United Kingdom' in s 64(3) of the Fair Trading Act 1973.

[69] See for example, *Chevron USA v NRDC*, 467 US 837 (1984) 84; P Craig, *Administrative Law* 3rd ed, (London, Sweet & Maxwell, 1994), pp 375–83.

the restrictions imposed by a measure must correspond proportionately to the ends which it seeks to achieve. The fundamental objection to proportionality is that it invites review of the merits of public decisions on the basis of a standard which is considerably lower than that of *Wednesbury* reasonableness and would involve the court in a process of policy evaluation which goes far beyond its allotted constitutional role. Proportionality requires the court to address questions involving compromises between competing interests which in a democratic society must be resolved by the legislature.[70] In the administrative context, they are plainly questions whose decision is entrusted by Parliament to the decision-maker. As Lord Lowry expressed it in *Brind*:

> The judges are not, generally speaking, equipped by training or experience, or furnished with the requisite knowledge or advice, to decide the answer to an administrative problem where the scales are evenly balanced, but they have a much better chance of reaching the right answer where the question is put in a *Wednesbury* form.[71]

As a general principle of Community law, proportionality is already an integral component of judicial review where the decision or measure under challenge falls within an area covered by EC legislation. It also plays a part in those cases where our courts currently have regard to the principles of the European Convention on Human Rights, and there are isolated instances of the application of proportionality in purely domestic contexts.[72] However, the prevailing judicial view is undoubtedly that of the House of Lords in *ex parte Brind*,[73] which rejected the application of proportionality outside the European context.

The refusal of the courts to adopt proportionality into the English law of judicial review is the high water mark of the courts' strict adherence to *Wednesbury* principles. There is no escape from an acceptance that a proportionality test would lower the *Wednesbury* 'threshold of unreasonableness'. True it is that under the European Convention, Member States are entitled to a 'margin of appreciation' in assessing

---

[70] Per Hoffmann J in *Stoke-on-Trent CC v B & Q plc* [1991] ch 48, 69, analysing the proportionality of the Sunday Trading provisions of the Shops Act 1950. But see J Jowell, 'Proportionality: neither novel nor dangerous' in Jowell and Oliver (eds) *New Directions in Judicial Review* (London, Sweet & Maxwell, 1988).
[71] Above n 16, at p 767.
[72] See for example, *R v Barnsley MBC, ex parte Hook* [1976] 1 WLR 1052; *R v Highbury Corner Justices, ex parte Uchendu, The Times*, 28 January 1994.
[73] Above n 16 cf Himsworth p 46 above.

whether a restriction of human rights can be justified,[74] but Neill L J was plainly correct in holding that 'this "margin of appreciation" [does not] cover so many degrees of latitude as that afforded by the traditional *Wednesbury* doctrine'.[75]

B. The Spillover Effect

The most significant effect of European influence in constitutional terms, has been the recognition of the European Communities Act as a species of fundamental law, which, unless and until it is repealed pursuant to a political decision to withdraw from the European Union, accords precedence to Community law over all inconsistent provisions of domestic law, past and future. Acts of Parliament may therefore be suspended,[76] disapplied,[77] or declared to be illegal,[78] to the extent that they conflict with the precepts of Community law. Furthermore, following the *Francovich* case,[79] the British courts must now provide a remedy in damages for loss caused by the impact of 'illegal' primary legislation. EC law therefore requires our courts to perform a number of tasks which would have been unthinkable even 20 years ago.

The effects of these new developments have been felt even outside the field of application of European law. The decision of the House of Lords in *M v Home Office*[80] to uphold the grant of an injunction against the Home Secretary in a matter which had no European element followed directly from *Factortame (No 2)* where, following a ruling of the European Court of Justice, the House made a limited exception to the rule that injunctions could not be issued against the Crown. *Pepper v Hart* is arguably another example of this spillover effect, reinforcing in domestic matters the purposive method of statutory interpretation

---

[74] A similar margin of appreciation for the decision-maker can be detected in the case-law of the Court of Justice: see, for example, *R v Minister for Agriculture, Fisheries and Food, ex parte FEDESA*, Case C–331/88 [1990] ECR 1–4023. And see Jones [1995] *PL* 430 on the margin of appreciation under the European Convention on Human Rights.
[75] *Ex parte NALGO*, above n 25, at p 798.
[76] *R v Secretary of State for Transport, ex parte Factortame Ltd (No 2)* [1991] 1 AC 603.
[77] For example, *Marshall v Southampton and South West Area Health Authority (No 2)* [1994] 2 WLR 292.
[78] *R v Secretary of State for Employment, ex parte Equal Opportunities Commission* [1995] 1 AC 1.
[79] *Francovich v Italy*, Case C–6/90 [1991] ECR 1–5357. And see Lewis [1993] *PL* 151.
[80] [1994] 1 WLR 377.

which is required when applying legislation in the Community law field.[81]

V.   JUDICIAL SUPREMACISM AND JUDICIAL SELF-RESTRAINT

It must be recognised, however, that the constitutional developments which have accompanied British membership of the European Union, startling as they may seem, have all been sanctioned by Parliament itself. Parliament enacted the European Communities Act 1972, and so gave effect to EC law within the UK Recently, however, a number of English judges, notably Lord Woolf, have written extra-judicially that in certain purely domestic circumstances the courts may hold invalid statutes duly passed by Parliament. Lord Woolf has argued that the courts could justifiably refuse to recognise and give effect to legislative action which sought to undermine the rule of law by removing or substantially impairing the powers of review of the High Court.[82] Laws J has asserted that:

> The democratic credentials of an elected government cannot justify its enjoyment of a right to abolish fundamental freedoms ... The need for higher order law is dictated by the logic of the very notion of a government under law ... the doctrine of Parliamentary sovereignty cannot be vouched by Parliamentary legislation; a higher-order law confers it and must of necessity limit it.[83]

He also maintained that sovereignty lies not in Parliament but in the constitution, which consists of a framework of principles, such as democracy and respect for human rights, which are fundamental and cannot be denied, even by Act of Parliament.[84] Further, Sedley L J has written that the Diceyan doctrine of the sovereignty of Parliament has given way to 'a bi-polar sovereignty of the Crown in Parliament and the Crown in its courts, to each of which the Crown's ministers are answerable—politically to Parliament, legally to the court'.[85]

---

[81] See *R v Registrar General, ex parte Smith* [1991] 2 All ER 88, *per* Staughton L J at p 95 and Le Sueur [1991] *PL* 326; on *Pepper v Hart*, see Oliver [1993] *PL* 5; see generally, A O'Neill, *Decisions of the European Court of Justice and their Constitutional Implications* (1994), ch 5.

[82] Lord Woolf, 'Droit Public—English Style' [1995] *PL* 57, 67–71.

[83] Laws J, 'Law and Democracy' [1995] *PL* 72, 81–93.

[84] *Ibid.*

[85] Sedley J, 'Human Rights: a Twenty-First Century Agenda' [1995] *PL* 386.

Similar views had earlier been expressed in New Zealand by Sir Robin Cooke, the distinguished President of the New Zealand Court of Appeal. In a series of cases and writings, he has advanced the view that the concept of a free democracy requires judicial limitation on legislative power. Some common law rights, he argues, such as the rights to democracy and to an independent judiciary, are so fundamental that even Parliament could not override them.[86] All this is a throwback to the language of Coke C J in 1610, the later judicial rejection of which I outlined at the outset.

Of these suggestions, four things must be said. First, they are contrary to the established laws and constitution of the United Kingdom and have been since 1688. I cite two judicial statements of the highest authority. Lord Wright has held:

> Parliament is supreme. It can enact extraordinary powers of interfering with personal liberty. If an Act of Parliament … is alleged to curtail the liberty of the subject or vest in the executive extraordinary powers of detaining the subject the only question is what is the precise extent of the powers given … In the constitution of this country there are no guaranteed or absolute rights. The safeguard of British liberty is in the good sense of the people and in the system of representative and responsible government which has been evolved.[87]

And Lord Reid has held:

> It is often said that it would be unconstitutional for the UK Parliament to do certain things, meaning that the moral, political and other reasons against doing them are so strong that most people would regard it as highly improper if Parliament did these things. But that does not mean that it is beyond the power of Parliament to do such things. If Parliament chose to do any of them the courts would not hold the Act of Parliament invalid.[88]

Secondly, many would regard as inconceivable, on the part of any Parliament which we can presently contemplate, any assault upon the basic tenets of democracy which might call for the invocation of the

---

[86] See for example, *New Zealand Drivers Association v New Zealand Road Carriers* [1982] 1 NZLR 374, 390; *Fraser v State Services Commission* [1984] 1 NZLR 116, 121; *Taylor v New Zealand Poultry Board* [1984] 1 NZLR 394, 398; *Te Runanga o Wharekauri Rekohu Inc v Attorney-General* [1993] 2 NZLR 301; 'Fundamentals' (1988) NZLR 158.
[87] *Liversidge v Anderson* [1942] AC 206, 260–61.
[88] *Madzimbamuto v Lardner-Burke* [1969] 1 AC 645, 723.

judicial power claimed. I am as conscious as any, however, of the need for eternal vigilance. But, if there ever were such an assault, it would surely be on the political battlefield that the issue would be resolved. I have to wonder whether it is not extra-judicial romanticism to believe that judicial decision could hold back what would, in substance, be a revolution.[89] Certainly, if such a tide in our affairs were ever to come, it would be for the judges of that time, and not of today, to decide how they should properly respond. The South African experience does show that the judges may have a role;[90] and I am ready to suppose that the judges of tomorrow might gain some comfort in their endeavours from the extra-judicial writings of distinguished judges of today.

Thirdly, the danger with any extra-judicial claim of right to review the validity of any Act of Parliament is that to many it smacks of judicial supremacism. The role and significance of the judiciary in our society will be hugely enhanced if the European Convention on Human Rights is incorporated by Parliament into our law. This is opposed in principle by the Conservative Party. It is supported by the Labour Party and the Liberal Democrats. Incorporation of the European Convention should be a strong candidate for prompt legislation by an incoming government. The traditional objection to incorporation has been that it would confer on unelected judges powers which naturally belong to Parliament. That objection, entertained by many across the political spectrum, can only be strengthened by fears of judicial supremacism.

Fourthly, it has to be made plain that those judges who lay claim to a judicial power to negate Parliamentary decisions, contrary to the established law and usages of our country, make an exorbitant claim that could only even be advanced were the courts ever to be presented with parliamentary decisions that were inconsistent with the fundamental tenets of a free democracy and therefore unworthy of judicial respect. The very basis of the claim, however—the superior political legitimacy of decision-making based on democratic processes—tells against greater activism in judicial review today where no-one would claim that the decisions for review, made under statutory powers, are other than democratically valid. It has therefore to be acknowledged that this claim serves only to underline the theme of my address this evening, that it is the constitutional imperative of judicial self-restraint which must inform judicial decision-making in public law.

---

[89] My views are echoed by Forsyth, 'Of Fig Leaves and Fairy Tales: The Ultra Vices Doctrine, the sovereignty of Parliament and Judicial Review' [1996] CLJ 122.
[90] See for example, *Harris v Minister of the Interior* [1952] 2 SA 428.

10

Principle and Pragmatism: The Development of English Public Law under the Separation of Powers*

I. INTRODUCTION

THE IDEA OF the separation of powers is one of the fundamental building blocks of constitutionalism. It can be traced back to ancient Greece, and to Aristotle, who wrote that every constitution should be divided into three parts: the deliberative, the magisterial and the judicial. More recently, the English philosopher, John Locke, and the French writer, Montesquieu, were at the forefront of advocating the importance of the separation of powers. Their message has been taken to heart by constitutionalists—the French Declaration of the Rights of Man goes so far as to say, 'Any society in which...the separation of powers is not observed has no constitution'.[1]

The idea which lies at the core of the modern doctrine of the separation of powers—that the legislative, executive and judicial functions of government should be discharged by independent institutions—is strikingly simple. So, too, is the rationale underlying the doctrine, which springs from a desire to prevent the over-concentration of power in the hands of a few. This, in turn, helps to ensure that government is conducted responsibly and accountably. It is the simplicity of these foundational principles, and their universal appeal, which explain why the separation of powers is embraced by so many developed legal orders.

In spite of this, the separation of powers has been subjected to a multitude of interpretations. No two legal systems which claim adherence to the doctrine have identical institutional arrangements. This is unsurprising. While the separation of powers is based upon certain shared values,

---

* Delivered as a lecturer in Hong Kong, 18 September 1998.
[1] Art 16.

the manner in which those values are given practical expression is naturally coloured by the individual traditions of national legal orders.

My purpose this evening is to explain the forces which have worked—and which continue to work—to shape the conception of the separation of powers which applies in the United Kingdom, and to discuss the implications of this for the constitutional role of the British judiciary.

II.   THE SEPARATION OF POWERS IN THE BRITISH CONSTITUTION

In the United Kingdom, the approach which is taken to the separation of powers—in common with so many other aspects of constitutionalism—is essentially pragmatic. Within the British constitutional order, the division of functions between the different branches of government is not set in tablets of stone. The separation of powers itself is not viewed as a single paradigm of institutional arrangements which can be achieved once and for all time. Rather, it is perceived as an ideal which must be pursued in a manner appropriate to contemporary circumstances. As political, legal and social conditions evolve over time so, too, conceptions change of what the respective institutions of government should do, and of the powers which each should exercise over the others. It is this flexible and pragmatic approach—which is the fruit of the unwritten constitution—that is central to the typology of constitutional development in the United Kingdom.

This, however, is only part of the story. In spite of the dynamism and fluidity of the British conception of the separation of powers, the doctrine also possesses hard edges which are rooted in the very bedrock of the constitution. They derive from the fundamentals—the paramountcy of democracy and the rule of law—on which the British polity is based. They find expression in the principles of parliamentary sovereignty and judicial independence, about which more later.

Thus, the institutional arrangements of governance in the UK are the product of both organic processes of reactive evolution, and the constitutional axioms which give practical force to the collective values of the polity. It is this interaction of principle and pragmatism which has both shaped the existing architecture of English administrative law and which influences its further development.

I shall come, later, to the Government's proposals for enhancing human rights protection in Britain. But, let me begin by examining the development of English public law to date, and the forces which have moulded it.

III. THE DEVELOPMENT OF JUDICIAL REVIEW: A PRODUCT
OF PRINCIPLE AND PRAGMATISM

A. The Growth of Judicial Review as a Pragmatic Response to a Pressing Constitutional Need

All systems of judicial review—including Britain's—must have some basis in constitutional principle. The doctrine of legality, which is the very essence of the rule of law itself, dictates that government should be prevented, by law, from exercising its power arbitrarily or capriciously—or, for that matter, from claiming power which it does not properly have. However, the judicial review jurisdiction in the United Kingdom—as in many other developed legal systems—has grown well beyond these narrow confines, by imposing increasingly sophisticated and intrusive limits on an ever broader range of governmental decisions. It is not difficult to discern a good deal of pragmatism in these developments.

Without any formal change to the constitution, a significant measure of responsibility for scrutinising the conduct of government has gradually passed from the legislature to the judiciary. This is not to say that Parliament does not continue to fulfil a vital role in the supervision of the executive. Nor does it mean that the respective tasks of the courts and Parliament do not continue to differ fundamentally in nature, the former being concerned with the *legality* of executive action, the latter with the broader question of *political* scrutiny. Nevertheless, it is undeniable that some transfer of responsibility—some change of emphasis—has taken place.

This modest, but significant, reorientation of the separation of powers has occurred as a practical response to important changes in the broader social and political contexts. Two factors are of particular significance.

First, the industrial revolution, and the urbanisation which attended it, changed—almost beyond recognition—the social landscape of nineteenth and early twentieth century Britain. As far as the role of government is concerned, the ethos of *laissez-faire* had, until then, been the order of the day. Indeed, it has been said that, 'Until ... 1914, a sensible lawabiding Englishman could pass through life and hardly notice the existence of the state, beyond the post office and the policeman.'[2] Although this may overstate the position somewhat, it certainly gives a flavour of the legal revolution which took place around the turn of the century, with the inception of

---

[2] AJP Taylor, *English History, 1914–1945* (Harmondsworth, Penguin, 1970), 1.

the welfare state and the massive expansion of governmental regulation. It is the rise of this spirit of interventionism which played an important part in the parallel growth of administrative law. If the state was to exercise greater control over individuals, the courts recognised that it would be necessary to develop some safeguards by, for example, requiring government to adopt fair decision-making procedures. Thus the courts began to create a corpus of administrative law capable of regulating the evolving relationship between British citizens and the burgeoning state.

It is not only the *fact*, but also the *nature*, of the courts' response to this challenge which illustrates the importance of informal pragmatism in British constitutional change. Lacking either a sovereign constitutional text or a legislative foundation on which to base a modern system of public law, the judges made the best use they could of those tools which lay ready to hand. For this reason, judicial review in Britain has been described as 'a largely do-it-yourself response ... to the growth of governmental power'[3] In the best traditions of the common law—according to which rights spring from remedies, rather than *vice versa*—the courts set about the task of adapting ancient remedies, such as the prerogative writ of *certiorari*, to more contemporary needs. Gradually, over many decades, the superstructure of administrative law which English lawyers know today emerged from these foundations which the judges themselves had laid.

As we approach the hundredth birthday of Lord Denning, which falls next January, it is appropriate to recall his profound contribution to the creation of modern administrative law in Britain. It is difficult to epitomise the approach of a judge whose output was as prolific as that of the former Master of the Rolls. However, one of his guiding principles was certainly a healthy repugnance of the abuse of public power. In Lord Denning's own words, 'The great problem before the courts in the twentieth century has been: In an age of increasing power, how is the law to cope with the abuse or misuse of it?[4] This pragmatic desire to subject government to the law can be observed in many of Lord Denning's judgments. It can be seen in the robust approach which he took to statutory provisions which purport to oust the jurisdiction of the courts,[5] and in his emphatic view that all public power, irrespective of its source, should be subject to control by the courts[6]—a view later adopted by the

---

[3] G Marshall, 'Postscript: The Courts, Law and Convention' in Lord Nolan and Sir Stephen Sedley, *The Making and Remaking of the British Constitution* (London, Blackstone, 1997), 102.
[4] *The Discipline of Law* (London, Butterworths 1979), 61.
[5] See *R v Medical Appeal Tribunal, ex parte Gilmore* [1957] 1 QB 574.
[6] See *Laker Airways Ltd v Department of Trade* [1977] QB 643.

House of Lords and now regarded as the new orthodoxy.[7] Similarly, in a number of cases, Lord Denning sought to give practical effect in domestic law to the European Convention on Human Rights.[8] His approach on this point was not ultimately followed because, according to the British legal tradition, the Convention can be made effective in national law only through legislation—something which, as I will explain later, forms an important part of this Government's programme of constitutional change. Nevertheless, Lord Denning's enthusiasm for human rights, at a time when few other judges shared this attitude,[9] illustrates his willingness to take practical steps to improve the position of citizens vis-a-vis the state.

A second important factor also underlies the courts' assumption of greater responsibility for scrutinising the executive. Just as the role of government was expanding, so the ability of Parliament to provide an effective check on the executive began to decline. This was largely a result of the growth of organised political parties. Since the majority of members of the House of Commons are also members of whichever party forms the government of the day, and in light of the highly disciplined nature of all modern political parties, the capacity of Parliament to hold the executive to account is necessarily limited.

It is against this background that the courts' development of administrative law can, once again, be seen as a pragmatic response to a pressing constitutional need. As Lord Mustill put it, 'To avoid a vacuum in which the citizen would be left without protection against a misuse of executive powers the courts have had no option but to occupy the dead ground [left by Parliament] in a manner, and in areas of public life, which could not have been foreseen 30 years ago.'[10]

B. The Limits of Judicial Review: Where Pragmatism Yields to Principle

It is important to understand, however, that while the flexible, unwritten constitution has conferred a good measure of freedom on the judges as

---

[7] See *Council of Civil Service Unions v Minister for the Civil Service* [1985] AC 374.
[8] See *inter alia, R v Secretary of State for the Home Department, ex parte Bhajan Singh* [1976] QB 198; *Ahmad v Inner London Education Authority* [1978] QB 36.
[9] A notable exception being Lord Scarman who, through his Hamlyn Lectures in 1974, is widely credited as having ignited the modern debate on human rights in English law. See L Scarman, *English Law—The New Dimension* (London, Stevens 1974).
[10] *R v Secretary of State for the Home Department, ex parte Fire Brigades Union* [1995] 2 AC 513, 567.

they have developed their public law jurisdiction, it has also imposed important constraints. Let me outline some leading examples of the way in which the hard-edges of constitutional principle have profoundly influenced the basic architecture of English administrative law, by dictating both its outer limits and its theoretical foundations.

a.   *The Distinction between Supervisory and Appellate Jurisdiction*

As every student of British public law quickly learns, the difference between appeal and review is axiomatic. Sir William Wade has succinctly explained that, 'On an appeal the question is "right or wrong?" On review the question is "lawful or unlawful?"'[11] Only by recognising this distinction is it possible for the courts to respect the constitutional authority of the other institutions of government. It is a function of Parliament's sovereignty—according to which it enjoys paramount and unbounded legal power—that it can choose in whom to vest decision-making power. If the courts enquired into the *merits* of decisions which a democratically-elected Parliament had remitted to the executive, the former would—contrary to Parliament's intention—act as the primary decision-maker. This, in turn, would undermine both the constitutional principle of parliamentary sovereignty and the democratic imperative on which it is based.

Consequently the courts have no choice but to exercise self-restraint. This is not a matter on which they enjoy the freedom which the unwritten constitution so often confers. Rather, it is an example of the hard-edged limits which the constitution occasionally—but with profound impact—prescribes, and which the judiciary almost invariably respects. It is, perhaps, unsurprising that in this sensitive area the courts have occasionally overstepped the mark. For instance, in the *Pergau Dam* case,[12] the issue was whether a grant of aid to help build a dam in Malaysia was 'for the purpose of promoting the development' of that country within the meaning of the relevant legislation.[13] The court held that, properly understood, this meant 'sound development', and concluded that the decision to make the grant was unlawful because, in the view of the court, the grant was economically unsound. By reading an additional requirement into the statute in this way, the court took away

[11] H W R Wade and C F Forsyth, *Administrative Law* 7th ed, (Oxford, Clarendon 1994), 38.
[12] *R v Secretary of State for Foreign and Commonwealth Affairs, ex parte World Development Movement Ltd.* [1995] 1 WLR 386.
[13] Overseas Development and Cooperation Act 1980, s 1(1).

from the executive a considerable degree of autonomy. It is this type of judicial activism which begins to blur the boundary between appeal and review, thereby undermining the constitutional foundations on which the courts' supervisory jurisdiction rests.

Nevertheless, in the vast majority of cases, the courts do respect the limits of their jurisdiction which the constitution sets, and which require a careful distinction to be made between merits and legality. Let me give just one example. At present, it is the policy of the British Government that persons of homosexual orientation may not serve in the armed forces. This policy was challenged by way of judicial review.[14] Delivering the leading judgment in the Divisional Court—which was later upheld by the Court of Appeal—Simon Brown L J felt that the arguments were finely balanced. Indeed, he went so far as to say that, in his view, those who sought to condemn the policy had the stronger case.[15] However, he accepted that, for the reasons I have outlined, it was not for a court of *supervisory* jurisdiction to evaluate the *merits* of the policy. Remarking that the judges 'owe a duty ... to remain within their constitutional bounds', Simon Brown L J acknowledged that the court could enquire only into the *legality* of the policy, which, in the end, was upheld.[16]

I shall explain later how the courts' approach will change in cases, like this one, which engage fundamental rights, once the new Human Rights Bill enters into force. For the moment, I simply emphasise that this case epitomises the sensitivity with which British judges have approached the development of administrative law, pushing forward with tenacious pragmatism where this has been appropriate, while, at the same time, respecting the proper limits of their constitutional province.

b. *Judicial Review of Administrative, Not Legislative, Action*[17]

The second way in which constitutional principle has confined the organic growth of judicial review relates to the range of decisions which

---

[14] See *R v Ministry of Defence, ex parte Smith* [1996] QB 517.
[15] Simon Brown L J said that the policy was based on 'a wrong view, a view that rests too firmly upon the supposition of prejudice in others and which insufficiently recognises the damage to human rights inflicted'. Nevertheless, the relevant question was whether it could 'properly be stigmatised as irrational'. See [1996] QB 517, 540.
[16] [1996] QB 517, 541.
[17] For present purposes, legislative action is taken to refer only to the enactment, by Parliament, of primary legislation; the rule-making power of the executive is treated as a species of administrative action.

can be challenged in the courts. The judges have liberated administrative law from a great number of fetters which previously confined the scope of their supervisory jurisdiction. The courts have dispensed with any requirement that, in order to be amenable to review, a power must be 'judicial' in character.[18] They have also rejected the notion that they can only supervise powers created by legislation, holding instead that all public power, whatever its source, is subject to judicial control.[19]

However, against this background of what has, at times, appeared to be the inexorable expansion of judicial supervision, the judges have—quite rightly—accepted one constant limit on their power. I refer, of course, to the principle of parliamentary sovereignty. Viewed in its contemporary setting, this constitutional axiom reflects the primacy which is attached to democracy in the United Kingdom. It traces an immovable perimeter of judicial power by absolutely precluding the courts from interfering with that which has received the imprimatur of the elected legislature. Judicial review of *legislative*, as opposed to *administrative*, action is therefore unknown in the English courts.

It is true that, in one very limited sense, this principle has been qualified. This has occurred as a consequence of British membership of the European Union. The task of harmonising the laws of all fifteen member states in those fields covered by EU law is immense. For this reason, the courts of member states are required to interpret national law as being compatible with EU law wherever possible.[20] Occasionally, however, it is simply not feasible for a national court to construe domestic law in this way. The European Court of Justice has held, and the British courts have accepted, that in such cases domestic tribunals must be willing to set aside national legislation in order to secure the effect of Community law.[21]

However, for three main reasons, this does not undermine the status of parliamentary sovereignty as a fundamental and ultimate limit on the powers of British courts, and as a hard-edged constraint on the organic and constantly evolving separation of powers. First, the ultimate sovereignty of Parliament remains intact. As Lord Denning explained in an early, but far-sighted, decision on EU law in 1979, 'If the time should come

---

[18] See *Ridge v Baldwin* [1964] AC 40.
[19] See *R v Criminal Injuries Compensation Commission, ex parte Lain* [1967] 2 QB 864; *Council of Civil Service Unions v Minister for the Civil Service* [1985] AC 374; *R v Panel on Take-overs and Mergers, ex parte Datafin plc* [1987] QB 815.
[20] See the decisions of the European Court of Justice in Case 14/83, *Von Colson v Land Nordrhein-Westfalen* [1984] ECR 1891 and Case C–106/89, *Marleasing SA v La Comercial Internacional de Alimentacion SA* [1990] ECR I–4135.
[21] *R v Secretary of State for Transport, ex parte Factortame (No 2)* [1991] 1 AC 603.

when our Parliament deliberately passes an Act with the intention of repudiating the Treaty [of Rome] ... or intentionally acting inconsistently with it and says so in express terms then...it would be the duty of our courts to follow the statute of our Parliament.[22] Secondly, this reversible modification of the sovereignty principle operates only in the limited fields in which EU law applies. Thirdly, and of greatest relevance to my theme this evening, this alteration to the sovereignty doctrine is emphatically not the result of a unilateral initiative on the part of the courts. Although it was the House of Lords (in its judicial capacity) which accepted that British courts have jurisdiction to set aside national legislation which conflicts with EU law, this conclusion followed inexorably from the very fact of British membership of the Communities. The modification of parliamentary sovereignty involved all three branches of government: the executive, whose treaty-making power facilitated British membership in the first place; Parliament, which enacted the legislation in which it is implicit that national courts must prefer Community law to national law, and the courts, which have accepted and acted upon that direction.

Thus, quite properly, the closer one gets to the constitutional bedrock, the harder it becomes to effect constitutional change. The hard-edged limits of the constitution do not yield easily—and it is for this reason that they have remained, and continue to remain, steady beacons in the otherwise ever-changing firmament of British public law.

c. The Theoretical Basis of Judicial Review

Constitutional principle has not only exerted a profound influence over *practical* matters, such as those which I have already mentioned. It has equally important implications for the *theoretical* foundations of English administrative law.

It has long been accepted that the juridical basis of the courts' powers of review is the ultra vires principle. This holds that the judges, in judicial review cases, are giving effect to Parliament's intention that executive power should be subject to legal control. Although these matters are not set out *explicitly* by Parliament, it is generally accepted that the judges are implementing an *implicit* legislative intention that public power must be exercised fairly, reasonably, and so on.

Recently, however, the adequacy of the ultra vires doctrine has been questioned by a number of academic commentators,[23] and even by

---

[22] *Macarthys Ltd v Smith* [1979] 3 All ER 325, 329.
[23] See D Oliver, 'Is the Ultra Vires Rule the Basis of Judicial Review?' [1987] *PL* 543; PP Craig, 'Ultra Vires and the Foundations of Judicial Review' [1998] *CLJ* 63.

some British judges.[24] Many writers have attempted to articulate a theory of English public law according to which the courts are viewed as enforcing autonomous principles of good administration which bear no relation to the intention of the Parliament.

Such approaches are fundamentally inconsistent with the essentials of British constitutionalism. In the UK, the three branches of government are not equal and co-ordinate. Parliament is the senior partner. As the House of Lords recognised in an important case which it decided earlier this year, it is crucial that this constitutional reality is reflected in the theoretical foundations of British public law.[25] This can only be achieved if it is possible to show that the judges' limitation of statutory power is consistent with what Parliament intended. If the courts enforce limits which Parliament did not intend should apply, the judiciary contradicts the legislature, and the constitutional order is undermined.[26]

It is for this reason that constitutional logic demands adherence to the ultra vires doctrine. Its great strength is its capacity to provide a theoretical framework which reconciles the organic growth of judicial review with the hallowed principle of legislative supremacy. It symbolises the importance of pursuing the instinctive desire to impose legal controls on government while respecting the established axioms of the constitutional order, and of tempering pragmatism with principle.

As an academic commentator has observed, 'By their ready acceptance of ultra vires the judges show that they are the guardians, not the subverters, of the existing constitutional order ... [I]t is a gentle but necessary discipline ... [which] marks the proper balance of powers between the elected and non-elected parts of the constitution.'[27]

---

[24] Lord Woolf, '*Droit Public*—English Style' [1995] *PL* 57; Sir John Laws, 'Law and Democracy' [1995] *PL* 72 and 'Illegality: The Problem of Jurisdiction' in M Supperstone and J Goudie (eds), *Judicial Review* 2nd ed; (London, Butterworths 1997), Sir Stephen Sedley, 'The Common Law and the Constitution' in Lord Nolan and Sir Stephen Sedley, *The Making and Remaking of the British Constitution* (London, Blackstone 1997).

[25] *Boddington v British Transport Police* [1998] 2 WLR 639. For comment on the significance of this decision for the constitutional foundations of administrative law, see MC Elliott, '*Boddington*: Rediscovering the Constitutional Logic of Administrative Law' [1998] *Judicial Review*.

[26] See CF Forsyth, 'Of Fig Leaves and Fairy Tales: The Ultra Vires Doctrine, the Sovereignty of Parliament and Judicial Review' [1996] *CLJ* 122; MC Elliott, 'The Demise of Parliamentary Sovereignty? The Implications for Justifying Judicial Review' (1999) 115 *LQR*; MC Elliott, 'The Ultra Vires Doctrine in a Constitutional Setting: Still the Central Principle of Administrative Law' [1998/9] *CLJ*.

[27] C F Forsyth, 'Of Fig Leaves and Fairy Tales: The Ultra Vires Doctrine, the Sovereignty of Parliament and Judicial Review' [1996] *CLJ* 122, 137.

d. Judicial Treatment of Preclusive Provisions

I should like to turn to one final example of the way in which constitutional principle has shaped the contours of English public law. The judicary's treatment of statutory provisions which—on their face, at least—exclude the jurisdiction of the courts provides perhaps the most graphic illustration of the interaction of hard-edged constitutional doctrine and the courts' practical desire to subject government to legal control.

The most striking example of the courts' jurisprudence in this area is found in the celebrated decision of the House of Lords in *Anisminic*.[28] The claimant had sought monies from the Foreign Compensation Commission as reimbursement for the expropriation of its property during the Suez crisis in 1956. Since the Commission refused to pay any compensation, the claimant sought to challenge the legality of the decision on the ground that the Commission had misunderstood the scope of its legal powers. However, the legislation which established the Commission provided that its determinations could not be 'called in question in any court of law'.[29]

The House of Lords was therefore faced with a difficult choice. On the one hand there was the pragmatic imperative of holding the government (and its agencies) accountable at law which, as we have seen, has been the driving force behind the development of judicial review. On the other hand, their Lordships were well aware that they could not disregard the expressed intention of the sovereign Parliament.

Ultimately it was held by a majority that, upon a proper construction of the legislation, Parliament had not intended to preclude judicial review entirely. The ouster provision had to be interpreted within the framework of the legislation. Since Parliament had set limits to the Commission's power, a strong presumption arose that Parliament must have intended those limits to be enforceable at law. 'What would be the purpose,' asked Lord Wilberforce, 'of defining by statute the limit of a tribunal's powers if, by means of a clause inserted in the instrument of definition, those limits could safely be passed?'[30]

By this reasoning, it was possible for the judges to pursue their familiar policy of favouring the subjection of government to legal control, without infringing constitutional principle by disregarding Parliament's

---

[28] *Anisminic Ltd v Foreign Compensation Commission* [1969] 2 AC 147.
[29] Foreign Compensation Act 1950, s 4(4).
[30] [1969] 2 AC 147, 208.

stated will. Lord Wilberforce was confident that the court had been faithful to legislative intention, and said of the decision that it would be 'a misdescription to state it in terms of a struggle between the courts and the elected branches of the constitution'.[31] Lord Reid also presented the decision as turning simply on the *construction* of the language which Parliament had used, explaining that, 'It is a well established principle that a provision ousting the ordinary jurisdiction of the court must be construed strictly—meaning, I think, that if such a provision is reasonably capable of having two meanings, that meaning shall be taken which preserves the ordinary jurisdiction of the court.'[32] And Parliament, of course, is well aware that it legislates against a background of such interpretative presumptions.

Nevertheless, it is undeniable that, in this case, the House of Lords came close to the perimeter of judicial power which is set by the bedrock principles of the constitution. Since *Anisminic*, Parliament has used other, stronger formulations in an attempt to oust the courts' supervisory jurisdiction in certain areas.[33] These new forms of ouster clause have not, as yet, been tested in the courts. It would not be appropriate for me to seek to pre-empt any judicial decision on the meaning of such provisions by expressing an opinion on them in this Lecture. However, constitutional logic dictates that some form of words must exist which would be sufficiently clear to insulate a given discretionary power from judicial review. If this was not the case, Parliament would not truly be sovereign.[34] Thus, if at some point in the future the courts

[31] [1969] 2 AC 147, 208.

[32] [1969] 2 AC 147, 170.

[33] See Foreign Compensation Act 1969, s 3(3) and (9), which provides that even 'purported determinations' are immune from review, and Interception of Communications Act 1985, s 7(8), and security Service Act 1989, s 5(4), which both seek to prevent review of decisions 'as to jurisdiction'.

[34] In fact, the courts have accepted Parliament's authority to exclude review. In *Smith v East Elloe Rural District Council* [1956] AC 736, the House of Lords gave literal effect to a provision which prevented review after the expiry of a six week time limit. This type of ouster provision does not threaten the rule of law as seriously as absolute ouster clauses (such as that which was considered in *Anisminic*), because judicial review is not wholly ruled out. More recently, in *R v Wicks* [1998] AC 92, the House of Lords accepted that the possibility of collateral challenge to the validity of administrative action can be displaced if such challenge is inconsistent with the statutory scheme which Parliament has enacted. However, as I explained in my speech in *Boddington v British Transport Police* [1998] 2 WLR 639, 653, the result in *Wicks* was influenced by the ample opportunity which existed for administrative challenge to the subordinate legislation in question. This further demonstrates that the courts' readiness to accept the limitation or exclusion of their public law jurisdiction turns (*inter alia*) on the extent to which this threatens the rule of law.

are presented with a sufficiently clear ouster clause, it will be their constitutional duty to give effect to it.

The courts' on-going endeavour to subject government to legal constraints rarely conflicts with parliamentary intention. This is because the rule of law, and the principles of judicial review to which it gives rise, represent a set of values which are both deeply-embedded and broadly shared within the British polity. For that reason the rule of law is almost invariably respected by all branches of government. Nevertheless, in the rare cases when the rule of law and the will of Parliament are not consistent, it is unquestionably the latter which must prevail. Logic requires that the profound impact of constitutional principle—and, in particular, parliamentary sovereignty—on British public law must extend to the courts' treatment of ouster clauses. In this area, as in all others, the considerable freedom which the courts enjoy in developing administrative law is ultimately bounded by the bedrock of the constitution.

IV. CONSTITUTIONAL REFORM AND HUMAN RIGHTS

I now turn from the development to date of English administrative law, to its future direction. The British Government is pursuing a comprehensive programme of constitutional reform. This includes the devolution of governmental power to a new Scottish Parliament and Welsh Assembly; the reform of the House of Lords; the creation of a legal right of access to official information; and the provision of a strategic authority and elected mayor for London. And now after the Good Friday agreement there will be a Northern Ireland Assembly with legislative and executive powers.

However, I focus in this lecture on another central part of the government's constitutional programme: the enhancement of human rights protection in the United Kingdom. This area provides an illuminating illustration of my theme this evening, the interrelation of principle and pragmatism in the development of the British constitution. I propose to examine two particular aspects of this subject: the way in which the reforms are being introduced, and the content of the reforms themselves. Let me take each in turn.

A.   Instituting a Human Rights Jurisdiction: The Need for Parliamentary Legislation[35]

English law is no stranger to fundamental human rights. The United Kingdom was at the forefront of the development of the European Convention on Human Rights, and was the first state to ratify it. Many of the freedoms which the Convention protects are based on the English common law's long tradition of liberty. British courts recognise and enforce human rights in a wide range of situations. They interpret ambiguous legislation as being compatible with international human rights law.[36] They vindicate a broad range of procedural rights through the existing law of judicial review. And they have singled out certain substantive rights, such as access to justice, as meriting special protection.[37]

Nevertheless, English courts have stopped short in the human rights field in one key respect. They have been unwilling to hold that executive action must comply with substantive rights such as those set out in the European Convention. Thus, while the courts insist that the government must act fairly and reasonably, they will not interfere with administrative action which infringes human rights unless the infringement is so unreasonable that no reasonable government could pursue such a course.[38] British citizens have not been wholly without protection in this field: since 1965, it has been possible for them to pursue human rights claims before the European Commission and the Court of Human Rights in Strasbourg.[39] And, although this route is both time-consuming and costly for litigants, it has provided an important safeguard in the absence of any domestic substantive human rights regime.

---

[35] For a more detailed discussion of the constitutional necessity of legislation as part of the institution of a human rights jurisdiction, see my 1998 National Heritage Lecture to the Historical Society of the United States Supreme Court, '*Constitutional Change in the United Kingdom: British Solutions to Universal Problems*' (Washington DC, May 1998; now chaper 4 in this volume).

[36] See *R v Secretary of State for the Home Department, ex parte Brind* [1991] 1 AC 696.

[37] For a recent example, see *R v Lord Chancellor, ex parte Witham* [1998] 2 WLR 849.

[38] This reasonableness test derives from the formulation of Lord Greene MR in *Associated Provincial Picture Houses Ltd v Wednesbury Corporation* [1948] 1 KB 223. That the *Wednesbury* test presently represents the outer limit of the courts' administrative law jurisdiction in human rights cases is clear from *R v Secretary of State for the Home Department, ex parte Brind* [1991] 1 AC 696 and *R v Ministry of Defence, ex parte Smith* [1996] QB 517.

[39] On the acceptance by the UK of the right of individual petition, see A Lester, 'Fundamental Rights: The United Kingdom Isolated?' [1984] *PL* 46 and 'UK Acceptance of the Strasbourg Jurisdiction: What Really went on in Whitehall in 1965?' [1998] *PL* 237.

Against this background, it may be thought that the judges have not been sufficiently concerned about human rights. Nothing, however, could be further from the truth. The judges have expressed their robust support for fundamental rights. Indeed, many senior members of the judiciary have argued strongly that British courts should be involved in enforcing substantive rights, and that the European Convention should be made part of UK law.

It may seem odd that the judges should speak up so strongly for human rights, and yet be unwilling to enforce substantive rights in court. However, within this paradox lies a revealing truth about the nature of constitutional change in Britain. The judiciary fully recognises the good sense in allowing British citizens to vindicate their rights in British courts. Equally, though, the judges appreciate that it would not be constitutionally proper for them unilaterally to create a human rights regime for the United Kingdom. This is, then, a further example of the way in which the organic development of judicial review is ultimately limited by the dictates of constitutional propriety: of how pragmatism must, in the final analysis, yield to principle.

The considerable freedom which the separation of powers allocates to the judiciary does not extend to such a sensitive task as instituting a fundamental rights regime. As always, it is to the underlying values of the polity that one must look in order to discern these hard-edges of the separation of powers doctrine. Two factors, in particular, explain why the creation of a human rights system lies beyond the judges' constitutional role.

First, it is not appropriate for judges to determine which substantive rights are sufficiently important to merit legal protection. Making these decisions involves difficult choices which are political in nature. If a catalogue of fundamental rights is to be created, this is surely a task for the elected elements of the constitution.

Secondly, the exercise of a human rights jurisdiction involves an important shift in the constitutional balance of power. It leads the courts to exercise a much more intensive form of scrutiny over the government. When they begin to review executive action on human rights grounds, the judges will no longer confine their gaze to the decision-making *process*. Nor will they assess the outcomes of that process by reference only to the *Wednesbury* doctrine, according to which the court will not intervene provided the executive does not act manifestly unreasonably. Instead, the courts will adopt an entirely new approach, deploying such concepts as proportionality and necessity, permitting the government to interfere with human rights only if it does so in response to a pressing social need. Moreover, the nature of *judicial* decision-making will itself become more explicitly ethical, as the courts begin to explore the substantive values on which democratic society is based. In short, the courts will impose more rigorous standards of legality on government.[40]

This does *not* mean that the courts will become the primary decision-makers. The judges will still have to respect the fundamental distinction between appeal and review, or merits and legality. Nevertheless, they will certainly exercise greater power—and power of a different type—over the executive. This is why it has been inappropriate for the judges to claim a human rights jurisdiction for themselves. The separation of powers in the United Kingdom is both flexible and dynamic. These characteristics often *do* permit the judges to push out the boundaries of judicial review, extending the constitutional role of the courts in response to changing circumstances. This elasticity, however, is not infinite. In the field of human rights, the necessary reorientation of power requires the input of Parliament. It is for this reason that the Government is promoting a Human Rights Bill to give effect in UK law to the European Convention. As Sir Stephen Sedley, a British High Court judge, has observed, '[T]here can come a point in even an organic constitution at which change has to be acknowledged to be contrary to the ground rules and—if it is to be legitimated—addressed and debated as such.[41] It is precisely that task with which Parliament is currently concerned, as it considers the Human Rights Bill.

B.   The Human Rights Bill's Respect for Constitutional Principle

This takes me from the *need* for legislation in this area, to my second point—the *content* of the legislation.

The guiding principle of the British Human Rights Bill has been the need to secure human rights protection while respecting constitutional propriety generally, and the doctrine of parliamentary sovereignty in particular. To this end, all public authorities will be placed under a wholly new obligation to respect human rights as they discharge their functions.[42] The courts themselves are directed to construe legislation, wherever possible, in a manner which is consistent with the rights listed in the

---

[40] These ideas are developed in further detail in my 1997 Tom Sargant Memorial Lecture, 'The Development of Human Rights in Britain under an Incorporated Convention on Human Rights' [1998] *PL* 221.
[41] 'Law and Public Life' in Lord Nolan and Sir Stephen Sedley, *The Making and Remaking of the British Constitution* (London, Blackstone 1997), 62.
[42] Human Rights Bill, cl 6(1).

European Convention.[43] This is a strong interpretative obligation.[44] Crucially, however, when national legislation cannot be construed consistently with the Convention rights, the judges will *not* be empowered to set aside parliamentary legislation.[45] In this manner, the British legislation, unlike the Hong Kong Bill of Rights Ordinance, is not entrenched.

In spite of this, the higher courts[46] will be permitted to declare that national law is incompatible with human rights.[47] This will trigger a fast-track procedure under which the Government may, subject to parliamentary approval, amend the offending legislation.[48]

This unique solution has been described by Lord Lester, a leading British human rights lawyer, as 'an ingenious and successful reconciliation of the principles of parliamentary sovereignty and the need for effective domestic remedies'.[49] I would add that the human rights legislation epitomises the typology of constitutional change in the United Kingdom, according to which principle and pragmatism exist side by side.

C. The Challenges of Constitutional Adjudication in Britain and Hong Kong

Hong Kong courts have already begun to adjudicate on constitutional texts, in the form of the Bill of Rights Ordinance and, more recently, the Basic Law. Indeed, their growing constitutional duties are evidenced by the Chief Justice's recent decisions to rename the Administrative Law List as the *Constitutional* and Administrative Law List, and to transfer to this List not only all civil cases which raise an issue under the Basic Law or the Bill of Rights, but also those which raise an issue under the Basic Law. In this manner, we are seeing the emergence of something akin to a Constitutional Court in Hong Kong.

---

[43] *Ibid*, cl 3(1).

[44] Lord Cooke, who, of course, has extensive knowledge of the New Zealand Bill of Rights Act 1990, has said that the interpretative obligation in the British draft legislation 'is, if anything, slightly stronger than the New Zealand section. If it is scrupulously complied with, in a major field the common law approach to statutory interpretation will never be the same again; moreover, this will prove a powerful Bill indeed.' See HL Deb, 3 November 1997, col 1273.

[45] Neither the courts' interpretative obligation nor the issue of a declaration of incompatibility under cl 4 shall affect 'the validity, continuing operation or enforcement' of any primary legislation. See Human Rights Bill, clauses 3(2)(b) and 4(6)(a).

[46] As defined in *ibid*, cl 4(5).

[47] See above n 45 cl 4.

[48] See above n 45 cl 10 and sch 2.

[49] H L Deb, 18 November 1997, col 521.

I have focused this evening on the importance of the courts' not pressing ahead with the expansion of judicial review at the expense of adherence to constitutional principle. However, it is equally important that the courts are not deterred from assuming new constitutional duties by overemphasising the limiting effect of constitutional doctrine or tradition. British courts will have to be astute to this as they begin to apply the European Convention on Human Rights. They will find it instructive to look at the experience of the Hong Kong courts.

On the one hand, as Lord Wilberforce explained in a passage which the Hong Kong courts have cited on many occasions, constitutional instruments must be given 'a generous interpretation avoiding what has been called 'the austerity of tabulated legalism', suitable to give to individuals the full measure of [their] fundamental rights and freedoms.'[50] However, as Lord Woolf cautioned, in a case on the Hong Kong Bill of Rights itself,

> it is ... necessary to ensure that disputes as to the effect of the Bill are not allowed to get out of hand. The issues involving the Hong Kong Bill should be approached with realism and good sense, and kept in proportion. If this is not done the Bill will become a source of injustice rather than justice and it will be debased in the eyes of the public.[51]

These two dicta do not necessarily contradict each other. Rather, they illustrate the difficult choices which courts have to make when applying—and particularly when *beginning* to apply—a human rights instrument. It is a matter of striking the correct balance between activism and restraint—or between *proper* deference to constitutional principle and the *exaggeration* of the constraints which the constitution imposes on the judicial branch.

As I would expect, the Hong Kong judges have had to feel their way carefully in this area. Some decisions have emphasised the importance of pressing forward and of not allowing traditional methodology to circumscribe unduly the new constitutional functions of the courts. In the very first Bill of Rights case to reach the Court of Appeal, Silke V P recognised the need to move away from the 'ordinary canons of construction', in favour of an 'entirely new jurisprudential approach'.[52] Other decisions have evinced greater attachment to the common law methodology. Waung J, for instance, has referred to the 'good sense' of the common law, and has said that the Bill of Rights should be 'subjected to the common law rules of interpretation with its concentration on the text of the statute'.[53]

---

[50] *Minister of Home Affairs v Collins MacDonald Fisher* [1980] AC 319, 328.
[51] *Attorney-General of Hong Kong v Lee Kwong-kut* [1993] AC 951, 975.
[52] *R v Sin Yau Ming* (1991) 1 HKPLR 88, 107.
[53] *R v Town Planning Board, ex parte Kwan Kong Co Ltd* (1995) 5 HKPLR 261, 300.

Thus the courts have questioned whether such tests as proportionality, necessity and pressing social need are appropriate to the Hong Kong system.[54] In these decisions—and many others like them—it is possible to see the outworking of the tension between activism and restraint which is present in all legal systems.

Most recently, the courts have been forced to confront the extent of their own powers in two cases of immense significance for Hong Kong. I refer, of course, to the decisions concerning the constitutionality of the legislation which identifies who are to be classified as permanent residents of Hong Kong, and which regulates the exercise by them of their right of abode in Hong Kong and, more fundamentally still, the legality of the Provisional Legislative Council itself.[55] As those cases demonstrate, the Hong Kong courts are still coming to terms with the nature of the new constitutional order. It is unclear, for example, whether they are entitled to test the laws and acts of the National People's Congress for compliance with the Basic Law of Hong Kong. The question has not yet been clearly answered whether the relationship between the courts of the Special Administrative Region and the People's Congress is the same as that which formerly existed between the courts and the Westminster Parliament prior to handover.[56]

---

[54] See for example, the decision of the Court of Appeal in *Tam Hing Yee v Wu Tai-wai* (1991) 1 HKPLR 261. The Court doubted the utility of 'some phrase such as "pressing social need" or considering whether the restriction [of the right] in question is reasonable and demonstrably justifiable in a free and democratic society'. For an interesting discussion of the jurisprudence of the Hong Kong courts on the Bill of Rights, see JMM Chan, 'Hong Kong's Bill of Rights: Its Reception of and Contribution to International and Comparative Jurisprudence' (1998) 47 *ICLQ* 306.

[55] On the compatibility of the immigration legislation with the Basic Law and the Bill of Rights, see *Cheung Lai Wah (An Infant) v Director of Immigration* [1997] 3 HKC 64 (Court of First Instance) and [1998] 1 HKC 617 (Court of Appeal). The Court of Appeal considered the constitutionality of the Provisional Legislative Council in *HKSAR v Ma Wai Kwan David* [1997] 2 HKC 315. It returned to that issue in *Cheung Lai Wah (An Infant) v Director of Immigration (No 2)* [1998] 2 HKC 382, holding itself bound by its earlier decision in the *David Ma* case. The *Cheung Lai Wah (No 2)* case is to be heard by the Court of Final Appeal. These proceedings will finally dispose of the question of the legality of the Provisional Legislative Council.

[56] In *HKSAR v Ma Wai Kwan David* [1997] 2 HKC 315, 334–35, Chan CJHC suggested that, following the resumption of Chinese sovereignty, the relationship between the regional courts and the National People's Congress was analogous to the relationship between the colonial courts and the Westminster Parliament. However, in *Cheung Lai Wah (An Infant) v Director of Immigration (No 2)* [1998] 2 HKC 382, 395, he questioned whether this analogy was appropriate: 'It may be that in appropriate cases ... the HKSAR courts do have jurisdiction to examine the laws and acts of the NPC which affect the HKSAR for the purpose of, say, determining whether such laws or acts are contrary to or inconsistent with the Basic Law ...' This issue may be resolved when the Court of Final Appeal adjudicates on the legality of the Provisional Legislative Council in *Cheung Lai Wah (No 2)*.

These uncertainties demonstrate that the Hong Kong courts are still in the process of discovering the contours of a new constitutional reality. In the short term, this can only make the task of the judges more difficult as they attempt to discharge their new public law duties. Nevertheless, as they come to terms with important constitutional changes, the same challenge faces the courts of both Hong Kong and Britain. In both legal systems, the judges must strive to achieve the correct balance between activism and restraint—developing their emerging constitutional jurisdictions while, at the same time, recognising the proper limits of their constitutional province.

V.   FROM JUDICIAL SELF-RESTRAINT TO A BROADER CONSTITUTIONAL IMPERATIVE OF SELF-RESTRAINT

I conclude by asserting that, properly understood, this doctrine of *judicial* self-restraint is actually only one aspect of a broader imperative of *constitutional* self-restraint.

The rationale which underlies the separation of powers is that each governmental function should be discharged independently. For this reason, provided that any given institution of government remains within its allotted constitutional province, it is crucial that it should be permitted to carry out its functions without interference from the other branches. The importance of this principle is nowhere more apparent than in relation to the judiciary—particularly in its relationship with the executive. It is central to the most basic conception of the rule of law that the courts should be left to dispense justice free from hindrance—or the fear of hindrance—by the government of the day. As the United Nations Commission on Human Rights observed in 1994, an independent judiciary is an 'essential prerequisite for the protection of human rights and for ensuring that there is no discrimination in the administration of justice'.[57]

This principle was, I am sorry to say, not always honoured by the previous British administration. Towards the end of its tenure, the last government began to criticise the judges when they held its policies and decisions unlawful on judicial review. The Special Rapporteur of the UN Human Rights Commission rightly expressed 'grave concern' at

[57] Resolution 1994/41 of the United Nations Human Rights Commission. See (1994) 20 *Commonwealth Law Bulletin* 957.

this behaviour.[58] The separation of powers, on which the British constitution is based, makes executive interference with the administration of justice wholly unacceptable.

Lord Nolan expressed the true position in terms that I doubt can be improved:

> The proper constitutional relationship of the executive with the courts is that the courts will respect all acts of the executive within its lawful province, and that the executive will respect all decisions of the courts as to what its lawful province is.[59]

The present administration recognises that this is how a mature, democratic government should relate to the courts.

It is only by respecting these elementary precepts of constitutionalism that a proper balance of power can be achieved, and democratic governance maintained. The unwritten constitutional order confers a great deal of flexibility not only on the judges but on all the institutions of government. Nevertheless, if any branch fails to respect the fundamental principles which determine the outer limits of its constitutional competence, the system cannot function. Judicial independence is just such a fundamental principle.

VI.   CONCLUSION

James Madison's *Federalist* papers on the separation of powers are widely regarded as one of the pre-eminent contributions to the subject. He asserted that, 'The accumulation of all powers ... in the same hands ... may justly be pronounced the very definition of tyranny.'[60] Madison devoted five papers to an analysis of how best to deal with this problem. His guiding principle was that 'a mere demarcation on parchment' was 'not a sufficient guard' against the over-concentration and abuse of power.[61]

This observation has particular resonance in relation to the British constitution, in which the division of power is based not on any written limits but, rather, on assent and cooperation between the various institutions

---

[58] Report of the United Nations Human Rights Commission's Special Rapporteur on the Indepedence of the Judiciary.
[59] *M v Home Office* [1992] QB 270, 314.
[60] *The Federalist Papers (No 51)* (London, 1987), 303.
[61] *Ibid*, at p 312.

of government. This characteristic accounts for the flexibility and the dynamism of the British conception of the separation of powers of which I have spoken this evening. Nevertheless, at the heart of the British constitution lies a longstanding and deeply-embedded agreement about the values on which the polity is based. From this consensus derives the hard-edges of the constitution, and the ultimate limits of the powers of the different branches of government.

It is this combination of the formal and the informal which has shaped the architecture of modern English public law. But care is needed on all sides if this uniquely British mode of constitutional evolution is to continue to work. As Lord Mustill has expressed it:

> Absent a written constitution much sensitivity is required of the parliamentarian, administrator and judge if the delicate balance of the unwritten rules [of judicial review] evolved ... in recent years is not to be disturbed, and all of the recent advances undone ... [T]he boundaries remain; they are of crucial significance in our private and public lives; and the courts should I believe make sure that they are not overstepped.[62]

These imperatives have been scrupulously observed by the judges as they have developed the modern law of judicial review, pushing the boundaries of public law forward where this has been appropriate, while being careful not to transgress the perimeter of their constitutional province. This philosophy also underlies the human rights legislation currently before Parliament, which will propel English administrative law into a new stage of its on-going evolution. And it is the same organic combination of principle and pragmatism which must guide the way as Britain faces up to the challenges of constitutional development that the next century is bound to bring.

[62] *R v Secretary of State for the Home Department, ex parte Fire Brigades Union* [1995] 2 AC 513, 567–68.

11

The Influence of Europe on Public Law in the United Kingdom

I. 'BRITAIN IN EUROPE': EUROPEAN LAW IN BRITAIN

I T GIVES ME great pleasure to address this Conference. I should like to congratulate the University of Oxford, its Institute of European and Comparative Law and Professor Markesinis for organising this Conference and bringing together some of the finest legal minds in Europe.

The theme of the Conference—'Britain in Europe'—is an expression which should be read as affirming our perception of Britain's role, in the new Millennium, as an active participant in Europe, within both the European Union and the Council of Europe. In order for the United Kingdom to play such a role, European law must influence and—to some extent—infiltrate our national legal order. In this sense, 'European law in Britain' is a necessarily and inevitable concomitant of 'Britain in Europe'. Although this phenomenon affects many branches of domestic law—as the contributions of other speakers today will demonstrate—I shall focus on the legal and constitutional implications of accommodating principles of European *public law* within the United Kingdom's legal framework.

There are two distinct (but related) aspects to this enquiry. First, how are principles of European public law to be given effect in Britain? How, in other words, does our constitution respond to the challenge of facilitating British membership of the European institutions? Secondly, once European law is thus received, what effect does it have on the future shape and direction of our system of public law?

II. THE LEGAL FACILITATION OF 'BRITAIN IN EUROPE'

I shall begin by considering the constitutional methodology by which principles of European public law are accommodated within the British legal framework. The ultimate challenge in this field is to facilitate Britain's full participation in matters European while remaining faithful to the enduring principles of domestic constitutionalism which lie at the heart of our legal system. This challenge—which engages constitutional theory at its most fundamental level—arises in relation to Britain's membership of both the European Union and the Council of Europe. Let me take each in turn.

A.   The British Constitution and the European Union

Central to the effective functioning of the European Union is the principle that European law should have uniform effect throughout all fifteen member states. As the Union expands, this will assume ever greater importance. National courts play a key role by seeking, wherever possible, to interpret national law consistently with Community law, thus ensuring that the latter takes effect throughout the Union.[1]

Occasionally, however, it is simply not feasible for a national court to construe domestic law in this way. As is well known, precisely this position was reached in the course of the *Factortame* litigation, in which the European Court of Justice held, and the British courts accepted, that in such situations domestic tribunals must be willing to set aside national legislation in order to secure effect for Community law.[2] In this way our courts have acquired a limited jurisdiction to review primary legislation and, to this extent, parliamentary sovereignty is curtailed so long as the United Kingdom remains part of the European Union. This, however, is to state the position in rather bald terms. In order properly to evaluate the constitutional implications of Community membership, it is essential to distinguish between what may be termed Parliament's *ultimate sovereignty* and its *contemporary sovereignty*.

Some commentators contend that the priority of Community law over national law can be rationalised so as to leave the theory of parliamentary supremacy in tact. Thus it is said that *Factortame* involved

---

[1] National courts do not, in fact, have any choice in this area. Community law directs that they must, by interpretative means, reconcile national and Community law whenever this is possible. This is known, in Community law, as the doctrine of indirect effect. See the decisions of the European Court of Justice in, *inter alia*, Case 14/83, *Von Colson v Land Nordrhein-Westfalen* [1984] ECR 1891; Case C–106/89, *Marleasing SA v La Comercial Internacional de Alimentacion SA* [1990] ECR I–4135.

[2] *R v Secretary of State for Transport, ex parte Factortame Ltd (No 2)* [1991] 1 AC 603.

nothing more than the application of a rule of construction.[3] I do not share that view. It is elemental that rules of interpretation yield in the face of sufficiently clear contrary enactment.[4] The rule of construction which was supposedly applied in *Factortame* did not, however, yield: it prevailed over a legislative scheme which was acknowledged to be incompatible. It follows that, as Professor Wade remarks, *Factortame* constituted 'much more than an exercise in construction'.[5] It is therefore quite clear that, for so long as the United Kingdom is a member of the European Union, Parliament's competence is limited in the sense that it may not enact legislation which is incompatible with directly effective Community law. For this reason, it can be said that the contemporary sovereignty of Parliament has been curtailed.[6]

However, it is necessary to keep in mind the distinct concept of Parliament's ultimate sovereignty which—according to Professor Trevor Hartley—entails that 'Community law will ... prevail [over inconsistent national law] *unless Parliament clearly and expressly states in a future Act that the latter is to override Community law*',[7] a view which derives support from Lord Denning's judgment in *Macarthys v Smith*.[8] On this approach, Parliament retains the theoretical capacity to derogate explicitly from Community law in exceptional circumstances. And, although not all commentators agree with this analysis,[9] it is universally accepted

---

[3] See *inter alios*, Sir John Laws, 'Law and Democracy' [1995] *PL* 72, 89. This construction-based view derives some support from the speech of Lord Bridge in *R v Secretary of State for Transport, ex parte Factortame Ltd* [1990] 2 AC 85, 140.

[4] Take, eg, the well-established rule of construction which holds that, when it legislates, Parliament is assumed not to intend to interfere with the right of the citizen to gain access to justice. The celebrated decision of the House of Lords in *Anisminic Ltd v Foreign Compensation Commission* [1969] 2 AC 147 demonstrates that this rule of interpretation will yield only in the face of extremely clear statutory provision. Nevertheless, as Laws J explained in *R v Lord Chancellor, ex parte Witham* [1998] QB 575, it is necessarily the case that the rule will yield if Parliament legislates to that effect with sufficient clarity. It follows from this that it would be futile—and quite meaningless—to seek judicial review of *legislation* (as opposed to judicial review of *executive action* carried out in purported reliance on a statutory authority) on the ground that it interfered with the constitutional right of access to the courts. Since that right is enshrined only in a rule of construction, it cannot prevail over contrary enactment. For further comment, see MC Elliott, 'Reconciling Constitutional Rights and Constitutional Orthodoxy' [1997] *CLJ* 474.

[5] H W R Wade, 'Sovereignty—Revolution or Evolution?' (1996) 112 *LQR* 568, 570.

[6] See also *R v Secretary of State for Employment ex parte Equal Opportunities Commission* [1995] 1 AC 1.

[7] TC Hartley, *The Foundations of European Community Law* 4th edn, (Oxford, Oxford University Press, 1998), p 255 (emphasis added).

[8] *Macarthys Ltd v Smith* [1979] 3 All ER 325, 329.

[9] Eg, H W R Wade, 'Sovereignty—Revolution or Evolution?' (1996) 112 *LQR* 568, 570–71.

that Parliament, if it wished, could enact legislation to effect the withdrawal of the United Kingdom from the European Union, thereby restoring its absolute supremacy. In this sense, therefore, Parliament's ultimate sovereignty undoubtedly remains intact.

The importance of this point should not be underestimated. The survival of Parliament's ultimate supremacy, although a theoretical point in one sense, does have some tangible implications. It serves to emphasise that the limitation of Parliament's competence which EU membership involves does not render sovereignty a dead letter. Community membership does not, therefore, open the door to a more thoroughgoing theory of limited sovereignty embracing a whole series of higher order laws to which Parliament would be subject;[10] and this, in turn, impacts upon a range of public law issues—such as the constitutional basis of judicial review[11] and the proper role of the courts in public law proceedings[12]—which have been, and continue to be, profoundly influenced by the supremacy principle. The crucial point, therefore, is that while the theory of parliamentary sovereignty has unquestionably been modified by our membership of the European Union, it nevertheless remains a key constitutional foundation that continues to shape the public law superstructure which it supports.

---

[10] A number of commentators have, in recent years, argued in favour of just such a thoroughgoing limitation of Parliament's legislative competence: see, *inter alios,* Sir Robin Cooke, 'Fundamentals' [1988] *NZLJ* 158; Lord Woolf, '*Droit Public*—English Style' [1995] *PL* 57 (although cf Lord Woolf, 'Judicial Review—The Tensions Between the Executive and the Judiciary' (1998) 114 *LQR* 579); Sir John Laws, 'Law and Democracy' [1995] *PL* 72 and 'The Constitution: Morals and Rights' [1996] *PL* 622. My own views on this subject can be found in 'Judges and Decision-Makers: The Theory and Practice of *Wednesbury* Review' [1996] *PL* 59. For a useful overview of this discourse, see R Mullender, 'Parliamentary Sovereignty, the Constitution, and the Judiciary' (1998) 49 *NILQ* 138.

[11] For an explanation of how the principle of parliamentary sovereignty profoundly affects the way in which judicial review is justified in constitutional terms, see H W R Wade and CF Forsyth, *Administrative Law* 7th edn, (Oxford, Oxford University Press, 1994), pp 41–6; CF Forsyth, 'Of Fig Leaves and Fairy Tales: The Ultra Vires Doctrine, the Sovereignty of Parliament and Judicial Review' [1996] *CLJ* 122; MC Elliott, 'The Demise of Parliamentary Sovereignty? The Implications for Justifying Judicial Review' (1999) 115 *LQR* 119; MC Elliott, 'The Ultra Vires Doctrine in a Constitutional Setting: Still the Central Principle of Administrative Law' [1999] *CLJ* 129. Opposing views are expressed by D Oliver, 'Is the Ultra Vires Rule the Basis of Judicial Review?' [1987] PL 543; Sir John Laws, 'Law and Democracy' [1995] *PL* 72; Sir John Laws, 'Illegality: The Problem of Jurisdiction' in M Supperstone and J Goudie (eds), *Judicial Review* (London, Butterworths, 1997); P P Craig, 'Ultra Vires and the Foundations of Judicial Review' [1998] *CLJ* 63.

[12] See below, s 3, and also my 'Judges and Decision-Makers: The Theory and Practice of *Wednesbury* Review' [1996] *PL* 59.

B.   The British Constitution and the European Convention on Human Rights

Let me turn, now, to the European Convention on Human Rights. Although states are not legally obliged to incorporate the Convention into national law,[13] the rights of the individual tend to be better protected when incorporation is effected.[14] This is particularly so in countries—like the United Kingdom—which do not possess domestic bills of rights. For this reason, incorporation of the Convention into our national law has long been overdue, and it gives me great personal pleasure to be able to say that this situation will be remedied on 2 October 2000, when the Act will be implemented.

I have already observed that one of the fundamental challenges posed by EU membership concerns the accommodation of Community law within the British constitutional framework. A comparable issue arises in relation to the European Convention—namely, how best to reconcile the need for an effective regime of rights protection with the constitutional structure of the United Kingdom?

The imperative of balancing these two objectives is central to the scheme of the new legislation. To this end, all public authorities will be placed under a wholly new obligation to respect human rights as they discharge their functions,[15] and the courts will be placed under a strong

---

[13] See *eg, The Guardian and The Observer v United Kingdom* (1991) Series A, v 216.

[14] A number of commentators have suggested that the courts, through the medium of the common law, *can* protect human rights adequately in the absence of incorporation: see, *inter alios*, Lord Browne-Wilkinson, 'The Infiltration of a Bill of Rights' [1992] PL 397; Sir John Laws, 'Is the High Court the Guardian of Fundamental Constitutional Rights?' [1993] *PL 59*; M Hunt, *Using Human Rights Law in English Courts* (Oxford, Hart Publishing, 1997). These theories are not, however, supported by the practice of the courts. Notwithstanding that the courts subject decisions which engage fundamental rights to 'the most anxious scrutiny' *(R v Secretary of State for the Home Department, ex parte Bugdaycay* [1987] AC 514, 531, *per* Lord Bridge), the courts, ultimately, have refused—for good constitutional reasons (on which see my 1998 National Heritage Lecture, 'Constitutional Reform in the United Kingdom: British Solutions to Universal Problems' (Washington DC, May 1998, now chapter 4 in this volume)—to depart from the *Wednesbury* standard of review. Incorporation, therefore, *will* mark the inception of a more rigorous system of rights protection, given that the emphasis will then shift, in human rights cases, from rationality to proportionality (on which see below and also my 1998 Tom Sargant Memorial Lecture, 'The Development of Human Rights in Britain under an Incorporated Convention on Human Rights' [1998] *PL* 221). For further discussion see below, s 3.

[15] Human Rights Act 1998, s 6(1).

duty[16] to construe legislation, wherever possible, consistently with the Convention rights.[17] Crucially, however, when national legislation cannot be construed in this way, the judges will *not* be empowered to set aside parliamentary legislation.[18] Instead, the higher courts[19] will be permitted to declare that national law is incompatible with human rights.[20] This will trigger a fast-track procedure under which the Government may, subject to parliamentary approval, amend the offending legislation.[21] This scheme, it has been said, effects 'an ingenious and successful reconciliation of the principles of parliamentary sovereignty and the need for effective domestic remedies'.[22]

As with the impact of EU membership, however, it is important to recognise that, while the ultimate principle of legislative supremacy is emphatically preserved by our new human rights system, there will nevertheless—quite rightly—be implications of a more practical nature for the sovereignty doctrine. The balance which the Human Rights Act seeks to strike will be secured by maintaining the sovereignty principle, while changing the environment within which it is exercised. The new powers of the higher courts to issue declarations of incompatibility,[23] and the duty incumbent upon Ministers to draw Parliament's attention to the human rights implications of draft legislation,[24] will focus legislators' minds more clearly than ever before on fundamental rights issues.

Consequently, while Parliament will unequivocally retain its sovereignty, it will be much less likely to use it in a manner that is insensitive to the values embodied in the Convention. What this will reduce to is a political doctrine of legislative self-restraint in

---

[16] Lord Cooke, who, of course, has extensive knowledge of the New Zealand Bill of Rights Act 1990, has said that the interpretative obligation in the British draft legislation 'is, if anything, slightly stronger than the New Zealand section. If it is scrupulously complied with, in a major field the common law approach to statutory interpretation will never be the same again; moreover, this will prove a powerful Bill indeed.' See HL Deb, 3 November 1997, col 1273.

[17] Human Rights Act 1998, s 3(1).

[18] Neither the courts' interpretative obligation nor the issue of a declaration of incompatibility under s 4 shall affect 'the validity, continuing operation or enforcement' of any primary legislation. See ss 3(2)(b) and 4(6) (a).

[19] As defined in s 4(5).

[20] See s 4.

[21] See s 10 and sch 2.

[22] Lord Lester of Herne Hill, HL Deb, 18 November 1997, col 521.

[23] See s 10.

[24] See s 17.

deference to human rights considerations. The fundamental parameters represented by sovereignty theory will therefore remain, but the dynamics of the relationships between the courts, the executive and Parliament will, within those ultimate limits, subtly change. In this manner, an accommodation is once again reached between, on the one hand, embracing the influences which inevitably follow from Britain's participation in Europe and, on the other hand, adhering to the hallowed principles on which our constitution has—for over three hundred years—been founded.

III. THE LEGAL CONSEQUENCES OF 'BRITAIN IN EUROPE'

I have concentrated, thus far, on how European influences are received into British law—how, in other words, 'Britain in Europe' is facilitated at the level of constitutional theory. I now turn to the second issue which I identified in my opening remarks—the question of how European public law influences the development of specific principles of administrative law in Britain. It will quickly become apparent that these two implications of Britain's being 'in Europe' are, in reality, two sides of the same coin, because the extent to which European influences may affect the development of English public law is ultimately a function of the constitutional framework within which that system of public law subsists. Let me illustrate this argument through two examples. I will turn, shortly, to the principle of proportionality. First, however, I wish to consider the doctrine of legitimate expectation.

A. The Doctrine of Legitimate Expectation

a. Introduction

That principle is well-established in the law of the European Union,[25] and our own courts have also embraced it, recognising its capacity both for protecting against arbitrary treatment and upholding the principle of legal certainty, both of which are central to the rule of law.[26] Thus it

---

[25] For an overview, see P P Craig, 'Substantive Legitimate Expectations in Domestic and Community Law' [1996] *CLJ* 289, 304–10.

[26] On the inception of legitimate expectation as an established ground of review in English administrative law, see CF Forsyth, 'The Provenance and Protection of Legitimate Expectations' [1988] *CLJ* 238.

is now well established in English law that expectations can be protected procedurally by, for example, requiring consultation or a hearing before established practice is departed from. The European Court of Justice, however, has gone further, holding that the expectation doctrine possesses a substantive, as well as a procedural, dimension.[27] The question whether English administrative law should follow suit has generated a good deal of controversy in our courts.

b.   Three Models of Legitimate Expectation in English Law

Consideration of the domestic case law discloses three competing conceptions of legitimate expectation. The first holds that the expectations of individuals can only ever be protected by the provision of some form of procedural relief. Laws J (now Laws L J) advocated this *procedural model* in the *Richmond* case, holding that 'the law of legitimate expectation ... only goes so far as to say that there may arise conditions in which, if policy is to be changed, a specific person or class of persons affected must first be notified and given the right to be heard'.[28]

Secondly, there is the *rationality model*. This holds that legitimate expectation offers a largely—but not exclusively—procedural protection. On this view, individuals' expectations will normally be protected by means of a court order requiring a certain procedure to be followed before the competent agency decides whether or not its policy should be changed. This second model, however, recognises that a given policy change may, exceptionally, cause such extreme prejudice to citizens that altering the policy is not a step which is open to rational decision-makers. The courts may therefore intervene in a substantive manner—by preventing the policy change from taking place, or by requiring the policy not to be applied to the applicant—when the agency's decision to change its policy was, in the first place, *Wednesbury*[29] unreasonable. Precisely this approach was adopted by the Court of Appeal in *Hargreaves*.[30]

---

[27] For discussion of the substantive legitimate expectation doctrine both in English and European law, see Craig, above n 25.

[28] *R v Secretary of State for Transport, ex parte Richmond-upon-Thames London Borough Council* [1994] 1 WLR 74, 93. See also *R v Secretary of State for the Home Department, ex parte Ruddock* [1987] 1 WLR 1482.

[29] *Associated Provincial Picture Houses Ltd v Wednesbury Corporation* [1948] 1 KB 223.

[30] *R v Secretary of State for the Home Department, ex parte Hargreaves* [1997] 1 WLR 906.

In the course of giving its judgment in that case, the Court of Appeal considered a third, *substantive model* of legitimate expectation. That approach had been advocated by Sedley J (now Sedley L J) in *Hamble Fisheries,* who opined that it is 'the court's duty to protect the interests of those individuals whose expectation of different treatment has a legitimacy which out-tops the policy choice which threatens to frustrate it'.[31] On this view, it is for the court to balance the merits of the relevant policy against the value of the individual's expectation and, whenever the latter—*in the court's opinion*—outweighs the former, substantive relief may be granted in order to preclude departure from the policy.

Although this fully substantive conception of legitimate expectation was emphatically rejected by the Court of Appeal in *Hargreaves*, it has now resurfaced in the decision of a differently constituted Court of Appeal in *Coughlan*.[32] The respondent health authority in that case was seeking to implement a new policy with regard to the service provided to those in long term nursing care. However, adoption of the new policy would have involved the closure of the residential facility where the applicant was being cared for which, in turn, breached an earlier undertaking given to the applicant to the effect that she would be able to remain at that facility for the rest of her life. This undertaking, said the Court, gave rise to a legitimate expectation. The question, therefore, was how it ought to be protected.

Had the Court of Appeal followed its earlier decision in *Hargreaves*, it would have concluded that the applicant was entitled to be consulted, but that substantive relief could not issue unless the policy change was truly irrational. The Court, however, did not follow its earlier decision.[33] Instead, it held that when an individual holds a legitimate expectation, it is for the judiciary to balance the public interest in allowing public bodies

---

[31] *R v Ministry of Agriculture Fisheries and Food, ex parte Hamble (Offshore) Fisheries Ltd* [1995] 2 All ER 714, 731.

[32] *R v North and East Devon Health Authority, ex parte Coughlan (The Times,* 20 July 1999).

[33] Lord Woolf M R, giving the judgment of the Court of Appeal, explained that the *Coughlan* case involved an 'abuse of power' which amounted to a 'failure of substantive fairness'. This distinguished it from cases—of which *Hargreaves* was presumably one—'where what is in issue is a conventional application of policy or exercise of discretion'. It is, however, difficult to understand what the exact distinction between *Coughlan* and *Hargreaves* is supposed to be. Because terms such as 'abuse of power' and 'failure of substantive fairness' do not appear to bear any precise meaning, their use creates the impression of an *ex post facto* rationalisation of a judicial decision to intervene, rather than the deployment of principled criteria which determine the proper scope of review in such cases.

to formulate new policies against the private interest of individuals who are, in some way, disadvantaged by policy changes. The Court could see no reason why the judiciary, rather than the public authority, should not ultimately determine whether the desirability of the new policy was sufficient to justify the frustration of the individual's expectation.[34]

It is strongly arguable that this conclusion is contrary to the fundamental principles on which our system of administrative law is founded and incompatible with the leading authorities. Let me explain why.

c.   Legitimate Expectation and Constitutional Theory

When a court protects an expectation by procedural means, this has a minimal impact on the administrative autonomy of the relevant authority. This is because the imposition of a procedural requirement merely constitutes a condition precedent to the proposed policy change, and does not attenuate the authority's ultimate freedom to alter its policy. This, in turn, means that procedural protection of legitimate expectations carries with it no risk of the courts transgressing their proper constitutional bounds, since they are concerned with *how*, not *whether*, the policy is changed. Hence no constitutional difficulty is disclosed: the courts remain within their proper sphere, and the ultimate autonomy of public authorities is never placed in jeopardy.

The position is very different if expectations are protected substantively. The provision of substantive relief may well have the effect of preventing the agency in question from departing from its existing policy which, in turn, represents a significant reduction in the freedom which the public authority enjoys in formulating and implementing policy. Substantive enforcement also has important implications for the role of the court since, once judges begin to adjudicate on the content and substance of executive decisions, the risk arises that they may, in effect, take over the role of the decision-maker, so exceeding their proper constitutional function.[35] These are precisely the issues which

---

[34] 'There is no suggestion in [the relevant case law] ... that the final arbiter of [the] justification [for departing from existing policy], rationality apart, is the decision-maker rather than the court,' *per* Lord Woolf M R.

[35] In *Coughlan*, the Court of Appeal stated that 'it is unimportant whether the unfairness [which affects an administrative decision] is analytically within or beyond the power conferred by law: on either view public law today reaches it'. (The Court of Appeal attributed this view to Lord Scarman, on the basis of his speech in *R v Inland Revenue Commissioners, ex parte National Federation for Self-Employed and Small Businesses Ltd* [1982] AC 617.) This, however, is fundamentally inconsistent with the

the Court of Appeal overlooked in *Coughlan,* and it is for this reason that it is strongly arguable that the decision is inconsistent with well-established constitutional principle.

It is certainly not my view that the courts should never review public decision-making on substantive grounds. However, in light of the constitutional implications which I have outlined, it is essential that they exercise particular caution in this area. The real issue, therefore, is not whether expectations should *ever* be protected substantively, but, rather, the *circumstances* in which substantive relief should be issued.

The difficulty with the approach adopted in *Coughlan* is that it permits a court to prevent a change in policy whenever it disagrees with the public authority's evaluation of the case. Arguably this discloses a fundamental misconception of the relationship which obtains, within our constitutional framework, between Parliament, the administration and the judiciary. It is not the constitutional function of a court to decide what the policy of the executive ought to be, and whether that policy can be changed. That is properly a matter for the decision-making agency which Parliament has designated.

It is for precisely this reason that our courts have long held that the appropriate standard of review in cases which engage issues of substance is the *Wednesbury* doctrine. By permitting judicial intervention only when the public authority has acted as no reasonable body could, the *Wednesbury* principle strikes the correct balance between judges and decision-makers. It reflects the constitutional philosophy on which our administrative law is founded, according to which it is the prerogative of the sovereign Parliament to choose upon whom decision-making power ought to be conferred, and that it is therefore unacceptable for the judicial branch to seize that power for itself.

The courts have accepted with striking consistency that—for these good constitutional reasons—*Wednesbury* traces the perimeter of their

---

orthodox position, affirmed by the decision of the House of Lords in *Boddington v British Transport Police* [1988] 2 WLR 639, according to which the ultra vires principle is the organising concept upon which the law of judicial review is founded. Once this is accepted, it becomes clear that judicial review is about identifying the precise location of the line which traces the perimeter of the competence which Parliament has conferred upon administrative agencies. Conceptualising administrative law in this way serves to emphasise the fact that the agency possesses a core of discretion with which the courts have no licence to interfere. It appears that the Court of Appeal's misconception, in *Coughlan,* of this foundational issue caused it to overlook the importance of drawing the limits of the supervisory jurisdiction in a manner which accords proper respect to the autonomy of executive decision-makers.

jurisdiction in matters of substance. Nowhere is this more readily apparent than in the field of human rights. Although British courts—it has been said—are 'straining at the leash' to give greater effect to fundamental rights,[36] they have recognised that, pending legislative intervention, it would be constitutionally improper for them to depart from *Wednesbury* as their guiding principle in matters of substance.[37] One of the most surprising aspects of the *Coughlan* decision is that it departs from this well-established line of authority without attempting to justify that departure.

Let me offer a final thought on this subject before moving on. The public law jurisprudence of other European countries quite properly forms a rich source of inspiration for our own courts: the scope for cross-fertilisation is immense. Nevertheless, the extent to which principles of European public law can influence and take root in domestic law is ultimately constrained by the constitutional framework within which English administrative law subsists. That framework quite clearly indicates that the concept of substantive expectation, as it exists in national law, must be kept within carefully defined limits—and it is the constitutional duty of our courts to recognise that.

B.   Proportionality

Let me now turn to doctrine of proportionality. In light of the important role which it occupies in the jurisprudence of the European Courts of Justice[38] and Human Rights,[39] I wish to examine the extent to which it has influenced—and ought to influence—English public law.

a.   Introduction

A good starting point is the *Smith* case,[40] which involved a challenge to the government's policy (since suspended) that prohibited persons of homosexual orientation from serving in the armed forces. This, said the

---

[36] MJ Beloff and H Mountfield, 'Unconventional Behaviour: Judicial Uses of the European Convention in England and Wales' [1996] *European Human Rights Law Review* 467, 495.

[37] The attitude of the courts to the *Wednesbury* principle in the human rights context is discussed below, s 3.2.

[38] See eg, Case 120/78, *Cassis de Dijon* [1979] ECR 649.

[39] See eg, *Sunday Times v United Kingdom* (1979) 2 EHRR 245.

[40] [1996] QB 517.

applicants, constituted a breach of Article 8 of the European Convention, which requires respect for an individual's private life. Having accepted that the applicants' human rights were engaged, Simon Brown L J, in the Divisional Court, went on to consider whether there existed a compelling public interest which could justify that policy. He concluded that the arguments were finely balanced, but that, in his view, those seeking to condemn the policy had the stronger case.[41] Thus it appears that, had the courts used the proportionality test in *Smith*, they may well have concluded that the qualification placed on the applicants' rights was not proportionate to the aim being pursued. Indeed, this was the conclusion which the European Court reached when it adjudicated on this case last year.[42]

However, the domestic courts did not analyse the facts of *Smith* by reference to the proportionality principle. Instead, they held that the government's policy would be unlawful only if it could 'properly be stigmatised as irrational'.[43] Although Lord Bingham M R held that the greater the prima facie human rights infringement, 'the more the court will require by way of justification before it is satisfied that the decision is reasonable [in the *Wednesbury* sense]',[44] it remains the case that, at the present time, English courts continue to evaluate the legality of decisions which engage human rights by reference to the rationality test, not the proportionality principle.

Against this background, I should like to address two specific points. I will consider, in a moment, the likelihood of proportionality taking root as a general principle of English administrative law. First, however, let me focus on the domestic role of proportionality in the particular context of human rights.

b.   Proportionality, English Law and Human Rights

It may, at first glance, seem odd that the English courts have refused to deploy the proportionality doctrine in human rights cases, particularly

[41] *Ibid*, at p 533.
[42] *Lustig-Prean and Becket v United Kingdom; Smith and Grady v United Kingdom* (*The Times*, 11 October 1999).
[43] *Smith*, above n 40, at p 540.
[44] Above n 40 at p 554, following the decision of the House of Lords in *R v Secretary of State for the Home Department, ex parte Brind* [1991] 1 AC 696, which—pending the entry into force of the Human Rights Act 1998—remains the leading authority on the status of the European Convention in English law and on the standard of review which is to be applied in human rights cases.

in light of the role which it plays at the European level. In order to understand why this position obtains, it is necessary to look to the constitutional framework within which our courts develop public law.

As I remarked earlier, the *Wednesbury* principle reflects a particular conception of the respective constitutional roles of the judiciary and the executive, according to which primary responsibility for decision-making rests with public authorities acting under powers conferred by Parliament. While the courts serve a crucial function—by ensuring that public administration is conducted according to law—their role is, ultimately, secondary. This means that a government decision cannot be overturned simply because a court disagrees with it.

There are three good reasons which explain why this is so. First, there exists a *constitutional imperative*: if Parliament confers decision-making power on a particular agency, the courts would frustrate Parliament's sovereign will if they arrogated that power to themselves. Secondly, there is the *pragmatic imperative*: the courts, particularly on substantive matters of policy, have considerably less expertise than the designated authority; it is, therefore, desirable that the authority itself should make such decisions because it is better equipped to do so. And, thirdly, there exists a *democratic imperative*: the electoral system operates as an important safeguard against misuse of public power by requiring many public authorities to submit themselves to the verdict of the electorate at periodic intervals. If this system of political accountability is to function, it is important that the decision-making role of those agencies is not usurped by the courts.

This is the constitutional philosophy which gives rise to the distinction between legality and merits, and which is given practical effect by *Wednesbury*, which permits judicial intervention on substantive grounds only when the court concludes that a decision is irrational.[45]

---

[45] The position is very different, of course, in relation to matters of procedure. It is open to the courts to impugn issues of decision-making procedure, and to require a better process to be followed, without first having to conclude that the original procedure followed by the agency was so defective that no reasonable agency would ever have adopted it. The *Wednesbury* doctrine therefore operates to confine the role of the reviewing court only in relation to matters of substance, not procedure. Space precludes detailed analysis of why this is so. However, the essential reasoning is captured well by J Jowell, 'Of Vires and Vacuums: The Constitutional Context of Judicial Review' [1999] *PL* 448, 451–52: '[T]he tenets of procedural fairness do not require a utilitarian evaluation of preferred outcomes. They are not based upon policy evaluations best suited to elected officials or their agents in a democracy ... [I]t is not seriously contended that the imposition of procedural norms is beyond the constitutional capacity of judges,

In contrast, the proportionality principle would require the judiciary to make a far more detailed evaluation of the merits of public decisions which, in turn, would fundamentally change the nature of the relationship which obtains between judges and decision-makers. As Simon Brown L J commented in *Smith*, although British judges fully recognise that 'the protection of human rights is ... a matter with which the courts are particularly concerned and for which they have an undoubted responsibility', they nevertheless 'owe a duty too to remain within their constitutional bounds and not trespass beyond them'.[46]

It is true that English courts will begin to use the tool of proportionality in cases which affect fundamental rights once the Human Rights Act enters into force in October.[47] Crucially, however, they will do so because Parliament will have ordained that they should. In our constitutional system, the three branches of government are not equal and coordinate: Parliament is the senior partner, and Parliament alone is able to change the constitutional ground rules. This explains why, notwithstanding the considerable influence exerted by the principle of proportionality, English courts have, until now, been unable to embrace it in the domestic context. This, in turn, illustrates one of the fundamental themes of my address today: that, while European public law strongly influences the development of domestic law, the extent to which those influences may actually take root is ultimately determined by the constitutional context within which English administrative law is located.

c.   *Proportionality: A General Principle of English Public Law?*

Let me address one final point. Once proportionality does come to be used by English courts in human rights cases, the critical question will become whether this will prompt a change in the standard of review, from rationality to proportionality, in *all* public law cases, whether or not they possess a human rights dimension.

who aim thereby not to achieve any particular social or economic objective but to ensure only that the decision was fairly arrived at.'

[46] [1996] QB 517, 541.

[47] Although the Act does not explicitly refer to the principle of proportionality, it is clearly implicit in the scheme of the legislation that the courts will be permitted to make recourse to that doctrine. In particular, s 2(1) directs that, when British courts and tribunals are dealing with issues which relate to the Convention, they must take into account (*inter alia*) the jurisprudence of the European Court of Human Rights which is, of course, imbued with the theory of proportionality.

Some writers urge that proportionality *should* be used as a general principle of administrative law,[48] arguing that it constitutes a more transparent and structured methodology than what has been termed the 'blunt tool'[49] of *Wednesbury* unreasonableness. However, I do not share this view. The fact that proportionality will become an established ground of judicial review in cases brought under the Human Rights Act does not mean that it will become the appropriate standard of review in every public law case. This follows for two related reasons.

The courts have rightly refused to use the proportionality test until the Human Rights Act is activated. The entry into force of that Act will not, of course, have any bearing on the consequences which follow from applying the proportionality doctrine: it will remain the case that, in using proportionality as a ground of review, executive action will be subjected to considerably more rigorous scrutiny than it is, presently, on *Wednesbury* review. The effect of the Act, therefore, is not to change the implications of proportionality-based review but, rather, to ordain that the use of proportionality is constitutionally acceptable notwithstanding that it carries such implications. In this sense, the Act will form a warrant which will confer constitutional legitimacy on proportionality-based review. It is, however, perfectly clear from the Human Rights Act that this warrant extends only to cases which, in the first place, engage fundamental human rights. It follows that the considerations based on constitutional propriety which have, to date, rightly deterred English courts from embracing proportionality will continue to apply to cases which do not fall under the new human rights legislation: it is the Act which will justify the courts' shifting from rationality—to proportionality-based review, and it is therefore the Act which ought to determine the compass of the proportionality principle.

A second factor points towards the same conclusion. It is already well-established that judicial review does not constitute a monolithic standard of supervision. Rather, the intensity of review in any particular case is determined by its facts and context. For instance, the courts accept that it is appropriate to adopt a relatively deferential attitude to

---

[48] See *inter alios*, J Jowell and A Lester, 'Proportionality: Neither Novel nor Dangerous' in J Jowell and D Oliver (eds), *New Directions in Judicial Review* (London, Stevens, 1988); PP Craig, 'The Impact of Community Law on Domestic Public Law' in P Leyland and T Woods (eds), *Administrative Law Facing the Future: Old Constraints and New Horizons* (London, Blackstone Press, 1997).

[49] This term was used to describe the *Wednesbury* principle by Craig, above n 48 at p 283.

decisions concerning national economic policy.[50] In contrast, although they are, at present, ultimately constrained by the *Wednesbury* principle, the courts certainly subject executive action which engages human rights to much more thoroughgoing scrutiny. Thus it is possible to envisage a continuum along which cases of different types lie, ranging from those which attract only a modest degree of scrutiny, to human rights cases which lie at the other end of the spectrum and which are, quite properly, examined with great rigour. This recognises that the need for judicial review varies according to the context. Different levels of intervention—and tools of differing intensity—are therefore required at the various points which lie along the continuum. Fundamental rights possess a normative resonance which makes the incisive tool of proportionality an appropriate method by which to uphold them. Such a high degree of judicial intervention in the administrative process is not, however, appropriate in other contexts. It is for this reason that the intrusive device of proportionality should be confined to the special area of human rights, and should not be perceived as a panacea which constitutes a standard of review suitable for every case.

IV.   CONCLUSION

This Conference is extremely timely. We are presently living in a period of significant constitutional change in the United Kingdom, and those changes are occurring within a public law environment that is no longer purely domestic, but which, instead, embraces the rich seam of jurisprudence and public law scholarship which subsists within Europe. Just as British administrative law can—and, once our judges begin to interpret the European Convention, increasingly will—influence the development of European public law, so the European principles enrich national law. Through these processes of cross-fertilisation we begin to see the emergence of common principles of European public law which, in turn, helps to ensure that all European citizens benefit from certain benchmark standards as they interact with national and transnational public bodies.

However, against this background of dynamic development, one challenge remains constant. I refer, of course, to the imperative of

---

[50] See eg, *Nottinghamshire County Council v Secretary of State for the Environment* [1986] AC 240.

embracing the influences which arise from our full participation in Europe in a manner which is consistent with the principles on which our own constitution is founded. The need to balance these objectives is a recurrent theme in modern British public law. It is reflected in the idea that, although Parliament's contemporary sovereignty is limited by the European doctrine of primacy, its ultimate supremacy remains. That same ethos of balance lies at the heart of the Human Rights Act, which unequivocally recognises the sovereignty of Parliament, while substantially changing the environment within which that sovereignty will, in the future, be exercised. And it is also possible to discern—in the way that our courts develop specific principles of administrative law—a clear awareness of the need to reconcile European influences with constitutional principle. Hence (with one or two exceptions) the courts' recognition that, pending legislative intervention, the *Wednesbury* principle marks the proper standard of substantive review.

Our constitutional landscape is changing, and administrative law in Britain and Europe are growing closer together. This is a natural consequence of Britain's presence in Europe, and it is of great benefit to the citizen. British public law's embrace of European influences is therefore as inevitable as it is desirable—but these developments must not occur at the expense of ignoring the constitutional foundation on which domestic public law rests. These two objectives are not, however, mutually exclusive. Far from it. They represent the twin principles on which administrative in Britain must be based in the twenty-first century, and which will ensure the existence of a system of public law that accommodates both the uniqueness of Britain's constitution and its place within the European legal family.

Part 3

British and International Perspectives on Law and Constitution

12

Judicial Independence and the British Constitution

W E IN THE UK are in the midst of a major programme of constitutional reform, as Lord Rodger has said, launched by the Government of which I am a member. Our reforms will have important consequences for the judges, and there is public debate, as there should be, about those consequences. I would like to offer my own thoughts. First, to set the scene, I will summarise how judicial independence is secured in the United Kingdom, and especially in England and Wales. Secondly, in the light of the forthcoming reforms, I will speak about the position of our senior judges, the Law Lords. And finally I will touch on my own, ancient but still highly functional, office of Lord Chancellor, and how it serves both judicial independence and accountability.

I. JUDICIAL INDEPENDENCE

The need for an independent judiciary is recognised throughout the free world. It is a cornerstone of Britain's constitutional arrangements, as it is of yours, for without judicial independence, there can be no rule of law.

In this country, our constitution does not embody a full separation of powers. Our Parliamentary democracy makes for a considerable fusion of the executive and legislative branches. Unlike, for example, the position in the United States, every Cabinet Minister is a member of one or other House of Parliament. Taken with our doctrine of Parliamentary sovereignty, and the powerful influence of the executive upon the legislature, the judicial arm is not as strong, yet it must ensure that the executive is kept subject to the rule of the law.

We have, therefore, to take especial care to guarantee our judicial independence. We do so by various means, the first of which is *law and convention*. The security of tenure of our senior judges has been guaranteed by statute ever since the Act of Settlement of 1701. A senior judge can only be removed on the joint address of both Houses of Parliament, and this has never happened to an English judge. Our judges are also given security of remuneration. Their salaries cannot be reduced by Government action. The judges are also granted high official rank and the legal immunities necessary to perform their judicial duties.

But judicial independence does not depend only on the law. It is also nourished by a *political and a professional culture*. With us, this derives from the free and self-confident legal profession from which our judges are drawn. This enables every judge to look the Government, his fellow judges, or anybody else in the eye and do his duty, in the words of the judicial oath, 'without fear or favour, affection or ill-will'.

Yet another important bulwark of judicial independence in our system is the office of Lord Chancellor, to which I will return.

In return for the independence we guarantee to our judges, the trust we place in them is that they will carry out their duties impartially. I define impartiality as the absolute recognition and fulfilment by judges of an obligation of fidelity to law.

Against this background, concern has been voiced in some quarters that this Government's programme of constitutional reform will 'politicise' the judiciary and threaten their judicial independence.

The aim of our constitutional reform programme has been to decentralise power in the United Kingdom, and to enhance the citizen's power to enforce his human rights, within a more open society. We have already carried the devolution and Human Rights Acts into law. We have recently published a draft Freedom of Information Bill. And we are now engaged on House of Lords reform—unfinished business of a century ago.

However, the new legislation has been carefully framed to preserve the traditional constitutional restraints on judicial interpretation of the law, particularly the sovereignty Parliament. The Human Rights Act, for example, will lead the courts to exercise a more intensive form of scrutiny over Government and public authorities. The judges will have to deploy such concepts as proportionality and necessity, permitting the Government to cut down human rights only if it does so in response to a pressing social need. The courts *will* be drawn into a greater number of politically controversial issues. But they will *not* as a result be enabled to strike down Parliamentary legislation, although they will be able to declare it incompatible with the European Human Rights Convention. Whilst changing the nature of the interpretative process, the Act does not confer on the courts a licence to construe legislation in a way which arrogates to the judges a power completely to rewrite existing law: that is a task for Parliament and the executive.

In my view, the advent of the Human Rights Act makes no material difference to the position of the judiciary. The judges in this country are used to interpreting the law in controversial cases in a way which may bring them into conflict with the executive, but which respects our constitutional settlement. Judges in the House of Lords, and below, have traditionally made decisions, under the law, which were highly controversial—in landmark cases on civil liberties; on trade union immunities; on citizens' rights in time of war; on natural justice; on freedom of expression and freedom of the press; on contempt of court; and on the whole modern development of judicial review under which the judges have struck down executive decisions as contrary to law. The most that our reforms will do is to make a difference of degree, not kind; and one which will rightly enhance the role and standing of the judiciary.

II.   THE LAW LORDS

The vital role of interpreting the new legislation will fall above all to our most senior judges, the Law Lords.

Our highest appellate court is unusual in western democracies, in that it is an organic part of our legislature. This is an example of our flexible approach to the separation of powers. The appellate function of the House of Lords goes back many centuries, but in its modern form, it dates from 1876. And it is important of course to appreciate that this function is not exercised by the peers at large, but by a small and highly professional court. Although this court sits in our Parliament building, it consists only of the Law Lords.

The Law Lords are full members of the House of Lords. They may take part in the House's legislative activities, under certain conventions. They are 'cross-benchers' who have no connection with any political party. In particular, they avoid making any comment in the House on any issue that is, or may come, before them judicially. Within these conventions, the Law Lords make a distinctive contribution to the work of the House of Lords in debates on the administration of justice, and in the valuable specialist contributions they make to many Select

Committees. Their knowledge in these areas is unequalled and the House would be the loser without them. Therefore, to the question whether the House of Lords in its legislative capacity must lose the benefits the Law Lords confer because of the doctrine of the separation of powers, I say 'no' for two reasons: first, because we do not apply the doctrine strictly; and, secondly, provided their role in the legislature does not prejudice their primary role as our final appellate judges, there is no need to change a beneficial system.

Some suggest that Article 6 of the European Convention, which is entitled 'right to a fair trial', requires Britain, by a side wind from the guarantee of that right, to change our long-settled constitutional arrangements. But Article 6 requires a fair and impartial hearing, not a strict separation of powers. Provided a Law Lord hearing a case in the House of Lords has abstained from expressing a concluded view in the legislative chamber, on an issue coming before him judicially, then there will be no breach in my view of Article 6 if he sits.

The reform of the House of Lords is the next plank of the Government's reform programme. A Bill is currently passing through Parliament to remove the rights of hereditary peers to sit and vote in the House of Lords. A Royal Commission has been appointed to make recommendations on the role and functions of a reformed second chamber, and on the composition required to meet those needs. The Royal Commission has been asked to report by the end of this year.

Some commentators suggest that the time has come for legislation to remove our highest appellate court from the House of Lords, and to establish a separate Supreme Court. The Government will of course give careful consideration to any recommendations which the Royal Commission may make, but at present it does not regard the case for this legislative change as made out.

III.　THE LORD CHANCELLOR

As Lord Chancellor, I am a senior member of the Cabinet and a Minister of Justice. But I am also, like my predecessors over many centuries, a judge. In this capacity, I am the president of the appellate committee of the House of Lords, as I am of the other superior courts in England and Wales. This role is a significant part of our constitutional arrangements to protect the independence of the judiciary. Let me explain why.

I have already said that the fusion of executive and legislative power in this country, coupled with legislative supremacy, leaves the judicial branch correspondingly weak.

The judicial branch as a whole must also shoulder a degree of accountability. This does *not* mean that the judges can be made answerable for their judicial decisions, duly made, although these may of course be subject to review in the appeal courts.

Judicial accountability requires that the public must be able to see that justice is being done. Just as judicial impartiality is the other side of the coin of judicial independence, so open justice as witnessed by an attentive media is a strong spur to judicial impartiality in practice. This was recognised by the authors of the European Convention on Human Rights, which guarantees a hearing which is not only fair, but also normally takes place in public.

However, a modern democracy also demands accountability to Parliament and the public for the overall efficiency and effectiveness of the system of justice. This includes the good conduct of the judges and the proper use of public resources. We also need to have procedures for selecting the judges which ensure appointment strictly on merit.

Proper accountability must never be allowed to develop into improper pressure, which could encourage the judiciary to make decisions with a view to public or Parliamentary popularity. That would turn judicial independence into a sham.

Striking the balance between accountability and independence is never easy. The problem is universal, and different countries have different solutions.

The office of Lord Chancellor has evolved as the English solution to this problem. The office dates back at least to the eleventh century, and probably earlier. It is older than our Parliament, older than our democratic system. The Lord Chancellor is the head of the judiciary and President of the highest courts in the country. In this capacity, he is a serving judge. He is also a member of the executive, as a senior Cabinet Minister, and he presides over the upper house of the legislature. The office carries significant authority within all three branches of Government. This makes the Lord Chancellor uniquely well-qualified to protect the independence of the judiciary in this country.

Lord Chancellors always come to the office after a long career in the law, whether as judges or as senior advocates. Their profession puts independent individual judgment above all else. They come to the office imbued with the values that underpin our democracy: the rule of law; the independence of the judiciary from any executive interference; the duty of the courts to stand between citizen and state; and to confine public authorities within the law. The public and the judges can have a well-founded confidence that, for any Lord Chancellor, these values, together with the authority of his office, would be armour against executive pressure.

The value of a Lord Chancellor is that he upholds judicial independence and can mediate between the executive and judiciary when need be. The judiciary has a representative in the Cabinet, and the Cabinet in the judiciary. The Lord Chancellor can also speak to the public on behalf of the judges, in a way that professional judges themselves cannot. The office of Lord Chancellor is the guarantor of judicial independence in our constitution. It holds the different parts together, and withstands pressure from all sides.

Let me give you two examples of how the office of Lord Chancellor protects the independence of the judiciary. I spoke earlier about the importance of an appointments system which ensures that judicial appointments are made on merit. With us, as in the majority of countries, judicial appointments are made by the executive. It is thus important that there are checks within the system, which prevent candidates from being appointed on the ground of their political beliefs or on any other grounds which seem convenient to the executive, but are not justified on merit. In this country, the appointment or recommendation for appointment of judges is one of the Lord Chancellor's most important responsibilities. He provides executive involvement in the appointments process, without compromising judicial independence, because of his dual role, and because he exercises these important functions away from the fierce party political controversies in the House of Commons.

Like my predecessors, I make judicial appointments strictly on merit, and I have effective systems and resources to do so. My central policy is to appoint, or recommend for appointment, those candidates who satisfy the statutory qualifications and who best meet the criteria for appointment. This is without regard to factors such as gender, ethnic origin, marital status or disability. I believe strongly in equal opportunities and encourage applications from any individual who meets the criteria for appointment. I have said time and again to ethnic minority audiences: 'Don't by shy, apply'. However, I am resolutely opposed to any proposition that our courts should be sculpted to conform to any notion of social, political, gender or any other balance.

No one appointments system has a monopoly on delivering appointments based solely on merit. Methods of appointment vary, and different systems must reflect the different traditions, cultures and conventions of individual states. But it is vital that judicial appointments command the respect and confidence of the legal community, and of Parliament and public. I firmly believe that in this country they do, and I am content to be judged by the quality of the judicial products.

My second example relates to judicial accountability. The position of the Lord Chancellor enables him to be responsible, as a Minister, through Parliament to the public for the overall efficiency of the justice system, in a way in which the judiciary cannot. The Lord Chancellor is accountable for the overall quality of the Bench; for the good conduct and discipline of the judges; and the proper deployment of the substantial resources voted by Parliament for the administration of justice. If these are not delivered to the satisfaction of Government or Parliament, the Lord Chancellor is responsible to the Prime Minister—as no other judge can be, or should be.

In exercising his responsibility for the administration of justice, the Lord Chancellor must work in close cooperation with the judiciary. The Lord Chancellor is in an ideal position to mediate between the interests of the executive and the interests of the judiciary on difficult issues, such as the resourcing of the courts.

The role exercised by the Lord Chancellor depends on his position as head of the judiciary. Without it, he could not command the same respect and confidence of the judges, which is essential since he is responsible for their good conduct and discipline. In this capacity, it is important that he sits as a judge. By being the head of the judiciary, not in name but in substance because he sits, the Lord Chancellor commands the professional respect and confidence of the Judges and their acceptance of his role in relation to their discipline and conduct. Until the middle of this century, Lord Chancellors sat judicially for most of their time. Although the demands of the Lord Chancellor's responsibilities in Cabinet in Government generally and in the legislative chamber now make it impossible for me to sit frequently, all my recent predecessors in this office have sat judicially, except one who was Lord Chancellor for only a few months.

Like my predecessors, I exercise my discretion not to sit where I consider it would be improper to do so. I have no doubt that any future Lord Chancellor would do likewise. Provided that the Lord Chancellor has abstained from expressing concluded views on an issue coming before him judicially; and he does not sit in any case where the interests of the executive are directly engaged; there is no reason at all why he should not sit and preside judicially.

There are those who think that the time has come to dismantle the office of Lord Chancellor. They base themselves in part on a purist view of the separation of powers—which if pursued with purity would lead them to drive every Cabinet Minister from the House of Commons or the House of Lords. In part they also argue that the Government's programme of constitutional change will produce more politically controversial cases and make it impossible for the Lord Chancellor to sit judicially.

I am not persuaded this view is correct and I am re-enforced by my experience of the office. The role of the Lord Chancellor is to compensate for the fusion of powers elsewhere. The new constitutional settlement gives the judges greater powers to settle vires disputes between the Scottish Parliament, the various Assemblies and Westminster. It gives them powers under the Human Rights Act to declare Westminster legislation incompatible with the Convention. I accept that these responsibilities will increase the potential for controversy between the executive and the judiciary. But I draw the opposite conclusion from the critics. I am clear that the only effect these changes will have on the office of Lord Chancellor is to make it more valuable and necessary than ever, as a buffer between executive and judiciary; and as a bulwark of our constitution.

So I conclude these short remarks, in summary, by saying that judicial independence in principle and practice is fundamental to the functioning of a parliamentary democracy and to freedom under the law. And that our constitutional settlement, including the Law Lords, and the office of Lord Chancellor, provides for both independence and accountability. *And* that these features of our constitution have as relevant and useful a part to play in the future as they have in the past.

You have now heard enough from me about how we deal with the balance of judicial independence and accountability in this country. I look forward to benefiting from the experience and thoughts of others; and I wish you every success with your discussions.

13

The Common Origins of English and American Law

I.   INTRODUCTION

T HE MILLENNIUM LECTURES explore our legal system at a
time—the arrival of a new Millennium—that must be as good
as any, I suppose, for a stocktaking. I suppose, also, that you
can stocktake by looking backwards or forwards and, if you are a
politician as Lord Chancellors have to become, you could try to look in
both directions at the same time. So that I will do.

Let me look to America. The American Bar Association's decision to
hold its Annual Meeting in London in July, gives me an opportunity to
look backwards and forwards, to explore the close ties and common
history of our two systems; and to send a strong early welcome to our
American friends and colleagues.

When an English lawyer opens a volume of American law reports,
his first impression is of familiarity. The details of the law being applied
are not always instantly recognisable. It may take a few moments to
become acclimatised to the language of anti-trusts or first degree murder. The context of the judgment may require careful reading, because
the English lawyer may be referred to a case involving the boundaries
of federal jurisdiction, direct judicial review of legislative action or a
civil case conducted before a jury.

But, once differences of circumstance have been overcome, there is
an inescapable feeling that the American judgment is a familiar product
of the common law.

This stems from features deeply embedded in the structure, style and
language of Anglo-American judgments.[1] In structural terms, the analysis

---

[1] A Taylor von Mehren, *Law in the United States: A General and Comparative View*
(Dordrecht, Kluwer, 1988), p 5.

will start in the past. The common law judge must always work retrospectively, looking back to previous authority to deduce the current law. This process of restrained activism characterises the judicial function in all common law systems.

In stylistic terms, the judgment will be practical. The common law judge is charged only with resolving the dispute at issue,[2] and anything said beyond this function is strictly *obiter*. This narrow function focuses attention on the immediate interests of the parties, and away from broad theoretical constructs or considerations of public policy.[3]

Yet surely most fundamental to our sense of familiarity is the common language of legal argument. English and American laws classify issues in almost identical, and equally esoteric, ways. The most striking example of this phenomenon may be the trust. It has flourished in the hands of English and American judges, providing a subtle body of jurisprudence that now governs the proprietary consequences of situations encompassing charitable donations, equitable wrongdoing,[4] insolvency,[5] and, increasingly, unjust enrichment.[6] The rules are not identical. It would take a certain amount of research before an English lawyer was comfortable with the principles of the remedial constructive trust operated in America. But the conceptual foundations are indisputably shared, and the division between legal and equitable ownership sits at the heart of Anglo-American property law.

II.   HISTORICAL FOUNDATIONS

A.   The Advent of the Common Law

The reason for a basic affinity between English and American law is well known—English law arrived with the first settlers. During the colonial

---

[2] NB: there is no provision of the United States Constitution that specifies the function of the judge in litigation. This is taken for granted as governed by the common law.

[3] C Harlow, 'American Influences on Judicial Review', in Loveland (ed), *A Special Relationship: American Influence on Public Law in the UK* (Oxford, Clarendon, 1995).

[4] See especially the judgment of the Privy Council in *AG for Hong Kong v Reid* (1994)1 All ER 1.

[5] See eg, *Re Kayford Ltd (In Liquidation)* [1975] 1 WLR 279.

[6] This emerges clearly from the judgment of Lord Browne-Wilkinson in *West-deutsche Landesbank Girozentrale v Islington London Borough Council* (1996) 2 All ER 961

period, Provincial Charters required all legislation to comply with the laws applied in England, and the ultimate redress of litigants lay with the Privy Council in London. It is unsurprising that the conceptual tools and values of the common law became entrenched in the American legal establishment. Aspiring lawyers came to be educated at the Inns of Court. Over 2,500 copies of Blackstone were sold as the key practitioner text prior to Independence.[7]

B.   Independence: A Challenge to the Common Law

The colonial period came to a tumultuous end in 1776, when momentous differences were opened up across the Atlantic.[8] A network of British colonies became independent states, with great moral and religious diversity. Their cultural transformation was dramatic.[9]

An entirely new philosophy lay behind Independence. The 1776 Declaration roundly renounced English tradition. It proposed a fresh start based upon 'self-evident truths' and new rights 'to life, liberty and the pursuit of happiness'.[10] The new America was founded upon a culture where the rights of man were paramount, and the absolute elevation of rights was seen as the safest precaution against future tyranny.[11] Across independent America, state legislatures began to enact Bills of Rights, expressing the common principle that:

> All men ... have certain inherent rights, of which, when they enter into a state of society they cannot by any compact deprive or divest their posterity.[12]

---

[7] R Pound, 'The Development of American Law and its Deviation from English Law' (1951) 67 *LQR* 49.

[8] R Stevens, 'Public Lecture given to British Institute of United States in Boston in April 1983', (1985) 6 *Journal of Legal History* 336.

[9] For the extent of unpopularity of English law, see P Miller, *The Life of the Mind in America* (1965), pp 99–116.

[10] *Ibid.*

[11] As evidenced by the diary entries of John Adams, second President of the United States: *Diary and Autobiography of John Adams*, v 1, *Diary* (L H Butterfield ed, 1962), p 278 (27 December 1765).

[12] Quotation from the Virginian Bill of Rights, drafted by George Mason shortly after the 1776 Declaration of Independence.

This philosophy, culminating in the federal Bill of Rights, was a radical departure from contemporary English thinking.[13] Both nations had solid democratic beliefs, under the conviction that government should obey the popular will. Both nations recognised the imperative of protecting individuals from the excesses of government. But in England, attention was focused on the democratic *structure* of government. Cromwell had encouraged experimentation with governmental structure, and English lawyers were proud of the mixed monarchy of King and Parliament which had emerged as the triumphant product of the Civil War. This inherent structural emphasis was advanced by the writings of Bentham.[14] He drove a firm wedge between law and morality and laid weight on the form, not the content, of law-making. In this way, the promise by early seventeenth century judges to annul Acts of Parliament that proved 'against common right and reason'[15] was soon forgotten, and constitutional reform in the nineteenth century was geared towards structural accountability.

Structural considerations never assumed such singular importance in America, for two reasons. First, it is argued that late eighteenth century America was a more egalitarian society, in which the need to protect the people from the ruling classes was less immediate than in an aristocratic England.[16] The most pressing need in America was to establish a legal framework that accommodated the country's great cultural pluralism. An instrument laying down the substantive entitlements of each party was essential for this purpose. Secondly, American federalism itself provided a highly effective structural control against tyranny. Montesquieu had already identified that smaller territories were less likely to be ruled despotically. Most importantly, the legal framework of federalism provided its own constitutional checks and balances that reduced the need for artificial structural safeguards.[17]

It is for these reasons that Americans saw the entrenchment of basic substantive rights as the safest guide to liberty. On this side of the Atlantic, fair democratic process became the touchstone of English liberty. While Jefferson was uniting a nation behind the slogan; 'No taxation without representation', England was moving towards the Great Reform Act.

---

[13] PS Atiyah and RS Summers, *Form and Substance in Anglo-American Law*. (Oxford, Clarendon, 1987).

[14] See particularly his influential *Fragment on Government*, published in 1776.

[15] *Per* Coke C J in *Dr Bonham's Case* (1610) 8 Co Rep 113b, 118a.

[16] H Steele Commager, *The Empire of Reason* (Weidenfeld & Nicholson, 1978), p 203.

[17] Steele Commager, n 16 above, pp 192–3.

C.   Meeting the Challenge of Independence

a.   *Reasons for the Reception of the Common Law*

But the common law survived in America as a 'necessary and safe guide'[18] in a turbulent time when states could not be expected to produce instant new laws, nor strong new legislative institutions. So Blackstone prevailed. His compilation of laws was both convenient and familiar to American practitioners.[19]

But the explanation runs deeper. The unique talent of the common law in post-revolutionary America was its principled flexibility, without the need to engage the politics of codification.[20]

The commentaries of Chancellor James Kent, 'the American Blackstone',[21] became staple practitioner texts, 'rolling through the decades before the Civil War like a juggernaut'.[22]

But common law *methodology* and philosophy was ideally suited to Independence.[23] Coke and Locke wrote of the common law as a libertarian institution within which a strong, independent judiciary protected individuals from monarchical extremes. The significance of *Entick v Carrington*[24] was not lost on Jefferson. He saw the common law as espousing the rights-based philosophy that the War of Independence had sought to achieve.[25] Government according to law was an obvious foundation stone for a new state with respect for the rights of man.

So independence did not quell the common law tide. It established the need for the active and effective judiciary which lies at the heart of any common law system.

---

[18] Chancellor James Kent, 1 *Commentaries* (1826), p 341.
[19] A Taylor von Mehren, *Law in the United States: A General and Comparative View* (Dordrecht Kluwer, 1988), p 7.
[20] See eg, *D'Hauteville v D'Hauteville* (rep Miller, Philadephia (1840)). As the Pennsylvania courts sought to determine the competing interests of maternal and paternal custody on separation, the approach of the English courts was closely scrutinised (although ultimately rejected). For an illuminating discussion of this case, see M Grossberg, *A Judgment for Solomon: The D'Hauteville Case and Legal Experience in Antebellum America* (CUP, 1996).
[21] JT Horton, *James Kent: A Study in Conservatism* (1939), ch 7 and Kent, 1 *Commentaries* (1826), p 471.
[22] Miller, n 9 above, p 156.
[23] M deWolfe Howe, 'The Migration of the Common Law to the United States of America' (1960) 76 *LQR* 49.
[24] (1765) 19 St Tr 1030.
[25] M White, *The Philosophy of the American Revolution* (New York, OUP, 1978), Beitzinger, 'The Philosophy of Law of Four American Founding Fathers' (1976) 21 *Am J Juris* 1.

b.   The Protection of Rights and the Democratic Imperative

But there were major differences in the protection of liberty. English law set a course of collective democracy, recognising that 'every citizen has a right to do what he likes, unless restrained by the common law or by Statute'.[26] Liberty was to be maintained by ensuring that those restrictions were democratic and fair. Post-revolutionary Americans set a course of individual rights, stipulating that every citizen has a core of basic rights that trump common law or statutory intervention.

III.   THE IDENTIFICATION OF CONSTITUTIONAL RIGHTS

A.   The Sources of Constitutional Rights

a.   Legislative and Common Law Constitutionalism

At first sight, any constitutional comparison between England and America is difficult. The United States is governed by a written constitution, the triumphant product of Independence. The United States is a federal structure. The Constitution of the United States incorporates a written Bill of Rights.

It places great symbolic weight on human rights. It elevates the basic rights of man to supreme constitutional status. It also lays down in general terms the principles of good practice that are to prevent federal interference with individual freedoms—such as the freedoms of speech, expression, religion, assembly, protest and peaceful domestic life.

To date, no such bold statement appears in the constitution of this country. English law observes rights as residual, comprising the range of conduct that has not been in terms cut down by statute or common law rules. Fundamental tenets have had to be expressed by the judiciary as a matter of common law.

I do not say that respect for basic freedoms has passed English law by. The writ of habeas corpus is a very early example of common law constitutionalism upholding the right to bodily integrity, and has often been expressed as a constitutional right to liberty.[27]

---

[26] *Attorney-General v Guardian Newspapers (No 2)* [1990] 1 AC 109, *per* Lord Donaldson M R.

[27] For the status of habeas corpus as a constitutional right, see the judgment of Lord Atkin in *Eshugbayi-Eleko v Government of Nigeria* [1931] AC.

More recently the judges have asserted common law constitutional rights. Take the recent decision of the House of Lords in *Simms*,[28] in which prisoners successfully challenged a government policy of preventing visits by professional journalists. Two constitutional rights—the right to freedom of expression and the right of access to justice—were at stake, and were attributed by Lord Steyn to 'the principle of legality'.

So an incomplete picture would be to assert that English constitutional rights are a product of the common law and therefore residual; whereas Amercia's derive from a single written statement.

b. Reducing the Divide: The Common Law Origins of American Constitutionalism

America itself readily identifies itself with the libertarian traditions of English constitutional history—Magna Carta, the 1628 Petition of Rights and the Bill of Rights of 1689.[29] So many of the 'self-evident truths' of Independence, trace their origins directly to existing common law principles including habeas corpus and the rule of law.[30]

Also, the grund norm of the rule of law, not expressed in the written constitution of America, is born out of the common law. Nor is the written Constitution of America an exclusive statement of rights. Principles of common law constitutionalism frequently bridge the gaps. I pass over *Marbury v Madison*. There are many other instances. In 1974, one of the turning points of the Watergate scandal—the issue whether President Nixon was obliged to disclose the contents of conversations with his advisers—came before the Supreme Court to determine the scope of Presidential privilege at common law.[31] More recently, the Court was asked to consider whether Congress could lawfully veto executive action, on which the Constitution was silent, but on which the separation of powers doctrine had much to say.[32]

---

[28] *R v Secretary of State for the Home Department, ex parte Simms* [1999] 3 WLR 328. See also *R v Lord Chancellor, ex parte Witham* [1998] QB 575.
[29] O'Day, *Understanding Comparative History: Britain and American from 1760* (Open University, 1997).
[30] Beitzinger, n 25 above.
[31] *United States v Nixon* 418 US 683 (1974).
[32] *Immigration & Naturalization Service v Chadha* 462 US 919 (1983).

B.   The Interpretation of Constitutional Rights

So, the written part of the American Constitution is a critical, but not an exhaustive, source of rights. There are precepts, but they have to be judicially interpreted.

Take *Roe v Wade*.[33] The Supreme Court had to consider the validity of a Texas law heavily restricting the availability of abortions. The law was struck down as a violation of the right to privacy contained in the Fourteenth Amendment. The judgment was radical in two ways: not only did it make a considerable extension of the right to privacy, but it adopted a tone that was almost legislative, specifying the date of foetal viability as the point where the right of privacy could legitimately be curtailed.

On any subsequent occasion that the Supreme Court has been faced with the abortion issue, reference is necessarily made to *Roe v Wade* as a starting point for analysis.[34] Thus the scope of the American right to privacy is no longer defined by the Fourteenth Amendment alone. Instead, the content of the right is marked out by a subtle combination of constitutional language and common law precedent.

So, as in *Simms* here, a broad right is identified in both cases as a principle of good constitutional practice. Then the interpretative function of the common law takes over, and the commonalities of English and American law regain their relevance as the court interprets the right and defines its scope. The similar legal reasoning, language and principles of substantive constitutionalism all modify the content of constitutional rights on both sides of the Atlantic.[35]

C.   Towards a Legislative Statement of Rights in England

Finally, let us note that our law is set to move even closer to the American model. From October, legislation will provide a formal source of basic rights in England. The Human Rights Act 1998 will identify essential constitutional values and set them on a proper democratic footing. While judicial interpretation will remain key to defining the scope of

---

[33] 410 US 113 (1973).

[34] See eg, *City of Akron v Akron Centre for Reproductive Health, Inc* 462 US 416, 103 S Ct 2481, 76 L Ed 2d 687 (1983) and *Webster v Reproductive Health Services* 492 US 490, 109 S Ct 3040, 106 L Ed 2d 410 (1989). The case was confined, although not formally overruled, in *Planned Parenthood of Southeastern Pennsylvania v Casey* 112 S Ct 2791, 120 L Ed 2d 674 (1992).

[35] Another example of external influences on the definition of constitutional rights in the United States may be found in the case of *Dred Scott v Sandford* (1857), discussed below.

these rights, future English judges will have at hand a clear legislative statement, a single source that will raise the prominence of human rights throughout English law.

IV. THE PROTECTION OF CONSTITUTIONAL RIGHTS

A. Direct Protection of Rights in Public Law Litigation

Let me first look at public law on both sides of the Atlantic.

a. The Common Law Origins of Administrative Law

Administrative law is a full-blooded product of the common law on both sides of the Atlantic. *Marbury v Madison* established that judicial review is inherent neither in federalism nor in a written constitution, but stems from two common law tenets: the rule of law and the separation of powers.

The rule of law is *the* foundation of rights enforcement in both countries. Individual liberties may only be upheld by acceptance that 'the King shall not be subject to men, but to God and the law: since law makes the King'.[36] The subordination of government to law explained why the courts could invalidate the Secretary of State's warrant for the search of Entick's property, and compel the delivery of Marbury's commission. I quote Chief Justice Marshall: 'it is the province and duty of the judicial department to say what the law is'.

So the search is for balance: the judicial branch must set itself boundaries that are sensitive to the dangers of usurping the executive or legislative function.[37]

b. Review of Executive Action: Common Constitutional Concerns

To keep check on their constitutional role, Anglo-American courts rely upon two particular concepts. They may be labelled 'interest orientation'[38] and 'agency autonomy'.[39]

---

[36] Bracton, quoted in F W Maitland, *The Constitutional History of England* (Oxford, Clarendon Press, 1908), p 100.

[37] Lord Irvine of Lairg, 'Judges and Decision-Makers: The Theory and Practice of *Wednesbury* Review' [1996] *PL* 59.

[38] See generally C Harlow, 'American Influences on Judicial Review', in Loveland (ed), *A Special Relationship: American Influence on Public Law in the UK* (Oxford, Clarendon, 1995).

[39] See generally P P Craig, 'Jurisdiction, Judicial Control and Agency Autonomy', in Loveland (ed), *A Special Relationship: American Influence on Public Law in the UK* (Oxford, Clarendon, 1995).

'Interest orientation' is how judges avoid acting as legislators. Common law methodology is inherently interest-oriented. So there are strict standing rules. The courts of both countries require public law litigants to establish, in the words of the Supreme Court, 'a sufficiently concrete and particularised or imminent injury'.[40] Thus the enforcement of rights is only effected by those directly concerned. Courts must refrain from granting a legal remedy where the appropriate solution is political.[41] Exceptionally, in both jurisdictions, public interest groups may bring actions to compel executive respect for human rights, but the qualification rules for these bodies are strict: they must be established, authoritative and truly representative of the public interest.[42]

The second restraint in both countries is 'agency autonomy'. This ensures that courts do not interfere improperly with the decisions of other branches of government.[43] Both systems uphold this principle by their strict distinction between appeal and review, avoiding consideration of whether the decision was substantively right. The questions asked in judicial review are confined to the legality of the decision in accordance with legal limitations on the decision-maker's powers: the 'fig-leaf' of *ultra vires*.[44]

In this way, the concept of jurisdiction assumes a centrality in administrative law, recognised by the House of Lords in *Boddington's* case.[45] So also in the focus of the Supreme Court in *Chevron v Natural Resources Defense Council*.[46] The Court was asked to consider the validity of environmental regulations, passed by an executive body under primary legislation[47] that permitted the licensing of newly modified sources of air pollution. The regulations set up a comprehensive scheme, requiring an entire plant to be licensed as soon as any part of it

---

[40] *Lujan v Defenders of Wildlife* 504 US 555 (1992).

[41] In *Lujan v Defenders of Wildlife*, the US Supreme Court was faced with a challenge to environmental legislation brought by members of environmental lobby groups. They argued that a new Endangered Species Act should be extended to apply outside the territory of the United States. The petitioners were denied standing to challenge the decision, on the ground that their claim was 'a generally available grievance about government' that should more properly be heard in a political arena, not a court of law.

[42] See eg, *R v Secretary of State for Employment, ex parte Equal Opportunities Commission* [1995] 1 All ER 545.

[43] See P P Craig, n 39 above.

[44] C F Forsyth, 'Of Fig Leaves and Fairy Tales: The Ultra Vires Doctrine, the Sovereignty of Parliament and Judicial Review' [1996] *CLJ* 122.

[45] *Boddington v British Transport Police* [1998] 2 WLR 639.

[46] *Chevron, USA, Inc v Natural Resources Defense Council, Inc* 467 US 837 (1984).

[47] Clean Air Amendments Act 1977.

was modified. The applicants objected that the regulations were unlawfully broad. In exercising its power of review, the court was careful to avoid discussion of the merits of the regulations. The judges' sole consideration was whether the regulations complied with the intention of Congress and fell within a 'permissible construction of the statute'. The court was entitled to ask whether the regulations had been made on a 'rational basis' as rationality was a limitation that Congress would clearly wish to impose. But regulations that were rational and legally accurate could not be challenged in a court of law. Our approach may be more 'hard edged'. If a statutory provision conferring powers on a body has one specific meaning only, which the statutory body did not follow, then it is not saved, even if its interpretation was reasonable or possible. On the other hand, if the provision lays down a criterion so flexible or imprecise that its application could rationally leads to different conclusions on the same facts, then it is only an irrational application that can be struck down.[48]

c. *Judicial Review of Legislation: A Major Divergence of Practice*

Thus no court, whether in England[49] or America,[50] will undermine the autonomy of executive agencies by investigating the merits of a decision. Decisions may only be challenged if they infringe a superior rule of law. Here this dictates that the enforcement of constitutional rights must stop at the level of parliamentary legislation.[51] Constitutional rights have traditionally been taken from the common law, and respect for the democratic imperative has resulted in the selfrestraint of English judges in attempting to impose common law rights over the express will of the legislature.[52]

---

[48] *R v Monopolies and Mergers Commission and another, ex parte South Yorkshire Transport Ltd* [1993] WLR 23, *per* Lord Mustill at 32 C-H.

[49] See *R v Secretary of State, ex parte Hargreaves* [1997] 1 WLR 906, where the Court of Appeal restored orthodoxy by refusing to hold a public body bound by any substantive legitimate expectations.

[50] See *Rizzo v Goode* 96 S Ct 598 (1976). Various citizens of Philadelphia brought a class action, alleging police brutality. The local court found that constitutional rights had been violated, and ordered city police officials to draft a complaint procedure consistent with 'generally recognised minimum standards'. The Supreme Court struck this judgment down: it infringed the 'latitude' necessary for a local administration 'in the dispatch of its own internal affairs'.

[51] *R v Ministry of Defence, ex parte Smith* [1996] QB 517.

[52] This principle is made particularly clear by Lord Hoffmann in *R v Secretary of State for the Home Department, ex parte Simms* [1999] 3 WLR 328.

In the United States, of course, it is very different. Like Parliament, Congress also represents an elected legislature giving effect to the popular will. But the laws of Congress are not the supreme laws of the United States. These are contained in the written Constitution of 1789, an instrument that delegates sovereign power from the people and the states to Congress, and entrenches basic rights at the heart of its provisions.

Let me recall how, in 1785, Justice Iredell expressed the nature of American constitutional review:

> ... no act [a legislature] could pass, could by any means repeal or alter the Constitution, because if they could do this, they would at the same instant of time destroy their own existence as a legislature and dissolve the government thereby established.

Therefore, Americans have no difficulty in holding *any legislature* bound to respect the principles of human rights. These rights form a superior body of democratically created law, and constitute an express restriction on *constitutional legislative authority*.

So, Britain has made its Parliament supreme to achieve individual freedom through democratic procedures. America has achieved freedom more directly, by expressly limiting the power of the legislature to ensure compliance with basic substantive precepts. Yet still American judges have by their decisions demonstrated their selfrestraint in determining the proper allocation both of constitutional powers and judicial process.[53]

Take *Dred Scott v Sandford in 1857*.[54] Dred Scott was a slave. He sought freedom under a Missouri law, known as 'once free, always free'. This well-established rule granted liberty to any man who had previously resided in a free state, but gave no protection to Scott—the Supreme Court of Missouri simply overruled the principle on hearing his case. He then made an appeal to the Supreme Court, but his appeal failed on the ground that it had no jurisdiction to intervene. First, blacks had no standing to bring actions before the Supreme Court, as the principle of racial segregation meant that United States citizenship was reserved to whites. Secondly, slavery was an issue in which federal authorities, including Congress, were powerless to intervene: the Constitution made no reference to slavery when delegating power to

---

[53] The clearest statement of these principles emerges from the case *Rescue Army v Municipal Court of Los Angeles* 331 US 459, 67 S Ct 1409, 91 L Ed 1666 (1947).
[54] 19 How (60 US) 393 (1857).

federal institutions. The Missouri Supreme Court had declared Scott to be a slave, and the US Supreme Court was bound to recognise this.

Dred Scott cannot be dismissed as an extreme example. Its influence lasted for a hundred years until the Supreme Court finally reversed its position on racial segregation in *Brown v Board of Education* in 1954.[55] So it must stand as a powerful illustration of constitutional sensitivities imposing severe limitations on the enforcement of rights.

B.   Wider Respect for Constitutional Rights

a.   Human Rights and the Interpretative Process

Let me return to judicial interpretation as an essential driver in the *definition* of rights. In both countries, statutes are interpreted consistently with the language to achieve the greatest respect for basic rights that can be achieved. Here our doctrine of Parliamentary supremacy has focused attention on interpreting, not challenging, legislative decisions. *Simms*[56] is a good illustration.

An insistence on basic rights is also key to the development of the common law.[57] This is clear to be seen from the judgment of the House of Lords in *Derbyshire*,[58] where the law of defamation was developed consonantly with the principle of freedom of expression, to prevent local authorities bringing libel actions.

b.   Wider Respect for Rights Throughout Anglo-American Law

But it has to be acknowledged that our approach to the construction of statutes, and judicial precedent, is typified by technical and literal reasoning.[59] Judges often rail in vain against unpopular common law rules, because their hands are tied by precedent.[60] Privity of contract doctrine presented an unpopular restriction on contractual autonomy for most of the twentieth century, but judges could go no further than express

---

[55] *Brown v Board of Education* (1954) 347 US 483.
[56] *R v Secretary of State for the Home Department, ex parte Simms* [1999] 3 WLR 328.
[57] *Attorney-General v British Broadcasting Corporation* [1981] AC 303, per Lord Fraser of Tullybelton at 352.
[58] *Derbyshire County Council v Times Newspapers Ltd* [1993] 1 All ER 1011.
[59] A Tunc, 'The Not so Common Law of England and the United States' [1984] *MLR* 150.
[60] *Woodar Investment v Wimpey Construction* [1980] 1 WLR 227.

their dissatisfaction with the rule—the weight of common law authority could not simply be ignored.[61]

The American approach has traditionally paid more direct concern to the immediate interests of the litigating parties. In the words of Roscoe Pound:

> [The American judge] conceives of the legal rule as a general guide to the judge, leading him to the just result, but insists that within wide limits he should be free to deal with the individual case, so as to meet the demands of justice between the parties and accord with the general reason of the ordinary man.[62]

So, American judges enjoy greater flexibility in the application of legal rules to suit the demands of individual cases.[63] Common law rules may be overruled if they are substantively dubious,[64] or likely to be overruled in the Supreme Court,[65] or if circumstances have changed since the previous decision to render the rule undesirable in modern times.[66] We might say that all this must be at the expense of certainty.

This argument should not be pressed too far. We can cite examples of American judicial restraint,[67] or English judicial activism,[68] in the development of rules to protect individual interests.[69] Here, we have seen great judicial activity in private law—unjust enrichment for

---

[61] Although, of course, statute has intervened with the Contract (Rights of Third Parties) Act 1999.

[62] R Pound, 'The Scope and Purpose of Sociological Jurisprudence' (1912) 25 *Harv LR* 489, 515.

[63] See *eg*, *Comunale v Traders & General Ins* Co 321 P 2d 768 (1958). For the position in English law, see Cross, *Precedent in English Law* 3rd edn (Oxford, Clarendon, 1977), ch III.

[64] *State v Baker* 15 Md App 73 (1971)

[65] Kniffin, 'Overruling Supreme Court Precedents: Anticipatory Action by United States Courts of Appeals' (1982) 51 *Fordham LR* 53.

[66] *Lemle v Breeden* 51 Hawaii 426, 462 P 2d 470 (1969): discarded common law rule of *caveat emptor* for residential tenancies.

[67] *Maki v Frelk* 85 Ill App 2d 439, 229 NE 2d 284 (1967): no judicial reform to contributory negligence rules, because this was a matter for the legislature.

[68] Witness the radical economic loss cases from *Anns v Merton LBC* [1978] AC 728 through to *Murphy v Brentwood DC* [1991] 2 All ER 908. Or even the recent leaps in the English law of restitution, where English judges are openly 'abrogating' (Lord Goff) and 'ending' (Lord Hope) old common law rules: *Kleinwort Benson v Birmingham CC* [1997] QB 380.

[69] The anti-abortion cases following *Roe v Wade* 410 US 113 (1973) (eg, *City of Akron v Akron Centre for Reproductive Health, Inc* 462 US 416, 103 S Ct 2481, 76 L Ed 2d 687 (1983) and *Webster v Reproductive Health Services* 492 US 490, 109 S Ct 3040, 106 L Ed 2d 410 (1989)) demonstrate that American courts are equally capable of becoming caught up in their own unpopular precedents.

example,[70] and judges are beginning to acknowledge more openly their role in shaping rules of law.[71] But the general mood of the law displays a difference of emphasis, suggesting that the language of rights is not here as deeply imbued as in America.[72]

Take an example of our more rigid approach from the private law of negligence.[73] Public authorities rarely owe a private duty of care to individuals in the exercise of their general statutory duties.[74] So, many actions brought against public authorities are struck out since it is not fair, just or reasonable to impose a duty of care. This practice was successfully challenged before the European Court of Human Rights in *Osman v United Kingdom*.[75] It was found that a general exclusionary rule would amount to a denial of a litigant's right of access to justice.

In *Barrett v Enfield London Borough Council*,[76] the House of Lords accepted this reasoning. It declined to strike out a claim against a health authority for causing psychological problems to a child in its care. Although the child's case 'faced considerable difficulties',[77] the child was at least entitled to have his arguments of public policy investigated at a full trial.

But we have also seen more restrictive judgments that confine the *Osman* principle to its narrowest and most formal limits. In *Palmer v Tees Health Authority*,[78] the Court of Appeal struck out a claim against a health authority where it was alleged that its negligent supervision of a diagnosed psychopath had led to the murder of a child. *Osman* was carefully distinguished. One line of reasoning[79] held that the real factor lying behind strike-outs against public authorities was not public policy, but proximity. As the European Court in *Osman* had only attacked

---

[70] See eg, the abolition of the mistake of law doctrine in *Kleinwort Benson v Birmingham CC* [1997] QB 380. An interesting mix of private and public law is also to be found in the judgment of the House of Lords in *Woolwich Building Society v IRC* [1993] AC.

[71] Lord Reed, 'The Judge as a Law Maker' (1972) 12 *Journal of the Society of Public Teachers of Law* 22.

[72] P S Atiyah and R S Summers, *Form and Substance in Anglo-American Law* (Oxford, Clarendon, 1987).

[73] See N Beresford (2000) 116 *LQR* 24.

[74] The principle is stated at its clearest in *Hill v Chief Constable of West Yorkshire* [1989] 1 AC 53.

[75] [1999] 1 FLR 193.

[76] [1999] 3 WLR 79.

[77] The words of Lord Slynn.

[78] [1999] All ER (D) 722.

[79] The judgment of Stuart-Smith L J.

strike-outs based on public policy, the principle of access to justice could be neatly sidestepped by reclassifying the legal issue. The other reasoned judgment[80] acknowledged the technicality of these subtle distinctions, but found instead that *Osman* applied only to strike-outs based on general, rather than specific, public policy concerns.

Such literal, technical judgments in the human rights field would be rare in the United States, where respect is accorded not only to the wording, but also the spirit, of rights. *Roe v Wade* reveals a greater willingness by the American judiciary to classify issues as raising questions of human rights, and a great sensitivity in their application. Here there is some evidence of an inclination to deny that rights are in issue at all.

C.   The Human Rights Act: Increased Awareness of Rights in England

Finally, the Human Rights Act will do much to reduce the gap between England and America. The large number of cases brought against us in Strasbourg show that our law's emphasis on collective democracy has too often failed to protect individual liberties. The fundamental point is that 'freedom under the law' ignores that the law, common law or statute, can deny or defeat basic human rights. In October the Human Rights Act will come into force and will provide a clear statement of fundamental rights with sufficient democratic credentials to be directly upheld by an English court.

It will prioritise rights throughout our system, and will require any departure from principle to be conscious and reasoned. Also judges are given strong interpretative powers so far as possible to read and give effect to legislation in a way compatible with Convention rights.

As in America, judges will be able to derive constitutional rights from a single source that will enable more effective judicial activism across a range of issues, but ever tempered by judgment and restraint.

Most importantly, the Act will provide a form of enforcement that is sensitive to English constitutional arrangements. Judges must still refrain from hearing a direct challenge to the content of legislation, but they will be enabled formally to question the compatibility of legislative acts with human rights. Ministers of the Crown will also be subjected to new duties in the promulgation of legislation, required to make

---

[80] The judgment of Pill L J.

formal declarations that their proposed legislation in their judgment complies with basic human rights.

V.   CONCLUSION: TOWARDS A COMMON FUTURE

So, is there a conclusion? Common law methodology lies at the heart of English and American law, even in areas such as the constitution, where American arrangements appear to be very different. Both countries have long traditions of protecting basic liberties, but there have been differing philosophical and cultural influences on the legal structure. In both countries the common law has delivered basic doctrines that facilitate the contrasting approaches of both systems.

The common law's capacity to respond to localising influences explains how both systems recognise differences of substance within strikingly similar legal frameworks.

Yet localising influences are diminishing.[81] The problems that will confront Anglo-American law in the twenty-first century are no longer parochial; they are of international proportions. The old common law concepts must soon be developed to encompass issues such as genetic reproduction and regulation of the Internet. Mutual guidance will inevitably be sought throughout the common law world. Our House of Lords is already beginning to look to American experience with increasing regularity when considering the response of English law to novel problems, such as sanctioning the withdrawal of life support from hospital patients in a permanent vegetative state[82] or fixing the boundaries of increasingly intrusive comment on the lives of public figures.[83] This tendency can only be expected to grow with the progressive convergence of cultural and scientific influences across the world.

The Human Rights Act provides a fine example of the ways in which English law can benefit from American experience. In October, our law will finally make the transition to the rights-based system that has existed in the United States for over 200 years. We have come to accept that American experience shows that a written declaration provides a more certain safeguard of individual rights than procedural democracy through a sovereign Parliament, indispensable though that is.

---

[81] Kahn-Freund, 'Uses and Misuses of Comparative Law' (1974) 37 MLR 1.
[82] *Airedale NHS Trust v Bland* [1993] 1 All ER 821.
[83] *Times Newspapers Ltd v Derbyshire* CC [1993] 1 All ER 1011. See also *Reynolds v Times Newspapers* [2001] 2 AC 127.

The British and American legal systems stem from common principled roots. We have gained, and continue to gain, each from the other. The links between us celebrate the quality of the common law and the institutions which underpin it: an independent judiciary, an independent legal profession, and our unshakeable commitment to the rule of law, without which no genuine democracy can exist.

14

Sovereignty in Comparative Perspective: Constitutionalism in Britain and America

I.   INTRODUCTION

'T HE AMERICAN CONSTITUTIONS,' said Thomas Paine, 'were to liberty, what a grammar is to language: they define its parts of speech, and practically construct them into syntax'[1] The central role which was played by James Madison, whose memory this Lecture commemorates, in the construction of the US Constitution is too well known to require elaboration this evening. It suffices to not that, as one American commentator recently put it, Madison's championing of the amendment of the Constitution was an accomplishment which 'entitles him to be remembered as father of the Bill of Rights even more than as father of the Constitution.'[2]

In the speech which he made to Congress introducing the Bill of Rights,[3] Madison acknowledged that 'paper barriers' have their limitations. But he also observed that, because 'they have a tendency to impress some degree of respect for them, to establish the public opinion in their favor, and rouse the attention of the whole community,' they are an important means by which 'to control the majority from those acts to which they might be otherwise inclined.'[4] By thus recognizing the potential of a Bill of Rights, Madison effected, for America, the constitutionalization of liberty—a process which, in the

[1] Thomas Paine, *The Rights of Man* (1791), reprinted in *Two Classics of the French Revolution* 270, 334 (1989).
[2] Leonard W Levy, *Origins of the Bill of Rights* (New York, Oxford UP, 1999) 34. For background information on the inception of the US Bill of Rights, see generally *ibid*, at 1–43.
[3] For the full text of Madison's celebrated speech, see 5 *The Roots of the Bill of Rights* 1016 (Bernard Schwartz ed, 1971).
[4] *Ibid,* at 1030.

ensuing two hundred years, many other legal systems rightly have emulated.

I hesitate, however, to categorise the United Kingdom simply as one of those 'other' jurisdictions. Of course, ever since Independence, there has existed a *formal* separation between our two systems. But the linkages of legal *culture* which connect them have proved more resilient. That is hardly surprising, not least because of the shared common law foundation on which modern English and American law both rest.[5] More specifically, many of the rights which were enshrined first in the state constitutions and, later, in the federal Constitution share much in common with the values articulated in English constitutional texts.

For instance, section 39 of the Magna Carta, which provided that '[n]o freeman shall be ... imprisoned ... except by the lawful judgment of his peers or by the law of the land,'[6] was clearly a forerunner of the Due Process Clause in the US Bill of Rights.[7] There are equally self-evident parallels between the provision in the 1689 Bill of Rights requiring 'that the freedom of speech ... ought not to be impeached or questioned'[8] and the guarantee enshrined in the US Constitution's First Amendment. More generally, the writings of English philosophers had a fundamental impact on the theory of government which took root in America, as the relationship between the Declaration of Independence and the work of John Locke illustrates.[9]

But in spite of the fact that we share so much in common, there are also obvious differences. My purpose this evening is to focus on one particular point of distinction between the British and American legal systems: the divergence between the American notion of *constitutional supremacy* and the British doctrine of *parliamentary sovereignty*. That distinction has long been viewed as symbolizing a fundamental difference of outlook between the United States and Britain on constitutional matters generally, and more specifically on the status of civil rights in our respective legal systems. I intend to examine the background to that

---

[5] See generally Lord Irvine of Lairg, 'The Common Origins of English and American Law,' Inner Temple Lecture to the Inner Temple, London (22 March 2000) (transcript available at http://www.open.gov.uk/lcd/speeches/2000/2000fr.htm).
[6] Magna Carta § 39 (1215), reprinted in 1 The Roots of the Bill of Rights, above n 3, at 8, 12.
[7] US Const amend V; see also *ibid*, amend. XIV.
[8] Bill of Rights (1689), reprinted in 1 *The Roots of the Bill of Rights*, above n 3, at 41, 43.
[9] See especially John Locke, *The Second Treatise of Civil Government* (J W Gough ed, Basil Blackwell 1946) (1690).

divergence, before going on to suggest that recent developments in the United Kingdom emphasize that the distinction between the two concepts, although real, should not be exaggerated.

II.   PARLIAMENTARY SOVEREIGNTY

Let me begin with the notion of parliamentary sovereignty.[10] The nuances of that principle are the focus of one of the most contentious areas of academic—and, on occasion, judicial—debate in English constitutional law.[11]

The sovereignty principle has not always been rigidly endorsed. In particular, certain judicial dicta from the early seventeenth century questioned whether the courts owed unqualified loyalty to Parliament's enactments. Most famously, in *Dr Bonham's Case*,[12] Chief Justice Coke said that the common law could 'controul Acts of Parliament, and sometimes adjudge them to be utterly void: for when an Act of Parliament is against common right and reason, or repugnant, or impossible to be performed, the common law will controul it, and adjudge such Act to be void.'[13] However, by the time he came to write his *Institutes*, Coke's views had become markedly more orthodox, and he accepted that Parliament possessed a 'transcendent and abundant' jurisdiction which could not be 'confined ... within any bounds.'[14]

---

[10] The work of Sir William Wade remains, for many, the classic exposition of sovereignty theory in the British context. See 'H W R Wade, The Basis of Legal Sovereignty,' 1955 *Cambridge LJ* 172; Sir William Wade, 'Sovereignty—Revolution or Evolution?,' 112 *LQ Rev* 568 (1996).

[11] The debate has been prompted both by the implications of European Union membership and, more generally, by a feeling in some quarters that the effective protection of fundamental rights is somehow incompatible with sovereignty theory. For a useful overview of the first aspect of the debate, see P P Craig, 'The Sovereignty of the United Kingdom Parliament After *Factortame*', 11 *Year Book of European Law* 221 (1991). On the debate's other dimension, see 'Geoffrey Marshall, Parliamentary Sovereignty: The New Horizons', (1997) *Pub L* 1; Richard Mullender, 'Parliamentary Sovereignty, the Constitution and the Judiciary', 49 *N Ir Legal Q* 138 (1998).

[12] 77 Eng Rep 646 (KB 1610).

[13] *Ibid*, at 652 Similar sentiments were expressed by Chief Justice Hobart in *Day v Savadge*, 80 Eng Rep 235, 237 (KB 1614) ('[E]ven an Act of Parliament, made against natural equity, as to make a man Judge in his own case, is void in it self.').

It is worth noting, however, that some historians suggest that Coke was arguing merely in favor of a particular approach to *interpretation*, rather than for a judicial power to *quash* such legislation. See, eg, J W Gough, *Fundamental Law in English Constitutional History* 40–41 (1955). Gough attributes a similar interpretation to the previously quoted passage from *Day. Ibid,* at 38–9.

[14] Sir Edward Coke, *The Fourth Part of the Institutes of the Laws of England: Concerning the Jurisdiction of the Courts* 36 (London, W Clarke & Sons 1817) (1644).

The correctness of that view was placed beyond doubt by the Revolution at the end of the seventeenth century.[15]

Although there exist myriad definitions of the doctrine of parliamentary sovereignty, the most enduring is that supplied by Albert Venn Dicey, the Victorian jurist and Vinerian Professor of Law at Oxford University. Writing in 1885, he described the Westminster Parliament as having 'the right to make or unmake any law whatever,' adding, for the avoidance of doubt it seems, that 'no person or body is recognized by the law of England as having a right to override or set aside' its legislation.[16] Although much of Dicey's (still influential) work has been criticised by many modern British commentators, I note with interest that, in an authoritative recent book on sovereignty, Jeffrey Goldsworthy concludes that Dicey's definition is still 'basically sound.'[17] Indeed, for the last three hundred years British courts have not questioned Parliament's capacity to enact any legislation which it chooses. As Lord Reid remarked:

> The idea that a court is entitled to disregard a provision in an Act of Parliament on any ground must seem strange and startling to anyone with any knowledge of the history and law of our constitution ... [S]ince the supremacy of Parliament was finally demonstrated by the Revolution of 1688 any such idea has become obsolete.[18]

It is true that some British judges now question—extracurially—whether sovereignty theory is apposite to the United Kingdom at the turn of the millennium.[19] In my view these criticisms are misplaced because they fail to appreciate that the notion of sovereignty is, in large measure, a function of the *context* within which it subsists. I shall argue that it is the *evolution* of that context which keeps fresh the idea of sovereignty,

---

[15] See generally Jeffrey Goldsworthy, *The Sovereignty of Parliament* 142–220 (Oxford, Clarendon Press, 1999).

[16] A V Dicey, *Introduction to the Study of the Law of the Constitution* 40 (ECS Wade ed, 9th ed London, Macmillan, 1956) (1885).

[17] Goldsworthy, above n 15, at 11.

[18] *British Rys Bd v Pickin*, [1974] AC 765, 782 (appeal taken from Eng CA).

[19] See Sir John Laws, 'The Constitution: Morals and Rights,' (1996) *Pub L* 622 [hereinafter Laws, Constitution]; Sir John Laws, 'Law and Democracy', (1995) *Pub L* 72 [hereinafter Laws, Law and Democracy]; Sir Stephen Sedley, 'Human Rights: A Twenty-First Century Agenda', (1995) *Pub L* 386; Lord Woolf of Barnes, 'Droit Public-English Style', (1995) *Pub L* 57. For similar sentiments, expressed in the New Zealand context, see Sir Robin Cooke, 'Fundamentals', (1988) *NZ LJ* 158. For rebuttals of the views of Sir John Laws (who is the most enthusiastic judicial critic of parliamentary sovereignty), see J A G Griffith, 'The Brave New World of Sir John Laws,' 63 *Mod L Rev* 159 (2000); Lord Irvine of Lairg, 'Response to Sir John Laws,' (1996) *Pub L* 636.

and which ultimately renders it an appropriate feature of the British constitution at the beginning of the twenty-first century. And I will suggest that it is that same evolutive context which reveals a *measure* of similarity between the British concept of parliamentary sovereignty and the American theory of constitutional supremacy, although those two ideas are, and will remain, *distinct*.

III.   CONSTITUTIONAL SUPREMACY

A.   The Notion of Constitutional Supremacy

Of course, legislative sovereignty has never been a feature of the US legal system. By 1787, eight of the thirteen colonies had incorporated judicial review into their constitutions. It is ironic that the views expressed by Sir Edward Coke in *Dr Bonham's Case*, although they had fallen out of favor in England by that time, were relied on in the *Writs of Assistance Case* in 1761,[20] and may have played some part in persuading the colonies to provide for judicial review in their constitutions.

The status of the Constitution as a higher order of law, prior and superior to the powers of the legislative branch, was articulated very clearly by Supreme Court Justice Samuel Chase in the case of *Calder v Bull* in 1798.[21] 'I cannot subscribe to the omnipotence of a State Legislature, or that it is absolute and without controul,' said Justice Chase.[22] 'An act of the Legislature (for I cannot call it a law), contrary to the great first principles of the social compact, cannot be considered a rightful exercise of legislative authority.'[23]

I note, however, that although constitutional review is as central to constitutionalism in America as parliamentary sovereignty is in the United Kingdom, some voices have been raised against it ever since its inception in *Marbury v Madison*.[24] One such voice was that of Judge John Gibson. In the dissenting opinion which he delivered in the case of *Eakin v Raub* in the Pennsylvania Supreme Court in 1825,[25] he observed that

---

[20] See Maurice H Smith, *The Writs of Assistance Case* (1978) 359–62.
[21] 3 US (3 Dall) 386 (1798).
[22] *Ibid*, at 387–8 (emphasis omitted).
[23] *Ibid*, at 388 (emphasis omitted).
[24] 5 US (1 Cranch) 137 (1803). For a useful account of the historical context in which *Marbury* was decided, see Robert G McCloskey, *The American Supreme Court* (2d ed 1994) 1–34.
[25] 12 Serg & Rawle 330 (Pa 1825).

[T]he Constitution is said to be a law of superior obligation; and, consequently, that if it were to come into collision with an act of the legislature, the latter would have to give way.... But it is a fallacy to suppose that they can come into collision *before the judiciary* .... The Constitution and the *right* of the legislature to pass the act may be in collision. But is that a subject for judicial determination?[26]

Although the jurisprudence of the Supreme Court has provided a clear, affirmative answer to this question, it is striking that the debate about the correctness of *Marbury*—both in terms of its fidelity to the intention of the Framers and, more broadly, whether it is desirable in normative terms—is still going on, two hundred years after the decision.[27]

B.   The Flexible Nature of Constitutional Supremacy

It is certainly not my intention this evening to attempt to evaluate the appropriateness of constitutional review in the United States,[28] although I *will* have something to say later about constitutional review in the United Kingdom. Instead, my purpose is simply to draw attention to the clear parallel which exists between the ongoing debate in America about the powers of the courts in relation to the Constitution,[29] and the discourse in Britain concerning the desirability of parliamentary sovereignty. Although our respective legal systems begin from different starting points—constitutional paramountcy and legislative supremacy—the two debates address essentially the same questions: How much power should the courts have over the other branches of government? And in what circumstances, if any, is it appropriate for the judicial branch to overrule elected legislators and administrators in order to safeguard individual or group interests?

[26] *Ibid*, at 347–8.
[27] For recent contributions to that debate, see Sylvia Snowiss, *Judicial Review and the Law of the Constitution* (1990); Mark Tushnet, *Taking the Constitution Away from the Courts* (1999).
[28] It is, however, an interesting question whether the United States would have been a less fair and just society had the courts not assumed the power of constitutional review. Compare Ronald Dworkin, *Law's Empire* 356 (Cambridge, Mass, Belknap Press, 1986) (arguing that judicial review has made US society more just), with Robert A Dahl, *Democracy and Its Critics* 189–91 (1989) (questioning effectiveness of judicial review to protect human rights).
[29] See for example, the seminal contribution to this debate made by Ronald Dworkin, *Taking Rights Seriously* 131–49 (London, Duckworth, 1977).

The fact that this same debate is ongoing within both the British and American legal systems points towards an important fact which is sometimes overlooked. Constitutional supremacy and parliamentary sovereignty are often perceived as concepts which are polemically opposed to one another, given that the former *limits* legislative power and *entrenches* fundamental rights, while the latter embraces formally *unlimited* power and *eschews* the entrenchment of human rights. However, the better view is that they represent two diffrent parts of a continuum, each reflecting differing views about how the judiciary and the other institutions of government ought to interrelate.

This conceptualisation follows (in part) from the fact that the notions of constitutional and legislative supremacy are themselves *elastic*. For instance, there exists a spectrum of opinions about precisely what constitutional supremacy ought to mean in the US context. Although it is firmly settled that the US Constitution *does* amount to a superior set of laws which *are* judicially enforceable,[30] this still leaves great scope for flexibility.[31] For instance, by 1858, the Supreme Court had held only two pieces of federal legislation to be unconstitutional.[32] The record of the Court in those early years contrasts sharply with the much more activist approach which was adopted by, for instance, the Warren Court.[33]

Such variation, over time, of the level of activism[34] which is evident in the Supreme Court's decisions reflects (among other things)[35] changing

[30] Academic debate notwithstanding. See above n 27.

[31] Perhaps the most vivid illustration of this flexibility is to be found in the Supreme Court's case law on the constitutionality of racial segregation. As is well known, the Court held in *Plessy v Ferguson*, 163 US 537 (1896), that the 'separate but equal' policy was not incompatible with the Constitution. However, in the celebrated case of *Brown v Board of Education*, 347 US 483 (1954), the Court came to the opposite conclusion. Chief Justice Warren concluded that the policy deprived the plaintiffs, and 'others similarly situated,' of the 'equal protection of the laws guaranteed by the Fourteenth Amendment.' *Ibid*, at 495.

[32] See *Dred Scott v Sandford*, 60 US (19 How.) 393 (1857); *Marbury v Madison*, 5 US (1 Cranch) 137 (1803).

[33] For a useful survey of historical and quantitative research on the judicial policies of the US Supreme Court, see David G Barnum, *The Supreme Court and American Democracy* (1993) 74–105.

[34] A discussion of the various meanings ascribed to the term 'activism' can be found in Bradley C Canon, 'Defining the Dimensions of Judicial Activism,' 66 *Judicature* 236 (1983). For a comparative analysis of the notion of activism in the fundamental rights context, see Lord Irvine of Lairg, 'Activism and Restraint: Human Rights and the Interpretative Process,' (1999) *Eur Hum Rts L Rev* 350.

[35] Of course, changes in the decisionmaking trends of the Supreme Court are also influenced by a large number of other factors. The study of such matters forms a discrete

judicial (and societal) conceptions of how the judiciary and the other branches should interrelate—and, in particular, of how the balance should be struck between, on the one hand, judicial intervention and, on the other hand, legislative and executive autonomy. This position is, of course, as inevitable as it is desirable. As Chief Justice Marshall remarked in *McCullough v Maryland*,[36] constitutions are 'intended to endure for ages to come, and consequently, [must] be adapted to the various crises of human affairs.'[37] Thus the necessary generality of a Bill of Rights makes it at once both timeless and evolutive. It follows that, while constitutional supremacy is a fixed feature of the US Constitution, the concept is a flexible one, the precise meaning of which is, ultimately, a product of contemporary legal and political thought. The notion of parliamentary sovereignty is, I will argue, similarly elastic.

This flexibility which inheres in the ideas of constitutional and legislative supremacy goes some way towards dispelling the myth that each is the antithesis of the other. Since they are each *catholic* principles which accommodate a *range* of views concerning institutional interrelationship, it is meaningless to suggest that they are inevitably opposed to one another. That is why I suggested earlier that the two theories are best thought of as different parts of a *spectrum* of views concerning how judges should relate to the other branches of government. I will return, later, to these *linkages* between the two theories.

IV.   TRADITIONAL POINTS OF DIVERGENCE

First, however, let me consider in more detail the *divergence* between the American principle of constitutional supremacy and British adherence to parliamentary sovereignty. There are important clues in the *historical* context which will help to illuminate the *contemporary* relationship

---

discipline in American legal scholarship and is beyond the scope of this Lecture. For analysis of the influences which shaped decisionmaking in the Supreme Court during its first two centuries, see, for example, David P Currie, *The Constitution in the Supreme Court: The First Hundred Years 1789–1888* (1985); David P Currie, *The Constitution in the Supreme Court: The Second Century 1888–1986* (1990); McCloskey, above n 24.
[36] 17 US (4 Wheat) 315 (1819).
[37] *Ibid*, at 413 (emphasis omitted); see also Alexander Hamilton, 'Third Speech at New York Ratifying Convention' (28 June 1788), in 5 *Papers of Alexander Hamilton* 114, 118 (Harold C Syrett ed, 1962) ('Constitutions should consist only of general provisions: The reason is, that they must necessarily be permanent, and that they cannot calculate for the possible changes of things.').

between the two theories. In particular, I wish to examine some of the key points of divergence which, traditionally, have been treated as pre-eminent in establishing a clear distinction between them. However, I will also suggest that the tide of history substantially has eroded some of those differences. Certainly, distinctions still remain, but they are more subtle, and less obvious, than once they were.

A. Philosophical Roots

The foremost method by which constitutional and legislative supremacy traditionally have been differentiated is by reference to their philosophical roots.[38] Those roots are relatively clear so far as the US notion of constitutional supremacy is concerned. As Chief Justice Marshall observed in 1821, '[t]he people made the constitution, and the people can unmake it. It is the creature of their will, and lives only by their will.'[39] Thus, the state and federal institutions acquire their legitimacy from the popular consensus which the constitutional texts evidence. In this sense, popular sovereignty is the *fundamental* principle, while constitutional supremacy is its *derivative*.

Later in this Lecture,[40] I will suggest that constitutional primacy is merely *one* possible derivative of popular sovereignty, and that, viewed in its contemporary setting, legislative supremacy also gives effect to the notion of sovereignty residing in the people. Historically, however, that is not the philosophical foundation on which the principle of parliamentary sovereignty was founded. Some writers suggest that the principle emerged through the translation of *religious* ideas about authority into a more *secular* conception of political sovereignty.[41] Whether or not this was so, one point is clear. The *origins* of the doctrine of legislative supremacy did not lie in a political philosophy which sought to give effect to any conception of popular sovereignty. This is plain, given that it was not until the nineteenth century (at the earliest) that it became possible, with the passing of the Reform Acts, to articulate any sort of

---

[38] See generally Roger Cotterrell, 'The Symbolism of Constitutions: Some Anglo-American Comparisons', in Ian Loveland (ed) *A Special Relationship? American Influences on Public Law in the UK* (Oxford, Clarendon Press, 1995) 25, 27–28. These themes are also touched upon by P P Craig, *Public Law and Democracy in the United Kingdom and the United States of America* 1, 3–9 (Oxford, Clarendon Press 1990).
[39] *Cohens v Virginia*, 19 US (6 Wheat) 264, 389 (1821).
[40] See below Part IV A.
[41] Eg, John Neville Figgis, *The Divine Right of Kings* 2d ed (1914) 258–9.

normative democratic justification for the sovereign power wielded by Parliament.[42]

From this primary distinction between the models of constitutional and parliamentary supremacy there flowed a number of other differences. Let me mention just two.

B.   The Relationship Between the Citizen and the State

First, the adoption of constitutional supremacy—and, hence, of popular sovereignty as the fundamental principle—served to place the relationship between the citizen and the state on a very different foundation in the United States from that which obtained in England. In particular, the *dynamic* of the relationship was different. Constitutional paramountcy reflects the notion of social compact, of a population which is engaged in the political process, and upon whose license the continued existence of the institutions of government depends. Thus it invokes the idea of participatory democracy.

In contrast, the concept of parliamentary sovereignty called to mind a more hierarchical structure of superiors and subordinates.[43] Since Parliament's sovereign power did not derive, in the first place, institutionally from the will of the people, there was little or no sense in which that power was felt to be held 'on trust' for the community at large.

C.   Legal Theory: Positivist and Normative Perspectives

Secondly, the traditional manner of distinguishing between legislative and constitutional supremacy has important implications when it is mapped onto the broader canvas of legal theory. Viewed in its *original* form, the doctrine of parliamentary sovereignty presented a visage which was relentlessly positivist[44] in outlook.[45] It constituted legal positivism in its paradigm form. By articulating a constitutional theory

---

[42] See below Part IV A for a discussion of reform of the electoral franchise.

[43] See Cotterrell, above n 38, at 39.

[44] Space precludes detailed discussion of the meaning of positivism. It is used, in the present context, in a general sense to describe that approach to legal and constitutional theory that treats legal and moral validity as distinguishable issues. Eg, HLA Hart, *The Concept of Law* 2d ed (Oxford, Clarendon Press, 1994) 185–93.

[45] As one commentator has noted:

which demands unqualified judicial loyalty to every Act of Parliament, it appeared to institutionalise the distinction between, on the one hand, legal validity and, on the other hand, considerations of morality.

As the great British judge, Lord Reid, remarked:

> It is often said that it would be unconstitutional for the United Kingdom to do certain things, meaning that the moral[] ... [or] other reasons against doing them are so strong that most people would regard it as highly improper if Parliament did these things. But ... [i]f Parliament chose to do any of them the courts could not hold the Act ... invalid.[46]

Viewed in this way, the doctrine of parliamentary sovereignty turns the pure theory of legal positivism into legal reality.

Constitutional supremacy, of course, is not amenable to such analysis. The fact that the Bill of Rights enjoys the status of fundamental law precludes a purely positivist approach to adjudication in America. Here, it is impossible to divorce legal validity from considerations of political and social morality. The existence of an entrenched Constitution enjoins an approach which embraces an ineluctable connection between questions of law and questions of morality.

Looked at in this manner, the divide between positivist and normative models of adjudication underscores still further the perceived distinction between the notions of constitutional and legislative supremacy.

V.   A MEASURE OF CONVERGENCE?

So much for *traditional perceptions*. What of *present realities*? I wish to demonstrate, in the time which remains, that although the picture I have just painted once may have described accurately the distinction between our two constitutional systems, it is now nothing more than an outdated caricature. In particular, I shall return to the idea which I

No greater testimony exists to the power and resilience of positivism in modern legal thought than the debate between constitutional lawyers about the nature of parliamentary sovereignty. At the root of almost all analyses of the nature and scope of the doctrine lies an unquestioned separation of legal from political principle.

TRS Allan, 'The Limits of Parliamentary Sovereignty', (1985) *Pub L* 614, 614 (footnote omitted).

[46] *Madzimbamuto v Lardner-Burke*, [1969] 1 AC 645, 723 (PC 1968) (appeal taken from S Rhodesia).

sketched earlier: that sovereignty, meaningless in abstract terms, is a creature of contemporary political and legal context. I will argue that, once this fundamental point is appreciated, it becomes apparent that the distinction between legislative and constitutional supremacy is *real*, but markedly more *subtle* than it once was.

Let me consider some specific features of modern British constitutionalism that fundamentally have changed the context within which the notion of parliamentary sovereignty must be understood and which, as a result, have important implications for any comparison of the principles of constitutional and legislative supremacy.

A.   The Modern Basis of Parliamentary Sovereignty

As a matter of legal history, the philosophical foundations on which those two concepts stand have been viewed as the fundamental point of distinction.[47] In particular, the idea that parliamentary sovereignty (unlike constitutional primacy) neither derived from nor depended upon an underlying popular consensus traditionally has exerted a strong influence on English constitutional theory. As Dicey put it, writing at the turn of the last century:

> [T]he courts will take no notice of the will of the electors. The judges know nothing about any will of the people except in so far as that will is expressed by an Act of Parliament, and would never suffer the validity of a statute to be questioned on the ground of its having been passed or kept alive in opposition to the wishes of the electors.[48]

At the beginning of the twenty-first century, the British doctrine of parliamentary sovereignty rests on rather different foundations. In common with most British constitutional developments, the change was evolutionary rather than revolutionary.[49] In particular, it was effected by gradual reform of the electoral franchise. Before 1832, the right to vote in general elections in the United Kingdom was based largely on

---

[47] See above Part III A

[48] Dicey, above n 16, at 73–4.

[49] For further discussion of the typology of constitutional change in Britain, see Lord Irvine of Lairg, 'Constitutional Change in the United Kingdom: British Solutions to Universal Problems,' *National Heritage Lecture* at the US Supreme Court (11 May 1998) (transcript available at http://www.open.gov.uk/lcd/speeches/1998/1998fr.htm).

property qualifications and extended to only five per cent of the adult population. The passing of the 'Great Reform Act'[50] in 1832 precipitated a period of fundamental reform which lasted for a full century.[51] Even by 1910, however, only twenty-eight per cent of the total adult population enjoyed the right to vote.[52] The most farreaching changes occurred in 1918:[53] Residency (as opposed to property entitlement) became the organizing principle, and, thanks to the sacrifices made by the 'suffragettes,' women over thirty years of age acquired voting rights.[54]

Those reforms demonstrate the emergence of representative and participatory democracy as the primary principle of constitutional and political theory in Britain. They evidence a paradigm shift in how the relationship between the state and the individual is conceptualized in the United Kingdom. In this way, the process of electoral reform fundamentally has changed the environment within which parliamentary sovereignty subsists, transforming the doctrine into the vehicle by which the modern commitment to democracy is institutionalised. Thus, the legal sovereignty exercised by Parliament now is viewed as deriving its legitimacy from the fact that Parliament's composition is, in the first place, determined by the electorate in whom ultimate political sovereignty resides.[55]

Indeed, this conception of sovereignty finds clear expression in the principle known as the Salisbury Convention.[56] In 1945, the Labour Party won an overall majority of seats in the House of Commons, yet the House of Lords was dominated by unelected Conservative peers

---

[50] Reform Act of 1832, 2 & 3 Will 4, c 65, §§ I, IV (Eng).
[51] Additional legislation was enacted in 1867 and 1884 that further widened the electoral franchise. See Representation of the People Act, 1884, 48 & 49 Vict, c 3 (Eng); Representation of the People Act, 1867, 30 & 31 Vict, c 102 (Eng).
[52] David Butler & Anne Sloman, *British Political Facts 1900–1979*, 5th ed (1980) at 227.
[53] Those changes were effected by the Representation of the People Act of 1918, 7 & 8 Geo 5, c 64 (Eng).
[54] In 1928, the franchise was broadened further by extending voting rights to women aged over twenty-one. See Equal Franchise Act of 1928, 18 & 19 Geo 5, c 12 (Eng).
[55] A V Dicey acknowledged the emergence of political sovereignty alongside the theory of parliamentary sovereignty, see, eg, Dicey, above n 16, at 82–85, although he was, perhaps, somewhat reluctant to embrace the full implications of their interaction.
[56] Although enunciated in its modern form in 1945 by the then Viscount Cranborne, the principle is known as the Salisbury Convention because it is founded upon the 'mandate' doctrine that was developed by the Third Marquess of Salisbury in the late nineteenth century.

who had inherited their seats. In a debate in the Upper Chamber, the then Viscount Cranborne argued that it would be 'constitutionally wrong' for the House of Lords to prevent the manifesto commitments of the elected Government from being enacted into law.[57] That argument was broadly accepted, and the Salisbury Convention thus emerged, according to which the unelected Chamber does not vote against legislation which seeks to give effect to electoral pledges that have been endorsed by the majority of voters.[58]

The present Government is pursuing a thoroughgoing process of constitutional renewal.[59] As part of that program, it has abolished the right of hereditary peers to sit in the House of Lords, subject to a temporary right of ninety-two to remain.[60] Although further reform of the Upper Chamber is presently being considered and is not yet firmly settled, the Royal Commission, which recently undertook a thorough investigation of this subject, has recommended clearly that the House of Lords can best fulfill its role as a Second Chamber if it is *not* fully elected.[61] Consequently, the Salisbury Convention, or a modern successor to that principle, will remain necessary in order to articulate the idea that, while the House of Lords has a pivotal role to play both in the legislative process and in holding the executive to account, the *elected* House of Commons is, in the final analysis, the senior partner.[62]

This view of how the two Houses of Parliament should relate to each other, which the Salisbury Convention institutionalises and which lies at the heart of the present reform program, acknowledges that the legitimacy of Parliament's legislative power is rooted firmly in the will of the

---

[57] See 137 Parl Deb, HL (5th ser) (1945) 47 (remarks of Viscount Cranbourne); see also 137 Parl Deb, HL (5th ser) (1945) 613–4 (remarks of Viscount Cranbourne).

[58] Formulated more precisely, the Convention requires that the House of Lords not oppose bills on their second or third readings. It also is accepted widely that the Upper Chamber should not subject draft legislation covered by the Salisbury Convention to 'wrecking amendments' that undermine the fundamental principles on which a bill is founded.

[59] For details of the Government's reform program vis-à-vis the House of Lords, see generally Modernising Parliament: Reforming the House of Lords, 1999, Cm 4183, available at http://www.official-documents.co.uk/document/cm41/4183/4183.htm. The reform program also encompasses the conferral of greater protection on human rights; the devolution of governmental power to Scotland, Wales, and Northern Ireland; the enactment of freedom of information legislation; and the establishment of a new strategic authority for Greater London.

[60] See House of Lords Act 1999, c 34, § 2(2) (Eng).

[61] See *A House for the Future*, 2000, Cm 4534, at 7, available at http://www.official-documents.co.uk/document/cm45/4534/4534.htm.

[62] The Royal Commission on the Reform of the House of Lords shares this view. See *ibid*, at 39–40.

electorate, for whom that power is held on trust.[63] This, in turn, clearly illustrates that the doctrine of parliamentary supremacy, seen from a modern perspective, is properly to be viewed as an expression of the political sovereignty of the people.

We therefore reach the position that the theories of government which obtain in both America and the United Kingdom are founded on the idea of popular sovereignty. The important implication of this is that, viewed from a contemporary perspective, the principles of constitutional and parliamentary supremacy are rooted in the same basic political philosophy which recognises that government depends, for its legitimacy, on the imprimatur of the people.[64] In this sense, the two theories are distinct species of the same genus. They constitute different methodologies by which the ultimate aspiration—to fully representative, participatory, and therefore legitimate governance—is translated into practical reality.

It is, perhaps, unsurprising that constitutional primacy was the solution which was preferred here, given that the Framers were starting from scratch and wished to constitute the United States on a different footing from that which obtained in the United Kingdom.[65] In Contrast, the British constitution is the product of evolution. That defining characteristic of British constitutionalism explains why, in the United Kingdom, the preferred solution has been to retain parliamentary sovereignty, but gradually to change the political and legal environment within which the principle exists. In that evolutive manner, the theory of parliamentary sovereignty, like the principle of constitutional supremacy, has come to represent the primacy which is attached to representative, democratic government, which is surely the most fundamental of all the values which our two countries have in common.

---

[63] The Parliament Acts enacted from 1911 to 1949, which provide, in certain circumstances, for the passage of legislation without the consent of the House of Lords, similarly institutionalize a conception of parliamentary sovereignty that roots its legitimacy firmly in the mandate conferred upon Parliament by the electorate.

[64] The arrival of British constitutional theory at this position has led some commentators to suggest that the democratic principle is prior—and therefore superior—to the doctrine of parliamentary sovereignty. See, eg, TRS Allan, *Law, Liberty, and Justice: The Legal Foundations of British Constitutionalism* (Oxford, Clarendon Press, 1993); Laws, 'Constitution,' above n 19; 'Laws, Law and Democracy,' above n 19; Woolf, above n 19. As I have indicated elsewhere, that is a view that I do not share. The fate of fundamentally antidemocratic legislation would, in the final analysis, be resolved in the political, not the judicial, arena. See Lord Irvine of Lairg, 'Judges and Decision-Makers: The Theory and Practice of *Wednesbury* Review,' (1996) *Pub L* 59 (now Chapter 9 in this volume).

[65] For a sophisticated and innovative analysis of the constitutional settlement adopted by the American Founders, see Bruce Ackerman, '*The New* Separation of Powers,' 113 *Harv L Rev* 633 (2000).

B.   Sovereignty, Constitutionalism, and Fundamental Rights

Thus far, I have been concerned with the common foundation which, viewed from a contemporary standpoint, the notions of constitutional and parliamentary sovereignty share. Let me turn, now, to the more specific issue of human rights protection.

I began my Lecture this evening by remarking upon the immense contribution which James Madison made to the adoption here of the Bill of Rights. The primacy which, as a result, US law accords to fundamental rights is perceived in other countries as the preeminent characteristic of the American Constitution. It is also regarded as a graphic practical illustration of the perceived fundamental divergence between the theories of parliamentary sovereignty and constitutional supremacy. I wish to challenge the correctness of that perception.

a.   *Political and Legal Control Mechanisms*

It is clear that our respective constitutions begin from different starting points. The US system, through its constitutional texts, articulates a positive approach to human rights: They are marked out, from the very beginning, as sacrosanct. In contrast, the United Kingdom has traditionally adopted a negative approach to fundamental rights. This is based upon the principle of legality: the idea that the citizen enjoys the freedom to do as he or she pleases and that any interference with individual liberties must be justified by law.[66] The primary focus of the British system therefore has been on the legislative process, given that the locus of the citizen's freedom is ultimately traced by Parliament's enactments. Thus arose the notion of the self-correcting democracy, according to which the protection of individuals' rights was effected by the political mechanisms of ministerial responsibility and parliamentary scrutiny. This focus on *political*, rather than *legal*, accountability underscored the distinction between the British and American approaches. The point was captured well by Lord Wright, who remarked that, because 'Parliament is supreme,' there exist in the British constitution 'no guaranteed or absolute rights. The safeguard of British liberty [therefore lies] in the good sense of the people and in the system

---

[66] The *locus classicus* of this approach is, of course, the decision in *Entick v Carrington*, 95 Eng Rep 807 (KB 1765). The infringement of the individual's rights in that case was held to be unlawful because no legal provision permitted their infraction, and a general plea of 'state necessity' was rejected.

of representative and responsible government which has been evolved.'[67]

However, although it is true that English law traditionally has emphasised political, rather than legal, control of government, this certainly does not mean that it has pursued the former to the exclusion of the latter. English judges have long recognised that, although Britain adheres to a version of the democratic principle which places enactments of the elected legislature beyond judicial control, Parliament 'does not legislate in a vacuum.'[68] Instead, it 'legislates for a European liberal democracy founded on the principles and traditions of the common law.'[69] The courts therefore approach all legislation on the well-founded presumption that Parliament intends to legislate consistently with such principles. By such interpretative means, the judiciary has been able to confer a high degree of protection on a range of fundamental norms, such as access to justice,[70] judicial review,[71] and rights of due process.[72]

Consequently, although British courts cannot strike down legislation,[73] they can often, by interpretative means, bring legislation which appears to be inconsistent with fundamental rights into line with them. This emphasises the point, to which I alluded earlier, that the notion of

---

[67] *Liversidge v Anderson*, [1942] AC 206, 260–61 (1941) (appeal taken from Eng CA).

[68] *Regina v Sec'y of State for the Home Dep't, ex parte Pierson*, [1998] AC 539, 587 (appeal taken from Eng CA) (Steyn, L J).

[69] *Ibid*, see also Lord Steyn, 'Incorporation and Devolution: A Few Reflections on the Changing Scene,' (1998) *Eur Hum Rts L Rev* 153, 154–5.

[70] See eg, *Regina v Sec'y of State for the Home Dep't, ex parte Leech*, [1994] QB 198 (Eng CA 1993); *Regina v Lord Chancellor, ex parte Witham*, (1998) QB 575 [1997]. For a discussion of access to justice and the interpretative process, see Mark Elliott, 'Reconciling Constitutional Rights and Constitutional Orthodoxy,' 56 *Cambridge LJ* 474 (1997).

[71] See preeminently, *Anisminic Ltd v Foreign Comp Comm'n*, [1969] 2 AC 147 (1968) (appeal taken from Eng CA), in which the House of Lords vouchsafed, by interpretative means, the availability of judicial review of administrative action.

[72] The law of judicial review, which safeguards a broad range of due process rights, takes effect as a consequence of judicial interpretation of enabling legislation, based on the presumption that Parliament wishes basic standards of fairness and rationality to be respected by those agencies upon which it confers power. For a detailed discussion of this 'modified ultra vires doctrine' as the juridical basis of judicial review, see Mark Elliott, *The Constitutional Foundations of Judicial Review* (2001); Mark Elliott, 'The Ultra vires Doctrine in a Constitutional Setting: Still the Central Principle of Administrative Law,' 58 *Cambridge LJ* 129 (1999); see also C Forsyth (ed) *Judicial Review and the Constitution* (Oxford, Hart, 2000).

[73] Unless it is irreconcilably inconsistent with directly effective European Union law. See *Regina v Sec'y of State for Transp, ex parte Factortame Ltd*, [1991] 1 AC 603 (1990) (appeal taken from Eng CA).

sovereignty is meaningless unless it is viewed within a particular context. The rule of law, and the values on which it is based, form a fundamental part of the constitutional environment within which the British doctrine of legislative supremacy subsists. In particular, it gives rise to an interpretative framework which is biased strongly in favor of fundamental rights and which thus shapes the context which gives color to Parliament's enactments.[74] Moreover, British courts have long been willing to take account of the European Convention on Human Rights in a number of contexts.[75] For instance, it is used to aid the construction of ambiguous legislation[76] and can influence the development of the common law when it 'is not firmly settled.'[77] It guides the courts when judicial discretion is exercised[78] and when they are called upon to decide what public policy demands, as well as taking effect in the United Kingdom by operation of European Union law.[79]

The perception of Britain as a self-correcting democracy, in which the rights of the individual are protected entirely by *political* rather than *legal* means, therefore has never been wholly accurate. Like the American principle of constitutional supremacy, the British doctrine of parliamentary sovereignty, understood within its proper setting, embraces both political

---

[74] TRS Allan has written extensively about the relationship between parliamentary sovereignty and the rule of law. See Allan, above n 64; TRS Allan, 'Legislative Supremacy and the Rule of Law: Democracy and Constitutionalism,' 44 *Cambridge LJ* 111 (1985); Allan, above n 45; TRS Allan, 'Parliamentary Sovereignty: Law, Politics, and Revolution,' 113 *LQ Rev* 443 (1997).

[75] See 573 Parl Deb, HL (5th ser) (1996) 1465–67 (remarks of Lord Bingham); Murray Hunt, *Using Human Rights Law in English Courts* 207–61 (1997); Francesca Klug & Keir Starmer, Incorporation Through the Back Door?, (1997) *Pub L* 223, 224–5.

[76] See eg, *Regina v Sec'y of State for the Home Dep't, ex parte Brind*, [1991] 1 AC 696 (1991) (appeal taken from Eng CA).

[77] *Attorney-Gen v British Broad Corp*, [1981] AC 303, 352 (appeal taken from Eng CA) (Fraser, LJ); see also *Rantzen v Mirror Group Newspapers* (1986) Ltd, 1994 QB 670 (Eng CA 1993); *Derbyshire County Council v Times Newspapers Ltd*, 1992 QB 770 (Eng CA 1992).

[78] See eg, *Regina v Khan* (Sultan), 1997 AC 558 (1996) (appeal taken from Eng CA) (exclusion of evidence in criminal proceedings), rev'd sub nom. *Khan v United Kingdom*, *Times* (London), 23 May 2000, Law Report, at 18 (Eur Ct Hum Rts 2000); *Attorney-Gen v Guardian Newspapers Ltd*, [1987] 1 WLR 1248 (HL 1987) (appeal taken from Eng CA) (provision of discretionary relief).

[79] For the European Court of Justice's case law, see principally, Case 4/73, *J Nold, Kohlen-und Boustoffgroßhandlung v Commission*, [1974] ECR 491; Case 11/70, *InternationaleHandelsgesellschaft mbH v Einfuhr- und Vorratsstelle fur Getreide und Futtermittel*, [1970] ECR 1125. For analysis, see, for example, Lord Browne-Wilkinson, 'The Infiltration of a Bill of Rights,' (1992) *Pub L* 397; Nicholas Grief, 'The Domestic Impact of the European Convention on Human Rights as Mediated Through Community Law,' (1991) *Pub L* 555.

and legal control of government, although the respective systems strike different balances between those two mechanisms.

b.   The Human Rights Act 1998

It has, however, been clear for some time that the balance struck in the United Kingdom has been premised on an outdated—and exaggerated— view of the efficacy of political accountability.[80] The former Prime Minister, John Major, remarked in a major speech opposing a Bill of Rights for Britain that '[w]e have no need of a Bill of Rights because we have freedom.'[81] This, however, overlooks the fact that constant effort is required in order to ensure that such freedom is preserved in the face of the legislative and executive activity associated with modern governance, both of which are well capable of trampling on basic human rights.

For precisely these reasons, the present Government introduced a Human Rights Act.[82] The legislation was enacted in 1998 and, after an intensive period of judicial training and preparation across Government, was implemented on 2 October 2000. It places public authorities under a new duty to respect fundamental rights,[83] and requires the Government to draw Parliament's attention to any new draft legislation which is likely to compromise civil liberties.[84] Most fundamentally, the Act directs the courts to interpret legislation compatibly with human rights whenever this is possible.[85] And when that is not possible, a 'declaration of incompatibility' may be issued,[86] which should lead to the offending legislation being amended by means of a 'fast-track' procedure.[87]

---

[80] See for example, the substantial number of judgments against the United Kingdom in the European Court of Human Rights. For discussion of the UK record before the Court, see AW Bradley, in Wilson Finnie *et al* (eds). 'The United Kingdom Before the Strasbourg Court 1975–1990', in *Edinburgh Essays in Public Law* (1991) 185.

[81] Robert Shrimsley, 'Future of the Constitution: Major Pledges to Defend "Freedoms",' *Daily Telegraph* (London), June 27, 1996, at 6, 1996 WL 3960465.

[82] Human Rights Act, 1998, c 42 (Eng). See generally *Rights Brought Home: The Human Rights Bill*, 1997, Cm 3782, http://www.official-documents.co.uk/document /hoffice/rights/rights.htm; Lord Irvine of Lairg, 'The Development of Human Rights in Britain Under an Incorporated Convention on Human Rights,' (1998) *Pub L* 221.

[83] Human Rights Act § 6(1) ('It is unlawful for a public authority to act in a way which is incompatible with a Convention right.').

[84] See *ibid*, § 19 (requiring government either to make 'written statement of compatibility' with Convention rights, or to note its inability to make such statement).

[85] Above n 83, § 3.

[86] Above n 83, § 4.

[87] Above n 83, § 10.

The Act does *not,* however, confer on British courts any authority to *quash* legislation which is irreconcilable with human rights norms.[88] Nevertheless, the issue of a declaration of incompatibility is very *likely* to prompt the amendment of defective legislation. This follows because such a declaration is likely to create considerable political pressure in favor of the rectification of national law and because a litigant who obtains such a declaration is likely to secure a remedy before the European Court of Human Rights if a remedy is not forthcoming domestically. Consequently, while British courts will not possess the power to strike down legislation which is incompatible with human rights, their power to issue a declaration of incompatibility is substantial, given that, in pragmatic terms, it very probably will lead to the amendment of defective legislation. In this *practical* sense, the Human Rights Act does introduce a *limited* form of constitutional review which is able fully to coexist with the theory of parliamentary sovereignty.[89] It also reconciles the dual democratic imperatives of governance *by the majority* in a manner which respects *minority interests.*[90]

c.   *British Constitutionalism and Legal Theory*

I will conclude, in a moment, by considering the broader significance of these developments for the relationship between the principles of constitutional and legislative supremacy. First, however, let me return to a specific point which I raised earlier.

---

[88] In contrast, full constitutional review *does* exist vis-à-vis the enactments of the Scottish Parliament, given that certain matters (eg, the competence to legislate on reserved matters or in contravention of the European Convention on Human Rights) lie beyond its powers. See Scotland Act, 1998, c 46, § 29 (Eng). Nevertheless, the position that obtains in Scotland remains distinguishable from that existing in the United States, given that the Scotland Act does not displace the capacity of the Westminster Parliament to legislate for Scotland on any matter (irrespective of whether it is reserved or devolved). *Ibid,* § 28(7). The possibility therefore remains for legislation (enacted by Westminster) to operate validly in Scotland notwithstanding its incompatibility with the Human Rights Act 1998.

[89] An approach to human rights that preserves the legislature's ultimate capacity to attenuate them also has been favored by a number of other common law countries. For instance, the New Zealand Bill of Rights Act, 1990 (NZ), http://rangi.knowledge-basket.co.nz/gpacts/public/text/1990/an/109.html, requires legislation to be interpreted consistently with fundamental rights, see above n 88, § 6, but leaves the legislature's power to restrict such rights ultimately intact, see above n 88, § 4. Similarly, Section 33(1) of the Canadian Charter of Rights and Freedoms permits legislative derogation from human rights provided that the derogation is explicit. See Canada Act, 1982, c 11, sched B, pt I, § 33(1) (Eng).

[90] See further 582 Parl Deb, HL (5th ser) 1234 (1997) (remarks of Lord Irvine of Lairg).

I noted that the sovereignty principle may appear to institutionalise a relentlessly positivist approach to law and adjudication: By commanding unyielding judicial fealty to every enactment of Parliament, it may seem to enshrine legal positivism in its paradigm form, apparently effecting a rigid separation between questions of legality and considerations of morality. To reach such a conclusion would be, however, to misunderstand the meaning of both positivism and sovereignty.

If positivism is simplistically defined as a theory which divorces questions of *validity* from considerations of morality, then sovereignty is, on any view, positivist in nature. However, the line which distinguishes adjudication on the *validity* of legislation from questions of *interpretation* is not watertight. Once this is appreciated, it becomes apparent that the British constitution is able to embrace sovereignty theory without institutionalising a purely positivist conception of law. The *interpretative* framework which exists in the UK legal order is based on a system of morality which can be traced back to the roots of the common law—which jealously guards the liberty of the individual—and whose most recent manifestation is to be found in the explicit commitment to fundamental rights contained in the Human Rights Act.[91] This reflects an approach which, far from being exclusively positivist, embraces an ineluctable connection between the meaning of law and the framework of values—based preeminently on respect for the rights and liberties of the individual—on which the British legal system is founded.

In this sense, the British and American legal systems both embrace approaches to adjudication which accept a connection between law and morality, albeit that linkage is given different institutional effect by each system. While the emphasis here is on morality (as it is given expression through the Supreme Court's interpretation of the Bill of Rights) as a determinant of the *validity* of legislation, the emphasis in the United Kingdom is on morality as a determinant of the *meaning* of legislation. Thus, while the ultimate objective of connecting law with morality is shared by our respective legal systems, the manner in which that goal is realised differs in order to reflect our distinct constitutional arrangements. This, in turn, reiterates one of my central themes

---

[91] For a more detailed discussion of the manner in which the Human Rights Act will institute an approach to adjudication that is more explicitly moral, see Irvine, above n 82, at 229.

this evening: That, while the principles of constitutional and legislative supremacy *are* clearly different, that divergence is often subtle rather than straightforward. It is to that theme that I finally return.

VI.   CONCLUSION

At first glance, it seems self-evident that American adherence to constitutional supremacy and British attachment to parliamentary sovereignty define a gulf which separates our respective approaches to constitutionalism. My purpose, this evening, has been to suggest that, while the two theories are clearly different, their divergence in formal terms should not be permitted to obscure a *measure* of convergence at the level of substance.

This follows because one of the defining characteristics of both theories is that their meaning ultimately is determined by the broader legal and political environment within which they subsist. Although the degree of their conceptual distinction is sufficient to ensure that they do not *overlap,* their inherent elasticity and context-sensitivity make it unduly simplistic to postulate a bright-line distinction between them. This conclusion applies with equal force both to their underlying foundations and their practical implications.

As I discussed earlier, reform of the British electoral franchise during the nineteenth and early twentieth centuries fundamentally changed the philosophical and political foundations on which parliamentary sovereignty rests, turning the doctrine into the vehicle which, like constitutional supremacy, gives effect to a notion of popular sovereignty. Thus, legislative and constitutional supremacy both institutionalise a theory of government which rests on the same philosophical basis, although they represent different interpretations of how that theory ought to be given effect.

Context is equally central to an appreciation of more practical matters, such as the protection which the theories of constitutional and legislative supremacy afford to fundamental rights. Viewed superficially, the former appears to render human rights absolutely secure, while the latter seems to make them precarious in the extreme. The position, however, is less straightforward in reality. The practical capacity of a written constitution to protect human rights is ultimately dependent upon the broader context within which it exists: 'If the judges are not prepared to speak for it, a constitution is nothing.'[92] It is the willingness of American judges to give practical effect to the Bill of Rights which has turned an aspirational text into enforceable law.

Equally, the extent to which parliamentary sovereignty renders human rights precarious is a function of the broader constitutional setting. As I argued earlier, the evolution of the context within which sovereignty theory exists has impacted fundamentally upon its implications for human rights protection. In particular, the new Human Rights Act creates an environment within which it is much more difficult, legally[93] and politically,[94] for Parliament to exercise its sovereignty in a manner which is inconsistent with civil liberties.

The fact that the United Kingdom does not embrace constitutional review continues to distinguish our system from that which applies here. But although such differences are important, they should not be allowed to obscure the fact that our respective systems share so much in common. The value of representative and participatory democracy lies at the very heart of both the American and British constitutional orders. And we share an appreciation of the importance of individual liberty whose roots can be traced back as far as the Magna Carta.

Writing in *The Federalist* in 1788, James Madison said that

> The aim of every political constitution is, or ought to be, first to obtain for rulers men who possess most wisdom to discern, and most virtue to pursue, the common good of the society; and in the next place, to take the most effectual precautions for keeping them virtuous whilst they continue to hold their public trust.[95]

---

[92] Sir Stephen Sedley, 'The Sound of Silence: Constitutional Law Without a Constitution', 110 *LQ Rev* 270, 277 (1994).

[93] This follows because the logical effect of section 3 of the Act is to introduce very clear statutory language as a condition precedent to legislative interference with human rights. See Human Rights Act, 1998, c 42, § 3 (Eng) (requiring that, insofar as possible, legislation be read to comply with Convention rights, thereby resulting in clarification of statutory language). The use of such language therefore has become a *legal* requirement that must be satisfied before Parliament is able to infringe fundamental rights.

[94] The Act makes it more difficult *politically* for Parliament to qualify human rights because, first, the use of clear language, see above n 93, and the § 19 statement of compatibility scheme, will draw parliamentary and public attention to the rights implications of draft legislation (and, therefore, will require the Government to justify the attenuation of human rights); and second, significant political pressure in favor of amendment is likely to attend a judicial declaration of incompatibility under § 4.

[95] *The Federalist* No 57 (James Madison).

Those words ring just as true today as they did two centuries ago. And the commitment to democratic and accountable government which they reflect remains the most fundamental of the many enduring factors which connect constitutionalism in Britain and America.

15

*The Spirit of Magna Carta Continues to Resonate in Modern Law**

I. THE LEGACY OF MAGNA CARTA: A JOINT COMMITMENT TO THE RULE OF LAW

FOR NEAR ON 800 years lawyers and parliamentarians have kept the spirit of Magna Carta alive. For their pains they have been accused of representing an essentially feudal Charter, that was motivated by self-interest and the demands of political expediency, as a constitutional document of enduring significance. On this view, it is the glint of the sword, not the spirit of liberty, which best characterises Magna Carta. The principal offender is said to be Sir Edward Coke, himself both judge and parliamentarian.[1] In his *Second Institutes*, he wrote that the Charter derived its name from its 'great importance, and the weightiness of the matter'.[2] He was wrong in this. It was so named to distinguish it from the separate and shorter Charter of the Forest.[3] Coke also considered that the terms of Magna Carta were 'for the most part declaratory of the principal grounds of the fundamental laws of England, and for the residue it is additional to supply some defects of the common law ...'[4] Coke certainly went too far, although it can be said that Magna Carta has had effect both as a statute and through the common law. The real issue, however, is whether Coke was closer than his critics to an enduring truth.

* This article is based on the inaugural Magna Carta Lecture, delivered by the Lord Chancellor in the Parliament Building in Canberra, Australia on 14 October 2002. The writer is grateful to Mr Tom Hickman. Research Student, Selwyn College, Cambridge, for his valuable assistance in the preparation of this lecture.
[1] The most notorious and vociferous condemnation was that of Edward Jenks, 'The Myth of Magna Carta' (1904) 4 *Independent Review* 260.
[2] *Institutes—Second Part*, v I (1642), *Proeme.*
[3] A B White, 'The Name Magna Carta' (1915) 30 EHR 472; (1917) 32 EHR 554. The terms of the Forest Charter were initially part of King John's Charter of Liberties, but they were separated from it in 1217 when it was reissued by his successor Henry III.
[4] Coke, above n 2, *Proeme.*

Magna Carta was re-issued four times, with various amendments, and is now thought to have been confirmed by Parliament on almost 50 further occasions.[5] The authoritative text, four chapters of which remain on the statute book in England,[6] is Edward I's *inspeximus* of 1297.[7] A copy of this version, the only one outside the United Kingdom, is displayed in Australia's new Parliament House. By accompanying words of confirmation, also still on the statute book,[8] it is said that the Charter of Liberties 'made by common assent of all the realm ... shall be kept in every point without breach';[9] and that the Charter shall be taken to be the common law.[10] In many respects Magna Carta has transcended the distinction between law and politics and its legacy represents a joint commitment by monarchs, parliamentarians and the courts, to the rule of law.[11] This legacy forms a central part of the shared constitutional heritage of Britain and Australia. It is in recognition of this that the monument to Magna Carta has been established in the Parliamentary Zone of Australia's national capital, incorporating the British Government's contribution towards the celebrations of the Centenary of Australia's Federation last year.[12]

For some, Magna Carta today represents no more than a distant constitutional echo. My proposition, to the contrary, is that the spirit of Magna Carta continues to resonate in modern law. However, let me first reaffirm Magna Carta's constitutional significance and refute suggestions that it was no more than a narrow baronial pact.[13]

---

[5] F Thompson, *Magna Carta—its Role in the Making of the English Constitution 1300–1629* (1972), ch 1.

[6] *Halsbury's Statutes*, v 10, Part I (2001), pp 14–17; the chapters are 1, 9, 29, 37.

[7] 25 Edw 1.

[8] *Halsbury's Statutes*, above, n 6, p 18.

[9] These words of confirmation refer to Henry III's re-issue, which is discussed below. This was the version on which Coke based his *Second Institutes*, since copies of John's Charter were unknown to him.

[10] See Coke, above n 2, *Proeme*.

[11] It is important to recognise, as Coke himself emphasised, that Magna Carta also provided a measure against which the acts of Parliament were to be judged. Coke stated that a 'good caveat to parliaments to leave all causes to be measured by the golden and straight metwand of the law and not the uncertain and crooked cord of discretion' and castigated parliamentary conduct that failed to observe the promises enshrined in Magna Carta (*Institutes—Fourth Part* (c 1669), 37, 41).

[12] Magna Carta Committee, Australia-Britain Society, *Magna Carta Place in Australia's National Capital: A Report on Its Naming and Development* (March, 2002).

[13] Modern texts frequently give only passing reference to Magna Carta or even entirely omit mention of it: *eg*, S De Smith and R Brazier, *Constitutional and Administrative Law*, 8th ed, (London, Sweet and Maxwell 1998); J Jowell and D Oliver (eds).*The Changing Constitution* 4th ed, (Oxford, OUP 2000); G Williams, *Human Rights under the Australian Constitution* (1999), pp 2–3; O Hood Phillips and P Jackson, *Constitutional and Administrative Law* 8th ed, (London, Sweet and Maxwell, 2001), para 2–007.

II.   MAGNA CARTA AND THE EMERGENCE OF THE
RULE OF LAW

The dramatic events surrounding King John's capitulation remain of central importance to understanding the constitutional significance and enduring message of Magna Carta. Indeed, the Australian monument to Magna Carta fittingly incorporates scenes from the period, which should continue to inspire generations of lawyers, laymen and parliamentarians alike.[14]

The story of Magna Carta is a chapter in the continuing history of the struggle between power and freedom. It is a chapter set in a time when ultimate power was concentrated in the hands of a single ruler. However, in a time before the principle of primogeniture had become established, the death of a king was usually followed by a contest for succession in which contestants relied both on might and right in enlisting the support of important magnates, the Church, and those in control of the treasury. It was at this stage that the privilege and power of kings was most clearly limited. Before coronation by the Church, new kings were required to make an oath to observe justice and equity and to uphold the peace. Abuses of the previous reign were stipulated and forbidden for the future. Such were the terms of Henry I's coronation oath, sworn in 1100. Henry had rapidly seized the throne after his brother died suddenly, if not a little suspiciously, while they were hunting; but his claim was weak and he had shaky baronial support. For these reasons he embodied his oath in a Charter of Liberties, which was the crude precursor of Magna Carta.[15] Nonetheless, once crowned, a coronation oath, even in the form of a Charter, was no restraint against a powerful king. Few expected such promises to be taken particularly seriously, and Henry broke every one of them.[16]

However, Magna Carta was not, as is often said, simply a reaction against the tyrannies and excesses of King John. Sir James Holt, the preeminent modern authority on Magna Carta, has argued that the predominant cause of the Charter was the manner in which the Angevin

---

Alternatively it is said to be a narrow document, the significance of which has been overestimated: eg, J Alder. *Constitutional and Administrative Law* 2nd ed, (Basingstoke, Macmillan 1994), 39, D Feldman, *Civil Liberties and Human Rights in England and Wales* 2nd ed, (Oxford, OUP, 2002) 71.

[14] Magna Carta Committee, above n 12, pp 13–21, 33–34.

[15] W Stubbs, *The Constitutional History of England—in its Origin and Development*, v I 4th ed, (1883), 328–330.

[16] W S McKechnie, *Magna Carta—a Commentary on the Great Charter of King John* (1905), 118.

Kings exploited England in an attempt to expand and defend their continental empire.[17] This process can be traced to the accession of Henry II in 1154 who, as Count of Anjou and Duke of Normandy, had dominions covering three-fifths of France. To sustain this empire Henry gave the administrative centres of England, the Curia Regis and the Exchequer, a new lease of life. He extended the jurisdiction of the King's Courts, and exploited the feudal obligations owed by his barons.[18] The momentum was increased by Henry's successor, Richard I, and his Chief Justiciar, Hubert Walter, since it was necessary to pay for Richard's prolonged and expensive crusades.[19] The Angevin Kings also eagerly seized new opportunities to raise revenue that were not open to other feudal lords, notably the taxation of trade and the control of weights and measures. Faced with this centralised and ruthlessly efficient governmental apparatus, the King's subjects required assurances that good practices would be observed and their liberties preserved.

Even so, it was no accident that the revolt occurred in the reign of King John. He was a capricious and inconstant ruler. Moreover, he inflamed his barons by demanding enormous scutages and aids to finance his unsuccessful military expeditions. He lost Normandy to the French King and his nickname, 'John Softsword', set him in unfavourable contrast with his lionhearted brother, Richard. A battle with Rome ended in his astute but ignominious offer of homage to the Pope.

When John determined on setting out across the Channel to stamp his authority on his lands in Poitou and Anjou and perhaps even re-take Normandy itself, he found many of his barons refusing to follow, in open defiance of their fealty. Instead John, with his mercenaries, set off northward to bring the most intransigent northern magnates to heel. Civil war was averted only by the bold intervention of Stephen Langton, the Archbishop of Canterbury, who persuaded John not to distrain his barons without lawful judgment of his court. Enraged, John had to settle for a fortnight's marching about his northern fiefdoms stamping his feet in frustration.[20] The following year in 1214 John renewed his assault on his enemies in France, but was this time deserted by his Poitevin barons. On his return to England his discontented

[17] J C Holt, *Magna Carta* 2nd ed, (1992), 24.
[18] *Ibid*, pp 29–33.
[19] Historians have recently revised views of Richard I's reign and administration, which were traditionally thought to have been retrogressive. See generally J Gillingham, *Richard Coeur de Lion—Kingship, Chivalry and War in the Twelfth Century* (1994), pp 95–118; M T Clanchy, *England and its Rulers* 1066–1272 2nd ed, (1998), pp 94–98.
[20] See W L Warren, *King John* (1997), p 214.

English magnates seized their opportunity and John was confronted by open revolt. As John's biographer has put it: 'it may well have seemed to men already inflamed to the point of conspiracy, that John had been obliged to come to terms with the Church and with the French king and that the next item on the agenda, as it were, was that he should come to terms with them'.[21]

It was likely to have been Stephen Langton who produced Henry I's Charter as a way of focusing and legitimating the baronial grievances.[22] While many of the barons, it is true, were principally activated by selfish desires for revenge and recompense, the Charter also appealed to moderates. It provided a point of compromise and a sure foundation for Magna Carta.[23] The terms of Magna Carta itself were hammered out during protracted negotiations in the meadow in Runnymede in 1215.[24] King John was undoubtedly trying to buy time and the country was still destined to descend into civil war. However, when the storm eventually subsided Magna Carta emerged as the rock upon which the constitution would gradually be built and the fulcrum upon which the constitutional balance would be struck.

The terms of John's Charter amplified and expanded Henry I's.[25] It was dominated by issues of contemporary importance as diverse as reliefs. Widows, wardships and fishweirs. Scutages and aids were only to be levied by the Common Council of the Kingdom.[26] The City of London, which had played host to the rebel barons, was to have all its ancient liberties and free customs.[27] There were several concessions to merchants, and weights and measures were regularised. The most

---

[21] *Ibid*, p 225.

[22] Langton's role is celebrated by the Australian Magna Carta monument. Modern historians, however, disagree over precisely what role he had. Certainly Warren regard him as the only person who deserves to be singled out from among Magna Carta's framers (above p 213, cf pp 217, 232, 245). He also believes that Langton produced Henry I's Charter, probably at the famous St Paul's meeting in 1213: above pp 226–8. Also Clanchy, Above n 19, p 138. Holt, however, is more circumspect and argues that the meeting never took place: above n 17, pp 219–20, 224–5, 269–70, 279–87.

[23] Warren, above p 231: Holt, above n 17, p 222.

[24] See Holt, above n 17, ch 7.

[25] Stubbs, above n 15, p 572.

[26] Chs 12 and 14: these provisions were altered in the 1217 Charter (see McKechnie, above n 16 pp 172–5) and were altogether excluded from later re-issues. Furthermore, this provision in no way limited the King's right to tallage London (*ibid*, p 281) and other towns. It thus contained only the germ of the later principle that taxation was only to be levied by the consent of property owners, as represented in Parliament.

[27] Ch 13, which later became ch 9.

famous chapters,[28] which later became the venerated chapter 29, stated that no free man was to be arrested, imprisoned, disseised, outlawed or exiled or in any way destroyed, except by the lawful judgment of his peers or by the law of the land. To no one in his realm, the King swore, would he sell, refuse, or delay right or justice. It is stretching imagination to find here a protection of jury trial, but Magna Carta manifestly asserted the superiority of the ordinary law and of regular over arbitrary justice.[29]

There is no reason to think, as is often suggested, that Stephen Langton was also solely responsible for the inclusion of 'free men' as addressees of the Charter. It was becoming clear to reflective lords and bishops that the Charter required a broader base than would be supplied by a simple baronial pact.[30] Coke later took the inclusion of 'free men' to encompass the entire citizenry, but, while it was certainly used broadly, it excluded the villein who was protected only by local custom in his lord's court.[31] Nonetheless, Sir James Holt has argued that the Charter was unique in accepting an exceptional degree of legal parity among free men, and also in its comprehensive application to a relatively cohesive community.[32]

By chapter 61, if the King transgressed, he was at the mercy of the 'community of the whole realm'.[33] Moreover, some provisions applied universally, such as the promise not to sell, refuse or deny justice. The provision which might have had the greatest popular significance was chapter 20.[34] By this chapter no man was to be fined except in proportion to the degree of the offence; and his livelihood was to be at all times preserved. Merchants were not to be deprived of their goods nor villein tenants deprived of their ploughs. These protections against destitution were not, as such, binding against all the world, only against the King;

---

[28] Chs 39 and 40.
[29] Other chapters likewise protected the citizenry's access to justice. Ch 17 (which became ch 11) stated that common pleas shall not follow the King's Court but shall heard in some fixed place; a provision that led to the separation of the Common Pleas and the King's Bench. Ch 38 (which became ch 28) provided that no man was to be put to wager his law except by the provision of an honest witness.
[30] Ch 1; Holt, above n 17, pp 269–70.
[31] See J H Baker, *An Introduction to English Legal History* 3rd ed, (London, Butterworths, 1990), pp 347–49, 531–40; McKechnie, above n 16, pp 341–4, 448–9.
[32] Holt, above n 17, pp 276–80; of cf P Vinogradoff. 'Magna Carta' (1905) 21 *LQR* 250 at p 253.
[33] It was the King's inability to satisfy the barons in respect of the contentious issues relating to the retrospective correction of previous transgressions that essentially led to the civil war which followed the events in Runnymede: Holt, above n 17, ch 10.
[34] Which became ch 14.

but further protection against the abuses of feudal lords was embodied in chapter 60, according to which they were to observe the same good practices in respect of their men as promised the King in respect of his.[35] This not only bestowed another dimension on chapter 20, but also extended the protections on such matters as wardships and marriage. The breadth of these protections is illustrated by the fact that in later times Magna Carta was most commonly relied upon in suits between private individuals.[36] This was, then, no mere private bargain between King and barons.

The great nineteenth-century constitutional historian, Bishop Stubbs, went as far as to declare Magna Carta the first great act of a united nation.[37] It is apparent that there was much insight in this assessment. Magna Carta was certainly the product of a shift in the structure of society. The Angevin Kings, with their powerful central administration, had been forced to concede that governmental power should be exercised according to principle, custom and law.[38] Although the crisis in 1215 was immediately and in great part a tussle between King and barons, under this surface the first great step was taken towards a new political theory of the state. Executive power could no longer be employed simply in pursuit of the King's own private projects, nor was it only limited by the rights of a narrow baronial class. Henceforth, government not only had to be just, but also had to consider the good of the community.[39] Significantly, the terms of the settlement were distributed in sealed charters throughout the realm and sheriffs, foresters, and other bailiffs, were ordered to read them in public.[40] In a time when most law was orally proclaimed, Magna Carta not only became 'the great precedent for putting legislation into writing',[41] but also an

---

[35] See Holt, above n 17, pp 276–7, who points out that this was 'not simply laid down as an airy principle' but was backed-up by chs 15 (no one shall levy an aid from his free men) and 16 (no one can be forced to perform more service for any tenement than is due there from). He concludes: 'When the framers of the Charter set out to protect the interests of under-tenants, they meant business'.

[36] Thompson, above n 5, ch 2.

[37] Stubbs, above n 15, pp 571 and 583.

[38] 'Magna Carta has thus been truly said to enunciate and inaugurate "the reign of law" or "the rule of law"' (McKechnie, above n 16, p 148), ' ... the permanent regulations which the Charter was intended to establish were, taken as a whole, a remarkable statement of the rights of the governed and of the principle that the king should be ruled by law' (Holt, above n 167, p 338).

[39] See in particular the analyses of Clanchy, above n 19, pp 97–8, and Warren, *above*, n 20, p 240.

[40] MT Clanchy, *From Memory to Written Record—England 1066–1307* (1979), pp 211–12.

[41] *Ibid.*

awesome record of the terms on which power was to be exercised; intended, as its terms read, to be observed 'in perpetuity'.[42]

King John's death in 1216 brought the child King Henry III to the throne. During his minority the Charter war re-issued three times. This was at the behest of the King's advisers and supporters, out of recognition that the continued legitimacy of government depended on the observance of certain principles of good administration, respect for the liberties of the subject, and adherence to the law. When Henry confirmed the Charter voluntarily and in full majority in 1237 its constitutional importance was secured. By 1300 copies of the Charter were being read and displayed in cathedrals and other public places across the land.[43]

We can conclude from this examination of the terms and historical context of Magna Carta that in celebrating its role in our shared constitutional heritage we need not fear that we are viewing history through rosetinted spectacles. Magna Carta is a defining document in the emergence of the rule of law and, however it came to acquire its name, certainly it is Great.

III.   MAGNA CARTA AND THE CONCEPTION OF MODERN HUMAN RIGHTS DOCUMENTS

If we shift our gaze from the thirteenth century to modern law, we find the modern-day equivalents of Magna Carta in agreements to respect human rights. Unlike Magna Carta, the abuses which inspired these documents became the concern of the whole world and they were conceived on the international plane. After the Second World War the international community resolved to spell out in writing the inalienable rights of individuals to ensure the future protection of, as the Preamble to the Universal Declaration of Human Rights puts it, 'freedom, justice and peace in the world'. These principles increasingly flesh-out the rule of law in modern democracies. However, the ancestral connection between Magna Carta and the modern human rights era, whilst there, must not be overstated. Magna Carta was framed in a time when tests of legal right might still be by battle or ordeal[44] and even the

---

[42] Ch 1.
[43] Clanchy, above n 40, p 213.
[44] Although ordeal was dying out, and from 1215 the clergy were forbidden from participating: Baker, above n 31, pp 5–6.

most beneficent of childhood folk heroes, Robin Hood, was said to have paraded the mutilated head of Guy of Gisborne on the end of his bow.[45] This is a far cry from the respect for human dignity and the fundamental worth of human life which underpins modern human rights documents. Also, despite its universality. Magna Carta still rested upon a system of inequality and feudal hierarchy.[46]

However, to reject Magna Carta's relevance and contribution to the modern human rights era would be to adopt a far too simplistic analysis. We should recall that the United States Constitution was held for many years to licence racial segregation; that, like Magna Carta, the American Declaration of Independence of 1776 consisted largely of a list of alleged wrongs committed by the Crown,[47] and that it was proclaimed agains a background of legalised slavery. The primary importance of Magna Carta is that it is a beacon of the rule of law. It proclaimed the fundamental nature of individual liberties; notwithstanding that many of the liberties it protected would not find direct counterparts in modern democratic states. That said, I shall discuss later its provisions protecting access to justice and illustrate their continued vitality in modern law.

Magna Carta influenced human rights documents in several, connected, ways. The first was through its role in the development of theories of natural rights.[48] Second, these documents owe a large debt to the various constitutions of the American States and the United

[45] J C Holt, *Robin Hood*, rev ed, (1989), pp 10–11, 32–3.

[46] Reflecting what were regarded as the good Christian ethics of the time, chs 10 and 11 of Magna Carta also explicitly discriminated against Jewish money lenders (one of the primary sources of credit at the time).

[47] 'The history of the present King of Great Britain is a history of repeated injuries and usurpations, all having in direct object the establishment of an absolute Tyranny over these States. To prove this, let Facts be submitted to a candid world ... [they are then listed].'

[48] It must be admitted that this was not always a positive contribution. Tom Paine was less than effusive about Magna Carta in *Rights of Man*, where he distinguished it from the French Declaration, arguing that it was not a founding constitutional instrument: B Kuklick (ed), *Thomas Paine: Political Writings*, (Cambridge Texts in the History of Political Thought, CUP, 1997), p 191. However, in *Common Sense* he had earlier called for an American Continental Charter of the United Colonies 'answering to what is called the Magna Charter of England' (*Ibid*, at pp 28–9). The Levellers generally admired Magna Carta and it was prominent in their thought and demands. A few, however, particularly William Walwyn, dismissed it. For example, Overton and Walwyn described Magna Carta as 'a beggarly thing containing many marks of intolerable bondage ...' ('A Remonstrance of many thousand citizens ...', 1646, in A Sharp (ed), *The English Levellers* (1998), 33 at pp 46–7). See generally on Magna Carta and Leveller thought, A Pallister, *Magna Carta—The Heritage of Liberty* (1971), pp 13–22.

States Constitution itself. In their turn these owe much to the legacy of Magna Carta, and in particular the writings of Blackstone and Coke.[49] American constitutional documents effectively married this constitutional inheritance with the ideology of natural and inalienable rights, best represented by the writings of John Locke and Tom Paine. I do not intend to pursue these avenues;[50] but I will nevertheless show that the spirit of Magna Carta played an important role in the conception of modern human rights documents and continues to resonate through them.

On 1 January 1942, the Allied powers included in their war aims the preservation of human rights and justice, in their own lands as well as in those lands in which human rights had been denied. From this point the Second World War can be seen as, in part, a crusade for what Winston Churchill termed, in an address to the World Jewish Congress that year, 'the enthronement of human rights'.[51] The United Nations Charter, signed after the conclusion of the war, included central commitments to human rights.[52] In 1948 the United Nations General Assembly adopted the Universal Declaration of Human Rights.[53]

Surprisingly perhaps, the most prominent voice demanding that the war be fought for human rights was the voice of the author, H G Wells, who had visited Canberra in the 1930s.[54] Wells sparked public debate in two letters to *The Times* in 1939. In the second he included a 'trial statement of the Rights of Man brought up to date'.[55] He introduced his declaration with the proposition that at various moments of crisis in history, beginning with Magna Carta and going through various bills of rights, it has been our custom to produce a specific declaration of

---

[49] AED Howard, *The Road from Runnymede—Magna Carta and Constitutionalism in America* (1968). For a short account see, DV Stivison, 'Magna Carta in American Law' in *Magna Carta in America* (1993).

[50] An account of the United Kingdom's contribution to human rights was given by Professor Palley as the 42nd Hamlyn Lecture Series. *The United Kingdom and Human Rights* (1991).

[51] 29 October 1942, *The Times*, 30 October 1942 (cited in H Lauterpacht, *An International Bill of the Rights of Man* (1945), p 86).

[52] Preamble and Arts 55 and 56. See my 'The Development of Human Rights in Britain' [1998] *PL* 221 at pp 221–24.

[53] General Assembly Resolution 217 (III), 10 December 1948.

[54] For accounts of Wells' role see DC Smith, *H G Wells—Desperately Mortal—a Biography* (1986), ch 17; J H Burgers, 'The Road to San Francisco: the Revival of the Human Rights Idea in the Twentieth Century' (1992) 14 *HRQ* 447 at pp 464–68; and A W B Simpson, *Human Rights and the End of Empire—Britain and the Genesis of the European Convention* (Oxford, Clarendon Press, 2001), pp 161–7, 204.

[55] 23 October 1939.

the broad principles on which our public and social life is based (perhaps better, on which our public and social life *should* be based).[56] The debate was conducted in the pages of the *Daily Herald*, and a drafting committee was established to refine the proposed declaration. It was nominally under the chairmanship of the former Lord Chancellor, Lord Sankey, whose name the declaration eventually bore. Wells produced a mass of material in this cause, and much was translated and published across the world. Some was even dropped by aircraft over the European Continent. His book, *The Rights of Man—or What are we Fighting for?*, is steeped in references to Magna Carta. He admits to having deliberately woven its terms into the provisions of the declaration itself, so that, he wrote, 'not only the spirit but some of the very words of that precursor live in this, its latest offspring.'[57]

The extent to which the enterprise of Wells and his colleagues influenced Anglo-American policy, or the framers of the United Nations Charter and the Universal Declaration of Human Rights, has not been conclusively established.[58] President F D Roosevelt, who was on good terms with Wells, commented upon his draft declaration in 1939.[59] In 1940 Wells conducted a lecture tour in the United States. Introducing the Universal Declaration to the General Assembly Mr Charles Malik, the Lebanese delegate, mentioned the contribution of six individuals. H G Wells was one, a second was Professor Hersch Lauterpacht, to

[56] In *The Rights of Man—Or What are we Fighting for?* (1940) Wells wrote:

> the first ... [necessity] is to do again what it has been the practice of the Parliamentary peoples to do whenever they come to a revolutionary turning-point of their histories, which is to make a declaration of the fundamental principles upon which the new phase is to be organised. This was done to check the encroachments of the Crown in Magna Carta. The Petition of Right made in 1628 repeated this expedient. It was done again in the Declaration of Right and the Bill of Rights which ended the 'Leviathan' and the Divine Right of Kings. Magna Carta and the Bill of Rights are an integral part of American law. The American Declaration of Independence was another such statement of a people's will, and the French Declaration of the Rights of Man derived its inspiration directly from that document (pp 28–9).

[57] *Ibid*, p 75.

[58] Wells' biographer, D C Smith, argues that Wells and the debate influenced the Atlantic Charter drawn up by Churchill and Roosevelt on 14 August 1941 (which was the sapling that later blossomed into the UN Charter) and Roosevelt's Four Freedoms (above n 54, p 604, n 16). He also states that Wells' views were introduced by Eleanor Roosevelt to the UN and even that 'final form' of the *Rights of Man* was the UDHR itself (*The Correspondence of H G Wells*, D C Smith (ed), v 1880–1903, pp xli–xlii). For criticism of these latter assertions see Simpson, above n 54, p 166. However, Simpson notes that some of wells' views were directly introduced to the San Francisco conference in another form (p 204).

[59] Burgers, above n 54, p 465.

[60] *Official Records of the Third Session of the General Assembly, Part 1, Plenary Meetings of the General Assembly, 21 September–12 December 1948*, 180th meeting, pp 857–8.

whom we will return, and a third was President Roosevelt.[60] It is rightly considered to be Roosevelt's famous 'Four Freedoms' address on the State of Union delivered in January 1941[61] that is the most direct ancestor of the United Nations Charter and the Universal Declaration of Human Rights, as well as the International Covenants that followed.[62] But if the spirit of Magna Carta was alive in the popular imagination in this period, so it was in political rhetoric. President Roosevelt himself appealed to Magna Carta and the heritage of freedom in his addresses to the American nation.[63] Similarly, in a broadcast to the United States after the conclusion of the war, Winston Churchill spoke of the 'great principles of freedom and the rights of man which are the joint inheritance of the English-speaking world and which through Magna Carta, the Bill of Rights, the Habeas Corpus, trial by jury, and the English common law find their most famous expression in the American Declaration of Independence'.[64]

Popular oratory of this sort would, of course, have had no direct effect on the jurisprudential developments of the time. Nonetheless, the spirit of Magna Carta was alive and well. It was in the minds of those who made the great political moves of the time and in the ears of those who had to put those moves into practice. After the Lincoln Cathedral copy of Magna Carta was transported to the United States Library of Congress for safe keeping in 1939,[65] an astonishing 14 million people

[61] S I Rosenman (ed), *The Public Papers and Addresses of Franklin D Roosevelt, 1940 Volume—War and Aid to Democracies* (1941), p 663. See also his State of the Union address, 11 January 1944, in I Rosenman (ed), *The Public Papers and Addresses of Franklin D Roosevelt, 1944–5 Volume—Victory and the Threshold of Peace* (1950), p 32.
[62] The direct influence can be seen from the preamble to those documents. The inspiration derived from Roosevelt's speech was repeatedly stressed in the General Assembly, see above n 60. For an excellent brief history, see L B Sohn, *Human Rights Movement: from Roosevelt's Four Freedoms to the Interdependence of Peace, Development and Human Rights* (1995).
[63] See The Third Inaugural Address, 20 January 1941; S I Rosenman (ed), *The Public Papers and Addresses of Franklin D Roosevelt, 1941 Volume—The Call to Battle Stations* (1950), 3 at 5; and A Radio Address Announcing the Proclamation of an Unlimited National Emergency, 27 May 1941, p 181 at p 193.
[64] M Gilbert, *Winston S Churchill 1874–1965, v VIII 1945–1965—Never Despair* (1988), p 200. Further eloquent testimony to Churchill's veneration for Magna Carta can be found in his *A History of the English-Speaking Peoples, v I—the Birth of Britain* (2002), ch VII ('Magna Carta').
[65] The Charter's evacuation was approved by Neville Chamberlain. It is an interesting aside to note that Churchill would not have allowed its removal and instructed that all national treasures, rather than be displaced from their homeland, be buried or hidden in caves: M Gilbert, *Winston S Churchill 1874–1965, v VI 1939–1941—Finest Hour* (1987), p 449.
[66] Sir Thomas Bingham M R (as he then was), discussing the long queue of pilgrims to the US Constitution that accumulates each day outside the National Archives in Washington,

queued to see it for themselves.[66] At a ceremony returning the Charter in 1946 the Minister representing the United Kingdom traced a lineage that he said was 'without equal in human history' and considered that the preamble to the United Nations Charter was the most recent of Magna Carta's 'authentic offspring'.[67]

In academic, but not physical, terms a far more weighty contribution than that of H G Wells to the development of modern human rights was Professor Lauterpacht's work. *An International Bill of the Rights of Man*, published in 1945.[68] Like Wells, Lauterpacht sought to emphasise the continuum between Magna Carta and his own enterprise, and to affirm its continued relevance to the modern world. He extolled the significance of the Charter in initiating the English constitutional practice of safeguarding the rights of subjects by way of general statutory enactment,[69] and even went as far as to declare that, 'in the history of fundamental rights no event ranks higher than that charter of the concessions which the nobles wrested from King John'.[70] The United Nations itself has suggested that the roots of the human rights movement can be traced to John's Charter of 1215.[71]And Eleanor Roosevelt, who chaired the Human Rights Commission responsible for drawing up the Universal Declaration,[72] proclaimed that it was a declaration of the basic principles to serve as a common standard for all nations and thus it 'might well become a Magna Carta of all mankind'.[73] If there was much in Stubbs' comment that Magna Carta was the first great act of a united nation, then there is also much to be said for the Universal Declaration of Human Rights as the first great act of a united world. Dr H V Evatt, the Australian President of the General Assembly, saw the Declaration as 'a step forward in a great

considered that 'the nearest we come, perhaps, is the Great Charter of 1215, an instrument of which the significance is, interestingly, much more generally appreciated in the United States than here' ('The Courts and Parliament' (1996–1997) 7 *KCLJ* 12 at p 12).

[67] John Balfour, *New York Times*, 11 January 1946 (cited in Thompson, above n 5, p v).

[68] Above n 51. The book was reprinted as part of H Lauterpacht, *International Law and Human Rights* (1950).

[69] Above n 51, p 55 and generally ch V.

[70] Above n 51, p 56.

[71] *The United Nations and Human Rights* (1978), p 1.

[72] For the influence of Eleanor Roosevelt on the UDHR see MG Johnson, 'The Contributions of Eleanor and Franklin Roosevelt to the Development of International Protection for Human Rights' (1987) 9 *HRQ* 19 at pp 27–48.

[73] Above n 60, p 862. However, Lauterpacht, criticising the Universal Declaration, rejected parallels with Magna Carta and other later declarations because, at least initially, it was primarily aspirational: see 'The Universal Declaration of Human Rights' (1948) 25 *BYIL* 354 at pp 371–2.

evolutionary process ... —the first occasion on which the organised community of nations had made a declaration of human rights and fundamental freedoms'.[74]

The Universal Declaration, whilst not as 'universal' as we might today wish, triumphed in uniting the common values and traditions of many seemingly disparate nations. The Commission contained representatives from 18 nations and republics. The Anglo-American legal tradition was a major element in its conception,[75] although the Chinese, French, Lebanese and Soviet Union representatives exerted influence.[76] Nonetheless, although the precise terms of Magna Carta found no place in the final document, we can see in the guarantee that 'no one shall be subjected to arbitrary arrest, detention or exile'[77] clear similarities with chapter 29 of Magna Carta.

The fact that the spirit of Magna Carta continues to resonate through modern human rights documents is reason enough for sparing it from that dusty cupboard of constitutional relics that have outlived their significance. There is, however, a further dimension to the relationship between Magna Carta and modern protections of human rights. This relates to the translation of international human rights guarantees into domestic law.

IV.   REINVIGORATING THE RULE OF LAW: GUARANTEEING HUMAN RIGHTS IN DOMESTIC LAW

The Universal Declaration is not directly binding on states, although it has largely become part of customary international law[78] and can be considered by domestic courts.[79] However, two years ago this month, the United Kingdom brought into effect the Human Rights Act 1998, which enables individuals to raise allegations of violations of the European Convention on Human Rights before domestic courts. The present Government's White Paper preceding the Bill stated an intention

---

[74] Above n 60, 183rd meeting p 934.

[75] For an unrivalled account of the English role, and the origins of modern human rights documents generally, see Simpson, above n 54.

[76] MG Johnson and J Symonides, *The Universal Declaration of Human Rights: a History of its Creation and Implementation, 1948–1998* (1998).

[77] UDHR, Art 9.

[78] Johnson and Symonides, above n 76, pp 67–8.

[79] See eg, *Hunter v Canary Wharf Ltd* [1997] AC 655 at p 714 (Lord Cooke of Thorndon).

[80] *Rights Brought Home: The Human Rights Bill*, Cm 3782 (1997).

to 'bring rights home'[80] and records comments made by Sir Edward Gardner Q C, M P during an earlier attempt to incorporate the European Convention. He noted that the Convention's language 'echoes down the corridors of history. It goes deep into our history and as far back as Magna Carta.'[81] Individual rights and freedoms are believed, rightly, to be held of birthright in our countries. The Government recognised in the UK context that the common law alone could not meet the demands of the modern age, and in particular the demands of our international obligations in Europe. The UK was persistently found wanting by the European Court of Human Rights and our own courts had no powers to make comparable findings. Since it is the joint responsibility of Parliament and the courts to protect the birthright of our citizens it was entirely fitting, and in accord with our constitutional heritage from Magna Carta through to the Petition of Right 1672, the Habeas Corpus Act 1679 and the Bill of Rights, for Parliament to set out new terms on which power is to be exercised; and so reinvigorate the rule of law in the UK.

Recently, in the Boyer Lectures, Chief Justice Murray Gleeson stated that 'human rights discourse is entering a new phase' in Australia and described how the question whether to enact a bill of rights is 'a controversial issue in current political debate'.[82] It is an issue which is obviously for Australians to decide. Since 1991 Australia has extended to individuals the protection of the International Covenant on Civil and Political Rights by allowing those claiming to be the victims of violations of protected rights to submit a communication to the Human Rights Committee. However, Australia has so far kept this protection beyond the jurisdiction of its own courts. We must not, however, underestimate the extent to which the Australian Constitution and the Australian Courts already protect individual rights. Nonetheless, if the number of adverse opinions of the Human Rights Committee increases then Australians may find, as was our experience in the UK, that pressure continues to grow for

---

[81] *Ibid*, 1.5 (*Hansard*, HC 6 February 1987, col 1224).

[82] 'Aspects of the Commonwealth Constitution—Part 2': *Boyer Lectures 2000—The Rule of Law and the Constitution* (2000), pp 64 and 67. A study published by the University of Wollongong has described this as a 'Millennium Dilemma' for Australia: J Innes, *Millennium Dilemma, Constitutional Change in Australia* (1998). The literature on this dilemma is voluminous, but for one comprehensive study which pays particular attention to the British heritage (considering Magna Carta a 'landmark document') see the Queensland Electoral and Administrative Review Commission, Issue Paper No 20, *Review of the Preservation and Enhancement of Individual Rights and Freedoms* (1992), especially pp 43–6.

[83] Cf Joint Committee on Foreign Affairs, Defence and Trade, The Parliament of the Australian Commonwealth, *A Review of Australia's Efforts to Promote and Protect*

a new settlement of individual rights.[83] Moreover, it occurs to me that, but for the generally amicable manner in which Australia became an independent nation, it might, like other successor nations to dependent territories, already have a bill of rights.[84]

V.　THE CONTINUING RELEVANCE OF MAGNA CARTA IN AUSTRALIAN AND UNITED KINGDOM LAW

The process of Federation meant that Magna Carta was given concrete legal effect in Australian jurisdictions in a complex way. Jurisdictions with Imperial Acts (the Australian Capital Territory, New South Wales, Queens-land and Victoria) all chose to enact chapter 29. This was not, primarily, for its potentially salutary legal effects, but rather to recognize Magna Carta's pivotal role in the constitutional legacy that these jurisdictions had inherited.[85] By contrast, in the Northern Territory, South Australia, Tasmania and Western Australia, Magna Carta was received by Imperial law reception statutes.[86] These jurisdictions find themselves in the surprising position of having almost all the provisions of Magna Carta theoretically still in force. I say surprising because, as I mentioned at the start of this lecture, only four chapters still remain on the statute book in the UK, but Magna Carta was largely received in these jurisdictions before this process of repeal began.[87] The position is also theoretical because the chapters of Magna Carta would have to be suitable to modern conditions there, and many clearly would no longer be.

The legacy of Magna Carta has also been inherited by Australia through the common law. Today, it can be seen to resonate most clearly through the fundamental common law doctrine of legality and the right of access to justice. We shall see, however, that the High Court of Australia in *Jago v District Court*[88] limited the extent of Magna Carta's contribution to the right of access to justice, at least in Australian law.

Human Rights (1992), which concluded that there are gaps in Australia's protection of human rights.

[84] For a brief account of the process of separation see G Sawyer, 'Government and Law' in J D B Miller (ed), *Australians & British—Social and Political Connections* (1987).
[85] D Clark, 'The Icon of Liberty: The Status and Role of *Magna Carta* in Australian and New Zealand Law' (2000) 24 *Melbourne L R* 866 at pp 869–70; AC Castles, 'Australian Meditations on Magna Carta' 63 *ALJ* 122 at p 124.
[86] Clark, *ibid*, pp 870–72.
[87] For an account of the process of repeal see Pallister, above n 48, ch 7.
[88] (1989) 168 CLR 23.

Nonetheless, Isaacs J, speaking in the High Court of Australia in 1925, was speaking truly when he proclaimed Magna Carta to be 'the groundwork of all our Constitutions'.[89]

I will return to the common law doctrine of legality shortly, but first let me address the right of access to justice. English courts attach considerable importance to the individual's right of access to justice; and now speak of it as a constitutional right.[90] The wellspring of the modern case law is the case of *Chester v Bateson*.[91] Regulations enacted during the First World War for the defence of the realm prevented certain landowners from recovering possession of their property from munition workers without the consent of the Minister of Munitions. This provision was held to deprive the subject 'of his ordinary right to seek justice in the Courts of Law',[92] and was consequently declared to be invalid. As a matter of 'constitutional law' Avory J was prepared to hold that the regulations were in direct contravention of chapter 29 of Magna Carta.[93] Darling J, however, recognised that, had the regulations been made within the authority of the parent statute, Magna Carta would have been of no assistance, since it cannot stand in the face of the doctrine of parliamentary sovereignty. However, he declared that the blanket sweep of the regulations, coupled with their draconian penalties, was unnecessary and represented an unjustified interference with individual rights.[94] The case foreshadowed the development of a common law method of constitutional interpretation, now routinely adopted by the English courts,[95] which demands that public officials justify their actions by reference to the principles of necessity and proportionality when they interfere with individual rights. Darling J's judgment, in particular, also illustrates the way that Magna Carta has

---

[89] *Ex parte Walsh and Johnson* (1925) 37 CLR 36 at p 79; he continued: '[Ch 29] recognizes three basic principles, namely, (1) primarily every free man has an inherent individual right to his life, liberty, property and citizenship; (2) his individual rights must always yield to the necessities of the general welfare at the will of the State; (3) the law of the land is the only mode by which the State can so declare its will'.

[90] *Raymond v Honey* [1983] 1 AC 1; *R v Secretary of State for the Home Department ex p Leech (No 2)* [1994] QB 198; *R v Lord Chancellor ex p Witham* [1998] QB 575; *R v Secretary of State for the Home Department ex p Simms* [2000] 2 AC 115. See my 'Activism and Restraint: Human Rights and the Interpretive Process' [1999] *EHRLR* 350 at pp 369–70.

[91] [1920] 1 KB 829.

[92] *Ibid*, p 834 (Darling J).

[93] Above n 91, p 836.

[94] Above n 91, pp 832–33.

[95] See *R (Daly) v Secretary of State for the Home Department* [2001] 2 AC 532; *Ex p Simms* [2000] 2 AC 115.

effect not only as a statute, but also resonates through the common law principles of interpretation developed to safeguard the liberties of the individual from the exercise of governmental power.[96]

Lord Scarman, a champion of human rights and an early and strong advocate of a Bill of Rights for the UK,[97] suggested judicially in 1975 that Magna Carta had been 'reinforced' by the European Convention.[98] Certainly it is now Article 6 of the Convention, which concerns the right to a fair trial, and its developing jurisprudence that will provide most assistance to UK courts in interpreting the right of access to justice. However, it is interesting to reflect on the fact that Article 6 itself makes no mention of any right of access to a court. This right has been read into is terms by the European Court. The Court argued that the 'principle whereby a civil claim must be capable of being submitted to a judge ranks as one of the universally "recognised" fundamental principles of law'.[99] In its turn, this fundamental principle found one of its first and most important expressions in Magna Carta.[100]

In Australia there has been some judicial disagreement about whether Magna Carta's promise not to delay or defer[101] right or justice supports a right to a speedy trial, or at least a right not to have one's trial

---

[96] In *Ex parte Walsh and Johnson* (1925) 37 CLR 36 at pp 79–80 Isaacs J stated:

> ... the Courts have evolved two great working corollaries in harmony with the main principles [of ch 29], and without which these would soon pass into merely pious aspirations. *The first corollary* is that there is always an initial presumption in favour of liberty, so that whoever claims to imprison or deport another has cast upon him the obligation of justifying his claim by reference to the law. *The second corollary* is that the Courts themselves see that this obligation is strictly and completely fulfilled before they hold that liberty is lawfully restrained. The second is often in actual practice and concrete result the more important of the two to keep steadily in vie ... it will be seen that the principles themselves and the corollaries are far more than mere academic interest. They materially help to solve disputed points ...

[97] 26th Hamlyn Lectures, *English Law—The New Dimension* (1974); 7th Lord Fletcher Lecture, 1985, 'Human Rights in the UK—Time for Change'.
[98] *R v Secretary of State for the Home Department ex p Phansopkar* [1976] QB 606 at p 626.
[99] *Golder v United Kingdom* (1975) 1 EHRR 524 at para 35.
[100] Lord Donaldson M R, speaking before important developments in the jurisprudence on Art 6, declared the common law, Magna Carta and Art 6 to be consistent: *R v Home Secretary ex p. Wynne* [1992] I QB 407 at p 418. See also *AB v John Wyeth & Bros Ltd* (1992) 12 BMLR 50. For a survey of the developments of the law on Art 6 since *Golder's case* see *Matthews v Ministry of Defence* [2002] EWCA Civ 773.
[101] This is the term adopted in the 1297 version.
[102] Relying on Magna Carta, McHugh J A (as he then was) powerfully argued that the common law recognised such a right: *Herron v McGregor* (1986) 6 NSWLR 246 at p 252; *About v Attorney-General for New South Wales* (1987) 10 NSWLR 671 at pp 691–92; *Jago v District Court of New South Wales* (1988) 12 NSWLR 558 at pp 583–85; *Brisbane South Regional Health Authority v Taylor* (1996) 186 CLR 541 at p 552. In this latter case McHugh J expressed apparently slightly modified views in

unreasonably delayed.[102] In *Jago v District Court* the High Court was faced with a claim for a permanent stay of criminal proceedings that were scheduled to be held over five and a half years after the accused had been charged. Refusing the stay, it held that no such right existed separate from either the court's duty to prevent injustice or from the accused's right to fair trial.[103] This view was subsequently adopted by the English Court of Appeal.[104] I agree that Magna Carta should not be read to require a stay of proceedings, or the quashing of a conviction, unless there has been an abuse of process or an unfair trial. However, it seems to me inescapable that there is, enshrined in Magna Carta, a right not to have justice delayed.[105] Deane J in *Jago*, differing slightly from the rest of the court, accepted that such a right exists. He pointed out that it was ordinarily vindicated through the ability of the accused to apply to the court for an appropriate order, and that it would only result in a permanent stay or quashing of a conviction in the circumstances envisaged by the whole court.[106] Michael Kirby in *Jago*, as President of the New South Wales Court of Appeal, considered that Magna Carta was sufficiently secured in Australian law,[107] but, in

---

stating that ch 29 of Magna Carta was protected by the power 'to stay proceedings as abuses of process if they are satisfied that, by reason of delay or other matter, the commencement or continuation of the proceedings would involve injustice or unfairness to one of the parties'. I will not discuss here Magna Carta's rather indirect contribution to the notion of 'due process of law', which has also been considered by Australian courts (see *Alder v District Court of New South Wales* (1990) 19 NSWLR 317) as well as by the Privy Council (*Thomas v Baptiste* [2000] 2 AC 1).

[103] (1989) 168 CLR 23; subsequently followed and affirmed in respect of new arguments in *Alder v District Court of New South Wales* (1990) 19 NSWLR 317. The case led KC Gould to remark that 'the Charter's place in the sun, if anywhere, rests largely on the towel of sentimentality' ('Australian Meditations on Magna Carta—a Postscript' (1990) 64 *ALJ* 376).

[104] *Attorney-General's Reference (No 1 of 1990)* [1992] 1 QB 630).

[105] For a discussion of the delay or denial of justice in the context of civil proceedings see *Allen v Sir Alfred McAlpine & Sons Ltd* [1968] 2 QB 229 at p 245 (Lord Denning MR).

[106] (1989) 168 CLR 23 at p 59.

[107] However, he did not recognise a separate right to a speedy trial. Nonetheless, by contrast, none of the other justices in either the High Court or the New South Wales Supreme Court (other than McHugh JA, on whose views see above, n 102) acknowledged that Magna Carta made any normative contribution to modern law. Brennan J considered that Coke's views on access to justice were merely aspirational (*Ibid*, p 42), and agreed with Toohey J Toohey J, *ibid*, pp 66–7, himself following Samuels J A in the court below (1988) 12 NSWLR 558 at pp 573–5), criticised Coke's interpretation of the Charter and argued that ch 29 was primarily intended to correct the worst abuse of royal justice while at the same time securing its pre-eminence. However, these provisions of Magna Carta can be regarded as reflecting an emerging view that justice was a community right and not simply a baronial privilege. It should also be recalled that by virtue of ch 60 of Magna Carta lords at each rung of the feudal ladder were expected to abide by the good principles of the Charter. Cf Holt, above, n 17, pp 279, 285–86, 327.

comments that have recently been reiterated by the High Court,[108] said that a more relevant source of guidance in interpreting the law was modern statements of human rights.[109] In the UK context the European Convention and the Human Rights Act have, indeed, fortified and reinvigorated the right, enshrined in Magna Carta, not to have justice delayed. Article 6 of the Convention confers a right to a hearing 'within a reasonable time'.[110] The Court of Appeal has recently held that a stay of proceedings or the quashing of a conviction will, as before, only be appropriate where there is an abuse of process or an unfair trial. However, in the event of an unreasonable delay the court can now mark a contravention of Article 6 and this can be taken into account when sentencing. Also, where appropriate, for example where there is a subsequent acquittal, UK courts can now make an enforceable award of damages to remedy such a violation.[111] This seems to me to be an example of a specific instance of the continuum between Magna Carta and the modern protection of human rights.

Finally, I promised that I would return to the doctrine of legality. The doctrine of legality mandates that government action cannot proceed arbitrarily and without lawful authority. It represents the kernel of the rule of law. A recent case has vividly illustrated how Magna Carta continues to underpin this doctrine in important respects.

Bancoult was an Illois, an indigenous inhabitant of the Chagos archipelago in the middle of the Indian Ocean. The islands were divided

---

[108] *Azzopardi v The Queen* (2001) 205 CLR 50 at p 65 (Gaudron, Gummow, Kirby and Hayne JJ). Cf M Kirby, 'The Australian Use of International Human rights Norms: from Bangalore to Balliol—a View from the Antipodes' (1993) 16 *UNSWLJ* 363. For a discussion of the protection of human rights in Australian domestic law: see J Doyle and B Wells, 'How Far Can The Common Law Go Towards Protecting Human Rights?' in P Alston, *Promoting Human Rights Through Bills of Rights: Comparative Perspectives* (Oxford, OUP, 1999).

[109] (1988) 12 NSWLR 558 at p 569.

[110] Kirby P in the Court of Appeal of New South Wales in *Jago* (1988) 12 NSWLR 558 at p 570) addressed Art 14.3 ICCPR which states: 'In the determination of any criminal charge against him, every one shall be entitled to the following minimum guarantees … (c) to be tried without undue delay'. He concluded that this did not protect an independent right to a speedy trial and, like ch 29 of Magna Carta, the provision was 'sufficiently secured' by the principles relating to unfair trials and abuse of process. Samuels J A adopted a wider interpretation of the ICCPR suggesting it did protect an independent right to a speedy trial, but took a narrower view about the value of international legal instruments regarding 'the normative tradition of the common law as a surer foundation for development' (pp 580 and 582).

[111] *Attorney-General's Reference (No 2 of 2001)* [2001] IWLR 1869; *R v Massey* [2001] EWCA Crim 2850. Damages may be awardable by virtue of HRA, s 8 which confers a broad remedial discretion on courts when a violation of the Convention has been found.

from the British colony of Mauritius in 1965, creating the British Indian Ocean Territory. Today these islands house a United States defence facility; but its establishment was at the expense of the islands' indigenous population, thought to have numbered around 400 people. This population was, in all relevant respects, exiled by an Immigration Ordinance in 1971. Aware that if the inhabitants of the Chagos Islands were recognised as indigenous their treatment of them would attract hostile scrutiny in the United Nations, successive British governments maintained that the inhabitants were only contract workers. Belatedly, almost 30 years later, the Divisional Court ruled that the enactment of the relevant provisions of the 1971 Ordinance had been unlawful.[112]

Relying on Magna Carta, it was argued that Bancoult had a statutory right not to be exiled unless it was by the law of the land. However, Laws L J held that direct reliance on Magna Carta could not assist Bancoult's case for two reasons. First, to find that the terms of Magna Carta had been breached the court would have to be satisfied that the Ordinance had been made without lawful authority. If there was no such authority the government's actions would be *ultra vires* in any event, although admittedly they would violate Magna Carta into the bargain.[113] Second, and more fundamentally, Magna Carta, as a statute, was held not to apply to the British Indian Ocean Territory because it was a ceded colony to which the benefit of UK statues had to be expressly extended.[114] But this was not the end of the matter. Laws L J stated that the 'enduring significance' of Magna Carta was that it was a 'proclamation of the rule of law' and in this guise it followed the English flag even to the Chagos archipelago.[115] Although Magna Carta did not provide the answer to this case, what did was that the 'wholesale removal of a people from the land where they belong' could not reasonably be

---

[112] [2001] QB 1067.

[113] Magna Carta often emerges behind the doctrine of legality in this manner: eg *Holden v Chief Constable of Lancashire* [1987] 1 QB 380; *Re B (Child Abduction: Wardship: Power to Detain)* [1994] Fam 607; *In re S-C (Mental Patient: Habeas Corpus)* [1996] QB 599; *R v Commissioners of Customs and Excise ex p a Company*, 15 October 1996.

[114] For a discussion of Magna Carta's extension to the Commonwealth see Sir I Jennings, 'Magna Carta and Constitutionalism in the Commonwealth' in S E Thorne, W H Dunham Jr, P B Kurland and I Jennings, *The Great Charter—Four Essays on Magna Carta and the History of Our Liberty* (1965).

[115] [2001] QB 1067, para 36. This phrase was coined by the Canadian Supreme Court, which stated in *Calder v Attorney-General of British Columbia* [1973] SCR 313 at p 395. (1973) 34 DLR (3d) 145 at p 203 that, 'Magna Carta has always been considered to be the law throughout the Empire. It was a law which followed the flag as England assumed jurisdiction over newly-discovered or acquired lands or territories.'

said to conduce to the territory's peace, order and good government. The Ordinance of 1971, therefore, violated the fundamental doctrine of legality and flouted the rule of law.[116]

VI.　THE CONTINUING RELEVANCE OF MAGNA CARTA IN MODERN LAW

Let me sum up this discussion briefly. The constitutions of the UK and Australia are distinct, but they share the same roots and Magna Carta and its legacy represent the sturdiest and the oldest. The fact that the provisions of Magna Carta rarely break the surface or provide explicit contributions to the outcome of modern cases should not obscure its contemporary importance.[117] I hope I have shown that in celebrating the legacy of Magna Carta in the UK and Australia we are not clinging to a constitutional relic, vastly overestimated by generations and without modern significance. The opposite is in fact true. Magna Carta can be truly appreciated as the foundation stone of the rule of law. Its terms continue to underpin key constitutional doctrines; its flame continues to burn in the torches of modern human rights instruments; and its spirit continues to resonate throughout the law.

---

[116] *Ibid*, para 57 and para 71 (Gibbs J). Despite the fact that the actions of the British Government infringed fundamental rights Laws L J felt that comments made in the Privy Council case *Liyanage v The Queen* [1967] 1 AC 259 precluded him from adopting a more rigorous constitutional standard of scrutiny of the legality of the Ordinance (although he was not strictly bound by the decision). He made no mention of whether he would have felt so compelled if Magna Carta had extended to the BIOT. Gibbs J, however, felt that if Magna Carta had applied to the BIOT 'I might have found assistance in the provisions of ch 29 in interpreting the legality of the Ordinance, at least in the resolution of any doubts on the point' (para 68). Laws L J has since suggested that Magna Carta might be one of a small number of fundamental statutes that the common law insulates from all but expressly stated repeal: *Thorbum v Sunderland City Council* [2002] 3 WLR 247 at para 68. However, the High Court of Australia has stated that Magna Carta does not 'legally bind the legislatures of this country or, for that matter, the United Kingdom. Nor ... [does it] limit the powers of the legislatures of Australia or the United Kingdom' (*Essenberg v The Queen*, 22 June 2000) and it is treated like any other statute.

[117] Concluding a comprehensive study of the continuing role of Magna Carta in Australian and New Zealand law, Dr David Clark states, ' ... the myth of *Magna Carta* has proved legally, and above all, constitutionally, useful to subsequent generations. While, as we have seen, it is of little practical use in actual cases, if remains an animating idea and one important basis upon which judges continue to found the legitimacy of the rule of law and constitutionalism generally' (above n 85, p 891).

16

Legislators, Liberty and the Law: A Comparative Analysis of the French and English Legal Systems *

I. INTRODUCTION

L ADIES AND GENTLEMEN, it is my great pleasure to be in Paris for this very special occasion. I am delighted to have been invited to deliver this Lecture, and my thanks goes to three distinguished jurists: Monsieur Canivet, Monsieur Guéna and Monsieur Denoix de Saint Mare. This evening's ceremony represents a unique joint endeavour between the *Cour de cassation,* the *Conseil constitutionnel* and the *Conseil d'État.* And this spirit of judicial cooperation echoes the judicial cooperation between our two countries, exemplified by the Anglo French Judicial Exchange and the work of the Franco British Judicial Committee. These initiatives, and our coming together this evening, remind us that what unites our two countries far outweighs our occasional differences.

This evening we celebrate two new expressions of our friendship and cooperation: an electronic resource which will share the jurisprudence of the French courts with English-speaking practitioners around the world; and the annual secondment of a French Supreme Court Justice to London. At the heart of both initiatives is our mutual friend, Professor Markesinis, to whom we are deeply grateful for his efforts at forging ever closer links between Britain and France. As Professor Markesinis and our hosts this evening have recognised, this is a time when lawyers—both in Europe and abroad—are looking increasingly to the experiences of other nations when approaching common problems.

* (Cour de cassation, 26 March 2003)

The jurisprudence of the French courts presents a challenging experience for those who have grown up with the idiom of the common law. In particular, the common lawyer looking into a French report will need time to familiarise himself with the context of the judgment, as the plurality of jurisdictions between the *Conseil constitutionnel, Cour de cassation* and *Conseil d'État* and the profound institutional differences between these jurisdictions is a feature which is largely unknown to the common law.[1]

Another striking feature has to be the style of French judicial reasoning. The language of a common law judge is pragmatic, reflecting a judicial activity of assessing historical rulings to find the principles which will decide the case. In comparison, the decision-making process in France is both analytical and more abstract. Unlike the common law judge whose first task is to identify the appropriate rule of law, the crux of French judicial reasoning—particularly in the *Cour de Cassation* where many of the legal rules are set out in comprehensive Codes or legislation—focuses on the interpretation and application of rules of law.

A well-known illustration of this process is the law of delict. Both Britain and France have highly developed principles governing liability for negligent acts, but while the basic norms of the French law derive from Articles 1382 to 1386 of the *Code Civil,* the foundation of English law is Lord Atkin's famous statement in the 1932 case of *Donoghue v Stevenson* that: '*You must take reasonable care to avoid acts or omissions which you can reasonably foresee would be likely to injure your neighbour.*'[2]

In the circumstances it is hardly surprising to find a difference between the styles of reasoning of the courts which are required to apply the principles of liability for harm. When deciding a novel case in negligence the British House of Lords must necessarily begin with previous authority—based on *Donoghue v Stevenson*—to see whether liability has ever been imposed in a similar situation before. The judge must then embark upon a journey of reasoning which draws out principles from the earlier cases imposing liability and decides whether they are relevant to the present facts. As Lord Hoffmann recently said:

> The [House of Lords] approaches the question … starting with situations in which a duty has been held to exist and then asking whether there are

---

[1] This is a result of the Supreme Court of Judicature Act 1873, before which English law did recognise a plurality of jurisdictions.
[2] *Donoghue v Stevenson* [1932] AC 562 at 580.

considerations of analogy, policy, fairness and justice for extending it to cover a new situation .... The trend of authorities has been to discourage the assumption that anyone who suffers loss is prima facie entitled to compensation from a person ... whose act or omission can be said to have caused it. The default position is that he is not.[3]

The role of the *Cour de cassation* is very different. Its judges are not required to reason from past authority but rather from the terms of the *Code Civil* itself, and this requires a very different analytical process. In the celebrated *arrêt Jand'heur*[4] *Cour de cassation* formulated a remarkable branch of jurisprudence: the liability for '*les actes des choses*' based on Article 1384 of the *Code Civil*. The judgment does not in any way reflect the historical approach of the British courts, but starts from an analytical interpretation of Article 1384 as the foundation for liability:

> Attendu que la présomption de responsabilité établie par cet article à l'encontre de celui qui a sous sa garde la chose inanimée qui a causé un dommage à autrui ne peut être détruite que par la preuve d'un cas fortuit ou de force majeure ou d'une cause étrangère qui ne lui soit pas imputable ....
> ... attendu que la loi, pour l'application de la présomption qu'elle édicte, ne distingue pas suivant que la chose qui a causé le dommage était ou non actionnée par la main de l'homme; qu'il n'est pas nécessaire qu'elle ait un vice inhérent à sa nature et susceptible de causer le dommage, l'article 1384 rattachant la responsabilité à la garde de la chose, non à la chose elle-même .... Par ces motifs, CASSE[5].

This short and analytical style of judicial reasoning, so very different from the approach of the common law, can often complicate the process of comparison between legal systems. However, the problem is not an insurmountable one. Differences in analytical style are commonplace even as between national institutions: the interpretative approach of the *Cour de cassation* is in principle quite different from that of the *Conseil*

---

[3] *Stovin v Wise* [1996] AC 923 at 949.
[4] Ch Reun 13 February 1931.
[5] '*Given that the presumption of responsibility established by this article as established against a person who has control of an inanimate object which has caused harm to another can only be displaced by proof of fortuitous circumstances of force majeure or by an alternative cause for which he is not responsible .... Given that the law, in applying the presumption which it requires, does not distinguish according to whether the object which caused damage was or was not operated by an individual, given that it is not necessary that there was an inherent defect liable to cause the harm, Art 1384 attaching liability to the keeping of the thing rather than to the thing itself .... For these reasons [the Court] quashes [the first instance decision]*'.

d'État and quite different again from that of the *Conseil constitutionnel.*
And, the published reports of the opinion of the *Avocat Général* of the
Commissaire du Gouvernement are rather longer and more similar to an
English judgment. So now that British and French lawyers have greater
facilities than ever before with which to investigate their mutual
jurisprudence, there is surely a great deal which lawyers on both sides
of the Channel can learn from their common experience.

This evening, I will explore some of this common experience and
investigate more closely the ways in which the two systems have
reached similar solutions to mutual problems.

II.   CONSTITUTIONAL LAW

No comparative exercise can proceed without an understanding of the
basic legal framework, so let me begin with an overview of the constitutional arrangements of Britain and France.

A.   Legislative and Common Law Constitutionalism

At first glance this is not an easy task, as differences appear more
obvious than similarities. Even the most basic source of French
constitutionalism—the written Constitution of 1958[6]—finds no parallel
in British constitutional arrangements.

To divine the principles of the British Constitution we must turn to
precedent. The most fundamental rules—including the principle that
ultimate legal sovereignty vests in Parliament[7]—derive from judicial
decisions rather than any instrument of constitutional legislation.[8]
Indeed, many important aspects of the British Constitution are not rules
of law at all, but simply aspects of custom and practice. For example,
there is no legal rule which expressly creates the office of Prime
Minister. The matter is left to convention, and whilst any departure
from this convention would be practically inconceivable there is no
positive rule to this effect.[9]

---

[6] Together with the key documents to which this Constitution refers, namely the
Constitutional Preamble of 1946 and the *Déclaration des Droits de l'Homme et du
Citoyen* of 26 August 1789.
[7] Dicey, *The Law of the Constitution*, 10th ed (London, Macmillan 1962) 39.
[8] See the review of earlier case law in *Madzimbamuto v Lardner-Burke* [1969] 1 AC 645.
[9] Dicey, *The Law of the Constitution*, 10th ed (London, Macmillan 1962) 24.

B.   Constitutional Commonalities—the Shared Libertarian Tradition

Amidst this picture is it even possible to find a basis for constitutional comparison between Britain and France? The answer is surely yes. Both countries are strong parliamentary democracies founded on the rule of law and with long experience of protecting basic rights. When we look beyond the structural and stylistic factors, what emerges is a clear common heritage of constitutional democracy and respect for basic rights.

In France, fundamental rights have provided a basic foundation of constitutionalism since the revolutionary *Déclaration des Droits de l'Homme et du Citoyen* of 26 August 1789. This document was a triumphant product of the revolution, and like the American Declaration of Rights thirteen years before[10] it heralded a modern era based on the self-evident truth that:

> *L'ignorance, l'oubli ou le mépris des droits de l'homme sont les seules causes des malheurs publics et de la corruption des gouvernements.*[11]

The principles of the *Déclaration* have since been reaffirmed and supplemented by a range of constitutional measures, including the political, economic and social principles of the Constitutional Preamble of 1946. The principles form part of the *Bloc de Constitutionnalité* which, in combination with international treaties and domestic legislation, have been powerfully developed by the French Courts to elevate rights to supreme legal status within France.

The recognition of rights has also been an overriding feature of British constitutionalism. As in France, statements of right such as *Magna Carta* in 1215 and the Bill of Rights in 1689 form a vital part of British constitutional history. More recently, the Human Rights Act 1998—a subject to which I will return shortly—has incorporated the principles of the European Convention on Human Rights directly into British law to ensure that they are protected across the ambit of governmental activity.

For the identification of rights in Britain we must also look to the courts. Writing in the 13th century, the English jurist Bracton declared

---

[10] See P Miller, *The Life of the Mind in America* (1965), pp 99–116.
[11] *'The ignorance, neglect or disregard of the rights of man are the sole causes of public grievances and of the corrupt practices of governments.'*

that '*the King shall not be subject to men, but to God and the law: since law makes the King*'.[12] In this way, by subjugating government to the rule of law, the English courts have carved out a prominent role in identifying and upholding the basic rights of man.

There is no more powerful illustration of this process than our historic decision, *Entick v Carrington*.[13] In 1765, the Secretary of State suspected a man of plotting against the government. Believing himself to have unlimited powers '*for the purpose of quieting clamours and sedition*', the Secretary of State ordered two of the King's messengers to break into the man's house and seize his papers. The court struck down the Secretary of State's actions as a violation of basic constitutional principle. In a strongly libertarian judgment, Lord Camden said:

> What would the Parliament say if the judges should take upon themselves to mould an unlawful power into a convenient authority, by new restrictions? That would be, not judgement, but legislation .... And with respect to the argument of State necessity, or a distinction that has been aimed at between State officers and others, the common law does not understand that kind of reasoning, nor do our books take notice of any such distinction.[14]

The judgment in *Entick v Carrington* has assumed an importance which is in many ways comparable with the 1789 *Déclaration*. Its libertarian ideology has influenced not only British constitutional arrangements but also common law constitutions around the world. History tells us that Thomas Jefferson had the case in mind when framing the Constitution of the United States, saying that its inherent liberalism—the concept of equality between men—espoused precisely the philosophy that the War of Independence had sought to achieve.[15]

Looking closely, there are some differences between the philosophy of *Entick v Carrington* and the principles of the 1789 *Déclaration*. Whilst the *Déclaration* lists the positive rights of man, Lord Camden did not refer to any positive rights at all. In substance, of course, the judgment upheld a range of basic rights—the right to privacy, the right

---

[12] Bracton, quoted in F W Maitland, *The Constitutional History of England* (Oxford, Clarendon Press, 1908), p 100.
[13] *Entick v Carrington* (1765) 19 St Tr 1030.
[14] At 1037.
[15] M White, *The Philosophy of the American Revolution* (OUP, NY 1978), Beitzinger, *The Philosophy of Law of Four American Founding Fathers*, (1976) 21 *Am J Juris* 1. See also O'Day, *Understanding Comparative History: Britain and American from 1760*, (Open University, 1997).

to freedom of conscience and expression, the right to have a fair hearing before a competent court. Yet the judgment approaches libertarianism as a blanket concept, under the principle that all liberties are sacrosanct unless an instrument of law provides otherwise.

C.   Reducing the Divide—Recent Trends Towards Convergence

This difference of emphasis is significant—it illustrates that English and French constitutional thinkers have to some extent approached the issue of rights protection from different perspectives. Yet the importance of this different emphasis as a matter of constitutional history should not be exaggerated. From the time of the *Déclaration* in 1789 we can clearly see the picture of a common constitutional heritage based on libertarian ideals. Indeed, if we look to more recent Anglo-French jurisprudence we can see that any difference of emphasis is more philosophical than real.

A common approach to the protection of rights and an increasing convergence of constitutional principle can be seen in two aspects of modern Anglo-French constitutionalism. On the one hand French constitutional doctrine—despite its legislative origins—is showing an ever-more prominent reliance upon judicial precedent for the identification and enforcement of general libertarian principles. On the other hand, English constitutional doctrine—despite its historical reliance on precedent—has recently moved strongly towards the legislative identification and protection of rights.

a.   *The Role of Precedent in Shaping French Constitutional Law*

As we have already seen, the basic principles of French constitutionalism have been carved out largely by the legislature, in the form of declarations of right following years of Revolution and World War. However, to say that the legislature has been uniquely responsible for upholding the rights of man would fail to do justice to the work of the French judiciary, particularly the recent jurisprudence of the *Conseil constitutionnel*.

It is well known that the *Conseil constitutionnel* was not expressly created as a supreme court for the protection of rights. Established amidst De Gaulle's presidentialising reforms of 1958, the *Conseil* was set up primarily to stand between Parliament and the Government, supervising the precise constitutional allocation of functions and ruling on constitutional competence when required.

Yet the *Conseil's* decision of 16 July 1971, about freedom of association radically altered this perception.[16] In a landmark judgment the *Conseil* held that Article 61 of the Constitution empowered it to rule not only on the form of proposed legislation, but also on whether such legislation complied with the substance of French constitutional values. Any proposed law which was incompatible with French constitutional principle—including the basic rights of man as proclaimed in the 1789 *Déclaration* and the social values set out in the 1946 Constitutional Preamble—could be struck down before promulgation as a violation of the Constitution.

This decision has often been described as a judge-led constitutional revolution,[17] and it has given rise to a substantial body of jurisprudence for the furtherance of basic rights in the face of proposed legislative infringements. Not only has the *Conseil* protected the basic liberties set out in the 1789 *Déclaration,* such as the decision of 12 January 1977, striking down proposed legislation granting sweeping powers of stop and search to the police,[18] but in other decisions its jurisprudence has far surpassed these basic freedoms and devised a sophisticated body of constitutional rights drawn from *la tradition republicaine.*

One example is the decision of 16 January 1982, when the *Conseil* ruled that nationalisation measures, providing unequal compensation for proprietors, contravened constitutional principles on rights to property, fairness and equality. The judgment contains a general statement of the right to property, set in this constitutional context:

> Les principes énoncés par la Déclaration des Droits de l'homme ont pleine valeur constitutionelle tant en ce qui concerne le caractère fondamental du droit de propriété dont la conservation constitue l'un des buts de la société politique et qui est mis au même rang que la liberté, la sûreté et la résistance à l'oppression ... [L]a liberté qui, aux termes de l'art.4 de la Déclaration, consiste à pouvoir faire tout ce qui ne nuit pas à autrui, ne saurait elle-même être préservée si des restrictions arbitraires ou abusives étaient apportées à la liberté d'entreprendre.[19]

[16] Cons Const 16.7.71, Rec 29.
[17] Art 61 of the Constitution now provides that sixty *députés* or *sénateurs* may refer proposed legislation to the Conseil, extending access for constitutional control of legislation to members of the opposition.
[18] DS 1978.173.
[19] *'The principles stated in the Declaration of the Rights of Man have full constitutional force as regards the fundamental character of the right of ownership. The preservation*

Another illustration of the *Conseil's* sophisticated rights-based jurisprudence comes from the decision on President Mitterand's proposed Amnesty Acts of May 1988. In rejecting the proposition that an employer could be forced to take back an employee who had been dismissed for violence in the workplace, the *Conseil* set out a range of principles concerning the underlying laws of the Republic deriving from *la tradition républicaine*:

> La contrainte qu'une telle réintégration ferait peser sur l'employeur qui à été victime de cet abus ou qui, en tout cas, n'en est pas responsable exéderait manifestement les sacrifices d'ordre personnel ou d'ordre patrimonial qui peuvent être demandés aux individus dans l'intérêt général … et que de telles dispositions dépassent manifestement les limites que le respect de la Constitution impose au législateur en matière d'amnistie.[20]

The powerful jurisprudence of the *Conseil constitutionnel* is a useful illustration of the importance of the judicial function in identifying and protecting basic rights, which in modern times has proved as prominent in France as in the judge-led English system.

b.   The Identification and Protection of Positive Rights in the British Constitution

At the same time, recent developments in British constitutionalism have illustrated the importance of Parliament working together with the courts to achieve fundamental libertarian ideals.

In the courts, judges have strengthened the libertarian principles of *Entick v Carrington* by seeking to identify a broad range of positive rights with constitutional status. A striking example is a decision of the House of Lords in 1999, in which a number of prisoners successfully challenged a government policy of preventing visits by

---

of this right constitutes one of the goals of political society and the principle has the same status as the right to personal liberty, safety and freedom from oppression … [T]he freedom which, under Art 4 of the Declaration, grants a general freedom to do anything which does not cause harm to another, could not itself be preserved if arbitrary or abusive restrictions were imposed on freedom of business.'

[20] Cons Const 20.7.88, [1988] AJDA 752 *'Such a reintegration would impose a burden on the employer who had been the victim of this abuse or in any event was not responsible. It would manifestly exceed the personal or proprietary sacrifices which can be demanded of individuals in the public interest …. Such provisions manifestly exceed the limits which respect for the Constitution imposes on the legislator in the field of amnesty.'*

professional journalists.[21] At the heart of the prisoners' case lay two constitutional rights—the right to freedom of expression and the right of access to justice—which found powerful expression in the judgment of Lord Steyn:

> One cannot lose sight that there is at stake a fundamental or basic right, namely the right of a prisoner to seek through oral interviews to persuade a journalist to investigate the safety of the prisoner's conviction and to publicise his findings in an effort to gain access to justice for the prisoner.[22]

The British Parliament has also taken an active role in this process. In 1998 the Human Rights Act was passed, incorporating the European Convention on Human Rights directly into British law and providing a legislative source of basic rights across the United Kingdom. While judicial interpretation has remained key to defining the scope of these rights, the importance of the Human Rights Act has been to provide judges with a single source of rights, enacted by a democratic legislature.

The Human Rights Act operates on a number of fronts. It imposes a positive obligation on public bodies to uphold the fundamental rights set out in the European Convention.[23] It also requires courts to interpret legislation, so far as possible, in a manner consistent with Convention rights.[24] And if an Act is clearly inconsistent with the principles of the Convention then the court should issue a 'declaration of incompatibility'.[25] This does not affect the continuing validity of the legislation, but triggers Parliament's power to pass fast-track remedial orders or amending legislation brought before it by the Government, in response to the declaration.[26] Finally, the Act subjects Ministers to new duties, requiring them to make written statements that their proposed legislation complies with the basic principles of the European Convention.[27]

Inevitably, there are some subtle differences of approach between the operation of the Human Rights Act and the recent jurisprudence of the *Conseil constitutionnel*. First, the source of rights is obviously different

---

[21] *R v Secretary of State for the Home Department, ex parte Simms* [1999] 3 WLR 328.
[22] *Ibid*, at 340.
[23] S 6.
[24] S 3.
[25] S 4.
[26] S 10.
[27] S 19.

because the Human Rights Act refers to the European Convention to define the types of basic right which are protected. More fundamentally, the British system of constitutional rights-based challenge is reactive, not pro-active. The Act does not set up a special jurisdictional order to be compared with the functions of the *Conseil constitutionnel*. Rather, it envisages that constitutional challenge to legislation will arise in the course of ordinary litigation before the ordinary courts whenever a party's basic rights have been infringed by legislation. And, whilst a common law court has the power to issue a 'declaration of incompatibility' requiring government to consider amending the offending provision, the ultimate decision on the content of legislation remains vested in Parliament.

D. Conclusion

It is fair to say that the constitutional traditions of Britain and France have traditionally displayed some disparities of style, and in light of their different historical experiences it is hardly surprising that some differences of constitutional doctrine remain today. However, while we can highlight differences in application, it is clear that the two nations share a common constitutional heritage based on the primacy of the rights of man. This heritage is surely strengthened by the enactment of the Human Rights Act, whose clear legislative statement of rights does much to bring British and French constitutional arrangements closer together. As with the French Constitutional Preambles, the Human Rights Act has provided the British legal system with a clear legislative statement of fundamental rights which carries genuine democratic credentials.

III.   ADMINISTRATIVE LAW

A.   The Structural Divide

Let me turn now to the principles of administrative law, as this is the field of litigation where constitutional rights most often fall to be considered.

As with constitutional comparison, the consideration of administrative law in France and Britain leads us immediately to a major structural divergence.[28] A British lawyer takes for granted the proposition that government is subject to the control of the common law courts, yet this proposition is directly contrary to the statement of principle which underpins French administrative law:

> Les fonctions judiciaires sont distinctes et demeureront toujours séparées des fonctions administratives. Les juges ne pourront, à peine de fortaiture, troubler de quelque manière que ce soit, les opérations des corps administratifs, ni citer devant eux les administrateurs par raison de leur fonction.[29]

This statement—contained in Article 13 of the Law of 16 August 1790—was a direct product of Revolution. It epitomised the revolutionary imperative of establishing a new system of government which was free from the interference of the unpopular *Ancien Régime*. It summed up also the thinking later espoused by De Tocqueville that the republican government should acquire the same inherent power of governance which formerly belonged to the King. But at the same time Article 13 reflected the basic premise—maintained today by Article 3 of the 1958 Constitution—that national sovereignty and the exercise of governmental power belonged above all else to the people of France.

In many ways the British experience could not be more different. As I have mentioned, Bracton's assertion in the 13th century that '*the King shall ... be subject to .... God and the law: since law makes the King*'[30] was taken up by an active and interventionist judiciary. As early as the sixteenth century the English courts had devised an effective system of control which allowed ordinary litigants to begin proceedings in the name of the Crown to seek review of improper governmental action. The remedies available in such proceedings—the ancient writs of prohibition, mandamus and certiorari—would enable the court to make binding orders requiring specific conduct on the part of the Crown.

---

[28] See Dicey, *The Law of the Constitution,* 10th ed, (London, Macmillan, 1962) 336, a caricature which has long been recognised as somewhat extreme: Wade & Forsyth, *Administrative Law,* 8th ed, (Oxford, OUP, 2000) 24.

[29] '*Judicial functions are distinct and will always remain separated from administrative functions. Judges may not—without abusing their authority—interfere in any way in the operations of the administrative branch, nor summon members of the administrative branch by reason of their function.*'

[30] Bracton, quoted in F W Maitland, *The Constitutional History of England* (Oxford, Clarendon Press, 1908) p 100.

B.   Commonalities Behind the Divide

Much has been made of this structural divide and the way in which it highlights the different constitutional experiences of the two nations. In addition there are differences of terminology, and the term 'administrative law' in France embraces not only the judicial supervision of government (as in Britain) but also the rules controlling public liability for wrongs which in Britain are not defined as administrative law at all. However, if we look to the area where the terminology does display consistency—the judicial control of government—the structural divisions should not close our eyes to some basic commonalities between Britain and France.

a.   *Government According to Law*

First, we should note that judicial review is a central feature of constitutional arrangements in both countries, notwithstanding the differences of constitutional structure to which I have referred. Fundamentally, powers of judicial review—however they are implemented—have arisen as a vindication of the principle that government must be conducted according to law.

Indeed, when we look more closely at the jurisprudence of the *Conseil d'État* and of the British Courts it is clear that jurisdictional control—the courts' insistence on identifying the source of governmental power—is central to both systems. Just as in *Entick v Carrington* Lord Camden ruled that the 'argument of state necessity' counted for nothing in the absence of clear legal powers, so in France the *Conseil d'État* is sure to strike down any act which is not founded upon a legitimate *base légale*.

A clear example of the operation of jurisdictional control in Anglo-French administrative law emerges from comparing the decision of the French *Conseil d'État* of 25 April 1994,[31] with the ruling of the British House of Lords in *Wheeler v Leicester City Council* in 1985.[32]

In its decision the *Conseil d'État* was asked to consider the legality of a local authority's decision to finance a leaflet opposing ratification

---

[31] CE 25 April 1994, *Président du Conseil Général du Territoire-de-Belfort* AJDA 1994.545.
[32] [1985] AC 1054.

of the Maastricht Treaty. The *Conseil* held that the decision was unlawful—local authorities have no responsibility for international affairs and in the absence of any recognised *base légale* the proposed measure had to fail.

This use of jurisdictional control to uphold the rule of law is closely paralleled by the decision of the House of Lords in *Wheeler*. There, a local authority withdrew access to public facilities from a local rugby club which had decided to play in South Africa during the time of apartheid. In formal terms the local authority had control over its public facilities. However, the House of Lords ruled that the local authority had no legal basis for imposing politically motivated punishments.

b.   Separation of Powers

Another fundamental doctrine underpinning the law of judicial review in both France and Britain is the separation of powers. This doctrine sets up a delicate constitutional balancing act. It requires those who are charged with the power of governmental supervision to give effect to the rule of law by protecting the rights of individuals against governmental encroachment. But at the same time it elevates the democratic imperative of respecting the acts of an elected legislature. The administrative courts must therefore set clear boundaries that are sensitive to the dangers of usurping the executive or legislative function.[33]

This is a particular concern in Britain, where the powers of controlling administrative conduct vest in the judicial branch of government under a procedure which is itself described as 'judicial review'.[34] In order to keep their constitutional role within proper limits, British courts must apply a number of doctrines, including strict rules of standing to ensure that the enforcement of rights is only effected by those directly concerned.[35] The courts also maintain

[33] Lord Irvine of Lairg, *'Judges and Decision-Makers: The Theory and Practice of Wednesbury Review,'* [1996] PL 59.
[34] Lord Irvine of Lairg, *'Judges and Decision-Makers: The Theory and Practice of Wednesbury Review,'* [1996] PL 59.
[35] In *Lujan v Defenders of Wildlife*, the US Supreme Court was faced with a challenge to environmental legislation brought by members of environmental lobby groups. They argued that a new Endangered Species Act should be extended to apply outside the territory of the United States. The petitioners were denied standing to challenge the

a distinction between the concepts of appeal, under which the court can substitute its view for that of the decision-maker, and review, under which the court examines only the legality of the decision. By this distinction the courts ensure that, in judicial review, they examine only the legality, and not the merits, of administrative decisions.[36]

But the British Courts also employ variable standards of review. Where the administrative act under review affects fundamental rights, for example the right to life, the Court's scrutiny should be more intense.[37]

This principle is critical to the sensitive application of administrative law. On the one hand it allows courts to intervene strenuously whenever the legality of a governmental act is in question, particularly whenever the rights of individuals are in issue. On the other hand it ensures a fair constitutional balance by keeping government policy outside the judicial domain. So in 1991 when a number of local authorities sought to challenge the government's policy on restraining local authority taxation and expenditure, the House of Lords refused to intervene on the basis that the decision raised sensitive issues of national economic policy and any challenge would amount to improper judicial interference in the political process.[38]

Similar principles are at work in French administrative jurisprudence. Of course, French administrative law does not recognise a clear *structural* separation between the executive and the judiciary. Whilst the *Conseil d'État* exercises a judicial function, in its ultimate supervisory authority over executive conduct, in structural terms it remains part of the executive branch.

Yet the jurisprudence of the *Conseil d'État* shows a clear concern for the dangers of illegitimate interference with executive decisions. As with the British courts, the *Conseil d'État* applies a variable standard of review, allowing decision-makers a broad scope of discretion in matters of public policy but considerably restricting their margin

---

decision, on the ground that their claim was 'a generally available grievance about government' that should more properly be heard in a political arena, not a court of law.

[36] C F Forsyth, *Of Fig Leaves and Fairy Tales: The Ultra Vires Doctrine, the Sovereignty of Parliament and Judicial Review* [1996] CLJ 122.

[37] *R v Secretary of State for the Home Department, ex parte Brind* [1991] 1 AC 696.

[38] *R v Secretary of State for the Environment, ex parte Hammersmith & Fulham LBC* [1991] 1 AC 521.

of latitude in cases involving fundamental rights. For example, in *Benjamin* the *Conseil* quashed a ban which had been imposed on a public speaker in violation of his right to free expression.[39] Although the authority had imposed the ban because of real concerns for the maintenance of public order, the *Conseil* would not permit these concerns to prevail over the right to free expression unless they were of a very serious character.

The concept of variable standards of review illustrates the courts' awareness of the separation of powers and the sensitivity of interference in governmental action. Notwithstanding the profoundly different regimes of administrative control in Britain and France, we can see that the risk of undue interference is a sensitivity common to both jurisdictions.

C.   Two Different Perspectives Underpinned by Common Principles

Yet this is not the only similarity of substance between the rules of French and British administrative law. To give another example, both systems maintain the importance of procedural fairness as expressed in the British concept of natural justice and the French *droits de défense*. Also the doctrines of *erreur de droit, faits matériellement inexacts* and *qualifications juridique des faits* find close parallels in the English rules governing errors of fact and law.[40]

Indeed, as with constitutional law, a close analysis looking beyond the initial structural differences shows that the founding principles of administrative control in France and Britain may not be as different as they first appear. It is true that in Britain the executive is subject to the jurisdiction of the ordinary courts whilst French government falls within its own entirely distinct jurisdiction. It is also true that this difference of practice highlights what was—at least two hundred years ago—a very different perception of the way in which governmental control should best be implemented. But looking deeper into the equation, we can see that the rules defining the control of government are motivated by similar concerns in England and France alike. On both sides of

---

[39] CE 19 May 1933, s 1933.3.1.
[40] *Anisminic v Foreign Compensation Commission* [1969] 2 AC 147; *R v Hull University Visitor, ex parte Page* [1993] AC 682.

the Channel these largely judge-made rules show some striking commonalities of substance.

IV. CONCLUSION

This pattern of structural divergences, underpinned by basic substantive similarities, is a pattern which can be seen in many areas of Anglo-French jurisprudence. Indeed, the localising influences which have often been responsible for this historical divergence are diminishing.[41] The problems that will confront Anglo-French law in the twenty-first century are no longer parochial; they are of international proportions. Old legal and constitutional values will have to be developed to encompass issues such as genetic reproduction and regulation of the Internet, and mutual guidance will inevitably be sought between nations. The House of Lords is already beginning to look to European experience with regularity when interpreting basic rights,[42] and this tendency can only be expected to increase with the progressive convergence of cultural and scientific influences across the world.

Perhaps the strongest impulse towards convergence is our countries' common membership of the European Union. The direct applicability of Community law now means that national courts on both sides of the Channel must look to each others' jurisprudence when seeking to implement the same law according to the same criteria. In the direct interpretation of Community law and indeed national legislation implementing rules of Community law, courts are beginning to define with ever greater precision the points of difference and accord among the various Community systems. For example, in a recent House of Lords case, the House was asked to interpret the Unfair Terms in Consumer Contracts Regulations, the British legislation passed to give effect to the Community Directive on Unfair Terms in Consumer Contracts.[43] Giving judgment, Lord Steyn acknowledged the need for harmonised European interpretations of Community legislation and referred to the comparative studies of the Commission of European Contract Law to explain that *'the purpose of the provision of good faith*

---

[41] Kahn-Freund, *'Uses and Misuses of Comparative Law'* (1974) 37 MLR 1.

[42] See for example, *R v Secretary of State for the Home Department, ex parte Brind* [1991] 1 AC 696.

[43] Council Directive 93/13/EEC (OJ 1993, L95, p 29).

and fair dealing is to enforce community standards of decency, fairness and reasonableness in commercial transactions'.[44]

This type of exercise shows that the comparison of European jurisprudence is not just a point of academic interest but a practical necessity. That is why the initiatives we are celebrating this evening are critical. They will help the legal systems of France and Britain to build upon the commonalities between their past and present experiences, to enable them to share in the development of their joint futures.

[44] *Director General of Fair Trading v First National Bank* [2002] 1 AC 481 at 500.

Part 4

Miscellaneous Essays on the Development of the English Legal System

17

*The Art of Advocacy and the Woolf Reforms**

G IVEN THE SUBJECT of this Conference, I feel as if I should be addressing my comments by way of submissions this afternoon to Mr Justice Hooper and not to the audience! As you may imagine, as Lord Chancellor, I have a fair number of opportunities to put my case before many different forums. I hope my own advocacy skills remain sufficient to live up to your expectations. But let me say at the outset what a pleasure it is to be here today.

More than 40 years ago, Norman Birkett argued that advocacy was the art of persuasion and presentation—an observation, he noted, that the Roman rhetorician Quintilian had originally made some 1800 years before. In the language of the 1990s, advocacy is, at base, the art of communication. And what could be more important in today's world?

Effective communication is central to modern existence. If I may be forgiven for using fashionable jargon, communication is all about knowing how to get your message across. And, before taking even that step, the effective communicator has to know what his message should be. To do that, he has to analyse the information he has at hand. And, in today's world, that can be easier said than done.

We are bombarded with a mass of information every day. Our ancestors had it easy. That old favourite, the grapevine, was the main source of information for most of human history. Then came the newspaper, libraries, the radio—all changing the way people communicated with each other, and changing the things that they wanted to know.

Today, we are in the age of 24 hours media coverage, bringing wars, technical and Scientific discoveries, and much more within easy reach of everyone. And the Internet adds yet another significant source of facts,

---

* Lecture delivered at the Worldwide Advocacy Conference, 29 June 1998.

figures, and opinion. Modern communication makes the concept of a 'global village' real.

As a priority, we have to learn to sift this information. We have to sort the wheat from the chaff. If we do not, we will be drowned by trivia. And, as advocates, we must ever remember that facts are sacred. Of course, we must present the facts in the way most favourable to whatever our cause may be. But we must never misrepresent the facts. The advocate works in a culture which outlaws misleading the court.

Nowadays, falsity often masquerades as truth and, if complaint is made, the reply often comes, 'but this is how it is perceived.' 'Perception' is the new false truth; but, to advocates, the *facts* are the truth, and are sacred. The advocate therefore works outwards from the facts into presentation and persuasion. So, having made the sift and found the information we need, we must marshal it in a way that is comprehensible to ourselves and others. A group of facts without a structure is as meaningless as random notes without a tune. These are, of course, exactly the skills an advocate has to deploy when dealing with a case.

The advocate has two prime duties: to use his skills to expose the truth; and to ensure that the judge and, if appropriate, the jury can see the case from his client's perspective. It is a role which goes to the heart of delivering effective justice. Excellent preparation is the backbone of successful advocacy—Longfellow's 'toiling ever upwards in the night'. Long hours over volume after volume of case papers, eyelids propped open over the law books—a familiar image to all of those here, including myself, who have made their careers in the law.

Eloquence can be learned, but nothing can beat knowing a case inside out. It is only when all the facts have been committed to memory, when all the different versions of events have been absorbed and analysed— all the permutations mastered—that the advocate comes into his own. For, armed with the facts, the advocate has a chance to see the chinks in the other side's armour—the opportunity to exploit the underlying weaknesses of the opponent's case. But he will fail to make the most of these opportunities if he has not learned one of the other key skills needed by an advocate: active listening. Not letting the words of witnesses float by unconsidered, not following blindly a prepared structure, but seizing each sentence and applying a forensic examination of every fact and assertion. The best cross-examination is a relentless progress in logic and probability.

Advocacy demands communication skills of the highest order; but it is much more than simply talking elegantly, or even convincingly. In fact, I believe the use of *advocacy* as a synonym for *speech* will become ever more misplaced as the justice system is reformed and modernised. There will always be a place for the advocate on his or her feet in open court, not least in criminal proceedings. The glories of the English legal system are in the oral dialogue between counsel and judge, testing arguments to destruction, and in the art of cross-examination. But in civil justice, the area I intend to focus on this afternoon, the wider skills of advocacy—including written advocacy—will become increasingly important and valuable. I will explain why in a moment.

First, let me remind you of the background. Previous governments allowed the civil justice system in England and Wales to stagnate. As Lord Woolf established during the course of his review, which resulted in two historic reports published in 1995 and 1996, over recent decades the system has developed five fundamental weaknesses. Civil justice is slow. Cases can take years to be resolved. And let us not forget that when we say 'a case', we are actually talking about people—individuals left hanging in the air, hoping for a good outcome, fearing the worst. People whose lives are blighted by the strain of waiting for justice to be delivered.

Civil justice is complex. The more sophisticated the laws are, the greater scope they give for excessive technicality. It is a real challenge to find a simplified route through the technicality of law and procedure. Sometimes a person with a grievance or dispute may be faced with a range of options for action, not all of them wise—but it can be difficult to work out which route to take for the best.

Slowness and complexity contribute to the third weakness: that civil justice is uncertain. When will a case reach its conclusion? And what will be the result? People involved in cases may have to put their lives on hold, for it can be difficult to plan ahead.

These weaknesses lead to the fourth: that civil justice can be unfair. In many cases, Lord Woolf found it was entirely feasible for the stronger party to exploit the slow, complex, uncertain nature of the system in order to grind down his opponents. The opponents might have a better case but, if they did not have the stamina for the contest, then they could be cheated of justice. And the last weakness Lord Woolf found was excessive cost. All the other problems contributed to pushing up costs—for the individuals involved in the case and for the long-suffering taxpayer too, not least because of legal aid.

Many of you will be familiar with the Government's plans for the reform of the civil justice system in England and Wales which I announced last Autumn. In sum, they are the provision of three routes to justice. First, an enlarged small claims procedure for most cases up to £5,000. Second, the new fast track for cases up to £15,000. And, third, the multi-track, for all cases above that level, and for those below that level which are more complex. I have heard it suggested that we do not intend—or will not be able—to keep to the ambitious timetable that I announced in October. Let me make our position absolutely clear. I said that radical reforms to the civil justice system would be brought forward in April 1999—and they will be. Those of you who work in the English civil justice system should have no doubt that significant change is on its way. You have just nine more months to prepare yourselves. And the message must be: 'Look to the future or be left behind".

Also on the horizon are a new set of challenges flowing out of the Human Rights Bill. Again, thorough and early preparation will be vital. For those of you considering these statements with trepidation, I can offer some comfort. Over the past year, my Department and I have conducted extensive consultation with the judiciary, the legal profession, and many other groups on how to approach the detail of the civil justice reforms. We have been listening to those who are already using case management techniques in our courts. We have been learning from their experiences. We have been able to take account of the concerns and fears some have expressed—and also, let me say, been encouraged by the many expressions of support for change.

The package of reforms we will introduce in April 1999 has been fully informed by this dialogue with the judiciary and profession. After April, we will continue to roll out the later stages of the reforms gradually and steadily. This will allow both court staff and court users to become familiar with all the changes and, hopefully, ensure that the system maintains and continuously improves its current performance during the transitional phase. The April reforms will include rules which introduce the fast track and multi-track, and which support the key tool to be used in achieving our objectives—judicial case management.

For those of you who are interested in seeing the details, I can announce that the current drafts of the rules will soon be available on my Department's website. We intend to initiate a debate on them in both Houses of Parliament next month, a clear signal of the importance which the Government attaches to them; and, following those debates, copies of the draft rules will be available on request from my officials for information. Our intention is to have a finalised version signed, sealed and delivered in *January 1999*—well before the implementation date of April.

A lot of hard work has gone into drawing up these rules. I want to thank all those judges and practitioners who have contributed to the process of debate and drafting because they have done us a valuable service. I have no doubt that these rules are the key to making the reformed civil justice system work efficiently. At the same time as we bring the new rules into effect, we will also be rolling out new supporting information technology. The High Court will be the first beneficiary. From April 1999, orders and notices in proceedings in the Queen's Bench Division, which are currently drawn up by hand, will be generated electronically.

At the same time, we will be updating our computer system in the county courts, which is called CASEMAN, so that it can be used to log new events created by the new rules, for example, the acknowledgement of service. Now, I am sure I am addressing an audience of people who are highly information technology literate. But even the most skilled computer users among you will acknowledge that learning how to use a new software package or a new piece of hardware takes time and is fraught with opportunities for making mistakes. I acknowledge my own special talent for error! So, we are taking a measured approach to putting in place updated information technology to support the civil justice reforms. As I have said, some elements, particularly in the High Court, will be brought into operation from April 1999, alongside the new rules. *Full* IT support for case management will follow in phases. The whole system is expected to be implemented early in 2000, around a year after the start of the process.

In the end, the efficient use of information technology will radically alter the way we do business in the civil justice system. But putting computers in place is not the only change the courts are facing. New practice directions are needed. There will be essential changes to court administration. There will be many new and revised court forms. That sounds mundane but, as any practitioner in the audience knows, a badly designed form can cause enormous difficulties.

With all this on the horizon, and the impact of the Human Rights Bill too, I believe that a cumulative approach is the only sensible way of proceeding. Our timetable remains ambitious and challenging—but realistic. We will begin the great process of change in April next year.

By the end of 2000, we should have a modern civil justice system of which we can be proud.

You may be thinking that I have come a long way from my starting point of the nature of advocacy. Well, let me explain where I see the connections between the civil justice reforms and the many important issues you will be discussing over the next few days. First of all, we can ask how advocacy itself may have contributed to creating the five weaknesses which were identified by Lord Woolf. A poor advocate will fail to make his case clearly and succinctly. He may ask badly expressed, or prolix questions; or fail to listen to the answers. He may emphasise the wrong points; bring in irrelevant material; or simply use language which is obscure and confusing; or ask three questions in one instead of one at a time. No question in cross-examination is justifiable unless it is relevant and nonrepetitious. I am sure we can all think of a few examples of bad practice—and may even, especially in our early days at the Bar, have been responsible for a few ourselves! Poor advocacy inevitably contributes to delay. If an advocate labours his argument, if he fails to come smartly to the point, he will be dragging out the length of the case for the benefit of no one—especially not his client. The best advocate is not the one who labours 17 points in logical order. He is the advocate who concentrates on the essentials and puts his best points first. Effective advocates are able to smooth the path of justice by making a case easier to understand—by making plain the most important facts and eliminating room for confusion by expressing submissions in simple language. They speed things up, not slow them down, by striking at the heart of a case quickly and cleanly.

Because of its adversarial nature, the effectiveness of our justice system is dependent on highly skilled advocacy. I am therefore pleased to know that the Inns of Court Law School regards it as a core element in the training of our young lawyers. The civil justice reforms will also contribute to promoting good advocacy. As I have already said, thorough preparation is the key. That preparation will be greatly assisted by an important new initiative in civil justice—pre-action protocols. These were recommended by Lord Woolf in his Final Report on Access to Justice.

Lord Woolf saw that streamlining and rationalising court procedures could not—alone—solve the problems which characterise today's civil justice system. He understood that it is all too easy for cases to be beset by delay, cost, and complexity long before they ever reach the door of the court. He recommended that action should be taken to modify the behaviour of parties at the earliest possible stage.

For some time, a number of Working Groups have, with the support of my Department, been drawing up pre-action protocols in a range of legal areas, including personal injury; road traffic accidents; and clinical negligence. All the major stakeholders in the civil justice system are involved, including legal practitioners; insurers; doctors; experts in various disciplines; and organisations representing the interests of litigants. With the agreement of the working groups, we intend to publish the prevailing drafts of the protocols later this Summer.

In essence, pre-action protocols set out codes of good practice, of best practice—of *sensible* practice—for all sides who are likely to become involved in legal action. They cover, for example, the content of standard letters; joint instruction of a single expert; and alternatives to litigation. They set out reasonable timetables for communication between parties; investigation of claims; early disclosure of documents; exchange of summaries of witness statements; and exchange of expert reports.

But, and I do want to emphasise this, protocols are so much pious aspiration unless the judges *insist* on compliance and impose the strongest available sanctions where there are material departures from the Protocols. The road to Hell is paved with good intentions—and Protocols are no more than good intentions, unless they are effectively enforced. Pre-action protocols are intended to facilitate early settlement where that is possible. If a settlement proves unachievable, then the pre-action protocol lays down a code which will help parties prepare thoroughly for litigation.

This is where the skills of the advocate come into play. The effective advocate marshals his facts, looks critically at his evidence, analyses his options. Preparation is his watchword. The pre-action protocols will help to shape that preparation. They will help to make it even more effective. And, have no doubt, careful preparation will become ever more vital in the reformed civil justice system, particularly for cases which are to be heard in the fast track. Those cases will be subject to tight—and judicially enforced strict—timetables.

Advocates should expect the fast track and the multi-track to have a profound impact on their working practices. They are going to have to learn new ways of deploying their skills. Written advocacy will grow in importance, as will ability to build a case on written evidence. Let me give you a few examples of what I mean.

Cases allocated to the fast track will be those which the procedural judge considered were capable of conclusion within one day in court.

This implies tight limits on the time available for oral argument and for cross-examination of witnesses. Advocates will have to prepare more focused questions and listen even more carefully to the responses they solicit in order to make the most of the time they have available.

Cases proceeding in the multi-track will be subject to strong judicial case management, so that the work done on a case will be proportionate to its value and complexity, both in preparation for the trial, and during the trial itself. This will usually involve early definition of the issues to be tried. And, in many cases, a timetable will be set for the trial, so that key elements, including oral argument, can be tailored to the nature of the issues in dispute—and limited as necessary.

And advocates will find they no longer have the same opportunities to question expert witnesses. Expert evidence will be allowed only with the court's permission. Even then, the emphasis will be on written evidence. Oral expert evidence will be the exception, not the rule, particularly in the fast track. This will require a considerable change in approach for some advocates.

Working within these boundaries, the advocate may find his opportunity for advocacy circumscribed; but he can still be highly effective. That will depend on two factors: his level of personal skill; and the thoroughness of his preparations before the case commences. Eloquence in court, of course, will still be vital, but so will all those other factors which make someone an excellent communicator.

So Ladies and gentlemen, I have laid my case before you at some length. It is time for me to draw to a close. Let me conclude by saying just this. The civil justice system in England and Wales will shortly be subject to radical change. No one should have any doubts about that. The use of pre-action protocols, enforced by the judges apply the toughest sanctions available to them; and the stricter rules governing the management of cases, will alter the culture of civil justice. The system will remain adversarial but, at the same time, it will take on more cooperative, inquisitorial features. But what will not change is the important place the advocate has within the system. The advocate will continue to be a key player in the court room, and in case preparation. The reason is simple: the delivery of justice depends on achieving understanding. No matter how the form and procedures of civil justice change, we will still need the services of effective communicators. And, as I said at the beginning, that, at base, is what advocacy is all about.

18

*The Feasibility of a Unified Approach to Proceedings Arising Out of Major City Frauds**

LADIES AND GENTLEMEN, I thank KPMG for its invitation this evening. My subject is whether there is a need to rationalise the response of the State and Regulatory bodies to major financial frauds; to reduce the multiplicity of different sets of proceedings which may arise when the possibility of wrongdoing is identified; and as a result, to avoid the delays which bedevill these proceedings.

The problem is complex. The Government knows no obvious, nor easy, solutions. This speech announces no decisions, and promotes no new policies by Government, nor personal initiatives. It asks questions and seeks views. In particular I offer my reflections on whether further unification of some proceedings, in one 'super-set', is feasible. What might that contribute to our ability to tackle major frauds? Unified proceedings would be consistent with the steps already being taken towards a more coherent and expeditious system.

The ability to respond effectively to major fraud is of the highest priority to the Government. We recognise that, in recent years, the public has at times felt that those responsible for major crimes in the commercial sphere have managed to avoid justice. Even when fraud is detected, the present procedures are often cumbersome, and difficult to prosecute effectively.

Many of you will know that our financial regulatory system is already undergoing something of a revolution. We are co-ordinating work across Departments, including my own, to build a new, modern, more unified regulatory system, designed to meet both our national and international needs. The Government announced legislation last year to integrate responsibility for banking, insurance and financial services

* Lecture given by the Lord Chancellor on 24 June 1998.

supervision under a single regulator. Also, we have given the Bank of England operational independence in monetary policy. Banking supervision has been moved to the Financial Services Authority, the new single regulator. The next stage will be covered in legislation, to be published in draft this summer.

The new Authority will be empowered both to retain the confidence of the City, and to protect consumers effectively. A vital part of its role will be to sustain confidence in the market. Specifically, to assist in the detection and prevention of financial crime. The Government is determined to ensure that our financial markets remain open and safe places to do business. For this, the Authority will take a pro-active role in regulating compliance with money laundering requirements. This will be made explicit in primary legislation requiring the Authority to monitor, detect, and prevent financial crime. It will have the power to make new rules prohibiting money laundering, and to bring criminal prosecutions for regulatory breaches.

The Government has also announced its intention to introduce a system of civil penalties for behaviour which, though falling short of criminal, might or actually does damage financial markets. This power will also be exercisable by the new Financial Services Authority. The Authority will be given new prosecution powers to tackle those who abuse the markets, including insider dealers. I would stress that the new civil fines regime is intended to *complement* not substitute for the criminal law. Criminal conduct will continue to be prosecuted.

The new regulator's powers will be tough and effective. And they will be exercised fairly. The Financial Services Bill will create a new single Tribunal, entirely independent of the Authority, to consider appeals against the exercise of its regulatory powers. The establishment of this Authority as a new 'super-regulator' for the financial sector illustrates the Government's commitment to a co-ordinated, coherent regulatory regime. This will ultimately benefit both the providers and the users of financial services. We believe that a strong, single regulator will further enhance the United Kingdom's reputation as one of the best governed and most attractive financial markets in the world. We value our standing as a clean market in which to do business. And we recognise the substantial economic benefit this generates for everyone in this country. We will not allow fraudsters, and their supposedly 'victimless' crimes, to damage that. All these measures will ensure that confidence in the integrity and vitality of the City of London, and its various institutions, will continue to grow under New Labour.

As I mentioned, the Government is working widely to combat different aspects of financial crime. In February, the Home Office consulted on alternatives to conventional juries in complex criminal fraud trials. The role of jury trials in these cases raises a number of difficult issues, on which the Government remains entirely open-minded. We must support both an effective, practical trial system, and the civil liberties of all defendants.

In drafting the fraud juries consultation document, we discussed the value of a fraud pre-trial procedures review. It is clearly important—no less for defendants than for prosecutors—to ensure, as far as possible, that cases are presented as clearly and straightforwardly as possible. Pre-trial procedures, which can significantly determine the eventual shape and scope of each case, must be efficient, effective, and broadly acceptable to all parties.

Last month, as part of my own contribution to these financial crime initiatives, I announced that my Department would undertake a review of these procedures. It will examine serious fraud trial procedures, from the decision to transfer or commit, to the start of the trial itself. The Review will seek to canvass directly the views and experiences of relevant practitioners throughout the process. I extend tonight an open invitation to anyone who wishes to make his or her views known to the Review, to do so as soon as possible.

I wish to look this evening, however, beyond the ongoing reform of financial criminal justice, and beyond the new regulatory regime. I want you to consider the multiplicity of proceedings which can, and often do, cascade out of a 'typical' serious fraud. The potential for a Gordian knot of overlapping proceedings can be illustrated by the following— entirely fictitious, you will observe—example.

A listed English bank, with international commercial lending, private, and investment banking arms, is taken over by a large American bank. This follows a contested bid which saw massive dealing in the bank's shares before and after the take-over. The bank's commercial lending portfolio includes secured lending to corporations in Ruritania, one of the so-called 'bull economies'. Proper provision seems to have been made for this. The bank's personal investment arm sells high yield personal pensions policies linked to the equity markets of these 'bull economies'.

Disgruntled ex-employees, redundant after the take-over, (its quite a good play this) make contact with friends in the media (they exist). Stories of irregularities in the bank's conduct begin to appear. There are allegations of undue closeness between the bank and its major customers.

Meanwhile, Ruritania's economy crashes, leading to mass unemployment and civil unrest. The bank's new auditors, brought in by the American parent, uncover substantial lending to Ruritanian customers, disguised through shell companies in various off-shore jurisdictions. Provision in the accounts appears to be wholly inadequate. The previous directors may have turned a blind eye to the absence of proper credit controls. They may have made misleading statements about the bank's financial performance at the time of the take-over, to manipulate the share price. Doubt is cast on the objectivity of previous audits.

Investigations by the FSA and PIA reveal that these pension policies, sold by the bank, are not linked to a 'pool' of 'bull economy' equities at all, but, rather, to equities in Ruritanian corporations which are customers of the bank itself. As the City reels from the bank's rapid implosion, the Secretary of State for Trade and Industry appoints inspectors, to investigate the affairs of the bank and dealings in its shares.

At this point the bank issues proceedings against its former auditors for negligence, and against its former directors for fraudulent misrepresentation. Mareva injunctions are obtained against the former directors, freezing their assets and restricting their spending on legal costs. The pensioners demand to be told how the regulators failed to spot the fraud. The Government appoints a Lord Justice of Appeal to begin a cross-departmental Inquiry into the bank's demise. The Inquiry hears much oral and written evidence. But this is unavailable for use in any subsequent proceedings, because of Public Interest Immunity. The Lord Justice's final report is inadmissible in any such proceedings, since it is deemed to be opinion evidence only.

Meanwhile, the Serious Fraud Office begins its investigation, seconding accountants from one of the major firms. It raids the bank's main offices, and uncovers what it believes to be false accounting. The bank's former directors are interviewed and charged. After numerous complaints, the Institute of Chartered Accountants begins an investigation into the conduct of the bank's former auditors. Unfortunately, it cannot find a major accounting firm to act for it—because by this stage they are all conflicted out. In any event, the auditors successfully judicially review the ICAEW's refusal to postpone its inquiry, pending the civil action. The civil action is itself stayed, pending the criminal trial, as are disqualification proceedings against the former directors brought under the Directors Disqualification Act 1986.

After two years, the criminal trial reaches preparatory hearings. The number of defendants and the complexity of the charges requires a series of trials. The directors begin proceedings which eventually reach the European Court of Human Rights, alleging a breach of their right to a fair hearing within a reasonable time. I trust that you are all still with me so far ...

The sheer number and complexity of proceedings generates an immense duplication of effort and expertise. A significant proportion of both the legal and accounting professions is making a healthy living— not, some may say, a crime in itself—from the fall-out of the bank's collapse. Indeed, in this fictitious scenario, the only major accounting firm to lose out is the defendant in the auditor's negligence proceedings!

Now I posit this example to highlight the procedural melee that can erupt from a major City fraud. In this scenario, I noted up to eight separate sets of proceedings, though I will offer a small reward, very small, to the first person to spot something I have missed. My count includes:

Criminal proceedings against some or all of the directors, brought by the SFO; an investigation under s 432 of the Companies Act 1985; an investigation into insider trading, under s 177 of the Financial Services Act 1986; disqualification proceedings against some or all of the directors under the Company Directors Disqualification Act 1986; in exceptional circumstances, a one-off inquiry, such as that following BCCI; an investigation by the relevant self-regulating organisations, leading to disciplinary proceedings; an investigation of the company auditors by the Institute of Chartered Accountants, leading to disciplinary proceedings: and civil proceedings, brought by or against the company.

The reason for this range of proceedings is that each of them serves a different function. Broadly speaking, criminal proceedings address retribution for and deterrence of wrongdoing. Companies Act and Financial Services Act investigations serve to calm the markets and assist the DTI in assessing the impact of the fraud. Special inquiries adduce general lessons to be learned from particular incidents. Disqualification proceedings protect the public from unfit company directors. Investigations and disciplinary proceedings by professional bodies punish misconduct by, for example, disbarring the defective practitioners. Finally, civil litigation serves as the vehicle for the vindication of individuals' private law rights.

So there is a considerable overlap between the functions of these various proceedings. Criminal proceedings may result in the harshest penalties, as well as the most severe stigma. So it must be right in principle that they attract the greatest procedural protections. These include the manner in which evidence may be presented to the Court, and the high standard of proof to be attained.

Also, the 'purity' of criminal proceedings is often protected by postponing other procedures concerning the same events until after the end of the criminal trial. This necessarily undermines the efficacy of the other procedures. It also means that at the end of a criminal trial, an individual cannot regard matters as closed, for better or worse. He or she may face yet further investigation of the same events.

Although the various procedures serve different functions, clearly they will still traverse much the same areas of factual investigation. For anyone less familiar with the very real complexities and difficulties inherent in this area, this welter of proceedings may look not dissimilar to the archetypal hole in the road, dug and redug in successive days to remedy the gas leak, the electricity supply, the gushing ruptured main. A huge duplication of effort can occur, and significant delays inevitably arise. We must, in good conscience, question whether this is the most efficient way for a modern state to deal with major financial wrongdoing.

But the problems go beyond 'mere' delay, expense and inconvenience. It seems increasingly likely that our present system for dealing with commercial fraud must change, in line with our international obligations under the European Convention on Human Rights. Article 6, thus far, has had the greatest impact. Article 6(1) provides a minimum guarantee of due process in both civil and criminal cases. It states that 'in the determination of his civil rights and obligations or of any criminal charge against him, everyone is entitled to a fair and public hearing within a reasonable time by an independent and impartial tribunal established by law.'

In *Saunders*, the UK Government was defeated before the Court of Human Rights over the use of answers given to DTI inspectors acting under section 432 of the Companies Act 1985. This compels persons under investigation to answer questions and produce documents, on pain of being held in contempt of court. The inspectors' powers of investigation per se were supported. The use of such information in any subsequent criminal trial was not.

Perhaps most tellingly, in a case brought only last year, the Commission ruled that there had been a breach of the Article 6 right to trial within a reasonable time, in respect of disqualification proceedings brought under the Company Directors Disqualification Act 1986.

In August 1991, the Official Receiver issued summonses seeking disqualification orders under the 1986 Act against the plaintiff and certain of his co-directors. Some co-directors were also the subject of criminal proceedings, so the hearing of applications under the 1986 Act was postponed until after the criminal trial. In August 1993, some directors were acquitted, and others convicted. The latter appealed, leading to a decision of the Court of Appeal in August 1994.

In early 1996 the High Court finally made a consent order staying the disqualification proceedings against the plaintiff. He complained, under the European Convention on Human Rights, that the UK had breached his right under Article 6(1) to a hearing within a reasonable time. The ECHR concluded that there *had* been a violation of Article 6(1), by virtue of a delay of about four-and-a-half years from the institution of disqualification proceedings against him, to the High Court order.

Article 6 requires us to ensure that persons accused of any wrongdoing—commercial or otherwise—have charges against them determined within a reasonable time. This raises most serious issues for the way in which we deal with City fraud. The case I have just outlined was unusual in its complexity, but sadly not unique in its length. More to the point, the delays in the prosecution of that case arose—at least in part—from problems caused by the multiplicity of proceedings. The fact is that substantial delays in determining proceedings can and do occur in the current system.

Now it is always dangerous to seek to draw general conclusions from individual cases in Strasbourg. But the last case I mentioned certainly demonstrates that delays inherent in the multiplicity of civil and criminal proceedings can support claims under Article 6 of the Convention. This problem is particularly pressing. The Commission regarded directors' disqualification proceedings as having so adverse an effect on their subjects, that special diligence is merited to bring them to a speedy conclusion.

Remember also that, under Article 6, signatory states will be obliged to ensure that their legal systems can deliver justice within a reasonable time. We cannot rely upon what might be termed 'intrinsic flaws' in the system, to justify delay. Inevitable and unexceptionable causes of delay can validly be blamed on the Government when a case reaches Strasbourg. Put bluntly, we cannot rely upon inadequacy of institutional resources to justify delays under Article 6. If the system gives rise to structural delays, we must remedy it.

This Government takes most seriously the need to ensure that our legal system meets the requirements of the European Convention on Human Rights. It is particularly important for us, because of our decision to give significant domestic effect to the rights conferred by the Convention. These—including that of trial within a reasonable time under Article 6—will affect domestic courts in two important ways. Courts will be obliged to interpret statutory provisions to conform with the Convention, so far as it is possible to do so. And public authorities, *including the courts*, will be required to act in a manner which is consistent with Convention rights.

Consider the practical effect of the Human Rights Act. Before, individuals like Saunders could complain to Strasbourg only about the *handling* of cases against them—and then only after domestic proceedings against them had run their course. The Act will let respondents and defendants rely directly upon Article 6 to influence *how their cases proceed*. For example, our courts already possess the power to dismiss or to strike out proceedings where there has been substantial delay. Now I cannot predict how courts might apply the requirements of Article 6. But I can easily anticipate arguments to the effect that the criteria for the exercise of existing powers should be adapted to meet Strasbourg requirements for trial within a reasonable time. The need to restructure is all the more pressing, when you consider that any actual or potential breach of Article 6 may lead to the frustration of domestic proceedings, not—merely!—an adverse judgment in Strasbourg some years after the event.

Although the case I mentioned earlier provides a good, if grim, illustration of how delay may arise out of the multiplicity of possible current proceedings, it is not the only possible mishap. I can envisage all manner of permutations of proceedings arising out of major frauds, causing delays which will be deemed to breach individuals' human rights. Nor should this problem be considered simply in the light of the European Convention and the Human Rights Act. The present system is inherently inefficient. This needs to be addressed in the interests of the proper administration of justice.

I have now, I hope, given some sense of the problems which we face under our present system, and some of the measures already in hand to counter them. As I said, the devising of a complete and practicable solution to these problems is an altogether more difficult task. I would like to encourage wide debate on how we should deal with major fraud. To provoke discussions, let me outline one possible way forward: a unified investigation, embracing punishment, deterrence, *and* public interest functions. This would need to include possible criminal conviction, civil fines, public reports, sanctions and directors' disqualifications. It may be that my theorising tonight raises more questions than answers. But it is good to question customary assumptions from time to time.

Consider the feasibility of a single set of proceedings, responsible not only for hearing any criminal charges, but also for producing reports on the lines of Companies Act and Financial Services Act investigations. And perhaps also for imposing disciplinary sanctions on directors and professionals. What might be envisaged would be proceedings heard by a High Court Judge and a jury, and also two expert assessors. The jury would participate only in the initial criminal stage of the proceedings, to be discharged when that stage was completed. The judge and expert assessors would then go on to consider any further sanctions and other steps to be taken.

In this scenario, the criminal stage of the proceedings would remain the most important feature of the procedure. The judge and jury would hear the case on the specific criminal charges first. The expert assessors are, at that stage, only observers. This would protect the 'purity' of criminal proceedings, and provide a safeguard against the *Saunders* situation, where investigative evidence was rendered inadmissible in the criminal prosecution. To minimise potential complexity, the prosecution might still be required to identify a few representative charges with the best prospects of conviction. The criminal case could proceed in conventional fashion. But the judge and expert assessors would be able to ask detailed questions of witnesses, being encouraged—within reason—to take an inquisitorial role.

Once verdicts had been given in the criminal case, the judge and expert assessors—by then well up the 'learning curve'—could proceed to consider any other issues beyond the criminal charges. If necessary, they could prepare a report along the lines of Companies Act or Financial Services Act investigations, and even provide for directors' disqualifications. A major part of the new Financial Services Authority's role will be to determine regulatory sanctions. This function could even, in theory, be incorporated into a unified trial-and-investigation procedure.

But then a question would arise. Should an appeal against criminal conviction have the effect of staying this second stage of the proceedings? This would tend to build delays back into the proposed unified procedure. As I have illustrated, in the current process these stays can be a major cause of excessive delay. But if the criminal trial is seriously defective, it could be argued that the Court of Appeal should rule at an early stage, before any further actions, which would run the risk of being based on erroneous premises. This would carry the risk that subsequent procedures could be nullified by a subsequent Court of Appeal decision. But that risk might be thought well worth taking, in the interest of concluding all proceedings within a time-frame which avoids the infringement of the defendants' human rights. So there seems to be no perfect solution.

But back to our scenario. At the second stage of the proceedings, evidence could be presented in accordance with the less stringent principles of DTI reports and rulings on directors' disqualification. As with the FSA in particular, incorporating investigations by regulatory and professional bodies into a unified procedure raises another problem. Who should undertake the investigations? The theory behind the delegation of policing functions to regulatory and professional bodies is that they will be both more efficient and better informed, because of their expertise in the professions in which their members work.

I can see two viable options. The first would charge the body exercising the new unified procedure to provide professional sanctions on behalf of regulatory and professional bodies. The post-criminal trial phase could include examining any misconduct charges against the professionals involved. The requisite expertise could be met by the appointment of expert assessors nominated by the regulatory and professional bodies.

The second alternative is for the regulatory and professional bodies' disciplinary procedures to be treated as a distinct, but related, procedure. The body in question could appoint its own disciplinary panel. This would have the right to follow the processes of the unified procedure, but would produce its own report and impose its own sanctions.

The first option, hoewer, is simple, and allows for the element of expert scrutiny. The case for a single body, to be responsible for judging and grading the many degrees of wrongdoing following the jury's decision on criminal liability, is also strong.

To assist a unified hearing regime, there might be a notification procedure between the relevant government departments and other regulatory and professional bodies. Each relevant entity could be alerted when another was considering taking action. The new Financial Services Authority could be used to devise notifying protocols. Notified entities would then have to decide whether to participate in the proposed proceedings, within a strict time limit.

To illustrate how this theory might work in practice, I return to the catastrophic collapse of my fictitious English bank. As the potential wrongdoing of the bank's former directors and auditors emerges, the various regulatory and professional bodies make a start on their investigations. The onus in this example is on the SFO to decide reasonably promptly whether to bring charges. Once it has, it will notify and report to the other regulatory bodies and government departments. They now have another four months, say, to continue with their investigations, providing information to each other, before deciding whether to join in the procedure and bring charges themselves. The panel of judge and two expert assessors is then appointed. It will exercise powers of case management, to keep the proceedings within reasonable bounds.

I use the language of Lord Woolf here deliberately, because in my view the problems presently associated with tackling major City fraud include those identified in his comprehensive survey of civil justice—cost, delay and complexity. The solutions in the fraud context are more complex, because the rights involved are more fundamental. In particular, the liberty of individual defendants may be at stake. Nonetheless, Lord Woolf's observations, on how the civil adversarial process can degenerate, without effective judicial control, into an unsupervised and inefficient battlefield, are apposite. His reforms will see a fundamental transfer of the management of civil litigation to judges.

In the unified procedure I have imagined, judges could control the overall conduct and management of proceedings, including the initial criminal trial stage. This rationalisation would provide no comfort to the white collar criminal. Rather, it would assist in a swift and proportionate response to any wrongdoing identified, and enable sanctions to be imposed, in a single set of proceedings.

Clearly, if solutions were easy to come by, the problems would have been tackled long ago. In speculating in this way, I invite you to consider two more potential problems. First, criminal cases in complex matters often take a very long time to prepare for trial. It could be argued that the usefulness of subsequent investigations would be diminished, if they could only proceed after the criminal proceedings end. However, there is a distinction between the process of gathering evidence for such an investigation, and the production of a report at the end of it. At the moment, publication of reports is often held up until after the criminal trial. Under a unified procedure, the tribunal which produces the report would itself conduct and observe the criminal trial. This would enable the most intensive scrutiny of events germane to the report to be produced. The criminal trial would become part of the investigation itself, rather than a wholly separate proceeding.

This demarcation between evidence which is to be used at the criminal stage of the proceedings, and that which is only for use at the second stage, might avoid the kind of difficulty raised by the *Saunders* case. Nevertheless, witnesses, even if not defendants themselves, could be concerned that their evidence might be used for a number of different purposes.

The multiple use of evidence obtained initially for a single purpose raises very basic legal issues. But a unified procedure would largely avoid this problem. Potential witnesses would know from an early stage who the various participating entities were, and therefore the potential uses to which their evidence would be put. Moreover, provided defendants are fully protected, the sharing of centrally-pooled evidence does accord with the efficient administration of justice. Indeed, one of the complaints made of the present system is that the statutory gateways for sharing evidence between regulators are too limited in their scope.

The second apparent problem is legal aid. When is it ever not? It may be available to defendants for the initial criminal phase, but not for the second, investigatory phase. Defendants might therefore find themselves unrepresented in the second phase. However, this would not be inconsistent with principle. It is in fact the position which already obtains, and reflects the greater significance of criminal proceedings for the individuals concerned.

In speculating thus, I have not tried to incorporate civil litigation into this imaginary unified procedure. I doubt it would be feasible to do so. The sheer number of parties involved and issues arising, would weigh down on the unified procedure unacceptably. Any civil trial would therefore need to be postponed until after the unified procedure had reached its conclusion. In a case where criminal convictions resulted, litigants in related civil proceedings would be able to rely upon s 11 of the Civil Evidence Act 1968, which provides that a conviction is admissible as evidence that the defendant committed the offence.

These difficulties serve to underline the tentative spirit in which I put forward these ideas. Whilst considering the subject of civil litigation, however, and mindful of my audience this evening, I will turn briefly to that aspect of the Woolf reforms which is likely to be of greatest consequence to forensic accountants. I mentioned the duplication of expert investigation into major frauds. Lord Woolfs report contended that a major cause of unnecessary cost in civil litigation was the uncontrolled use of expert evidence. He found that the growth of a litigation support industry based upon an ethic of partisanship was anathema to the principles of proportionality and access to justice.

Accordingly, in his interim report, Lord Woolf recommended that the use of expert evidence should be under the complete control of the court. From that starting point, he argued for the wider use of *single, neutral* experts, to be selected by the court or jointly by the parties. These proposals provoked more opposition than any others during the extensive consultation process. It resulted in revisions to his final recommendations in favour of a more flexible approach to the use of expert evidence.

The approach being adopted as a result of the Woolf report continues to favour the use of single court-appointed experts and assessors, answerable to and working for the court itself. Under this system, it will be to the court itself that expert reports will be addressed. However, it is also recognised that some issues lie outside a substantially established area of knowledge, where it is appropriate for the court to sample a range of opinion. In these cases, experts may be appointed by the parties as well as by the court. Even in those instances, however, a high degree of private cooperation between opposing experts will be expected. The aim is a consensus of opinion, without the hindrance or restraining influence of the lawyers or the parties themselves. Wherever possible, a joint investigation will be carried out, resulting in a single report to the court, identifying any areas of disagreement.

Far from diminishing the importance of the expert witness, this new approach will enhance the status and influence of the expert in civil litigation. A different kind of responsibility will grow from reporting directly to the court. The adversarial culture will give way to the qualities of impartiality, independence and objectivity which are so integral to the work of the accountancy profession. The Woolf reforms herald an exciting phase for all involved in forensic accountancy, as the enhanced role of the expert witness becomes established within our modernised civil justice system.

In this address, I have sought to identify a major problem, to outline some of the work already being undertaken by the Government to address it, and to put before you my own reflections on where further answers may lie, in particular by examining the feasibility of a unified procedure. The Government welcomes the views of all professionals regularly charged with grappling with the fall-out from major City fraud. The task of ensuring a just, speedy and commercially sensitive procedure for coping with large-scale City crime is one in which we all have a major interest. The Government is working towards this; will continue to do so as a matter of urgency; and invites and welcomes informed comment and advice from those who are in the front line of addressing these problems on a daily basis.

19

The Patient, the Doctor, their Lawyers and the Judge: Rights and Duties

I. INTRODUCTION

IN RECENT YEARS, there has been a marked increase in the number of cases coming before the civil courts involving the medical profession in one way or another. Claims for medical negligence have given rise to increasingly complex factual issues for the courts to resolve and, on occasions, to what some have thought to be startlingly high awards. A number of much publicised challenges about the proper allocation of resources have provoked emotive issues but the courts, however sympathetic, have had to remain dispassionate. Most striking of all has been the development of an almost new medical jurisprudence involving equally complex and emotive issues but issues which have often been as much about ethics as the law. I have in mind recent cases concerning the right to life and the right to terminate life. The courts have had to consider the rights of a patient to refuse treatment, however drastic the consequences of the patient's refusal, set against the duty of the professional to provide that treatment in order to save the patient's life. Other cases have been concerned with the rights and obligations of the more vulnerable members of society: the infirm, the mentally ill and the mentally handicapped.

These developments must be seen against the background of a more consumerist, and arguably more litigation-prone population, on the one hand, and on the other, the rapid progress that has been made in medical technology. It is now possible to cure the previously incurable, and to preserve life despite injuries which, only a few years ago, would inevitably have led to death within a very short time. These advances carry enormous benefits, but can raise new problems as well. Expectations are much greater and sometimes over-optimistic. Doctors cannot guarantee success. Also, there may be questions about what is to be achieved by applying the whole panoply of advanced technology to a particular case. And our recognition of just how rapid and revolutionary tomorrow's advances could be, also has some influence on the decisions which have to be made today.

So the courts have been presented with major challenges. I want to examine how they have responded. Have they been content to allow the medical profession to dictate the standards as new problems present themselves, or have they become more interventionist? Have they been too cautious, or too proactive? Is their approach likely to be modified as a result of a changes in attitudes to the medical profession, or as a result of the Human Rights Act just passed giving further effect to the European Convention on Human Rights? I begin with the field of clinical negligence because this provides a classic measure of the Courts' general approach.

II.   CLINICAL NEGLIGENCE

The key controlling feature of the modern law of negligence is the concept of duty. Medical negligence is no exception. Duty is the means by which the law regulates the conduct of the doctor towards the patient. The duty, whether it arises in contract (in the private sector), or tort (in the public sector), is a duty to exercise reasonable care and skill.

Of course, it is easy to say that a duty is owed. But it is not so easy to say what the duty is. It is a duty of care. But, defining the *standard* of care required does not go far enough. It does not tell us what *quantum* of care is to be expected. The former is universal and uniform throughout the law of negligence: it is to behave as a reasonable person in the circumstances. However, the *quantum* of care which is to be demanded, is where the interesting law begins. 'In the circumstances' means, in the context of medical negligence, in the circumstances of the practice of medicine. First, what do the cases say?

A.   Bolam

The invariable starting point in answering this question is the case of *Bolam v Friern Hospital Management Committee* decided in 1957.[1] Mr Justice McNair directed the jury in these terms:

> The test is the standard of the ordinary skilled man exercising and professing to have that skill. A man need not possess the highest expert

[1] [1957] 1 WLR 582.

skill ... it is sufficient if he exercises the ordinary skill of an ordinary competent man exercising that particular art.[2]

Later, he said:

[A doctor] is not guilty of negligence if he has acted in accordance with a practice accepted as proper by a responsible body of medical men skilled in that particular art.[3]

As medical negligence claims began to increase, *Bolam* took on a near holy writ status. Although it was only a first instance judgment, its authority and correctness were not doubted. It was not until 1980 that it came to be considered, and endorsed by the House of Lords.[4] Although in one sense, McNair J's direction to the jury in *Bolam* is as sound now as it was then, it came in for considerable criticism from commentators because of the way the principle came to be regarded.

The crucial question in liability in negligence is not so much the standard of care as the *quantum* of care. Rightly or wrongly, McNair J's view in *Bolam* came to be seen as meaning that the *quantum* of care owed by a doctor to a patient was a matter for doctors, as a class, or as a subgroup within a class, to decide. All that the doctor needed to do, to answer a claim of breach of duty, was to show that he or she had done what fellow doctors would have done. And, if doctors disagreed among themselves, it was enough to avoid liability, to show that the defendant doctor had complied with a standard of care accepted as reasonable by some of his or her peers. The quantum of care to be demanded of doctors by the law, and so the very definition of duty, had become, or so it appeared to some, the preserve and prerogative of doctors.

B. Sidaway

If this tended to give doctors a considerable measure of self-regulation in the treatment of their patients, the precise ambit of the treatment to which the principle applied remained open to debate. In particular did treatment include the information given to a patient about the risks of an operation? If so, did *Bolam* apply to the duty to give that information?

---

[2] *Ibid*, at 586.
[3] Above n 1 at 587.
[4] *Whitehouse v Jordan* [1981] 1 WLR 246 (HL), *per* Lord Edmund-Davies at 258. See also, *Maynard v West Midlands RHA* [1984] 1 WLR 634 (HL). But note also, *Chin Keow v Government of Malaysia* [1967] 1 WLR 813 (PC).

The House of Lords had to consider this question for the first time in a case called *Sidaway*, in 1985.[5] The authority had relied upon expert evidence that a body of skilled and experienced neurosurgeons would have regarded it as acceptable not to warn of a slight, but well recognised, risk of serious damage which Mrs Sidaway did in fact suffer following surgery. It was held that the *Bolam* test applied and that in the light of the defendant's expert evidence her claim must fail. Lord Diplock, the Senior Law Lord, saw the duty to warn as an integral part of the doctor's treatment of his patient and held that the courts should not interfere with the profession's approach to these issues. He said:

> In matters of diagnosis and the carrying out of treatment the court is not tempted to put itself in the surgeon's shoes; it has to rely upon and evaluate expert evidence, remembering that it is no part of its task of evaluation to give effect to any preference it may have for one responsible body of professional opinion over another, provided it is satisfied by the expert evidence that both qualify as responsible bodies of medical opinion.[6]

The only dissenting voice was Lord Scarman's. To him, the proper approach of the law, to what has come to be commonly referred to as 'informed consent', was one of rights. The doctor's duty fell to be determined by the patient's rights.[7] Such a rights-based approach could, perhaps, be expected of Lord Scarman, given his long commitment to human rights and his advocacy of the incorporation of the European Convention on Human Rights (ECHR) into English law. But, his view did not carry the day in *Sidaway*. A proposition that the patient should have the right to choose whether to accept a slight, but well recognised, risk of serious damage, did not prevail.

So, *Bolam* and, in particular, an interpretation of *Bolam* which appeared to leave the content of a doctor's duty for doctors to decide, occupied centre stage in medical negligence in this country.[8] Elsewhere in the world, the courts were less keen to embrace the principle.

C.   Australia

In a case called *Rogers v Whittaker* in 1992,[9] the Australian High Court, a highly distinguished court in the Commonwealth, departed

---

[5] *Sidaway v Board of Governors of the Bethlem Royal Hospital and the Maudsley Hospital* [1985] AC 871 (HL).
[6] *Ibid*, at 895.
[7] Above n 6 at 882 and 885–6.
[8] See eg, *Gold v Haringey H A* [1988] QB 481 (CA).
[9] (1992) 67 ALJR 47 (Aust H Ct).

both from *Sidaway* and *Bolam*. For them, the content of the doctor's duty, the *quantum* of care, was for the court to determine, not the profession. This, the High Court held, was particularly so of the information to be given to a patient to obtain consent, but it was equally true of diagnosis and treatment. The evidence from doctors of current or approved practice was, of course, relevant and, certainly, very important. But it could not and should not determine what the law required. The ground for this landmark decision had already been prepared by the earlier decision of the Supreme Court of South Australia in *F v R*[10] in which King C J remarked pithily that '... professions may adopt unreasonable practices'.

D.   Canada

In Canada, *Bolam* never took root. As early as 1949 in *Anderson v Chasney*,[11] the Manitoba Court of Appeal had held that, if the doctor's plea that he had acted in conformity with general practice was to serve as a complete answer to any claim against him, '... a group of operators by adopting some practice could legislate themselves out of liability for negligence ... by adopting or continuing what was obviously a negligent practice'.[12]

Furthermore, in the landmark decision of *Reibl v Hughes* in 1980,[13] the Supreme Court of Canada had stated clearly that, when it comes to informing a patient so as to obtain consent to treatment, the doctor's duty was to pass on that information which a reasonable patient would wish to know, and not merely that which doctors might think appropriate. No room there for the *Bolam/Sidaway* approach.

E.   Bolitho

The *Bolam* principle was recently reviewed by the House of Lords in *Bolitho*.[14] Its facts are instructive because they illustrate the temptation for a trial judge to move into the area of professional judgment, a temptation which the judge had, however, resisted. A young boy in hospital suffered two episodes of acute respiratory problems and, as a result of a

[10] (1983) 33 SASR 189 (Sup Ct SA) at 194.
[11] [1949] 4 DLR 71 (Man CA); on appeal, [1950] 4 DLR 223 (Can Sup Ct).
[12] *Ibid, per* Coyne J A at 85.
[13] (1980) 114 DLR (3d) 1 (Can Sup Ct).
[14] *Bolitho v City and Hackney Health Authority* [1998] AC 232 (HL).

third, sustained cardiac arrest and severe brain damage. The health authority admitted negligence, in that a doctor did not attend when she was called, but said that, even if the doctor had attended, she would not have intubated the child, and such a decision would not have been negligent. The issue, therefore, was whether, as experts called by the plaintiff asserted, any doctor who had attended and had not performed prophylactic intubation, would have been negligent, so establishing the necessary chain of causation. The defendant's experts said that a decision not to intubate would have been reasonable. The judge took a favourable view of the defendant's experts despite being attracted, as a layman, by the argument that their views were simply neither logical nor sensible. However, as he said, to disagree with them would effectively mean he was substituting his views for those of the medical experts. This he declined to do and the plaintiff's claim failed. In upholding his approach, the House of Lords stressed that, although such cases would be rare, the Court *will* hold that a body of opinion is not reasonable or responsible, if it is demonstrated that body of opinion is not capable of withstanding logical analysis.

A similar view had been ventured by the Canadian Supreme Court in *ter Neuzen v Korn*.[15] Sopinka J stated that the courts could 'consider and hold that the standard practice was itself below the required legal standard', where this standard practice was 'fraught with obvious risks'.[16] The decision in *Bolitho* has been seen as heralding a new era and of signalling a more interventionist approach by the courts. Professor Kennedy had said in his authoritative work on the subject that the decision in *Sidaway* will soon be 'consigned to history'.[17]

I am not convinced that, *by itself*, *Bolitho* heralds such a change. The trial judge had considerable reservations about the evidence given by the defendants' experts. However, he accepted it, not simply because the views emanated from eminent members of the medical profession, but also because he was not satisfied that those views were unreasonable. That assessment was not faulted on appeal.

I say 'by itself' because there are two other matters that need to be considered. The first is a possible change in the climate affecting the medical profession. Without commenting on the detailed facts which Professor Kennedy will be considering in his inquiry, it would be naive

---

[15] (1995) 127 DLR (4th) 577 (Can Sup Ct).
[16] *Ibid*, at 588 and 591, *per* Sopinka J.
[17] I Kennedy and A Grubb (eds), *Principles of Medical Law*, (Oxford OUP 1998) at para 3.137.

not to anticipate that the recent events will in themselves have had a considerable impact on the way the medical profession views itself and is viewed. I refer, of course, to the Bristol Royal Infirmary Inquiry, whose terms of reference are 'to inquire into the management of the care of children receiving complex cardiac surgical services at the .... Infirmary between 1984 and 1995 ... to make findings as to the adequacy of the services provided ... to reach conclusions ... and to make recommendations which could help to secure high quality care across the NHS.' Even in the last few days, much attention has been focused on the adequacy of surgical services provided to women in another part of the country. It may not be surprising if conspicuous illustrations of what could be described by some, neutrally, as the fallibility of some members of the profession were to lead to more critical scrutiny of what might formerly have been presented and taken as standard views, within the profession, of what is acceptable practice.

Secondly, the impact of the incorporation of the ECHR by virtue of the Human Rights Act 1998 must be addressed. The Act will bring rights home, so that they can be enforced in the national courts, without going to Strasbourg. The principles of the Convention will gradually reshape the climate in which the courts view any case concerned with human rights. Many aspects of the doctor–patient relationship connected with these rights may be profoundly affected. We ought therefore to consider some details of the relevant Articles of the Convention.

III.   THE CONVENTION

Which Convention rights may be relevant in the medical field? The answer, here, and I suspect elsewhere, is 'more than you might guess'. There is, of course, the first right secured by the Convention, in *Article 2*, that 'everyone's right to life shall be protected by law'. Advocates and opponents of abortion and euthanasia may well be looking to the case law of the European Commission and Court of Human Rights for support for their views. In such controversial areas, however, the Commission and the Court have preferred to be cautious, conscious of the fact that national laws vary considerably. There are no clear-cut answers to be found by looking to Strasbourg. In the case of *Paton v UK*[18] the Commission held that a foetus had no absolute right to life. But it left open the controversial question whether the foetus did have some right to

---

[18] (1980) 19 DR 244 (E Com HR).

life, although subject to special limitations, such as perhaps the primacy of the mother's health. In *H v Norway*[19] the Commission held that the abortion of a 14-week-old foetus for social reasons was not contrary to Article 2. It was 'a delicate area', in which contracting states must have greater discretion to determine what the law should be than they have where some of the other Convention rights are concerned. To use the Strasbourg language, states are allowed a wide margin of appreciation.

Article 2, like most other Articles, cannot be considered in isolation. It has been argued—although the point was not decided—that the right to privacy conferred by Article 8 confers a right to an abortion. Any programme of compulsory abortion or sterilisation—of course inconceivable in this country—could be challenged under Article 12, which provides for the right to found a family.

Article 3 provides that 'no one shall be subjected to torture or to inhuman or degrading treatment or punishment'. Article 3 has proved to be particularly relevant in the case of prisoners and mental patients. It could also have relevance in the context of the treatment given to mental patients for their medical, as opposed to mental, conditions.

In *Herczegfalvy v Austria*[20] the Court held that there was no breach of Article 3 where a violent, mentally ill patient who was incapable of taking decisions for himself was given food and drugs forcibly. They also held, disagreeing with the Commission, that keeping the applicant handcuffed to his bed for a week was also justified since in accord with 'the psychiatric principles generally accepted at the time'. The Court said that 'it is for the medical authorities to decide, on the basis of the recognised rules of medical science, on the therapeutic methods to be used, if necessary by force, to preserve the physical and mental health of patients who are entirely incapable of deciding for themselves'. You may hear echoes from Europe of the *Bolam* approach there.

Again, in this case, another Article came into play. The applicant also complained that the treatment amounted to an interference with his private life under Article 8. The Court, however, reached the same conclusion as it had on Article 3.

Also of relevance to prisoners and mental patients is *Article 5,* which secures the right to 'liberty and security of the person'. Article 5, has been considered in a recent case involving the United Kingdom, *Johnson v UK*[21] A defendant who had been convicted and detained

---

[19] No 17004/90 (1992) (E Com HR).
[20] [1993] 15 EHRR 437 (E Ct HR).
[21] (1998) 2 EHRLR 224–6 (E Ct HR).

under a Mental Health Act hospital order, because he was held to be suffering from schizophrenia, came before a Mental Health Review Tribunal after five years. The Tribunal discharged him—because he was no longer suffering from mental illness—but only discharged him on certain conditions. These meant that he had to remain in detention until alternative supervised accommodation could be found. The Court held that there had been a breach of Article 5(1). It was legitimate not to order his absolute discharge, but, in imposing the residence requirement and deferring his release, the Tribunal lacked the powers to guarantee his relocation to a suitable hostel within a reasonable time. The onus was on them to secure a hostel willing to take him. On the general question of the detention of mental patients, the Court ruled that a person could not be detained by reason of unsoundness of mind unless (i) he was reliably shown by objective medical opinion to be of unsound mind; (ii) the mental disorder was of a kind or degree warranting compulsory confinement; and (iii) the continuation of the confinement depended on the persistence of the disorder.

The lawfulness of an individual's detention and his capability of taking decisions for himself, may arise in the same case. In *St George's Healthcare NHS Trust v S*[22] a pregnant woman, who would not consent to a Caesarean section was admitted, also without her consent, to a hospital for assessment on an application under section 2 of the Mental Health Act, and then transferred to another hospital where the Caesarean section was carried out. The Court of Appeal reaffirmed the principle of the autonomy of the individual and the right of self-determination. The individual has the right to refuse medical treatment, even though it seems unreasonable to do so. And even if the decision is considered to be unusual, or eccentric, or even irrational, it does not follow that the person must be mentally disordered and ought to be detained in hospital. The person must come within the carefully prescribed circumstances set out in the Mental Health Act. The woman's detention in both hospitals was unlawful, and the Caesarean section amounted to trespass to her person.

The right to refuse medical treatment may also be bolstered, in some cases, by reliance on *Article 9*: 'everyone has the right to freedom of thought, conscience and religion [and] to manifest his religion or belief, in worship, teaching, practice and observance.' As in so many cases, a balancing exercise may have to be carried out here, because of the need to protect the rights and freedoms of others.

[22] [1998] 3 WLR 936 (CA).

So, the practices of the medical profession must be affected by the Convention, and often by the combined effect of two or more Articles at the same time. But Article 2, and the right to life, is likely to be the main focus for the medical profession. I will therefore say a little more about it.

Everyone has a right to life, but not a duty to live. There will not necessarily be a corresponding duty on others, including doctors, to do everything which they could do to increase the chance that an endangered life may continue, whatever the surrounding circumstances. At one extreme, harrowing though it may be, the individual who uniquely could donate tissue to save another's life, is under no obligation to do so. And where the life under threat is that of a person, of full mental capacity, who is determined to end his or her own life, intervention may—far from being a duty—amount to an unwarranted interference with his or her own rights. Yet I wonder how many of us, abruptly faced with the sight of a person on the point of taking his or her own life, would pause to analyse the relevant rights and duties before deciding whether or how we should intervene. These are extreme examples, but courts, as well as the profession, are regularly being asked to find the answers to equally difficult questions.

What are the surrounding circumstances which can make it seem so difficult to find the answers? There can be no exhaustive list. But recent cases have provided some striking illustrations.

IV.   RESOURCES

That is not to say that the questions to be answered are always entirely novel. Sometimes they are age-old questions, set in a new context. *The Doctor's Dilemma* dramatised by Shaw, was, I think, that there had been fifty patients but only treatment enough for ten. Ten might live but the others would die. It was not easy to explain why it was impossible to take on just one more patient—without pushing one of the existing ten off the life-raft. A stark choice. That was possibly a starker choice than whether a large proportion of resources which are not limitless should be channelled into expensive experimental treatment for one patient who might not benefit at all, and would certainly have to undergo additional suffering as a result of the treatment.

In the much publicised case of *R v Cambridge Health Authority, ex parte B*,[23] the patient was a little girl suffering from leukaemia.

[23] [1995] 1 WLR 898 (CA).

The Health Authority decided that treatment, which could be provided privately and might give a 20 per cent chance of success, was not in her best interests and scarce resources should not be allocated to it. The decision was challenged by way of judicial review. The judge upheld the application,[24] but the Court of Appeal felt bound to overrule his decision. The Master of the Rolls acknowledged that difficult and agonising judgments have to be made how a limited budget is best allocated to the maximum advantage of the maximum number of patients, but said that this was not a judgment which the court could make.[25]

Although at one stage it had been suggested that the Health Authority had failed to have regard to the wishes of the child and her family, the Master of the Rolls recognised that their keen desire for the treatment to be tried was one of the reasons which made the decision such an agonising one to make.[26] However, in many other cases, (as we shall see) the agonising part of the decision-making process is that because of the patient's lack of capacity, it is not possible to know what his or her wishes actually would be.

The absence of a bottomless pool of resources is by no means a new realisation. A recent important decision of the House of Lords about the computation of damages serves as a salutary reminder of how meeting one set of needs will make it more difficult to find the resources to meet other needs. In *Wells v Wells*,[27] they considered what discount rate should be applied in calculating a lump sum award of damages to compensate for future losses. There has to be a discount because the plaintiff will be paid the whole sum at once, and it could and should be invested so that, over the years, a mixture of capital and income can be drawn down to make up for the anticipated future losses. The question was whether it was right to assume a conventional rate of four to five per cent, as the courts had done for many years, or whether the discount should reflect the lower rate of return available on the safer, Index-Linked Government Securities. The unanimous decision was that, to produce the full compensation to which plaintiffs are entitled, awards should be calculated to reflect the lower rate of lower investment, which was three per cent. At first sight, the difference may not seem very great. But the sums of money involved can be very large. Inevitably, the damages payable in cases of catastrophic injury will be

---

[24] (1995) 25 BMLR 5 (Laws J).
[25] Above at 906, *per* Sir Thomas Bingham M R.
[26] *Ibid*, at 905.
[27] [1998] 3 All ER 481 (HL).

very substantial. This week, newspapers reported a 'record' award of nearly four million pounds in a clinical negligence case. In claims like that, the smallest variation in the discount rate can make an enormous difference to the final sum. The House of Lords were fully aware of that, but rightly said that the court was not concerned with affordability, the impact on the NHS. Commentators however have pointed out that a substantial increase in the cost of clinical negligence claims may divert much needed funds away from the real job of treating patients.

V.   CAPACITY

Many of the recent cases have been concerned with the patient's capacity to consent to or refuse treatment, both where the capacity itself is in question,[28] and where the patient is manifestly incapable of making decisions about his or her future,[29] most extremely where he or she is in the condition which has come to be known as 'persistent vegetative state'.[30]

We have already seen, in the case of *St George's Healthcare NHS Trust v S*,[31] that in cases of acute emergency, the right questions may not be asked, and the right people may not be contacted at the ideally right time. Actions may be taken with the best possible intentions, but nevertheless amount to serious infringement of the patient's rights. Where the urgency has been less great, the courts have been able to reflect, and provide guidance when applied to, by the medical profession. Usually this takes the form of declaratory relief.

This is a very limited remedy but nevertheless an important one for those charged with the care of the patient. The court can only declare what the legal position *is*. It cannot say what should happen. Nor can it sanction something which would otherwise be unlawful. However, its declaration, whichever way it goes, can give some comfort to the doctors, who at least will have the protection of the court's finding as to the patient's competence. The Family Division of the High Court has now devised a specific procedure for such applications which is designed to be speedy and to ensure that applications are dealt with by judges with

---

[28] See *eg, Re MB (Medical Treatment)* [1997] 2 FLR 426 (CA) and *St George's Healthcare NHS Trust v S* [1998] 3 WLR 936 (CA).
[29] See *eg, Re F (Mental Patient: Sterilisation)* [1990] 2 AC 1 (HL).
[30] See *eg, Airedale NHS Trust v Bland* [1993] AC 789 (HL) and *Frenchay Healthcare NHS Trust v S* [1994] 1 WLR 601 (CA).
[31] [1998] 3 WLR 936 (CA).

experience in this area. It applies to all cases involving capacity when surgical or invasive treatment may be needed by a patient.

Of course the question for the court is not always whether it is lawful to give treatment to a patient who lacks the capacity to consent for himself or herself. The facts in the case of Anthony Bland are well known: the 17-year-old patient who was in a 'persistent vegetative state' following the Hillsborough disaster.[32] There, the question was whether it would be lawful to discontinue artificial nutrition and hydration, and medical treatment. Unusually, the House of Lords dealt specifically in declaratory proceedings with the question of criminal as well as civil liability. Again, in a new context, the House applied the *Bolam* principle and relied on the views of responsible medical experts who had concluded that the patient's existence in the permanent vegetative state was of no benefit to him.

The government recognises that these are controversial issues which need careful consideration. Last year we issued our Green Paper *Who Decides?*[33] seeking views on proposals made by the Law Commission for a legal framework to enable decisions to be made on behalf of incapacitated people on questions of health care and personal welfare, as well as on financial issues.[34] We have received over four thousand responses, and we are now considering the way forward. Because so many of the responses have referred to the subject of euthanasia, it is important to stress, here, that the Law Commission's Report made no recommendations about that subject and neither did the Green Paper seek views on it. Euthanasia is a deliberate intervention undertaken with the express intention of ending a life, albeit at the person's own request or for a merciful motive, and it is illegal. The government unqualifiedly supports the view of the House of Lords Select Committee on Medical Ethics that euthanasia is unacceptable.

VI. CONCLUSION

It is obviously impossible, in the course of one short lecture, to do more than touch on a small sample of the difficult, sensitive issues about rights and duties in the doctor-patient relationship. The climate is changing more rapidly than ever before. Naturally, we are all immensely grateful for the new skills, treatments and cures now available to save lives and

---

[32] *Airedale NHS Trust v Bland* [1993] AC 789 (HL).
[33] *Who Decides? Making Decisions on Behalf of Mentally Incapacitated Adults* (Cm 3803) (LCD 1997).
[34] Law Commission Report No 231, *Mental Incapacity* (1995).

improve the quality of lives. Yet we have to recognise that these beneficial additions to the profession's armoury also bring with them new challenges and new dilemmas. Expectations are greater, sometimes unrealistically so. I repeat, doctors cannot guarantee success. Expenditure too escalates, and the high cost of many new treatments inevitably makes it harder to make decisions about the allocation of the resources we have. Another catch is that we rely on pioneers to make these advances. By definition they are at least one step ahead of their more traditionally minded colleagues, so that the application of the *Bolam* test to their practices may seem contradictory and an impediment to further progress. Attitudes are changing within and outside the profession. As we have seen, historically the courts have been reluctant to appear to trespass on the expertise of another, senior profession. But I think there is movement towards recognition of circumstances in which practices considered appropriate by a body of doctors may not always be the benchmark by which their actions must be judged. And if incorporation of the European Convention of Human Rights encourages the courts to focus more on the patient's rights, this may prove not entirely compatible with what doctors have traditionally seen as their duties, and suggest an approach closer to that of the other Commonwealth courts.

But finally before concluding, I would like to turn away for a moment from questions about when or whether particular treatment was (or will be) properly given to an individual patient. I will ask you to think about whether our traditional approach to putting right what has been found to have gone wrong is necessarily the best one. I have mentioned the escalating cost of compensating plaintiffs by paying them lump sum awards. Of course, wrongs must be properly righted. But we should perhaps question (as did the House of Lords) whether making large lump sum payments is the best way of providing for the future care of patients and others who have suffered injury as a result of negligence.

The problem is that, however well intentioned the lump sum, and the chosen interest rate, may be, the sum determined can turn out too much, or too little. It cannot, surely, be beyond our wit, perhaps through the medium of an insurance backed indemnity to devise a means of allowing these plaintiffs, through the balance of their lives, to be compensated according as their fluctuating needs actually require. Certainly it would be difficult not to conclude, in all the areas I have touched on in this Lecture, that the decade that lies ahead is likely to see major development and change in the law's responses to the acutest issues arising out of the practice of medicine in a mature and increasingly rights conscious society.

20

Intention, Recklessness and Moral Blameworthiness: Reflections on the English and Australian Law of Criminal Culpability

I. INTRODUCTORY REMARKS

ONE HUNDRED AND fifty years ago William Charles Wentworth had the vision, against the tide of popular opinion, to see a place for advanced education in Sydney's bright future. He fought long and hard to found Australia's first university here. Teaching began in 1852, with 24 students studying Greek, Latin, Mathematics and Science. The University had three professors: one from Oxford, one from Cambridge and one, I am pleased to say, from Aberdeen. Today, you have more than 160 professors, and more than 37,000 students. Almost one tenth of your students come from overseas and many great world figures have passed through your hands, among them two Nobel Laureates, James Wolfensohn, the President of the World Bank and Robert May, the Chief Scientific Adviser to the British Government.

Law has long been taught at Sydney University. You have provided Australia with three Prime Ministers, including John Howard, four Chief Justices of the High Court, including Chief Justice Gleeson, nine Chief Justices of the Supreme Court of New South Wales and, of course, Sir William Deane, the Governor-General. Many fine legal scholars have graced the Faculty. The list is a roll of honour, but I confine myself to three: Professor Julius Stone, one of the great figures of the school of sociological jurisprudence; William Morison, a remarkable legal theorist who made substantial contributions in judicial procedure and torts; and, more recently, Ross Parsons who was instrumental in establishing the study of taxation as an academic discipline in law schools.

As a Scot, however, let me mention another name, not as distinguished as the others as a lawyer, but certainly one identified with an enduring image of the Australian spirit. George Patterson, also known as 'Banjo' Patterson, was an Australian-Scottish solicitor practising in this city in the 19th century. In 1895, on a visit to friends in the outback at Dagworth station, he heard his hostess, Christine MacPhereson, play on the piano a haunting tune called 'Craigielea'—in Scotland originally called 'The Bonnie Wood of Craigielea'. It was to this tune that Banjo Patterson eventually composed a new set of words. By the time of the Great War his song had become the most popular in Australia; today it ranks alongside Auld Lang Syne among the best loved around the world. But out of consideration for the feelings of others, I shall not detain you today with my own rendition of 'Waltzing Matilda'.

Instead, let me move from the sublime to the deeply serious to consider how the concept of culpability has influenced the development of mens rea doctrines in Australia and England over recent decades; particularly the two best-known forms of fault in criminal law: intention and recklessness.

II.   OPENING

The State can deliver no stronger condemnation than a finding of criminal guilt. Its reach can extend beyond the punishment itself—to loss of employment, or professional status, or even the freedom to travel abroad. These extra-judicial consequences record the social truth that, implicit in a criminal conviction, is the judgment that the defendant has done something reprehensible, warranting serious moral blame. Ultimately, it is the implicit moral condemnation in a conviction that gives the word 'criminal' its cultural resonance.

It is unsurprising, therefore, that the common law has been reluctant to inflict these labels without an integral finding of culpability. *Actus non facit reum nisi mens sit rea* may be a clumsy maxim, and dubious Latin, but it gestures toward something profound in the criminal law: that people should not be branded criminals on the basis of accidents or misfortunes. Especially in cases of serious crime, there must first be some finding of fault—typically, some finding of mens rea. As Kenny put it, at the beginning of the 20th century, 'no external conduct, however serious or even fatal its consequences may have been, is ever punished unless it is produced by some form of mens rea.'[1]

In practice, however, shaping mens rea doctrines so as best to serve these underlying notions of culpability has generated many difficulties for courts throughout the Commonwealth.[2]

Let me begin with two conceptions of criminal fault: *subjective* and *objective*.

A long-standing debate in modern criminal law is whether criminal mens rea is to be measured by a subjective or an objective standard. Should culpability be assessed subjectively, by reference to the defendant's own characteristics and state of mind, and especially his own deliberate choice to do, or risk doing, a criminal act? Or should it be assessed objectively, by reference to his actions, and perhaps the characteristics, and hypothetical beliefs and choices, of the so-called reasonable man?

This long-standing debate is also a foundational one. Among its other roles, mens rea is the bridgehead between an actus reus perpetrated by the accused and a finding that the defendant is culpable for perpetrating that actus reus. Mens rea links action to blame, supplying the moral warrant for a conviction. When criminal lawyers dispute the merits of the 'objective' against the 'subjective' approaches to blame, their dispute is about the conditions under which a condemnatory finding of criminal 'guilt' is justified. Under a fully subjective standard of fault, for example, convictions are warranted only when an offence is done intentionally, or perhaps recklessly. Justifying criminal liability for negligence, on the other hand, requires commitment to a more objective theory of blame.

In the courtroom, the same debate lies behind some pressing doctrinal questions. Courts must decide whether particular mens rea elements, such as 'intention' and 'recklessness', should be interpreted to require 'subjective' foresight of risk by the accused. And, if liability may sometimes be imposed for an inadvertent failure to avoid

---

[1] Kenny, *Outlines of Criminal Law* 2nd ed, (1904) 39.
[2] The same underlying concern with culpability has also motivated judicial activism in common law defences. The courts of Australia, England, and elsewhere, have wrestled in recent decades with such questions as the proper effect of unreasonable mistakes made in self-defence; the inculpatory or exculpatory effects of intoxication: the extent to which defences such as duress and provocation should require levels of fortitude or self-restraint of which the defendant himself was incapable; and so forth. Time, however, does not permit me to address these questions today.

harm, on the basis of an 'objective' standard of foreseeability, what standard of behaviour are we entitled to expect of the accused? Suppose an anaesthetist makes a mistake. His patient dies. On a charge of manslaughter by gross negligence, to what standard must the accused be held?[3] Is it sufficient to exculpate the accused that he did the best that he knew how? Or should he be required to meet the standard of behaviour expected of a reasonable person, irrespective of his own experience or capacities? These are legal questions of immediate practical importance, yet go to the foundations of the criminal law.

Today, I confine myself to intention and recklessness. My thesis is this: over the past 40 years, Australian and English courts have not always seen eye to eye over these doctrinal questions, despite their centrality. Looking back, the Australian courts, and the High Court in particular, have been the more consistent. Australian criminal law has more rigorously followed the subjective path when approaching questions of mens rea. By contrast, English courts, and the House of Lords in particular, have sometimes deviated from that path. Yet, over time, we in England have tended to find our way back to that subjective path, so that our jurisdictions have begun our new century more closely aligned on these issues than in recent decades.

III.   INTENTION

Let me begin with intention. In 1960, the House of Lords decided *DPP v Smith*.[4] Smith was driving a car that contained, on its back seat, stolen scaffolding clips. A police officer saw the clips and, suspecting they were stolen, instructed Smith to pull over to the kerb. This Smith failed to do. He accelerated away. The police officer clung to the side of the car and was dragged along with it. Apparently in an effort to shake off the officer, Smith repeatedly tacked across the road, travelling by now at considerable speed. Ultimately, the officer was dislodged; but directly into the path of an oncoming car. He was run over and killed.

Smith was convicted of murder. He appealed, claiming that the trial judge, Donovan J, misdirected the jury about proof of the mens rea

---

[3] Compare *Adomako* [1995] 1 AC 171 with *Yogasakaran* [1990] 1 NZLR 399.
[4] [1961] AC 290 (hereinafter *Smith*).

element in murder. Donovan J had directed the jury, *inter alia*, that they were permitted to infer Smith's intention from the surrounding circumstances, including 'the presumption ... that a man intends the natural and probable consequences of his acts.'[5]

The Court of Criminal Appeal upheld the appeal. It ruled that the judge had failed to make clear that the jury's ultimate task was to decide what, subjectively, was Smith's own intention, and that the presumption that people intend the natural and probable consequences of their actions was merely evidential and capable of being rebutted.

But the House of Lords reversed that decision and restored Smith's conviction, holding that Donovan J made no error at all. The presumption was much more than a matter of evidential inference. It was an irrebuttable rule. Mental incapacity cases aside, a person should be *deemed* to intend a consequence if a reasonable person would foresee it as probable.[6]

The effect of *DPP v Smith* was to change the legal definition of intention. It was surely a major change of approach: although the then Lord Chancellor, Viscount Kilmuir, was able to draw upon some authority to support his conclusions,[7] the balance of the case law favoured a more narrow conception of intention that focused on the subjective state of mind of the defendant himself.[8]

A. The Australian Response

To the credit of the High Court of Australia, it was not for a moment tempted to rechart its own course. Prior to *Smith*, in a sequence of its own decisions, it had affirmed the subjective view that, under the

---

[5] See *Smith*, above n 4 at 299–300 (CA); 325 (HL).

[6] '[O]nce the accused's knowledge of the circumstances and the nature of his acts has been ascertained, the only thing that could rebut the presumption would be proof of incapacity to form an intent, insanity or diminished responsibility.' *Smith*, above n 4 at 331.

[7] Most notably *Ward* [1956] 1 QB 351 at 356, which is criticised in the note at (1956) 72 *LQR* 166 and by S Prevezer, 'Murder by Mistake' [1956] *Crim LR* 375.

[8] See for example, Rupert Cross, 'The Need for a Re-definition of Murder' [1960] *Crim LR* 728; HR Stuart Ryan, 'The Objective Test of Intention in Criminal Liability' (1960) 3 *Crim LQ* 305; *Smith*, above n 4, noted at [1960] *Crim LR* 765; Glanville Williams, 'Constructive Malice Revived' (1960) 23 *Mod LR* 605; Rex A Collings, 'Negligent Murder' (1961) 49 *Calif LR* 254; S Prevezer, 'Recent Developments in the Law of Murder' (1961) 14 *CLP* 16; Sir Cyril Salmon, 'The Criminal Law Relating to Intent' (1961) 14 *CLP* 1; JL Travers & Norval Morris, 'Imputed Intent in Murder' (1961) 35 *ALJ* 154.

common law in Australia, it must be proved beyond reasonable doubt that the accused himself had the requisite intention. These decisions had culminated in the 1957 case of *R v Smyth*,[9] in which the defendant was convicted of murder after striking his victim several times with a wrench. At trial, the judge directed the jury in terms remarkably similar to the language used later by Donovan J.[10] But his direction, said the High Court, had been wrong:[11]

> [w]e think that the direction complained of is not in accordance with law and ought not to be given. In this Court disapproval has been expressed on more than one occasion of the use, where a specific intent must be found, of the supposed presumption, conclusive or otherwise, that a man intends the natural, or natural and probable, consequences of his acts ....[12]

The discrepancy between our two legal systems soon came to a head in *Parker v R*,[13] a case where the defendant had killed his wife's lover by running him over with a motor car. The High Court took the opportunity fully and clearly to endorse its earlier decisions, a move of considerable constitutional as well as criminal law significance. The Court set itself directly against the decision of the House of Lords, which was described by Dixon CJ as 'misconceived and wrong'. Thus, *DPP v Smith* had proved a valuable catalyst in Australia, contributing to the development of its distinctive juridical identity. Formerly, the High Court had regarded itself as bound by decisions of the House of Lords on issues of general legal principle, even in the face of contrary High Court precedents.[14] By refusing to follow *Smith*, the High Court in *Parker* was forced explicitly to sever the yoke of English legal authority.[15]

---

[9] (1957) 98 CLR 163.

[10] *Ibid*: 'If you think that grievous bodily harm ... was a natural and probable consequence of what the accused man might be found by you to have done, then the law is that he is presumed to have intended those very consequences.'

[11] Above n 9 at 166–7. Application for special leave to appeal was nonetheless refused.

[12] Citing *Stapleton v R* (1952) 86 CLR 358 at 365; *Baily v Baily* (1952) 86 CLR 424 at 427; *Deery v Deery* (1954) 90 CLR 211 at 219–223; *Gow v White* (1908) 5 CLR 865 at 876.

[13] (1963) 111 CLR 610; reversed on other grounds (1964) 111 CLR 665.

[14] *Piro v W Foster & Co Ltd* (1943) 68 CLR 313; *Brown v Holloway* (1909) 10 CLR 89 at 102; Zelman Cowen, 'The Binding Effect of English Decisions Upon Australian Courts' (1944) 60 *LQR* 378.

[15] 'Hitherto I have thought that we ought to follow decisions of the House of Lords, at the expense of our own opinions and cases decided here, but having carefully studied

B.   The Path Back

Time has proved the High Court right. The presumption endorsed in *Smith* was effectively undone by statute in England, with the passing of the *Criminal Justice Act* 1967 (UK).[16] At common law, too, the case has since been disavowed by the Privy Council.[17] An objective test of intention, at least in murder, has no place in the common law.

But it is important to observe that pressure on the definition of intention in murder did not end with the demise of *Smith* at the hands of the *Criminal Justice Act* 1967 (UK). Although it is sometimes unnoticed, *Smith* involved not one, but two, derogations from a subjective test of intention. The first was to equate *foreseeable* consequences with *foreseen* ones: if it was a natural and probable consequence, then Smith would be taken to have foreseen (and in turn intended) it. This extension blurs the boundaries between recklessness and negligence. The second derogation from a subjective test of intention was to equate foresight of a probable consequence with intention: if Smith foresaw the police officer's death, then he *intended* it. This extension blurs the boundary between recklessness and intention. At the time, it was the first extension that attracted notoriety and a statutory response. But the boundary between recklessness and intention has proved the more enduring difficulty.

In part, this second problem persisted because the mental element of murder in England is narrower than in Australia. It requires an intention to kill or inflict grievous bodily harm;[18] by contrast with the law in Australia's common law jurisdictions, where foresight of probable death or grievous bodily harm is sufficient.[19] Sometimes, this generates moral and legal pressure-points in cases where our instinct may be that

---

Smith's Case [1961] AC 290 I think that we cannot adhere to that view or policy .... I wish there to be no misunderstanding on the subject. I shall not depart from the law on the matter as we had long since laid it down in this Court and I think *Smith's* Case [1961] AC 290 should not be used as authority in Australia at all.' (1963) 111 CLR 610 at 632 (Dixon CJ, in a passage endorsed by the entire bench).

[16] S 8. See also RJ Buxton, 'The Retreat from Smith' [1966] *Crim LR* 195, who shows that the decision was being ignored by trial judges even before the 1967 Act.

[17] *Frankland and Moore v R* [1987] AC 576 at 594.

[18] *Vickers* [1957] 2 QB 664 at 672; *Smith*, above n 4; *Hyam* [1975] AC 55 at 68; *Leung Kam-Kwok v R* (1985) 81 Cr App R 83.

[19] *Crabbe* (1985) 156 CLR 464; *Knight* (1992) 175 CLR 495, 501; *Crimes Act* 1900 (NSW), s 18; *Crimes Act* 1900 (ACT), s 12. The fact that it makes no practical difference in this context explains the *dicta* in *Crabbe* at 469 and *Vallance* (1961) 108 CLR 56 at 59, 82 noting that the law sometimes treats foreseen probable consequences of an

the accused ought to be convicted of murder, but where it cannot be proved that he intended the victim's death, in the full sense of having sought to bring that about.

In *Hyam*,[20] for example, a vengeful Mrs Hyam poured petrol through the letterbox of Mrs Booth's house, after Mrs Booth had supplanted her in the affections of a Mr Jones. She set the petrol alight, intending only to frighten Mrs Booth, but recognising that serious injury was likely to follow. Two people died, and Mrs Hyam was charged with murder. In Australia, she could be convicted without the need to describe death or grievous bodily harm as intended, because foresight that serious injury is probable is sufficient mens rea for murder in Australia. In England, however, because murder requires a finding of intent, in order to uphold her conviction the House was compelled to regard Mrs Hyam's foresight that serious harm was highly probable as establishing, in law, an intention to inflict that harm.

It was not until 1985, in *Moloney*,[21] that the House of Lords clearly differentiated between actual intention and foresight of probable outcomes. Subsequent cases[22] have confirmed and refined the division between these two forms of mens rea. They culminate most recently in *Woollin*,[23] a decision that would have been inconceivable at the time of *Smith*, or even *Hyam*. The accused in that case lost his temper and apparently threw his three-month-old son against a hard surface. The child's skull fractured and death ensued. In Woollin's trial for murder, the prosecution alleged that Woollin had foreseen the risk of serious injury with sufficient certainty for this to be, in law, a case of intention. The House accepted the possibility of this analysis in principle.[24] Nonetheless, it quashed Woollin's conviction and substituted

---

act as intended. See Peter Gillies, *Criminal Law* 4th ed, (1997) 51–6. Contrast the law in codified States, where recklessness *per se* is insufficient but is compensated for by varieties of constructive murder: *Criminal Code Act* 1899 (Qld), Schedule 1 s 302; *Criminal Code Act* 1924 (Tas), Schedule 1 s 157; *Criminal Code Act Compilation Act* 1913 (WA), Schedule 1 ss 278–9; also *Criminal Code Act* (NT), s 162.

[20] *Hyam*, above n 18.

[21] [1985] AC 905 at 928: 'foresight of consequences, as an element bearing on the issue of intention in murder, or indeed any other crime of specific intent, belongs, not to the substantive law, but to the law of evidence.'

[22] Notably *Hancock and Shankland* [1986] 1 AC 455 (HL) and *Nedrick* [1986] 1 WLR 1025 (CA).

[23] [1999] 1 AC 82.

[24] Compare, in Australia, *Hurley* [1967] VR 526 at 540 ('fully aware that the result would follow'); *Hatty v Pilkinton* (1992) 108 ALR 149 at 158 ('a virtual inevitability').

a conviction for manslaughter because the trial judge had misdirected the jury by requiring only that the accused foresaw a 'substantial risk' (rather than the 'virtual certainty') of serious injury or death. In the leading judgment, Lord Steyn explicitly rejected the possibility that a person's intention can be inferred, as a matter of substantive law, from his foresight of a risk falling short of virtual certainty. Any such inference is merely evidential. Thus intention is, at last, unequivocally a subjective legal concept in England, and one clearly distinguished from recklessness: the defendant must either seek deliberately to bring about the relevant consequence, or recognise that the consequence is a virtually certain concomitant of some other outcome sought. It is not enough that the consequence was foreseeable, or even foreseen as probable.

It has been about 40 years since *Smith* was decided. During the intervening years, the reluctance to acquit of murder those wrongdoers who deliberately put at risk the lives of others, yet did not actually seek to cause death, has inevitably put pressure on the definition of intention. English law has made some wrong turnings. But the shadow of *Smith* is now fully lifted. English law has, at last, a definition with which Australian courts might again feel comfortable.

IV.   RECKLESSNESS

In recklessness, the controversial decision corresponding to *Smith* is *Commissioner of Police of the Metropolis v Caldwell* in 1982.[25] The accused had been working for the proprietor of a residential hotel. He developed a grievance against the proprietor, and, after drinking too much one evening, decided to set the hotel on fire. This he did, although the amount of damage caused was fairly minor. Caldwell was charged, *inter alia*, with an offence against s 1(1) of the *Criminal Damage Act 1971* (UK). This makes it an offence to damage another's property 'being reckless as to whether any such property would be destroyed or damaged'. The House of Lords held that a person is reckless in law if:[26]

---

[25] [1982] AC 341.
[26] *Ibid*, at 354. This definition enabled the House to uphold D's conviction also for the more serious charge under s 1(2), of damaging property being reckless whether life would thereby be endangered. D had claimed that, being drunk, he had not considered the risk to life that his actions posed.

(1) he does an act which in fact creates an obvious [and serious]²⁷ risk
that property will be destroyed or damaged and (2) when he does the act
he either has not given any thought to the possibility of there being any
such risk or has recognised that there was some risk involved and has
nonetheless gone on to do it.

The ruling was a radical departure from the traditional understanding of recklessness. According to well-known precedents,
such as the 1957 decision in *Cunningham*,²⁸ recklessness was a
subjective concept, requiring actual foresight of the risk by the
accused. The essence of *Caldwell* was to create a second category
of recklessness in criminal law, by which the defendant will also
be counted reckless if he fails to think of a risk when that risk is a
glaring one. In effect, as Professor Fisse has observed,²⁹ recklessness
under *Caldwell* embraces both advertent wrongdoing and gross
negligence.

May I interpose that I am well aware of the recent tragedy at Childers
in Queensland and my reference to *Caldwell* is not, of course, intended
to have any bearing upon it.

Rather like the House's foray into intention in *Smith*, *Caldwell*
introduced two dimensions of objectivity into the law governing
mens rea. First, the decision extends liability beyond the traditional
subjective requirement for actual foresight on the part of the
accused, so that it is sufficient if the consequence is obvious to a reasonable man. Secondly, the foreseeability standard supplied by the 'reasonable man' test is applied without reference to the defendant's own limitations.

The effect of this second dimension of objectivity was seen in
1983 in *Elliott v C (a minor)*,³⁰ where a 14 year old girl of low
intelligence had wandered away from home and spent the night
outdoors without sleep before ending up in a garden shed.
She then destroyed the shed while playing with matches and some
white spirit. Even though it was found as a fact that the risk of setting
fire to the shed would not have been obvious to someone of her
limited capacities, she was convicted of criminal damage. The
Divisional Court held, on the authority of *Caldwell*, that the test of

---

²⁷ Interpolated in *Lawrence* [1982] AC 510 at 527.
²⁸ [1957] 2 QB 396.
²⁹ Brent Fisse (ed), *Howard's Criminal Law* 5th ed, (1990) 444.
³⁰ [1983] 1 WLR 939.

obviousness is itself objective: would the risk be obvious to an ordinary adult, rather than, should it have been obvious to the particular defendant.[31]

A.   The Australian Response

At the time, *Caldwell* was criticised quite forcefully by Australian academic lawyers,[32] whereas the Australian courts seem to have regarded it as going only to the interpretation of a specific statute, and so of no general significance.

The High Court has ignored *Caldwell* almost entirely.[33] Exceptionally, McHugh J's judgment in *Royall v R* [34] mentions *Caldwell* when considering the mens rea element of 'reckless indifference to death' contained in s 18 of the *Crimes Act* 1900 (NSW). However, like the rest of the High Court, he went on to reject an objective interpretation, ruling that the section requires foresight of the probability or likelihood of death.[35] The Court's analysis explicitly echoed the leading case of *Crabbe*,[36] where the mens rea element of malice aforethought in murder at common law was said to require, at least, foresight of the probability of death or grievous bodily harm. *Crabbe*, decided in 1985, and *Royall*, decided in 1991, bear close resemblance to the subjective analysis of malice aforethought and recklessness found, back in 1957, in the English case of *Cunningham*. In these cases, one can see that English and Australian law are true cousins. Correspondingly, according to the critics,[37] it is the bloodline of *Caldwell* that was moot.

---

[31] See also *R Stephen* (1984) 79 Cr App R 334.

[32] See in particular, Editorial, 'The Demise of Recklessness' [1981] 5 *Crim LJ* 181; Fisse, above n 29 at 444 ('a radical departure from principle'); and in New Zealand, KE Dawkins, 'Criminal Recklessness: Caldwell and Lawrence in New Zealand' (1983) 10 *NZULR* 364.

[33] Apart from parenthetical references to *dicta* in the case which do not touch on the definition of recklessness: *Peters v R* (1998) 192 CLR 493 at 543 n 249 (theft); *Crabbe*, above n 19 at 471 (noting that a passage by Glanville Williams was cited in Edmund-Davies' *dissenting* judgment).

[34] (1991) 172 CLR 378 at 455.

[35] See also *Annakin* (1988) 37 A Crim R 131; *White* (1989) 17 NSWLR 195; *Solomon* (1980) 1 NSWLR 321.

[36] *Crabbe*, above n 19.

[37] Even in England: see, for example, *Smith* [1981] *Crim LR* 393 at 410; Glanville Williams, 'Recklessness Redefined' [1981] *CLJ* 252; Griew, 'Reckless Damage and Reckless Driving: Living with *Caldwell* and *Lawrence*' [1981] *Crim LR* 743; Jenny

Nonetheless, Australian law has not always been immune to the charms of an objective concept of recklessness. There are a number of reported cases in which Australian courts have used the term 'reckless' to refer, in effect, to gross negligence—or 'reckless negligence', as Windeyer J once memorably expressed it.[38] This is accepted, for example, in *MacPherson v Brown*, a South Australian case, where Chief Justice Bray recognised that Australian law knows two senses of the word:

> The term 'recklessness' is sometimes confined to advertent conduct and sometimes used to include inadvertent conduct ... In this [second] sense recklessness is synonymous with criminal negligence.[39]

Chief Justice Bray's own preference was that 'the word 'reckless' should be confined to action where the relevant consequences are adverted to'. But it is clear from this and from other cases[40] that *Caldwell* recognises a strain of analysis to which voice had previously been given even in Australia.

Despite these divergent authorities, however, it is right to say that by the time of *Caldwell* the subjective meaning of recklessness was predominant in Australia.[41] It had already been endorsed in a series of cases at state level,[42] and blessed by the High Court in such cases as *Vallance v R*[43] and *Pemble v R*[44] *Caldwell* elicited no change in this position.[45] Even the phrase 'reckless indifference', found in the South

---

McEwan & St John Robilliard, 'Recklessness: the House of Lords and the Criminal law' (1981) 1 *LS* 267; George Syrota, 'A Radical Change in the Law of Recklessness?' [1982] *Crim LR* 97; RA Duff, 'Professor Williams and Conditional Subjectivism' [1982] *CLJ* 273; RA Duff, *Intention, Agency and Criminal Liability* (Cambridge, CUP, 1990) ch 7; Glanville Williams, 'The Unresolved Problem of Recklessness' (1988) 8 *LS* 74.

[38] *Mamote-Kulang v R* (1964) 111 CLR 62 at 79.

[39] (1975) 12 SASR 184 at 188, quoting, in part, from Colin Howard, *Criminal Law* 2nd ed, (1970) at 56–7. The two possible senses of 'recklessness' are noted also by Windeyer J in *Phillips* [1971] ALR 740 at 756–7.

[40] For example, *Evgeniou v R* (1964) 37 ALJR 508 at 513; Compare *Sivewright v Casey* (1949) 49 SR (NSW) 294, in the context of contractual rescission.

[41] However, in order to avoid confusion, a direction that avoids use of the term itself has often been preferred: *La Fontaine v R* (1976) 136 CLR 62 at 76–7 (Gibbs J); *Pemble v R* (1971) 124 CLR 107 at 120–21 (Barwick CJ); *Crabbe*, above n 19.

[42] *Nydam v R* [1977] VR 430 at 437; *MacPherson v Brown*, above n 39; *Stones* (1955) 56 SR (NSW) 25 at 34; *Ashman* [1957] VR 364 at 366.

[43] Above n 19 at 64 (Kitto J).

[44] (1971) 124 CLR 107 at 119 (Barwick CJ).

[45] See for example, *Smith* (1982) 7 A Crim R 437 at 440, 446–7; *Taylor* (1983) 9 A Crim R 358.

Australian statutory offence[46] of criminal damage—surely a phrase and an offence redolent of *Caldwell*, if any were—has been said by the Supreme Court of that state to require proof of the accused's knowledge of the risk.[47]

B. The Path Back

If *Caldwell* failed to take hold elsewhere in the Commonwealth,[48] its roots have proved shallow even in England. Although the decision exercised considerable influence during the 1980s, its importance has diminished. For example, it no longer governs the English law of manslaughter,[49] rape,[50] or assault.[51] In effect, its application is now restricted to the offence in *Caldwell* itself (criminal damage), and to a few other statutory offences.[52] Professor Ashworth has observed rightly, that 'the *Caldwell* definition is now of little practical significance.'[53] Subjective recklessness of the variety found in *Cunningham* and *Royall* now predominates and, once more, English law is aligned with Australian.[54]

At least, mostly aligned. I mentioned earlier that there were two objective dimensions to *Caldwell*. The second dimension of *Caldwell* may yet survive. Where an offence can be committed negligently, or with gross negligence, *Caldwell* and *Elliott v C* remain authorities that the criminal law makes no allowance for personal characteristics of the defendant, such as low intelligence, when assessing foreseeability. Contrast *Boughey v R*,[55] a murder case from

---

[46] *Criminal Law Consolidation Act* 1935 (SA) s 85.

[47] *Durwood v Harding* (1993) 61 SASR 283; *Tziavrangos v Hayes* (1991) 55 SASR 416. See too *Athanasiadis* (1990) 51 A Crim R 292 (rape); *Hemsley* (1988) 36 A Crim R 334 (sexual assault).

[48] See apart from Australia, *Sansregret v R* (1985) 17 DLR (4th) 577; *Harney* [1987] 2 NZLR 576.

[49] *Adomako* [1994] 3 All ER 79, reversing *Seymour* [1983] 2 AC 493.

[50] *Satnam and Kewal Singh* (1983) 78 Cr App R 149.

[51] *Spratt* (1990) 91 Cr App R 362.

[52] For example, *Large v Mainprize* [1989] Crim LR 213.

[53] Andrew Ashworth, *Principles of Criminal Law* 3rd ed, (Oxford, OUP, 1999) 191.

[54] Note the discussion here is concerned primarily with consequences. In respect of circumstances, especially the victim's lack of consent in an offence of sexual violence, both England and Australia have indicated a preference for what is at least a partially objective test: *Tolmie* (1995) 37 NSWLR 660; *Evans* (1987) 30 A Crim R 262 at 267–8, 273–274; *Satnam and Kewal Singh*, above n 50.

[55] (1986) 161 CLR 10. (Application for special leave to appeal was refused).

Tasmania in which the accused, a medical practitioner, had strangled his partner in the course of somewhat unconventional but consensual sexual activity. Section 157(1)(c) of the *Tasmanian Criminal Code* provides that a culpable homicide is murder if perpetrated by 'any unlawful act or omission which the offender knew, *or ought to have known*, to be likely to cause death in the circumstances...' [Emphasis added].

The High Court endorsed a more subjective approach to the section than is found in *Caldwell*. According to the Court:

> The starting point of the inquiry on the question whether an accused ought to have known that his or her actions were likely to cause death must be the knowledge, the intelligence and, where relevant, the expertise which the particular accused actually possessed. The relevant question is not whether some hypothetical reasonable person in the position of the accused would have appreciated the likely consequences of the applicant's act. It is what the particular accused, with his or her actual knowledge and capacity, ought to have known in the circumstances in which he or she was placed.[56]

Boughey is irreconcilable with *Elliott v C*. Yet even here, there are signs that English law is moving toward a more subjective approach.[57] Given that the accused in *Caldwell* was not burdened with abnormal capacities, the decision can be regarded as obiter on that point. Moreover, in *Adomako*, in 1995, a case of grossly negligent manslaughter by an anaesthetist, Lord Mackay, the then Lord Chancellor, suggested that gross negligence involves conduct so bad that it may be characterised as reckless 'in the ordinary connotation of that word'.[58] If that is the test then, surely, in ordinary language, 'recklessness' involves an assessment of the offender's conduct by reference to his own capacities. As Goff LJ pointed out in *Elliott v C*,[59] the accused in that case was not reckless in any ordinary sense of that word. Indeed, given her limited intelligence, she would probably not even be negligent.

---

[56] *Ibid*, at 28–9 (Mason, Wilson & Deane JJ).
[57] See also *Hudson* [1966] 1 QB 448 at 455. In Canada, the Supreme Court has favoured taking account of personal incapacities. See *Creighton* [1993] 105 DLR (4th) 632.
[58] Above n 3 at 187. See the note by Simon Gardner, 'Manslaughter by Gross Negligence' (1995) 111 *LQR* 22 at 23–4.
[59] Above n 30 at 949.

There are also dicta from the decision of the House in *Reid* in 1992,[60] a reckless driving case, to the effect that fault should be assessed by reference to the capacities of the particular defendant.[61] And, only a little time ago in *Smith*,[62] the House has ruled that the sufficiency of provocation is to be assessed by having regard to all the circumstances, including the accused's own state of depression, and not against a fully objective standard of reasonableness. While none of these cases is decisive, each suggests a more sympathetic awareness of involuntary human frailties; a recognition that criminal culpability must sometimes allow for personal limitations that the defendant cannot transcend.

V.   CONCLUSION

The requirement for some form of mens rea in offences is venerable. It can be traced as far back as the time of Henry I.[63] But the interpretation and application of mens rea principles has not been static. The past century, in particular, has seen an evolution in the general doctrines of mens rea at common law, a trend toward the incorporation of subjective principles of criminal culpability. Through both legislation[64] and judicial reform,[65] constructive liability crimes, such as felony murder, have become increasingly uncommon. Most serious offences now require some element of foresight of the actus reus by the accused.

Sometimes, English courts have been innovative in developing subjective doctrines, such as the rule that mistakes made in self-defence need not be reasonable, and the recent decision in *Smith* that provocation must take account of the defendant's own capacity for self-restraint. For these defences, the law in England is now more subjective than it is

---

[60] [1992] 3 All ER 673.

[61] In particular, Lord Keith states that a defendant should not be liable where his inadvertence is owing to 'some condition not involving fault on his part' (at 675c); Lord Goff similarly mentions 'illness or shock' (at 690J); while Lord Browne-Wilkinson refers to 'sudden disability' (at 696F).

[62] [2000] 3 WLR 654.

[63] *Leges Henrici Primi* c 5, § 28. A very valuable paper is Sir Owen Dixon's 'The Development of the Law of Homicide' (1935) 9 *ALJ (Supp)* 64.

[64] For example, s 1 of the *Homicide Act* 1957 (UK).

[65] *A–G's Reference (No 3 of 1994)* [1997] 3 All ER 936.

in Australia.[66] Yet on questions of mens rea, as I have suggested today, the English have often lagged behind their antipodean counterparts. Australian courts have more consistently developed a subjectivist theme, resisting the siren voice of objectivism and the ostensible moral pull of the facts in particular cases. There has, perhaps, been a greater willingness to acquit a particular accused, or to convict him only of a lesser offence, rather than to stretch the fibres of mens rea concepts beyond their natural tolerances.[67] Perhaps, too, English appellate courts were hampered in earlier decades by their previous inability to order a retrial after a misdirection—an impediment that fortunately now is removed.

Indeed, 'the persistent heresy of objective guilt',[68] as Chief Justice Bray once characterised it, is not always heresy in England, even today.[69] In offences of strict liability, for example, the *Proudman v Dayman*[70] defence of reasonable mistake is unavailable in England. That much has been recently confirmed by the House in *B (a minor) v DPP*,[71] a decision that otherwise gives resounding support to the presumption of subjective mens rea espoused by Lord Reid in *Sweet v Parsley*.[72]

Quite apart from applauding Australian lawyers for their consistency, there is much to be said for taking a subjective approach to culpability. The most culpable form of wrongdoing is the knowing, deliberate infliction of harm; and we can be sure that a subjective interpretation of such mens rea concepts as intention and recklessness will highlight these cases in particular. Moreover, there is much to be said for recognising personal limitations. It is surely wrong to blame people for failing to achieve the impossible. It is certainly undesirable that criminal

---

[66] Compare *Beckford* [1988] AC 130 with *Zecevic v DPP (Vic)* (1987) 162 CLR 645 (self-defence); also *Smith*, above n 62 with *Masciantonio v R* (1995) 183 CLR 58 (provocation).

[67] The judgment of Lord Steyn in *Woollin* [1999] 1 AC 82 at 94 provides a striking modern contrast: 'It is true that [the test of foresight of virtual certainty] may exclude a conviction of murder in the often cited terrorist example where a member of the bomb disposal team is killed. In such a case it may realistically be said that the terrorist did not foresee the killing of a member of the bomb disposal team as a virtual certainty. That may be a consequence of not framing the principle in terms of risk-taking.'

[68] *MacPherson v Brown*, above n 39.

[69] Contrast, for example, the more objective rules governing intoxication in English law (*DPP v Majewski* [1977] AC 443) with the straightforwardly subjective approach taken in Australia (*O'Connor* (1980) 146 CLR 64).

[70] (1941) 67 CLR 536.

[71] [2000] 1 All ER 833.

[72] [1970] AC 132; *He Kaw Teh v R* (1985) 157 CLR 523, the leading Australian decision on mens rea in statutory offences.

sanctions should be inflicted because a person is less intelligent than the rest of us and, like the defendant in *Elliott v C*, cannot foresee the damage her actions may cause.

But I finish on a note of caution. Subjectivism is simple and appealing. Yet, although it captures the most graphic types of fault, it is incomplete. Not all wrongdoing is deliberate. A purely subjective law of mens rea would, for example, leave manslaughter by gross negligence unpunished. More generally, objective standards will always have a role to play in our law. They help articulate the limits on individual freedom that the criminal law exists to impose. Without external standards of reasonableness, frequently it would be impossible to distinguish wrongful acts from accidents or from cases of justification. This is why there remain requirements of proportionate response, for instance, in defences such as self-defence and duress.

Let me recall the point with which I began. Our legal doctrines should reflect the public implication of moral fault that accompanies a criminal conviction. Often, to achieve that, the courts must select between objective and subjective versions of the law. My claim now in closing is that neither theory offers a sufficient explanation of culpability by itself. History has sided with the High Court of Australia on the interpretation of intention and recklessness, but a more general arbitration between objective and subjective views is likely to be impossible, and probably misguided. This is all the more true when we take account of the practical constraints that surround the operation of the criminal legal system. Not every moral nuance can be reflected by the law, and the mens rea concepts of intention and recklessness cannot be expected to accommodate all the subtleties to which diverse cases can give rise. Certainly, they have not borne the weight of *Smith* and *Caldwell* without controversy. Yet, even under Australian law, analogous difficulties have arisen. We know that intention here is a subjective concept and that foresight of a risk falls within the ambit of recklessness. Australian courts have avoided *Smith* only at the price of a different problem, one that the English law of murder does not encounter. According to the High Court,[73] foresight of a *possibility* of death is insufficient to support a conviction for murder at common law. But if that is so, what *degree* of probability of death suffices? In this context, words like 'substantial', 'probable', and 'likely' are frequently deployed.[74] These are

[73] *Crabbe*, above n 19; *Boughey*, above n 55.
[74] See *Smith* (1982) 7 A Crim R 437; *Hallett* [1969] SASR 141 at 153; *Sergi* [1974] VR 1 at 10.

intractable terms, and necessarily objective. They involve a risk of death that the accused must foresee. But it is surely not for the accused himself to decide what level of risk he is permitted to run. That must be for the law to decide. And we have to decide these perplexing questions, with a level head and an open mind, perhaps best 'under the shade of a coolabah tree'.

21

*The Law: An Engine for Trade**

M Y SUBJECT IS commercial law and its role as an engine for trade. English law is practically unique among the legal systems of the world because its commercial rules are entirely integrated into the general practice of the law, with business disputes heard in the same courts, using the same principles, as other litigation.

This sets commercial principles in context. It avoids stark distinctions between commercial contracts, private contracts and consumer contracts and stands in the way of overclassification. The explanation for separate commercial systems elsewhere is that they should reduce legal burdens on business, whilst an integrated system may not provide the fast and sensitive procedures traders require.[1]

English law, however, is highly regarded in the international commercial community. Out of seventy-two trials heard in the Commercial List in the High Court during the last year, forty-four involved foreign parties.

Let us consider the four principal ways in which commercial law serves our free market economy. First, commercial law is clear and predictable, providing a firm body of rules on which traders can depend. Secondly, it contains a strong and positive law of contract to uphold trading agreements. Thirdly, the law has been shaped by the needs and expectations of merchants, and much business practice has been incorporated into law. Fourthly, Parliament and the courts have made genuine

---

* A lecture delivered to the British Academy on Wednesday 22 November 2000. I acknowledge my indebtedness to Neil Beresford, Barrister-at-law, for his invaluable assistance in the preparation of this lecture.
[1] In France, for example, commercial contracts are an exception to the strict rule, contained in Civil Code, Art 1341, that contracts must be proved by signed documents. Art 109 of the Commercial Code allows commercial contracts to be evidenced *par tous moyens*. The limitation period is also shorter (being 10 years) than the 30-years period applicable to general contractual transactions: Commercial Code Art 189.

innovations to lead the market economy forward, building on business practice to provide strong frameworks for industry.

I.   LEGAL PREDICTABILITY

The very first need of the business community is legal predictability. An unpredictable legal climate is unacceptable to business, forcing traders into necessary legal advice and insurance cover to secure against the risk of their deals being defeated. In 1774, Lord Mansfield said:

> In all mercantile transactions the great object should be certainty; and therefore, it is of more consequence that a rule should be certain, than whether the rule is established one way or the other. Because speculators in trade then know what ground to go upon.

A.   The Commercialisation of the Common Law

Before 1750, commerce was hindered by a division between the law merchant and the common law.[2] Common law was the unified law of the land,[3] yet it was slow to innovate in commerce, since it had become preoccupied with its own technicalities and procedures rather than the requirements of business.[4] A misplaced word in a property transfer would often defeat entire transactions.[5] Businessmen had to have some reprieve from these stern rules, and the solution was to let merchants rely on their own customs as exceptions to the common law. If a transaction accorded with a practice recognised in the mercantile community, its validity could be assessed by reference to that practice rather than the insensitive common law.[6]

---

[2] Maitland, 'Select Pleas in Manorial Courts' (1889) 2 *Selden Soc* 132.
[3] J Holden, *The History of Negotiable Instruments in English Law* (London, University of London, Athlone Press, 1955) 27–36, M Postan, *Medieval Trade and Finance* (Cambridge, Cambridge University Press, 1973) ch 2. For a different perspective on the nature of *lex mercatoria* (but a similar conclusion on the question of incorporation) see J Baker, 'The Law Merchant and the Common Law Before 1700' [1979] *CLJ* 295.
[4] P S Atiyah, *The Rise and Fall of Freedom of Contract* (Oxford, Oxford University Press, 1979) ch 12.
[5] J Powell, *Essay upon the Law of Contracts and Agreements* (1790) I, 152–60.
[6] If he did not adduce such evidence, the merchant would be 'stuck' in the common law doctrine of *assumpsit*, and the custom would only be relevant to 'explain the *assumpsit*', that is to justify the implication of a liability: *Oaste v Taylor* (1612) Cro Jac 306.

The solution was an obvious compromise, the price of which was legal certainty.[7] Litigating businessmen invariably put evidence of local customs before their judge,[8] and the success or failure of commercial transactions then came to depend on the judge's acceptance of this factual evidence.[9]

It was not until Lord Mansfield became Lord Chief Justice in 1756 that positive measures were taken to combat the uncertainty permeating commercial litigation. Mansfield's approach was to incorporate mercantile customs directly into the common law. When a merchant led evidence of a local custom, Mansfield evaluated its content by consulting businessmen[10] and applying his renowned expertise in foreign systems.[11] If the custom was accepted, it would become binding law,[12] and no subsequent court could admit further evidence on the point.[13]

Through this process, Lord Mansfield laid the foundation of the modern commercial system. Commercial law was transformed from propositions of fact into a rational corpus of law, capable of consultation by businessmen, lawyers and judges alike.[14]

B.   Late Nineteenth-Century Codification Projects

In the nineteenth century the exponential growth in commerce from the Industrial Revolution fuelled the demand for clear and accessible commercial rules. Digests of cases on core commercial subjects were perceived as inadequate when traders looked to the commercial codes

---

[7] See the complaints of Buller J in *Lickbarrow v Mason* (1793) 2 TR 73.

[8] This in fact appears to be what the majority of business litigants did: *Death v Serwonters* (1685) Lutw 885.

[9] It was eventually settled that merchants wishing to rely on trade customs were obliged to meet two heavy burdens of proof: that the custom had immemorial antiquity and limited geographical application: *Brown v London* (1669) 1 Lev 298.

[10] See, for example, his evaluation of the rules of contract in *Loveacres d Mudge v Blight* (1775) 1 Cowp 352.

[11] In the leading case of *Lewis v Rucker* (1761) 2 Burr 1167, Lord Mansfield determined the method of quantifying an insurer's liability for partial loss by first 'conversing with some gentlemen of experience in adjustments'.

[12] *Edie v East India Co* (1761) 2 Burr 1216.

[13] Evidence in future would thus be admissible only on matters which had not yet been resolved: *Long v Allen* (1785), detailed in J Park, *Marine Insurance* (1st ed) 446.

[14] Commentaries were soon produced to rationalise particular areas. Among the earliest commentators were Paley, *Principles of Moral and Political Philosophy* (1785), see Powell, n 5 above. These were soon followed by famous works on more specific subjects, such as Chitty's *Treatise on the Law of Bills of Exchange* (1799) and Byles' *Treatise on the Law of Bills of Exchange* (1829).

of Continental Europe and India,[15] and the Associated Chambers of Commerce seized the initiative.[16] During the 1880s, leading commercial minds of the day[17] were commissioned to collate the case law into a cluster of codifying legislation in the four key areas of commercial activity: bills of exchange, factoring, partnerships and sales of goods.[18]

The codes were a huge advance in the quest for legal clarity. Adopted throughout the Commonwealth, they condensed a hundred years of common law understanding into individual statutory statements. Their format relieved traders of the need to refer to the vast body of case law when ascertaining commercial rules. In *Bank of England v Vagliano Brothers*,[19] concerning the Bills of Exchange Act 1882, Lord Herschell said:[20]

> The purpose of (a codifying) statute surely was that on any point specifically dealt with by it, the law should be ascertained by interpreting the language used instead of, as before, by roaming over a vast number of authorities in order to discover what the law was, extracting it by a minute critical examination of the prior decisions.

The statutes were a triumph, described by one judge as 'the best-drafted Acts of Parliament ever passed'.[21] Not only did they make the law accessible,[22] but they yielded such effective principles that the law has required little reform since.[23]

---

[15] M Chalmers, 'An Experiment in Codification' (1886) 2 *LQR* 125; J Dove-Wilson, 'Concerning a Code of Commercial Law' (1884) 28 *Journal of Jurisprudence* 337.

[16] For the role of business in instigating the codification process, see B Rodger, 'The Codification of Commercial Law in Victorian Britain' (1992) 108 *LQR* 570.

[17] Sir Frederick Pollock, author of a highly influential digest on the law of partnership, drafted the Partnership Bill. The rest were entrusted in large part to Sir Mackenzie Chalmers.

[18] The cost of the draft Bills was ultimately shared between the Chambers of Commerce and the Institute of Bankers: Executive Council of the Associated Chambers of Commerce, 11 March 1881.

[19] [1891] AC 107.

[20] At 144–5.

[21] MacKinnon,LJ in *Bank Polski v Mulder & Co*[1942] 1 All ER 396.

[22] Another argument in favour of codification was that it would offer a single coherent statement of English business law at a time when numerous international conventions were being held to undertake the global harmonisation of trade laws: T Barclay, 'Assimilation of Mercantile Law' (1886) 2 *LQR* 66.

[23] The codes also gave the opportunity for the assimilation of laws in England and Scotland. These laws remained very different even following the investigation of a Royal Commission in June 1853. The Commission published a first Report in 1854, and legislation followed in 1856. However, it was unpopular and widely criticised at

This is not to say that the law has stood still. Many details have required modification to reflect changing commercial and social values, but this modification has taken place well within the original framework. In sales law for example, demand from consumers has tightened the legal duties imposed on sellers,[24] and demand from business has necessitated the legal recognition of coownership in mixed goods.[25] Parliament has introduced these changes without compromising the clarity of the original code, by passing consolidating legislation. The Sale of Goods Act 1979 brings together the disparate Sales Acts passed since 1893, reproducing the original Act and its subsequent reforms in a single instrument. This consolidation does not serve the same function as codification, since earlier materials are not replaced, merely republished. However, the combination of both measures—codification and consolidation—has ensured that our commercial laws remain both relevant and accessible.

Parliament has even added entire branches of law without disturbing the integrity of the original legislation. This summer Parliament passed the most important partnerships legislation since the original Act of 1890 in the shape of the Limited Liability Partnerships Act.[26] The Act will add another form of business entity to the existing armoury, providing an attractive means of incorporation for multinational accountancy and legal firms.

Nineteenth-century codification was therefore a great success, which has led some to question why the process should not be expanded across a broader ambit of commercial transactions.[27] The reason for this lies in the law's inherent pragmatism. During the nineteenth-century projects, full codification was considered to be too difficult within the British parliamentary system, and lawyers concluded that the complexity of formulating and enacting a large commercial code would not be

---

the time for making unsatisfactory and superfluous changes to the law: 'English Amendments of Scotch Law', 1 *Scottish LJ* 1 (1858).

[24] The most significant amendments were made by the Supply of Goods (Implied Terms) Act 1973, which introduced a distinction between consumer and non-consumer transactions and introduced an implied term of merchantable (now *satisfactory*) quality where the seller is in the course of a business. It also took measures to prevent sellers from restricting their liability and consolidated the terms implied into contracts of sale with those implied into contracts of hire purchase. For details, see I Carr, 'The Supply of Goods (Implied Terms) Act 1973' (1973) 36 *MLR* 519.

[25] See the Sale of Goods (Amendment) Act 1995.

[26] See N Beresford 149 (1999) *NLJ* 1647.

[27] See eg, R Goode, *Commercial Law in the Next Millennium* (London, Sweet & Maxwell, 1998) ch 4.

justified by positive benefits.[28] Experience from France and Germany has added little momentum to the campaign, as the commercial codes in these countries have yielded only equivocal benefits. No code can be entirely comprehensive,[29] and in Germany a trader now refers to the commercial code for the content of his agreements, to the civil code for the existence of his agreements, and to judicial precedent for the validity of his agreements.[30]

In Britain, the absence of full-scale codification has brought a significant advantage: legal flexibility. Since it is founded on general principles, commercial law has evolved in tandem with wider legal values. For example, in the Victorian era from which the Sale of Goods Act dates, a contract formed under the influence of illegitimate pressure would only be set aside if this pressure took the form of a physical threat.[31] Today we recognise a subtle body of rules that regards all illegitimate threats as capable of amounting to duress.[32] By a process of steady evolution, the law has moved far from its unforgiving Victorian roots.

II.   LAYING THE FOUNDATIONS FOR A FREE MARKET ECONOMY: THE LAW OF CONTRACT[33]

The second keystone of commercial law is its recognition of private agreements. Today it goes without saying that most types of business

---

[28] It was said by no less a reformer than Lord Selborne LC, chief proponent of the Judicature Acts, that a wholesale commercial code would create enormous difficulties in Parliament, and would be unlikely to pass through both Houses without so much scrutiny as to destroy the utility of the project: 'Codification of Commercial Law' (1885) 78 *Law Times* 321.

[29] The German commentator Köndgen writes of the 1897 *Handelsgesetbuch* (Commercial Code) 'Its choice of transaction types seems selective at best, arbitrary at worst; and its provisions are often fragmentary. While we find adequate provisions relating to the carriage and storage of goods, or commercial agency, the Code is silent on banking, secured transactions or commercial leases; the provisions on commercial sales cover merely ten sections.' ('Commercial Law', in W Ebke and M Finkin (eds), *Introduction to German Law* (The Hague/London, Kluwer, 1996).

[30] Under the principle of good faith, devised by German courts in response to hyperinflation during the 1920s and 1930s and based upon s 242 BGB.

[31] *Skeate v Beale* (1841) 11 A & E 983.

[32] *The Dimski Shipping Corporation SA v International Transport Federation (The Evia Luck)* [1992] 2 AC 152. The law is, of course, commercially sensitive. Careful distinctions are drawn between those threats which are illegitimate and those which are legitimate business practices: *CTN Cash & Carry v Gallagher Ltd* [1994] 4 All ER 714.

[33] See generally n 4 above; A W B Simpson, 'Innovation in 19th Century Contract Law' (1975) 91 *LQR* 247.

contract may be freely made and enforced in the courts, with the obvious exception of contracts which have unlawful or immoral purposes.[34] In any free market system, a large proportion of wealth is concentrated in speculative interests held on share and futures exchanges. For this market to operate, it is essential that traders be kept to their promises.

A. The Absence of Any Law of Contract at the Turn of the Nineteenth Century

Yet the modern law of agreements is a surprisingly recent phenomenon. In the wake of the Glorious Revolution, secure property rights assumed supreme political importance[35] and legal policy was focused on the protection of ownership.[36] Any financial speculation undermining this security was frowned upon, and even criminalised. As late as 1800, traders were being prosecuted for offences such as *regrating*, buying goods for resale at the same market.[37]

This economic climate had no need for an autonomous law of contract. Agreements did little more than facilitate property transfer,[38] and the law gave no support to market speculation. Agreements to purchase goods were unenforceable until the goods had in fact been delivered,[39] so parties could simply escape from a bargain if a change in the market price made it unprofitable. Even when goods had been delivered, a supplier could not insist on the agreed contract price, but damages in any court proceedings would be confined to the objective value of the goods provided.[40]

---

[34] See *Lipkin-Gorman v Karpnale* [1991] 2 AC 548.

[35] J Plumb, *The Growth of Political Stability in England 1675–1725* (London, Macmillan, 1967).

[36] As Thompson points out: 'Millers and—to a greater degree—bakers were considered as servants of the community, working not for a profit but for a fair allowance': E Thompson, 'The Moral Economy of the English Crowd in the Eighteenth Century' (1971) 50 *Past & Present* 76, 83.

[37] *R v Ruby* (1800) Peake Add Cas 189.

[38] It is of particular interest that in Blackstone's *Commentaries*, contract is dealt with under *Volume ii* ('*Rights of Things*').

[39] In *Walker v Moore* (1829) 10 B & C 416, Littledale J went so far as to say: 'It is contrary to the policy of the law that a man should offer an estate for sale before he has obtained possession of it'.

[40] *Flureau v Thornhill* (1775) 2 W BL 1078. The reason for this is that promises were enforced not for the subjective reason that the parties had reached agreement, but only in so far as the transaction had a binding moral force.

B. Nineteenth-Century Revolutions—the Age of Freedom of Contract

A developed law of contract did not really begin until the 1820s, led on by the pressures of railway capitalism.[41] Steam railways demanded an unprecedented financial outlay which could only be met through public subscription and they offered healthy profits in return. Speculation took off on an unprecedented scale,[42] but the framework for this speculation was simply not in place. With no adequate legal backing, the market experienced three devastating crashes in the space of twenty years.[43]

In response to the vast increase in trade during the Industrial Revolution, a new and principled law of agreements emerged.[44] Its rules were focused on the original intentions of the parties to the agreement, so bringing three crucial advantages to business. First, technical and artificial constructs gave way to new simple rules for the interpretation of agreements.[45] Secondly, the law began to enforce speculative bargains without requiring prior performance by either party, preventing recalcitrant traders from evading unprofitable transactions.[46] Thirdly, damages began to be assessed on a realistic basis, the court looking to the terms of the original agreement to calculate a party's loss.[47]

In this way the law has evolved into a fine engine for financial speculation. By 1877, less than eighty years after Kenyon LC had condemned regrating as contrary to the common law,[48] Bacon VC said in the case of *Noble v Edwards*,[49]

---

[41] See generally R Kostal, *Law & English Railway Capitalism* 1825–1875 (Oxford, Clarendon Press, 1994).

[42] N McKendrick, J Brewer and J Plumb, *The Birth of a Consumer Society: The Commercialisation of Eighteenth-Century England* (London, Europa, 1982).

[43] The crashes took place in 1826, 1836 and 1845 Contemporary businessmen pilloried the legal system for its shortcomings. The harsh verdict of the *Railway Gazette* (26 May 1849) was that 'the public have waited in vain for three years for some speedy means of bringing to justice those who robbed them.... They have hitherto been helplessly and hopelessly without redress.'

[44] Such work was founded on the work of Lord Mansfield, who half a century earlier had championed the intentions of the parties as a means of contractual interpretation in cases such as *Pillans & Rose v Van Mierop & Hopkins* (1765) 3 Burr 1663.

[45] See *Kingston v Preston* (1773) 2 Doug 691.

[46] Simpson, n 33 above.

[47] This was achieved by the time of *Hadley v Baxendale* (1854) 9 Ex 341.

[48] *R v Ruby* (1800) Peake Add Cas 189.

[49] (1877) 5 ch D 378.

A man who speculates in land means always to get as much profit from it as he can. If, by his superior skill, he foresees that he can advantageous profit by working, cultivating and improving a farm, certainly if it is worth his while he can do that, and it would be quite worth the while of anybody buying from to pay him whatever in their respective judgments, the land is worth, without considering what the then vendor gave for it himself. What is more common? It is everyday practice in this court.

III.   UPHOLDING THE EXPECTATIONS OF MERCHANTS—LEGALISING MERCANTILE PRACTICE

The law of contract gives traders the flexibility to establish business arrangements tailored to their own requirements. But a business agreement will rarely make express provision for every detail of the bargain, and so the law must fill the gaps, giving effect to the presumptions and expectations of the traders entering the agreement.

English law achieves this objective in two ways: by creating legal rules based on realistic trade customs, and by recognising that traders often wish to incorporate standard terms and practices into their agreements.

A.   Conferring Positive Legal Status on Mercantile Institutions

Let me turn to three specific illustrations of how the law has facilitated trade by creating bodies of law based on trade custom.

a.   Bills of Exchange

First, bills of exchange. A debtor wishing to make a payment may approach his bank for a bill of exchange, to be drawn in favour of the creditor. The bill is sent to the creditor, who has two options: either he may present the bill to the bank or its local agent for payment, or he may transfer the bill to a third party, who then receives the right to payment from the bank.

The institution holds many advantages for business, and has been operated by merchants since the thirteenth century. Its greatest attraction is the attribute of free transfer, or *negotiability*. The creditor receives a promise of payment that can readily be transferred to third parties with the minimum of formality.

Bills of exchange were not easy to integrate into the law. Their negotiability sits in stark contrast to the inflexible common law rule that contractual rights may not be transferred to third parties.[50] For this reason, early decisions set bills of exchange outside the common law, in the law merchant.[51] By the late seventeenth century, however, bills of exchange had become such a central feature of commercial transactions that they were finally recognised by the common law,[52] and a full set of rules was swift to develop. These rules were modelled firmly upon the practice of traders.

For example, in a case of 1695[53] the court was asked to rule upon the appropriate rule for the settlement of foreign bills. Evidence was led, proving that universal practice in the business world was to allow three days' grace for payment. This practice was accepted as law.

Much further development and consolidation took place during the eighteenth and nineteenth centuries—the numerous digests on the law[54] culminating in Sir Mackenzie Chalmers' Bills of Exchange Act 1882. Its principles derive directly from the practice of businessmen and that is the reason for its enduring success.

b.   Bills of Lading

The innovation of the international shipping community provided another fertile source of inspiration. Of particular importance to modern shipping is the bill of lading, a document issued by the carrier both to evidence the shipping contract and to prove the shipper's title to the cargo. Yet bills of lading are another legal oddity. Once issued by the carrier they may be freely conveyed to third parties, and this conveyance operates to transfer not only title to the cargo, but also the rights of the shipper under the contract of carriage.[55]

---

[50] In *Three Rivers v Bank of England* [1996] QB 92, the court summed up the common law's refusal to countenance the assignability of contractual rights. Assignment is only recognised in equity or in exceptional cases by statute. See Law of Property Act 1925, s 136.

[51] See *Burton v Davy* (1437) ss 49, 117.

[52] This achievement is credited to *Woodward v Rowe* (1666) 2 Keb 105, 132.

[53] *Tassell and Lee v Lewis* (1695) 1 Ld Raym 743.

[54] Eg, Chitty's *Treatise on the Law of Bills of Exchange* (1799), Byles' *Treatise on the Law of Bills of Exchange* (1829).

[55] Since the Carriage of Goods by Sea Act 1992.

Given the conflict between bills of lading and the common law's refusal to sanction transferable contracts, these bills were slow to be recognised. It took the decision of a special jury in the historic decision of *Lickbarrow v Mason*[56] in 1793 to establish that transfer of title to the cargo accompanied transfer of the bill and that became the common law. However, it took the Bills of Lading Act, 1855, to provide that the rights of the shipper under the contract of carriage also accompanied transfer of the bill.

Two unusual features highlight the unique commercial origins of the law governing bills of lading. First, legal intervention has been kept to a bare minimum, to the extent that many central doctrines remain as presumptions, not rules of law. Indeed, the first principle of shipping law—that carriers may always be compelled to issue a bill of lading—stands entirely unsupported by legal authority.[57] The law has intervened only as required, as for example in 1992, when the Carriage of Goods by Sea Act was passed to close a serious lacuna identified in a case before the House of Lords when a carrier escaped all liability for negligently damaging a cargo sold in transit.[58]

The second unique feature of shipping law is the extent of international harmonisation. At the turn of the twentieth century, international practice began to grow disparate. Individual states had introduced legislation regulating the rights and duties of parties to shipping agreements,[59] but this piecemeal approach could not be sustained in an increasingly global marketplace. The international trading community moved for standardisation, and a body of international rules was introduced at The Hague

---

[56] (1793) 2 TR 73.

[57] L D'Arcy, *Ridley's Law of the Carriage of Goods by Land, Sea and Air* 7th ed, (London, Shaw, 1992) 82.

[58] See *Leigh & Sillavan v The Aliakmon Shipping Company Ltd, The Aliakmon* [1986] AC 785, where the buyer of steel coils was left without a remedy when the goods were negligently damaged in transit at a time when they still belonged to the sellers. The sellers had no remedy as they had suffered no loss, and the contractual rights under the agreement had not passed to the buyers until a point in time after the damage had already occurred.

[59] The first legislation of the modern age was the Harter Act, enacted in the United States in 1893. This was followed by the Australian Sea Carriage of Goods Act 1904 and the 1910 Water Carriage of Goods Act in Canada.

[60] The International Convention for the Unification of Certain Rules of Law Relating to Bills of Lading, 25 August 1924. The Convention was implemented into English law by the Carriage of Goods by Sea Act 1924, which came into force on 1 January 1925.

[61] This amendment was necessary to take account of the container revolution. It was signed at Brussels on 23 February 1968, and implemented into English law by the Carriage of Goods by Sea Act 1971.

on 25 August 1924.[60] The Hague Rules (as amended in 1968)[61] have been highly successful in establishing a worldwide framework for contracts of carriage by sea. The rules stand as testament to the role of the law as an engine for trade. By harmonising conditions of carriage across the globe, they have lowered the costs of negotiating international contracts and established minimum standards to set a level playing field for traders.

c.   Letters of Credit

My third example of business-led development in commercial law comes from international finance. Letters of credit are financing mechanisms operated between parties to an international sale. The buyer opens at his bank a credit in favour of the seller subject to specific instructions, usually that the bank withholds payment until it receives valid shipping documents. The buyer's bank then sends a letter of credit to the seller, either through its own offices or through another bank in the seller's country. Once the goods have been dispatched, the seller must present the requisite documents to the bank, and payment will be made.

Letters of credit provide traders in the international market with a guaranteed means of payment, which oils the flow of international trade. Yet letters of credit contain two legal surprises. First, they are anomalous within the common law. By mercantile usage, the bank's payment undertaking is considered binding by virtue of its issue alone without the need for consideration or reliance by the beneficiary. A second surprise is the complete absence of statutory intervention in this area. Both these features are understandable, however, since letters of credit have developed almost entirely through the initiative of businessmen.

In 1933, the International Chamber of Commerce published a set of Uniform Customs and Practice for Documentary Credits to establish an international standard for letters of credit. Revised on a regular basis,[62] the Uniform Customs and Practice are incorporated into letters of credit worldwide.[63] They are a prime example of commercial development taking place outside the legal arena, but recognised by the law. Of course,

---

[62] Revisions occurred in 1951, 1962, 1974, 1983 and 1993.

[63] See the comments of Mustill LJ in *Royal Bank of Scotland v Cassa di Riparmio delle Provincie Lombard* [1992] 1 Bank LR 251 at 256, and for a full discussion, see B Kozolchyk, 'Letters of Credit' 9 *International Encyclopaedia of Comparative Law*.

letters of credit have come before the courts and judges have upheld their legality as an aspect of mercantile practice, but these judgments owe their content largely to the terms of the Uniform Customs and Practice. In 1983, the House of Lords was asked to determine a point on which there was no prior authority in English law: whether, when the seller had unwittingly tendered to the confirming bank documents containing a false statement, the bank was obliged to pay.[64] The House of Lords found that the bank *was* obliged to pay, after evaluating the possible solutions to the problem with one eye to the Uniform Customs and Practice and another to the demands of commerce. Lord Diplock dismissed the proposition, that the bank was not obliged to pay if the documents, although conforming on their face with the terms of the credit, contained some inaccurate statement of material fact, thus:[65]

> The more closely this bold proposition is subjected to legal analysis, the more implausible it becomes; to assent to it would, in my view, undermine the whole system of financing international trade by means of documentary credits.

Letters of credit are thus another prime example of the law responding to change by adapting its rules with keen commercial sensitivity to the customs and expectations of traders.

B. Soft Law—Incorporating the Understandings of Merchants into Commercial Agreements

The second way in which the law has acted to uphold the expectations of traders is by giving effect to standard business practices in commercial agreements. Widely accepted practices are of great value to business, as they provide ready-made bodies of rules that adapt to change and avoid the need for direct legislation. This is particularly true in international trade, where the commercial pressure for legal harmonisation is great but the potential for agreement among governments is low. The legal vacuum remains to be filled by the initiative of businessmen.

At an international level, much positive work has been carried out by the International Chamber of Commerce, (the ICC), an organisation

---

[64] *United City Merchants v Royal Bank of Canada* [1983] 1 AC 168.
[65] At 184.

run by businessmen from over 130 member states. We have already seen the value of the Uniform Customs and Practice for Documentary Credits. The ICC has also been active in international shipping, by drawing up a set of standard terms for international shipping contracts. INCOTERMS are drafted by lawyers and businessmen and updated regularly.[66] They are so widely accepted throughout the world that INCOTERMS are likely to be implied into shipping contracts even if the parties make no direct election themselves.

Such permissive forms of regulation are also evident in domestic trade law. The Companies Act 1985 contains a model constitution for limited liability companies, whose provisions may be adopted or excluded at will. These measures are a highly efficient way of supervising business, as they give entrepreneurs commercial freedom to select the most appropriate rules for their individual needs.[67]

So, we have seen various means in which the law has facilitated trade by giving full effect to business customs. In some instances the law has followed the initiative of business by turning commercial practice into law. In others it has maintained a deliberately low profile, allowing businessmen to make their own rules and giving legal effect to these rules only when required.

IV.   SENSITIVE REGULATION OF TRADE

Next, let me turn to instances where lawyers have led the way.

Early political economists declared that the sole objective of business law was to follow the lead of merchants. In his *Wealth of Nations*, Adam Smith concluded that man's pursuit of his own self-interest provided the key to prosperity, and that legal intervention was unwelcome in the free market process.[68] Of course, the idea has much truth.

---

[66] The latest version is INCOTERMS 2000.
[67] B Cheffins, *Company Law: Theory, Structure and Operation*, (Oxford, Oxford University Press, 1997), ch 5.
[68] G Brennan and J Buchanan, *The Power to Tax: Analytical Foundations of a Fiscal Constitution* (Cambridge, Cambridge University Press, 1980).
[69] As Professor Cheffins writes in his economic analysis of company regulation, 'The enactment and amendment of legal standards can be a process plagued by delays .... The individuals who promulgate and administer laws governing market behaviour may not have sufficient expertise concerning the conduct being regulated to judge accurately the impact of the decisions they are taking.... Government regulation can suffer from problems which can undermine the case for intervention': n 67 above, 364.

Healthy market freedom is an important interest, and modern economists continue to stress the importance of minimum commercial regulation.[69]

However, at some point regulation becomes inevitable. At the time of the first railway company flotations in the 1820s, there was an entirely unregulated share market.[70] Prevented from forming public companies by the notorious Bubble Act of 1721,[71] entrepreneurs offered shares to the public unlawfully by trading under 'deed of settlement' associations. Disreputable enterprises flourished. Of the 624 associations floated in 1824, only one fifth survived until 1827.[72] When the practice of public subscription was legalised in 1825, businessmen were able to operate within the law but little overall benefit was achieved. In the absence of any regulatory framework, commercial standards remained reprehensibly low. Dishonest businessmen floated thinly-capitalised companies,[73] and devastating stock market crashes occurred in 1826, 1836 and 1846.[74]

This experience highlights the first danger of an unregulated market: the inevitable temptation to perpetrate fraud.

The second danger is the so-called externalities problem.[75] Businessmen are likely to operate to maximise their own profits, although this may prejudice society as a whole. Thus, law must regulate to ensure that the driving force of commerce does not undermine wider public interests.

Self-regulation is one possible solution to these two dangers, allowing business to take collective notice of public policy. For this reason, self-regulation is an essential feature of the English business system, and is directly encouraged by law. The Financial Services Act 1986

---

[70] AB DuBois, *The English Business Company After the Bubble Act* (London, OUP, 1938).

[71] See generally P L Davies, *Gower's Principles of Modern Company Law* (London, Sweet & Maxwell, 1997), chs 2–3.

[72] H English, *A Complete View of Joint Stock Companies Formed in 1824 and 1825* (London, Sweet & Maxwell, 1827).

[73] BC Hunt. *The Development of the Business Corporation in England 1800–1867* (New York, Russell, 1969).

[74] M Reed, *Investment in Railways in Britain 1820–1844: A Study in the Development of the Capital Market* (Oxford, Oxford University Press, 1975), 14–16; Pollins, 'The Marketing of Railway Shares in the First Half of the Nineteenth Century' (1954–55) 7 *English Historical Review* 233.

[75] As identified in the ground-breaking article by Professor Ronald Coase, 'The Problem of Social Cost' (1960) 3 *Journal of Law & Economics* 1.

[76] R Bagott, 'Regulatory Reform in Britain: The Changing Face of Self-Regulation' (1989) 67 *Public Administration* 435.

established a comprehensive scheme of self-regulation in the supervision of equity markets,[76] with daily operations overseen by Recognised Investment Exchanges, run by market practitioners, with ultimate authority in the Securities and Investment Board, itself a private company. The most recent Statute is the Financial Services and Markets Act 2000, which established the Financial Services Authority.[77]

However, self-regulation is not always adequate, and the law must often take a positive lead in prescribing commercial standards. In taking this lead, the law recognises three key principles. First, the principle of minimum regulation: the regulator must avoid tying the hands of business with an excessive number of rules. Secondly, the principle of appropriate regulation: selecting the correct type of rule for the context. Broad mandatory rules are rarely required, and it is often possible to regulate in less intrusive ways by providing standard practices in which industry is strongly encouraged to participate. Thirdly, there is the principle of continuing relevance: the regulator must ensure that the rules passed are capable of frequent and effective updating to take account of commercial developments.

By respecting these principles in all forms of regulation, English law has been consistently sensitive to commercial needs.

A.   Company Law—Sensitivity in Parliament and the Courts

The boom-and-bust experience of railway capitalism illustrated the need for state intervention in the companies' market. Yet, at the same time, a middle course was required between total deregulation and the stifling administrative requirements formerly imposed by the Bubble Act.[78] In the aftermath of the appalling market crashes came the modern corpus of company law.

The answer to companies regulation was devised by Gladstone in 1844.[79] Since that time, the company as a business vehicle has taken off

---

[77] The regulation of markets and financial services is now supervised by the Financial Services Authority under a new statutory framework created by the Financial Services and Markets Act 2000. The Act lays down four central objectives to be respected in the regulation of financial markets: market confidence, public awareness, the protection of consumers, and the reduction of financial crime.

[78] As the *Railway Gazette* recorded in 1859: 'Each separate railway company which has been under the necessity of applying to Parliament for powers ... has been mulcted in an enormous amount of money for no earthly purpose but to fill the pockets of parliamentary lawyers': *Railway Gazette*, 5 March 1859.

[79] *Parliamentary Papers*, Commons (1844) VII Q 2054. See also F Hyde, *Mr Gladstone at the Board of Trade* (1934).

as an unequivocal success. In 1885, there were 60 listed companies. Today, the total number of companies registered at Companies House is around 1.14 million,[80] and 2,450 of these are listed on the London Stock Exchange.

The modern system rests on three key principles: free incorporation, limited liability and minimum external interference.

The first principle is that businessmen must have freedom to seek access to public money by incorporating as companies. There is of course the danger that incorporated companies will be used as a sham to swindle investors, but this danger cannot be addressed by burdensome regulation, or else promoters will operate outside the law as they did in the 1820s. The solution is a model of free market theory, a system of public company registration which is convenient for businessmen, yet informative for potential investors. Individuals now have the right to incorporate as companies, but the price of this right is the publication of details including the company's constitutional documents and annual accounts at Companies House.

The second principle is that the public must be actively encouraged to subscribe in business ventures, which generally requires that they be protected from the risk of business failure. In 1855, the Companies Act was amended to allow the liability of members to be limited to the value of their shareholdings. Again, however, there must be a price for this broad right, and Parliament has evolved protective mechanisms to ensure that limited liability is not abused at the expense of company creditors. For example, it is a rule of fundamental importance that the share capital of a company—that proportion of assets which has been contributed by shareholders—must be kept intact for the benefit of creditors. The Companies Act strictly controls the circumstances in which a company can reduce its share capital, and court approval must be sought before making a formal reduction of the capital fund.[81] The common law has also evolved doctrines to prevent fraud, and shareholders will be personally liable for a company's debts if they have formed the company to perpetrate a fraud.[82]

Thirdly there is the principle of minimum interference in company management. Informed market freedom underlies the operation of

---

[80] Figures taken from DTI Consultation Paper: *Modern Company Law for a Competitive Economy* (1998).
[81] This was achieved by a legislative reform of 1928. See Company Law Committee, s 151 *Companies Act 1985* (Law Society Legal Practice Directorate, 1990) 21–32.
[82] *Williams v Natural Life Health Foods Ltd* [1997] 1 BCLC 131.

English companies legislation, and supervision of company management is generally left to the shareholders acting through the general meeting. Of course, there has been some legislative intervention to provide for cases where the principle of informed market freedom has failed. Under the Company Directors Disqualification Act 1986, dishonest or incompetent company directors can be disqualified from company management. The Insolvency Act 1986 contains provisions to hold directors criminally liable for fraudulent trading,[83] and liable at civil law for trading in the knowledge that the company cannot pay its debts.[84] The Law Commission has recently recommended that the law impose a strict objective standard of care on company directors to ensure the better protection of those dealing with companies.[85] This would be a considerable development from the position at the turn of the twentieth century, which merely required a company director to exercise diligence in the conduct of his duties.[86]

Companies regulation should not only be effective, but it must also be clear. The original Companies Act 1844 has now been amended on many separate occasions, and while these amendments are presently consolidated in the Companies Act 1985, the profusion of company law sources remains a cause for some concern. A major review of company law is currently underway at the Department of Trade and Industry to streamline the regulation of companies, to eliminate unnecessary bureaucracy and to ensure the greatest respect for the principle of minimum regulation. The consultation document proposes:

> To strip out obsolescent and over-complex provisions and repair defective ones …. We need clear and simplified arrangements which, starting from first principles, better capture the balance of obligations, protections and responsibilities which are required to underpin the modern marketplace so as to ensure that the participants can be confident about fair dealing.[87]

The review is also considering a reformulation of the duties imposed upon directors. In the manner of a nineteenth-century code, these duties

---

[83] Insolvency Act 1986, s 213.
[84] *Ibid*, s 214.
[85] Law Commission Report No 261, *Company Directors: Regulating Conflicts of Interests and Formulating a Statement of Duties*. This development may already have been pre-empted by the common law. See *Re D'Jan of London Ltd* [1994] 1 BCLC 561; (1994) 110 *LQR* 390.
[86] *Re City Equitable Fire Insurance Co* [1925] ch 407.
[87] DTI Consultation Paper: *Modern Company Law for a Competitive Economy* (1998) para 3.8.

would be taken from the common law and laid out in a single statutory statement to make the principles clear and accessible.

All stages of the review will enjoy full public consultation, through representative working groups and the regular publication of key findings for comment. All proposals will undergo economic analysis to ensure that the new law strikes an appropriate balance between regulation and facilitation.

B. Patents—Sensitivity in Legislation

Another example of successful legislative intervention in the free market has been the patent system, originating in the Statute of Monopolies 1624. Patents are a clear compromise of free market principles, as they prohibit businessmen from taking the obvious and profitable step of copying other people's ideas. However, the compromise is entirely necessary. Without patents, inventors would have little incentive to innovate and technological advance would be substantially impaired.

The modern patent system is again a product of the Industrial Revolution. Before the formation of the Patent Office in 1852, the administrative burden of obtaining patents was overwhelming. Applications demanded attendance at 10 different offices, and the process had to be carried out separately in Scotland, Ireland and England and Wales.[88]

The reforms of 1852 have transformed the patent system into an outstanding engine for commercial innovation. Last year alone almost 29,000 applications were made. Four features in particular have been instrumental in achieving appropriate regulation.

First, patents do not create wholly controlled monopolies. They confer on their owners the narrower benefit of exclusive commercial exploitation for a duration limited to twenty years. Even during the currency of the patent, members of the public[89] are free to conduct experiments on the patented invention.[90] The law only intervenes if the copier derives commercial advantage.

---

[88] H Dutton, *The Patent System and Inventive Activity During the Industrial Revolution* (Manchester, Manchester University Press, 1984), ch 5. Charles Dickens portrayed the abound process and its expense in his *Tale of a Poor Man's Patent*.
[89] Patents Act 1977, s 60(5)(a).
[90] *Ibid*, s 60(5)(b).

Secondly, the patent application procedure ensures that full technical details of inventions are disclosed to the public.[91] Not only does this requirement ensure that patent applications are genuine, but crucially it facilitates technological advance. As Grove J said in a case of 1884:

> [The applicant] is bound so to describe it in his specification as that any workman acquainted with the subject … would know how to make it; and the reason of that is this, that if he did not do so, when the patent expired he might have some trade mystery which people would not be able actually to use in accordance with his invention (although they had a right to use it after his invention had expired), because they would not know how to make it.[92]

Thirdly, patents protect only novel and non-obvious inventions.[93] Applications are subject to intensive review, by the Patent Office before grant and by judicial scrutiny after grant in any infringement proceedings.[94] This confines the rights of commercial exploitation to meritorious cases, and prevents abuse by those seeking monopoly rights on the basis of no real innovation.

Fourthly, patents have been applied in a manner that is friendly to commerce. In particular, the judge-made rules of construing patent specifications display commercial sense and subtlety. Judges do not read patent documents literally, but search for their *pith and marrow*. In the leading case,[95] Lord Reid said:

> Claims are not addressed to conveyancers: they are addressed to practical men skilled in the prior art, and I do not think that they ought to be construed with that meticulousness which was once thought appropriate for conveyancing documents.

That was under previous legislation but is still the modern approach of the judges.

The patent system is strongly marked by commercial sensitivity at all levels, both in its legislative infrastructure and in its judicial application.

---

[91] This has been the case since the great reforms of 1883.
[92] *Young v Rosenthal* (1884) 1 RPC 29.
[93] Patents Act 1977, s 1.
[94] *Ibid*, s 74.
[95] *Rodi & Wienenberger AG v Henry Showell Ltd* [1969] RPC 367.

C. Equity: Sensitivity in Judicial Rule-Making

In addition to these major legislative schemes, the continuing role of the judiciary in commercial regulation must not be overlooked. There is strong international confidence in our specialised Commercial judges.[96]

Of particular interest is the way in which the courts have developed principles of equity—an institution originally conceived to mitigate unfairness in the common law—in the commercial context. In the *Romalpa* case, in 1976,[97] the Court of Appeal was asked to adjudicate on the ownership of aluminium foil which had been sold to a company on the following terms:

> The ownership of the material to be delivered will only be transferred to purchaser when he has met all that is owing to seller .... Until the moment of full payment of what purchaser owes seller purchaser shall keep the objects in question for seller in his capacity of fiduciary owner.

These terms were intended to prevent ownership from passing to the buyer until the price had been paid. This turned out to be important security, as the buyer went into receivership before making payment. The seller's only effective means of recovery was to rely on these terms and claim ownership of the foil it had supplied.

The court accepted that the seller could claim the aluminium remaining in the buyer's yard. This proved a milestone in the law of secured credit, giving suppliers the opportunity to protect themselves against the insolvency of their buyers without the need for formal security in the shape of a mortgage or a charge. Since the original *Romalpa* decision in 1976, there has been a flourishing case law in this field.[98]

The court also accepted that the seller was entitled to claim ownership of £35,000 in the buyer's bank account representing the proceeds of foil that had been sold on to third parties. The claim was revolutionary, as

---

[96] For a positive appraisal of the sensitivity of the specialised commercial judiciary in England, see R Austin, 'Commerce and Equity-Fiduciary Duty and Constructive Trust' (1986) 6 *OJLS* 444. A very different system of judicial specialisation operates in North American jurisdictions, and this has been criticised: see, for example, H Butler and L Ribstein, 'Opting Out of Fiduciary Duties: A Response to the Anti-Contractarians' (1990) 65 *Wash LR* 1.

[97] *Aluminium Industrie Vaassen BV v Romalpa Aluminium Ltd* [1976] 1 WLR 676.

[98] Key cases have been *Re Bond Worth Ltd* [1980] ch 228, *Re Peachdart Ltd* [1984] ch 131, *Armour v Thyssen Edelstahlwerke AG* [1991] 2 AC 339, and *Compaq Computer Ltd v Abercorn Group Ltd* [1993] BCLC 602.

orthodoxy suggested that the seller's claim to ownership of the foil had lapsed in favour of a bare contractual claim to the proceeds of sale. Yet the court looked to principles of equity to uphold the seller's claim. It has long been established that when a party is appointed to serve the interests of a principal, whether as a trustee or an agent, he must not take unauthorised profits from the transaction. If he does, the profits belong in equity to the principal. In *Romalpa*, the court took this rule and set it in a commercial context, holding that the terms of the sale contract created a fiduciary relationship, and that any profits obtained by the buyer would belong in equity to the seller.

This is not the only example of judicial creativity in the commercial world. In company law, judges have relied on the law of fiduciaries to regulate company management, prescribing minimum standards of honesty and loyalty with which directors must comply. In these ways, the judiciary has played an important and creative role in commercial regulation even during the twentieth century.

V.   CONCLUSION—COMMERCIAL LAW INTO THE FUTURE

In this brief review, we have seen that the unique English system, without any distinct corpus of commercial rules, has proved an outstanding success. In particular, three features have marked the law's approach since it began the process of commercialisation in the eighteenth century: faciliation, integration and regulation. The law has *facilitated* trade by recognising the effect of commercial agreements and practices, giving effect to the intentions of contracting parties to support the free market economy. The law has *integrated* key mercantile customs into its structure, establishing coherent and predictable legal frameworks in a number of areas important to business, from bills of exchange to sales of goods. The law has also *regulated*, particularly in recent times, prescribing rules to ensure that the free market operates with the greatest internal efficiency and without detriment to the community at large.

Each of these features has assumed its greatest importance at different stages of legal development. Facilitation and integration were early objectives, as the common law courts had to reform their rules and procedures to accommodate a body of mercantile custom which had for centuries been regarded as a separate institution. Regulation is a more recent phenomenon, as increasingly sophisticated economic theories of markets have called for measures of state intervention, and governments have become more eager to act in the interests of market openness and fairness.

Yet all three processes remain relevant to the law-making process as we begin the twenty-first century.

The law continues to facilitate, by encouraging flexible frameworks that give traders the freedom to set their own standards of conduct. In the last five years, the approach to dispute resolution has been undergoing radical change to reduce the burden of litigation on business. Court procedures have been streamlined to enhance the speed and effectiveness of litigation, and in a broader context, other procedures such as strengthened arbitration,[99] and mediation,[100] and alternative dispute resolution, are being actively promoted.

The law continues to integrate, particularly in the international arena. Legal cooperation within the European Union has been considerable, and Community Directives have now harmonised large areas of commercial practice, from public company mergers[101] to the use of unfair terms in consumer contracts[102] and the mutual recognition of professional qualifications.[103] In the field of intellectual property, the European Patent Office in Munich has provided an invaluable service to business since its inception in 1973. It allows inventors to secure patents in every Member State with just a single application, and the Office now receives over 100,000 applications every year. Global cooperation is also an increasing reality. I have emphasised the valuable work of the International Chamber of Commerce in formulating standard practices, and the importance of the Hague Rules in setting standards for international shipping. International instruments for the

[99] As a result of the Arbitration Act 1996, the arbitration mechanism has been substantially expedited, parties have been given greater freedoms to fix their own procedures, and arbitration has been asserted as a true source of dispute resolution independent of the courts.

[100] In June 1996 the Commercial Court issued a practice statement encouraging judges to adjourn proceedings at an early stage if alternative dispute resolution, particularly mediation, would be appropriate.

[101] The 1st Company Law Directive of 1968 (Directive 68/151) made provision for compulsory disclosure of company information, registration, pre-incorporation contracts and ultra vires and exhaustive grounds of nullity. To date, a further four Company Law Directives have been adopted and implemented, two are awaiting implementation and five remain under negotiation.

[102] Directive 93/13 (Unfair Terms in Consumer Contract).

[103] See especially Directive 89/48 on the mutual recognition of diplomas, and Directives 77/249 and 98/5 on legal qualifications.

harmonisation of trade are a striking feature of the modern legal scene. In July, the International Law Association met in London to discuss proposals for international conflict of laws rules, and next month in Geneva the World Intellectual Property Organisation will consider an international instrument for the protection of audiovisual performances.

The law also continues to innovate through regulation. The limited liability partnership and the current Company Law Review are prime examples of an increasingly sophisticated law reform process led by government in consultation with the Law Commission and business.

Thus the law has been and is an essential engine for trade. By devising a principled reconciliation of laissez-faire and excessive regulation, giving scope for market freedoms while prescribing firm rules when required, English law has been the creative mediator to resolve diverse interests into a congruent whole.

Index